D0568380

Java Programming
with Oracle JDBC

Java Programming
with Oracle JDBC

Donald Bales

O'REILLY®

Beijing · Cambridge · Farnham · Köln · Paris · Sebastopol · Taipei · Tokyo

Java Programming with Oracle JDBC
by Donald Bales

Copyright © 2002 O'Reilly & Associates, Inc. All rights reserved.
Printed in the United States of America.

Published by O'Reilly & Associates, Inc., 1005 Gravenstein Highway North, Sebastopol, CA 95472.

O'Reilly & Associates books may be purchased for educational, business, or sales promotional use. Online editions are also available for most titles (*safari.oreilly.com*). For more information contact our corporate/institutional sales department: (800) 998-9938 or *corporate@oreilly.com*.

Editor:	Jonathan Gennick
Production Editor:	Matt Hutchinson
Cover Designer:	Ellie Volckhausen
Interior Designer:	David Futato

Printing History:

January 2002: First Edition.

Nutshell Handbook, the Nutshell Handbook logo, and the O'Reilly logo are registered trademarks of O'Reilly & Associates, Inc. Many of the designations used by manufacturers and sellers to distinguish their products are claimed as trademarks. Where those designations appear in this book, and O'Reilly & Associates, Inc., was aware of a trademark claim, the designations have been printed in caps or initial caps. The association between the image of hummingbird moths and Oracle JDBC is a trademark of O'Reilly & Associates, Inc.

Java and all Java-based trademarks and logos are trademarks or registered trademarks of Sun Microsystems, Inc., in the United States and other countries. O'Reilly & Associates, Inc., is independent of Sun Microsystems. Oracle® and all Oracle-based trademarks and logos are trademarks or registered trademarks of Oracle Corporation, Inc., in the United States and other countries. O'Reilly & Associates, Inc., is independent of Oracle Corporation.

While every precaution has been taken in the preparation of this book, the publisher assumes no responsibility for errors or omissions, or for damages resulting from the use of the information contained herein.

ISBN: 0-596-00088-X
[M]

Table of Contents

Part V.   Essentials

Preface

Oracle is the write-once-run-anywhere database. Since the mid-1980s, Oracle has been available on almost every operating system. With the release of Oracle RDBMS Version 6, you could develop a database schema on your desktop knowing it could be implemented unchanged on multiple large-scale platforms. With the release of Oracle7, stored procedures could be written using PL/SQL, and once again, these could be ported to any supported operating system. Oracle8 brought object orientation, and Oracle8i brought internal support for Java™. These releases represent 15-plus years of demonstrated commitment by Oracle Corporation to make Oracle the write-once-run-anywhere database. But platform independence alone did not make Oracle the dominant database in the marketplace. Other factors contributed as well:

Open-systems initiatives
> Oracle grew up with Unix and therefore carries an open-systems attitude that has fostered innovation and acute customer awareness.

Configurable resources
> The Oracle RDBMS resources, such as filesystem and memory usage, are configurable and manageable by the DBA. As a result, an Oracle database can be tuned for the task at hand, whether that task is transaction processing, batch processing, or decision support.

Leading technology
> Oracle has consistently led the relational database industry technologically. From time to time, competitors have temporarily leaped ahead of Oracle in a niche, but Oracle has always retaken the lead.

You may have already guessed that I am an Oracle advocate. I have had 16 years of experience with Oracle and its competitors, and this alone has taught me to respect the product. A more telling story is how many developers who have worked with Oracle tell me all the things they miss when they work with another product.

I got involved with Oracle accidentally. The company I was working for had acquired one of its competitors, and I was sent to the West Coast to convert the reports from something called a relational database to COBOL VSAM/ISAM programs on a minicomputer. The reason for the conversion was the poor performance of the acquired company's reports. During the conversion, I heard all the badmouthing going around at that time about relational technology. My thoughts at the time were that, performance aside, relational technology greatly simplified decision-support development. And, had the reports I was converting been done right, performance would not have been an issue.

After that experience, I felt that eventually, relational database technology would dominate the development market, so I decided to research the products available and pick the one that I thought would emerge as the market leader. After several months of research, I decided on Oracle, which at the time was just in Version 5. Since that time, I have been working with Oracle and, from time to time, its competitors. Over the years, I have used COBOL, Pro*COBOL, C, Windows SDK, Pro*C, OCI, C++, Smalltalk, Visual Basic, PowerBuilder, PL/SQL, and Java as client development languages—all to access an Oracle database. With my varied experience, I still remember my first mistakes with Oracle—performing that conversion was the very first.

I have learned more than anything else that the only reason a relational database performs poorly is because we don't use it like a relational database. On that first project with Oracle, the previous programmers were performing data processing the slow way: they opened cursors on different tables and did fetches until they found a match between tables, essentially doing full table scans and not using the database to perform the joins. There was really no reason to badmouth relational technology back then, except for our own ignorance. Boy, I sure could have used a good O'Reilly book on Oracle back when I did that conversion.

While Oracle was growing as the database product of choice, Sun Microsystems released Java in the mid-1990s. Since that time, Java has gone from being considered an applet language, a client-side language, a server-side language, an enterprise application language, and now, with Oracle8i, an object-relational database language. That is so cool. Now we can leverage the strength of relational technology and object orientation in our enterprise applications on both client and server. But to leverage this technology to build enterprise applications, we need to have a solid foundation. That is what this book is all about. Oracle Java DataBase Connectivity (JDBC) is the foundation for all your Java/Oracle applications.

Why I Wrote This Book

I am a firm believer that good foundational knowledge is a must if you, as an application developer, are going to write a robust application. Your knowledge of the fundamentals of the technologies you're using makes or break not only any application you write, but your programming career as well. I was extremely pleased to write a book about Oracle JDBC, because it is the foundation for using Java with Oracle.

This is a book written by a programmer for programmers. I try to include enough detail to get the novice up and running without boring the experienced programmer to death. My hope is that this book will guide you through the process of making a connection and executing SQL statements while maintaining database integrity and enabling you to use all the database technologies offered by Oracle.

This Book's Intended Audience

This book covers a lot of material about Oracle's implementation of JDBC. It provides both the beginner and the advanced Oracle or Java user with all the information needed to be successful. However, a certain amount of basic knowledge about SQL, Java, and object orientation is a must.

I am often asked, "What's the best way for me to learn Oracle?" Wow! Now that's a loaded question. To learn Oracle is a big task, because Oracle is a big product. But I always respond with these suggestions:

- Go to *http://technet.oracle.com/membership/* and sign up on the Oracle Technology Network (OTN, or Technet) as a member. It doesn't cost you anything to become a member, and you get access to all of the Oracle documentation online. You also get access to the discussion forums, where others like yourself post questions when they're having problems. And you can download the most recent Java drivers and other software for free.

- Better yet, sign up for a technology track or two. Technology tracks cost $200 each. For your $200, you get four updates a year on a CD of all the software for a track. For $400, you can get either the NT Servers or Linux Servers tracks along with the NT Development Tools track and have a complete setup for learning Oracle.

- Do some serious studying. Read the *Oracle Concepts Manual*. Then read *Oracle: The Complete Reference*, by George Koch and Kevin Loney (Osborne McGraw-Hill). Follow that with the *Oracle Developer's Guide*. Then finish your beginner's work by reading *Oracle PL/SQL Programming* by Steven Feuerstein with Bill Pribyl (O'Reilly). O'Reilly has several other books on Oracle that you will find helpful. Check them out at *http://oracle.oreilly.com/*.

- If you have the funding, send yourself to all the Oracle developer classes and a couple of DBA classes, too—so you can keep your DBA honest. The DBA classes will also help you when you try to create your own database in your "learning" environment.

Usually when I offer this advice, I get a response such as: "Gee, that sounds like a lot of work." True, it is a lot of work, but I've been studying Oracle for 16 years and I still don't know all of it. How else do you expect to make the big bucks?

As far as Java goes, reading *Learning Java* by Patrick Niemeyer and Jonathan Knudsen (O'Reilly) is an excellent starting point. O'Reilly has an entire series of books on Java that take each major area and cover it exhaustively—for example, *Database Programming with JDBC and Java* by George Reese (O'Reilly). George's book covers basics that are not database-specific while pursuing a more abstract or advanced approach to examining the various ways you can utilize programming models with JDBC. Check out all the Java series titles at *http://java.oreilly.com/*.

If you're into electronic documentation, you can download a copy of the JDBC Java specification from Sun Microsystems at *http://java.sun.com/products/jdbc/*. The standard JDBC API Javadoc can be found in the *doc* directory of the JDK you install. If you want a complete JDBC API Javadoc, you can download a copy of Oracle's JDBC Javadoc at the OTN web site.

Structure of This Book

This book attempts to be both a tutorial and a reference. It's divided into five parts and includes 20 chapters. The material builds upon itself as you go along. So if you skip ahead in any section, be forewarned that you may have to backtrack. The book is packed with fully functional examples that demonstrate each concept as it is discussed.

Part I, *Overview*
> Chapter 1 introduces the JDBC API, defines the term client-server, and uses that definition to identify four different clients that JDBC programmers may encounter. These client definitions create a context for the material covered in Part II.

Part II, *Connections*
> Chapters 2–7 cover topics related to establishing a connection. While most books cover this material in a couple of pages, too many developers suffer with the nuances of establishing a connection under the four different client types not to warrant a more in-depth coverage of the material.

Part III, *Relational SQL*
> Chapters 8–13 cover topics related to the use of traditional relational SQL. They also cover the use of large binary objects (LOBs) and batching.

Part IV, *Object-Relational SQL*
> Chapters 14–16 cover topics related to the use of Oracle's object-relational SQL. You will learn how to work with user-defined database types using JDBC.

Part V, *Essentials*
> Chapters 17–20 cover topics related to transaction management, data integrity, locking, detection, and troubleshooting. While not strictly part of JDBC, these are essential topics that every JDBC programmer should understand.

Conventions Used in This Book

The following typographical conventions are used in this book:

Italic

> Used for filenames, directory names, table names, field names, and URLs. It is also used for emphasis and for the first use of a technical term.

`Constant width`

> Used for examples and to show the contents of files and the output of commands.

`Constant width italic`

> Used in syntax descriptions to indicate user-defined items.

`Constant width bold`

> Indicates user input in examples showing an interaction.

UPPERCASE

> In syntax descriptions, usually indicates keywords.

lowercase

> In syntax descriptions, usually indicates user-defined items such as variables.

[ ]

> In syntax descriptions, square brackets enclose optional items.

{ }

> In syntax descriptions, curly brackets enclose a set of items from which you must choose only one.

|

> In syntax descriptions, a vertical bar separates the items enclosed in curly or square brackets, as in {TRUE | FALSE}.

...

> In syntax descriptions, ellipses indicate repeating elements.

 Indicates a tip, suggestion, or general note.

 Indicates a warning or caution.

Software and Versions

This book covers Oracle8*i*, Release 2, Version 8.1.6, which is the first version of Oracle to support JDBC Version 2.0. Accordingly, the examples used in the book were tested with JDK Version 1.2.2 and J2EE Version 1.2. Don't be discouraged if you're still using JDK 1.1.x. Most of the examples, except for some of the J2EE stuff, work fine with JDK 1.1.5+. Even some of the features that are new to JDBC 2.0, such as prefetching and batching, are supported under JDK 1.1.5+ via an additional Oracle import. All the program examples are available online at *http://examples.oreilly.com/ javajdbc/*.

Oracle8i, Version 8.1.7, and Oracle9i both introduce new features that represent incremental improvements to Oracle JDBC. We'll discuss the most important of these new features in Chapter 20. Even though I used Oracle8i, Version 8.1.6 for all the examples in this book, everything you read still applies to Oracle8i, Release 3, Version 8.1.7 and to Oracle9i.

Most of the filenames in my examples use the Windows path notation using back-slashes instead of forward slashes. I use this notation not out of preference for a particular operating system (my preference is Unix), but because I feel most of you will be learning how to use Oracle JDBC on a Win32 platform. So for you Unix/Linux programmers, forgive me for making you reach over the Enter key.

Comments and Questions

Please address comments and questions concerning this book to the publisher:

O'Reilly & Associates, Inc.
1005 Gravenstein Highway North
Sebastopol, CA 95472
(800) 998-9938 (in the United States or Canada)
(707) 829-0515 (international/local)
(707) 829-0104 (fax)

There is a web page for this book, which lists errata, examples, or any additional information. You can access this page at:

http://www.oreilly.com/catalog/jorajdbc

To comment or ask technical questions about this book, send email to:

bookquestions@oreilly.com

For more information about books, conferences, Resource Centers, and the O'Reilly Network, see the O'Reilly web site at:

http://www.oreilly.com

Acknowledgments

A Native American medicine man once told me, "A man needs a woman to teach him how to live." With this I could not agree more. That said, I never would have been in a position to write this book had it not been for the profound way in which my wife Diane has taught me how to live. With her love, honesty, and tireless support, no matter how wacky some of my adventures or ideas have been, she has always been there as a friend, pointing out that the only limits to my ability were the ones I imagined. As a writing teacher, her advice has been immensely valuable. I am truly grateful to have her help and advice. For the last year, while I have been writing this book, she has pretty much lived without me. Yet she has been my sounding board on many issues related to the book, and it all must have sounded like I was speaking another language. I can't express in words how intensely I love her, but having the time to write this book is good indication of how much she loves me. Thank you Diane!

This book was only half as good as it is now when I first turned my chapters over to my editor Jonathan Gennick. The other half came from Jonathan's feedback. You can't imagine how humbling it is to write a chapter of a book, edit yourself several times, send it to your editor, and then get it returned to you with so many edit marks that it looks like it's the first paper you wrote in your freshman year of high school. Nonetheless, through the process of editing emerges a work that is better, better because of the teamwork between writer and editor. Thank you Jonathan! And thank you also to Matt Hutchinson, production editor for the book, and to the entire O'Reilly production team.

Also, a special thanks goes out to my technical reviewers: Kuassi Mensah, Java Products Group Manager, Oracle Corporation; Shiva Prasad, Senior Product Manager, Oracle Corporation; Ekkehard Rohwedder, SQLJ Development Manager, Oracle Corporation; Alan Beaulieu, President, APB Solutions, Inc.; and Charles Havranek, President and CEO, xde.net. Your efforts improved this book and are greatly appreciated!

Overview

Part I consists of a single chapter that introduces the JDBC API, defines the term client/server as it will be used in the book, and provides a framework of four different client types. Each of the four client types, which require a different treatment when establishing a database connection, will be discussed in detail in Part II.

Introduction to JDBC

Oracle JDBC is where the write-once-run-anywhere database meets Java, the write-once-run-anywhere programming language. JDBC acts as the bridge between Oracle and Java. But what is JDBC? JDBC is a Java API for executing dynamic SQL statements. Oracle JDBC is for executing dynamic SQL statements in a standard way and for leveraging Oracle's extended functionality. Consequently, when you use Oracle as your persistent storage, you have to make a decision early on as to whether to program for portability or for additional performance and functionality.

Before we start our discussion on how you can use JDBC, I think it's appropriate to cover some required background information. In this chapter, we'll start by looking at the architecture of the JDBC API. Then we'll continue by defining client/server and four different types of Oracle clients. Finally, we'll finish with my soapbox speech about how it's important to use the set capabilities of SQL.

The JDBC API

In this section, I will try to give you the big picture of the JDBC API. Given this overview, you'll have a contextual foundation on which to lay your knowledge as you build it chapter by chapter while reading this book.

The JDBC API is based mainly on a set of interfaces, not classes. It's up to the manufacturer of the driver to implement the interfaces with their own set of classes. Figure 1-1 is a class diagram that shows the basic JDBC classes and interfaces; these make up the core API. Notice that the only concrete class is DriverManager. The rest of the core API is a set of interfaces.

I'll take a second to explain some of the relationships in the diagram. DriverManager is used to load a JDBC Driver. A Driver is a software vendor's implementation of the JDBC API. After a driver is loaded, DriverManager is used to get a Connection. In turn, a Connection is used to create a Statement, or to create and prepare a PreparedStatement or CallableStatement. Statement and PreparedStatement objects are used to execute

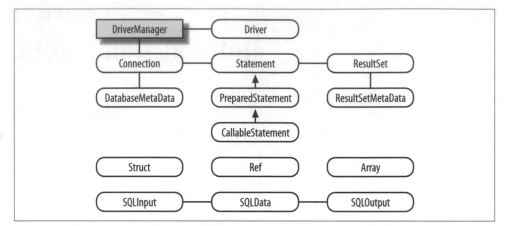

Figure 1-1. The interfaces of the core JDBC API

SQL statements. CallableStatement objects are used to execute stored procedures. A Connection can also be used to get a DatabaseMetaData object describing a database's functionality.

The results of executing a SQL statement using a Statement or PreparedStatement are returned as a ResultSet. A ResultSet can be used to get the actual returned data or a ResultSetMetaData object that can be queried to identify the types of data returned in the ResultSet.

The six interfaces at the bottom of Figure 1-1 are used with object-relational technology. A Struct is a weakly typed object that represents a database object as a record. A Ref is a reference to an object in a database. It can be used to get to a database object. An Array is a weakly typed object that represents a database collection object as an array. The SQLData interface is implemented by custom classes you write to represent database objects as Java objects in your application. SQLInput and SQLOutput are used by the Driver in the creation of your custom classes during retrieval and storage.

In Oracle's implementation of JDBC, most of the JDBC interfaces are implemented by classes whose names are prefixed with the word Oracle. Figure 1-2 shows these classes and is laid out so that the classes correspond positionally with those shown in Figure 1-1.

As you can see from Figure 1-2, the only interface not implemented by an Oracle class is SQLData. That's because you implement the SQLData interface yourself with custom classes that you create to mirror database objects. Now that you've got the big picture for the JDBC API, let's lay a foundation for understanding what I mean when I used the term *client* with respect to JDBC.

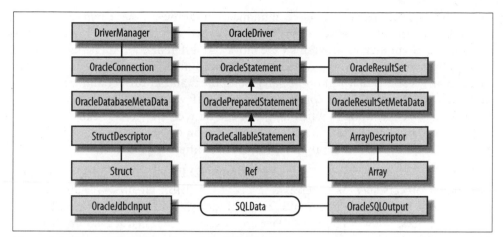

Figure 1-2. Oracle's implementation of the JDBC API interfaces

Clients

In Part II, we'll examine how to establish JDBC connections from four types of Oracle clients: an application, an applet, a servlet, and an internal client. But first, I need to define what I mean by client. Let's begin that discussion by clarifying the term client/server.

What Is Client/Server?

Over the years, I've heard countless, sometimes convoluted, definitions for the term client/server. This has led to a great deal of confusion when discussing application architecture or platforms. So you have a consistent definition of the term client/server, I propose we use Oracle's early definition for client/server and then define the four different types of clients we'll encounter in this book.

It's my opinion that Oracle is in large part responsible for the definition and success of the so-called client/server platform. From its beginnings, Oracle has been a client/server database. Here's my definition of *client/server*:

> Any time two different programs run in two separate operating-system processes in which one program requests services from the other, you have a client/server relationship.

In the early days, before the use of networks, Oracle applications consisted of the Oracle RDBMS running on one operating-system process as the server and one or more end users running their application programs in other operating-system processes. Even though this all took place on one physical computer, it's still considered client/server. The Oracle RDBMS represents the server, and the end-user application programs represent the clients.

With the use of networks, the communication between the client and server changed, but the client/server relationship remained the same. The key difference was that client and server programs were moved to different computers. Examples of this are the use of C, C++, VisualBasic, PowerBuilder, and Developer 2000 to develop applications that run on personal computers and in turn communicate with an Oracle database on a host computer using TCP/IP via Net8. This type of scenario is what most people think of when they hear the term client/server. I call this type of client/server architecture *two-tier* because the division of labor is a factor of two, not because the client and server programs run on two different computers.

Now, with Java and the Java 2 Enterprise Edition (J2EE), which includes servlets and distributed objects such as Enterprise JavaBeans™ (EJB), client/server applications have become multitiered. Such multitier applications, which can have three, four, or even more tiers, are referred to as *n-tier* applications (in which *n* is more than two tiers). For example, someone using a browser on a PC can execute a servlet on another host computer. The computer on which the servlet runs is known as an *application server*, and it in turn might execute EJB on a third host computer, which would be known as a *component server*. The component server might contact yet another server, a *database server* running Oracle, to retrieve and store data. In this example, we have four tiers: personal computer, application server, component server, and database server. Distributing the software over four computers is one means of scaling up an application to handle a larger volume of transactions.

With respect to the *n*-tier application, it's possible to deploy that application so the application server, component server, and database server are all on the same host computer. In such a scenario, we would still call it an *n*-tier application because the division of labor among programs is a factor greater than two. The key point to note is that while we can run all the server software on the same host computer, the *n*-tier architecture allows us to distribute the application over multiple servers if necessary. Did you notice in these last two examples how a server might also be a client? The servlet running on the application server was the client to the EJB running on the component server, and so forth.

Now that you have a better understanding of the term client-sever, let's continue by looking at the different types of clients that utilize JDBC and Oracle.

Types of Clients

As far as application development using Java is concerned, prior to Oracle8*i*, there were two types of clients: an *application* and an *applet*. Both run in a Java Virtual Machine (JVM), but an applet runs in a browser, which in turn runs as an application. Typically, an application has liberal access to operating-system resources, while an applet's access to those resources is restricted by the browser. I say typically, because using the Java Security API can restrict an application's access to operating-system resources, and with a signed applet, or security policies, you can gain access to operating-system resources. Another distinction between applications and applets is that while an application has a main( ) method, an applet does not. Yet another distinction is how they are programmed to connect to the database. Because of these distinctions, it is useful to consider applications and applets as two different types of clients.

With the coming of J2EE, servlets and EJB both became new types of clients. A *servlet*, a Java replacement for a CGI program, is a Java class that runs inside a servlet container similar to how an applet runs inside a browser. Typically, a servlet takes the input of an HTML form submitted by a browser and processes the data. A servlet may also generate an HTML form or other dynamic content. Servlets differ from applications in a couple of ways. Like applets, servlets have no main( ) method. There are also differences in how you program a servlet to connect to a database. More importantly, a servlet is an application component. One or more servlets are written to create an application.

Moving on to component technology, EJB is a Java component model for creating enterprise applications. EJB is a software component that runs in a component server, which is usually referred to as a Component Transaction Monitor or EJB Container. Like applets and servlets, EJB has special considerations when it comes to connecting to the database and performing transactions. Therefore, we'll consider EJB as a fourth type of client.

With the release of Oracle8i, Oracle stored procedures could be written in Java and became a new type of client. Connectivity for Java stored procedures is very simple. Because EJB and Java stored procedures are both internal clients, we'll consider both of them as the fourth type, an internal client. In summary, we have defined four different types of clients that may utilize JDBC:

- Applications
- Applets
- Servlets
- Internal objects

The important point is that each of these client types has a different set of requirements when it comes to establishing a connection to the database. An application is the easiest type of client to connect. That's because it has liberal access to operating-system resources; you typically just make a connection when you start your program and then close it before you exit. An applet, on the other hand, has to live with security, life cycle, and routing restrictions. A servlet has life cycle and possible shared connection issues, and an internal client such as EJB or a stored procedure has security issues.

It's common for programmers to have problems establishing a JDBC connection to an Oracle database. Consequently, I'll discuss each type of client's requirements separately, and in detail, in the chapters that follow. This should get you started on the right foot. Chapter 2 covers most of the general knowledge you'll need, so even if you're interested only in connecting from applets, servlets, or internally from Java stored procedures, read Chapter 2 first.

Using SQL

OK. Get ready. Here's my soapbox speech. A final word before you start. Don't make the mistake of becoming dependent on a procedural language and forgetting how to use the set-oriented nature of SQL to solve your programming problems. In other words, make sure you use the full power of SQL. A common example of this phenomenon is the batch updating of data in a table. Often, programmers will create a program using a procedural language such as PL/SQL or Java, open a cursor on a table for a given set of criteria, then walk through the result set row by row, selecting data from another table or tables, and finally updating the original row in the table with the data. However, all this work can be done more quickly and easily using a simple SQL UPDATE statement with a single- or multicolumn subquery.

I can't emphasize enough how important it is for you to know the SQL language in order to get the most from using JDBC. If you don't have a lot of experience using SQL, I suggest you read *SQL in a Nutshell*, by Kevin Kline with Daniel Kline (O'Reilly) or *Oracle: The Complete Reference*, by George Koch and Kevin Loney (Osborne McGraw-Hill).

PART II

Connections

In Part II, we'll look at how to establish database connections within the context of each one of the four clients defined in Chapter 1:

- Applications
- Applets
- Servlets
- Internal objects

As part of our discussion on servlet connections, we'll look at various strategies for managing pools of connections. Following the chapters on connections, we'll continue by covering Oracle's advanced security features. Finally, we'll investigate the JDBC optional package's connection pooling framework.

CHAPTER 2

Application Database Connections

In Chapter 1, I defined four client types. In this chapter, I'll discuss how to make a database connection from the first type of client, an application. Establishing a database connection may sound like an easy task, but it's often not, because you lack the necessary information. In this chapter, I'll not only explain the ins and outs of making a connection but also talk about the different types of connections you can make and point out the advantages of each.

JDBC Drivers

In order to connect a Java application to a database using JDBC, you need to use a JDBC driver. This driver acts as an intermediary between your application and the database. There are actually several types of JDBC drivers available, so you need to choose the one that best suits your particular circumstances. You also need to be aware that not all driver types are supported by Oracle, and even when a driver type is supported by Oracle, it may not be supported by all versions of Oracle.

Driver Types

Sun has defined four categories of JDBC drivers. The categories delineate the differences in architecture for the drivers. One difference between architectures lies in whether a given driver is implemented in native code or in Java code. By native code, I mean whatever machine code is supported by a particular hardware configuration. For example, a driver may be written in C and then compiled to run on a specific hardware platform. Another difference lies in how the driver makes the actual connection to the database. The four driver types are as follows:

Type 1: JDBC bridge driver

This type uses bridge technology to connect a Java client to a third-party API such as Oracle DataBase Connectivity (ODBC). Sun's JDBC-ODBC bridge is an example of a Type 1 driver. These drivers are implemented using native code.

Type 2: Native API (part Java driver)

This type of driver wraps a native API with Java classes. The Oracle Call Interface (OCI) driver is an example of a Type 2 driver. Because a Type 2 driver is implemented using local native code, it is expected to have better performance than a pure Java driver.

Type 3: Network protocol (pure Java driver)

This type of driver communicates using a network protocol to a middle-tier server. The middle tier in turn communicates to the database. Oracle does not provide a Type 3 driver. They do, however, have a program called Connection Manager that, when used in combination with Oracle's Type 4 driver, acts as a Type 3 driver in many respects. Connection Manager will be covered in Chapter 3.

Type 4: Native protocol (pure Java driver)

This type of driver, written entirely in Java, communicates directly with the database. No local native code is required. Oracle's Thin driver is an example of a Type 4 driver.

It's a popular notion that drivers implemented using native code are faster than pure Java drivers because native code is compiled into the native op-code language of the computer, whereas Java drivers are compiled into byte code. Java drivers have their CPU instructions executed by a Java Virtual Machine (JVM) that acts as a virtual CPU, which in turn has its commands executed by the computer's real CPU. On the other hand, the code for native code drivers is executed directly by the real CPU. Because the JVM represents an additional layer of execution, common sense would seem to dictate that native code would execute faster. However, as you will see in Chapter 19, this is not always the case. Most of the time, Oracle's Java driver is faster than its native driver.

Oracle's JDBC Drivers

Oracle provides Type 2 and Type 4 drivers for both client- and server-side use. *Client-side* refers to the use of the driver in an application, applet or servlet, whereas *server-side* refers to the use of the driver inside the database. Here's a list of Oracle's JDBC drivers:

JDBC OCI driver

This is a Type 2 driver that uses Oracle's native OCI interface. It's commonly referred to as the OCI driver. There are actually two separate drivers, one for OCI7 (Oracle release 7.3.x) and another for OCI8 (Oracle release 8.x). This driver is for client-side use and requires that the Oracle client software be installed.

JDBC Thin driver

This is a Type 4, 100% pure Java driver for client-side use.

JDBC internal driver

This is a Type 2, native code driver for server-side use with Java code that runs inside the Oracle8*i* database's JServer JVM. It's also called the *kprb driver*.

JDBC server-side Thin driver

This is a Type 4 100% pure Java driver for server-side use with Java code that runs inside the Oracle8*i* database's JServer JVM that must also access an external data source.

Figure 2-1 shows the JDBC driver architecture on the Win32 platform. On the client side are the JDBC-ODBC bridge (supplied by Sun, not Oracle), the JDBC OCI driver, and the JDBC Thin driver. All three communicate with the listener process on the server. The difference in architecture is in the software layers between the JDBC driver and the listener. As you can see from Figure 2-1, the JDBC Thin driver communicates directly with the listener. The JDBC OCI driver, on the other hand, must communicate with the OCI native software, which in turn communicates with the listener. Even more removed from the listener is the JDBC-ODBC Bridge. The JDBC-ODBC Bridge driver communicates with an ODBC driver. In turn, the ODBC driver communicates with OCI native software, which in turn finally communicates with the listener. The fact that the JDBC Thin driver communicates directly with the listener is probably why it performs just as well as its native-mode counterpart in most cases.

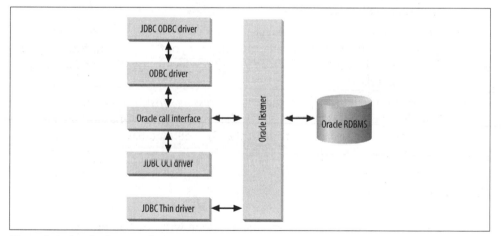

Figure 2-1. Oracle driver architecture

In order to keep things concise, from now on I'll refer to the JDBC OCI driver as the OCI driver and the JDBC Thin driver as the Thin driver. Whenever we discuss server-side drivers, I'll qualify the Thin driver as the server-side Thin driver. Otherwise, we're always talking about client-side drivers.

Guidelines for Choosing a Driver

Given that the drivers have subtle variations in their capabilities and are not applicable to universal client usage, you must decide ahead of time which driver to use for any given application. As you progress through this book, you'll learn about the varying capabilities of the drivers, but for now, here are some guidelines for choosing an appropriate driver for your applications:

Two-tier client/server application
> I suggest you use the Thin driver for all two-tier, client/server applications. The one exception is for applications making heavy use of stored procedures. For those, you should use the OCI driver. Note that this is contrary to Oracle's recommendation. Oracle recommends that for maximum performance, you always use the OCI driver with two-tier, client/server applications. I disagree with Oracle's recommendation because the difference in performance between the OCI driver and the Thin driver is nominal in most instances, yet installing the Oracle client software to support the OCI driver can become a costly software configuration management issue.

Servlet or applet
> I suggest you use the Thin driver for portability when writing servlets and applets. For an applet, you have no choice but to use the Thin driver. It is a pure Java driver that allows a direct connection to the database by emulating Net8's protocol on top of Java sockets (TCP/IP).

Middle-tier program residing in a database
> I suggest you use the server-side internal driver if your program resides in a database and uses only resources, such as Enterprise JavaBeans (EJB) and stored procedures, in that database.

Middle-tier program residing in a database, but accessing outside resources
> For a middle-tier program such as EJB that resides in an Oracle8*i* database but requires access to resources outside of the Oracle8*i* database in which it resides, use the server-side Thin driver.

Versions

Table 2-1 lists the Oracle JDBC driver versions along with the database versions and JDK versions supported by each and the driver types that are available for each.

Table 2-1. Oracle drivers and the JDKs they support

Driver release	Database versions						JDK			Client side		Server side	
	7.3.4	8.0.4	8.0.5	8.0.6	8.1.5	8.1.6	1.0.x	1.1.x	1.2.x	OCI	Thin	Thin	Internal
7.3.4	X						X	X		X	X		
8.0.4	X	X					X	X		X	X		
8.0.5	X	X	X				X	X		X	X		
8.0.6	X	X	X	X			X	X		X	X		
8.1.5	X	X	X	X	X		X	X	X	X	X		X
8.1.6	X	X	X	X	X	X		X	X	X	X	X	X

There are a few important issues to consider about the information in Table 2-1:

- The server-side internal driver only supports JDK 1.2.x.
- Beginning with driver Version 8.1.6, JDK 1.0.x is no longer supported.
- Also beginning with Version 8.1.6, the OCI driver uses the standard Java Native Interface (JNI). This means you can now use the OCI drivers with JVMs other than Sun's. Prior to 8.1.6, the OCI driver used an earlier native call specification named Native Method Interface (NMI). This prevented the use of OCI drivers with non-Sun JVMs.

As you can see by examining Table 2-1, Oracle supports JDBC for database versions 7.3.4 through 8.1.6. Each new release of the driver software maintains backward compatibility with earlier versions of the database. In addition, as long as you don't try to use newer functionality with an older driver release, you can use an older driver release with a newer version of the database. For example, you can use the 7.3.4 driver to access an 8.1.6 database, as long as you don't try to use features that did not exist in the 7.3.4 version of the database. This can be a handy workaround when planning the migration of a large application. Let's say you had an application that you migrated from database Version 7.3.4 to 8.1.6. You could continue to use the 7.3.4 driver in the client until you start utilizing features, such as object views, that are specific to database Version 8.1.6. However, I still recommend you use the newest drivers whenever possible.

Oracle Class Files

Each Oracle client software release has its own set of class files stored in a zip format: *classes102.zip* for use with JDK1.0.x, *classes111.zip* and *nls_charset11.zip* for use with JDK 1.1.x, and *classes12.zip* and *nls_charset12.zip* for use with JDK 1.2.x. From here on I'll refer to these sets of class files as *classesXXX.zip*.

Installation

Installing the JDBC drivers varies depending on whether you use the OCI driver or the Thin driver. Let's start with the OCI driver installation.

Installing the OCI Driver

To install the OCI driver software, follow these steps:

1. Install the Oracle client software from its distribution CD.
2. Add the appropriate *classesXXX.zip* file to your CLASSPATH environment variable.
3. If you are using Java 2 Enterprise Edition (J2EE), add the appropriate *classesXXX.zip* file to your J2EE_CLASSPATH environment variable.
4. Add the client binaries to your PATH environment variable.
5. On Unix or Linux, add the client binaries to the LD_LIBRARY_PATH environment variable.

Install the Oracle Client

If you are going to use the OCI driver, you'll need the Oracle8*i* Oracle Client distribution media or the Oracle Enterprise Edition distribution media (typically, these are on CD-ROM) to install the client software. Follow your operating-system-specific instructions to execute the Oracle Universal Installer. Then simply follow the installation instructions from the Oracle Universal Installer's screen.

The Oracle Universal Installer creates several directories during the installation of the client software on your computer. The directories of interest to you are all under *ORACLE_HOME\jdbc*. *ORACLE_HOME* refers to the directory where the Oracle client software was installed. Typically, these directories are:

demo/samples
> Contains Oracle's sample programs, demonstrating the use of SQL92 and Oracle SQL syntax, PL/SQL blocks, streams, objects (user-defined types and extensions), and performance extensions.

doc
> Contains the API documentation for the JDBC drivers.

lib
> Contains the following *classesXXX.zip* files:
>
> *classes111.zip*
>> For JDK 1.1.x support
>
> *classes12.zip*
>> For JDB 1.2.x support

---

nls_charset11.zip and nls_charset12.zip
> For National Language support

jta.zip
> For the Java Transaction API

jndi.zip
> For the Java Naming and Directory Interface API

The files *jta.zip* and *jndi.zip* are part of the standard JDK, but Oracle recommends you use those included in the *lib* directory (and those that Oracle distributes) for compatibility with Oracle classes in the *classesXXX.zip* file.

The content in these directories varies with the version of JDBC drivers installed. The preceding directories and files are from Version 8.1.6.

Setting environment variables

After the client software installation, add the name of the appropriate *classesXXX.zip* file to your CLASSPATH environment variable setting. If you are using J2EE, also add the appropriate *classesXXX.zip* file to your J2EE_CLASSPATH setting. Be sure to specify only one *classesXXX.zip* file; otherwise, you will encounter unexpected behavior and errors. For example, if your Oracle Client software is installed on Microsoft Windows NT in the *C:\Oracle\Ora81* directory, then you need to add the following file to your CLASSPATH and J2EE_CLASSPATH environment variables:

```
c:\oracle\ora81\jdbc\lib\classes12.zip;
```

In addition, you also need to add the Oracle Client binaries to your PATH. For example, if your Oracle Client software is installed on Windows NT in *C:\Oracle\Ora81*, then you need to add the following to your PATH statement:

```
c:\oracle\ora81\bin;
```

For Unix, you need to add the Oracle Client binaries to your LD_LIBRARY_PATH setting. For example, if your Oracle Client software is installed in */u01/app/oracle/product/8.1.6*, then you need to add the following to your LD_LIBRARY_PATH setting:

```
/u01/app/oracle/product/8.1.6/lib:
```

Installing the Thin Driver

To install the Thin driver software, follow these steps:

1. Install the Oracle Thin driver from the Oracle client distribution CD.
2. Add the appropriate *classesXXX.zip* file to your CLASSPATH environment variable.
3. If you are using Java 2 Enterprise Edition (J2EE), add the appropriate *classesXXX.zip* file to your J2EE_CLASSPATH environment variable.

Install the Thin driver class files

If you are going to use the Thin driver, you can use the Oracle Universal Installer as I specified for the OCI driver, but this time select only the appropriate Thin driver for installation. Alternatively, you can simply locate the appropriate *classesXXX.zip* file on the distribution media and copy it to an appropriate location on your computer. Then add the desired *classesXXX.zip* file to your CLASSPATH and J2EE_CLASS-PATH settings. Once again, be sure to specify only one *classesXXX.zip* file; otherwise, you will encounter unexpected behavior and errors.

You can also obtain the Thin driver, and an updated version of the OCI driver, via the Oracle Technology Network (OTN) at: *http://technet.oracle.com/software/tech/ java/sqlj_jdbc/software_index.htm*. To get access to the drivers you must be an OTN member. Membership is free, and there is a wealth of valuable information available, such as documentation, discussion forums, and technology tracks that allow you as a developer to get a developer copy of all the software for a particular operating system for about $200/year. I encourage you to take advantage of this resource.

Be aware, however, that while the OCI driver updates are available at OTN, the rest of the OCI client software is not. You must get this by installing the client software from your distribution media. Further, if you get a newer *classesXXX.zip* file, say for 8.1.6, you can use it only with Version 8.1.6 client software. The Java class files must match the version of the client software. Many problems flood the JDBC forum about this issue. Of course, you can avoid this problem by using the Thin driver, which does not use any client software.

Setting environment variables

After you've installed the Thin driver, or copied its *classesXXX.zip* file to an appropriate directory, you'll need to set several environment variables. Add the desired *classesXXX.zip* file to your CLASSPATH and J2EE_CLASSPATH settings. For example, if you copied the *classes12.zip* file to */u01/app/oracle/product/8.1.6/jdbc/lib* on Unix, then you need to add the following to your CLASSPATH and J2EE_CLASS-PATH environment variables:

```
/u01/app/oracle/product/8.1.6/jdbc/lib/classes12.zip;
```

Using Sun's JDBC-ODBC Bridge

This discussion on installation would not be complete if I did not at least acknowledge Sun's JDBC-ODBC Bridge. If you are going to use the Bridge, then you'll have to install the Oracle Client and ODBC software, because the Oracle ODBC drivers use the OCI software.

Connecting to a Database

After you've installed the appropriate driver, it's time to get down to some programming and learn how to establish a database connection using JDBC. The programming involved to establish a JDBC connection is fairly simple. Here are the steps to follow:

1. Add `import` statements to your Java program so the compiler will know where to find the classes you'll be using in your Java code.

2. Register your JDBC driver. This step causes the JVM to load the desired driver implementation into memory so it can fulfill your JDBC requests.

3. Formulate a database URL. That is, create a properly formatted address that points to the database to which you wish to connect.

4. Code a call to the `DriverManager` object's `getConnection( )` method to establish a database connection.

Package Imports

Import statements tell the Java compiler where to find the classes you reference in your code and are placed at the very beginning of your source code. To use the standard JDBC package, which allows you to select, insert, update, and delete data in SQL tables, add the following imports to your source code:

```
import java.sql.* ;        // for standard JDBC programs
import java.math.* ;       // for BigDecimal and BigInteger support
```

If you need to use JDK 1.1.x, you can still get most of Oracle's JDBC 2.0 features by including the following `import` statement in your program:

```
import oracle.jdbc2.*     // for Oracle interfaces equivalent to
                          // JDBC 2.0 standard package for JDK 1.1.x
```

Keep in mind, however, that when you do start using JDK 1.2.x or higher you'll have to modify your code and remove this `import` statement.

Without the `imports` shown here you'll have to explicitly identify each class file with its full package path and name. For example, with `imports`, you'll normally write the following code to create a connection object:

```
Connection conn = DriverManager.getConnection(
  "jdbc:oracle:thin:@esales:1521:orcl", "scott", "tiger");
```

Without `imports`, however, you'll have to type the following longer statement instead:

```
java.sql.Connection conn = java.sql.DriverManager.getConnection(
  "jdbc:oracle:thin:@esales:1521:orcl", "scott", "tiger");
```

As you might expect, Oracle provides a number of extensions to the JDBC standard. These extensions support the use of Oracle-specific database features such as the methods to write database object types. To use Oracle's extended functionality, add the following imports to your source code:

```
import oracle.sql.* ;        // for Oracle type extensions
import oracle.jdbc.driver.*; // for Oracle database access and updates
                             // in Oracle type formats
```

Now that you have your last bit of housekeeping done, you can move on to registering the appropriate driver in order to establish a JDBC connection.

Registering a JDBC Driver

You must register the Oracle driver, oracle.jdbc.driver.OracleDriver, in your program before you use it. At this point, you may be confused because we've been talking about the OCI and Thin drivers, but now we refer only to one class when registering. That's because the same class file implements both drivers.

Registering the driver is the process by which the Oracle driver's class file is loaded into memory so it can be utilized as an implementation of the JDBC interfaces. You need to do this only once in your program. You can register a driver in one of three ways. The most common approach is to use Java's Class.forName() method to dynamically load the driver's class file into memory, which automatically registers it. This method is preferable because it allows you to make the driver registration configurable and portable. The following example uses Class.forName() to register the Oracle driver:

```
try {
   Class.forName("oracle.jdbc.driver.OracleDriver");
}
catch(ClassNotFoundException e) {
   System.out.println("Oops! Can't find class oracle.jdbc.driver.OracleDriver");
   System.exit(1);
}
```

The second approach you can use to register a driver is to use the static DriverManager.registerDriver() method. Use the registerDriver() method if you are using a non-JDK compliant JVM, such as the one provided by Microsoft. For example:

```
try {
   DriverManager.registerDriver(new oracle.jdbc.driver.OracleDriver());
}
catch(SQLException e) {
   System.out.println("Oops! Got a SQL error: " + e.getMessage());
   System.exit(1);
}
```

The third approach is to use a combination of Class.forName() to dynamically load the Oracle driver and then the driver classes' getInstance() method to work around noncompliant JVMs, but then you'll have to code for two extra Exceptions. To call the getInstance( ) method for the dynamically loaded class, you can code the call as Class.forName().newInstance( ):

```
try {
  Class.forName("oracle.jdbc.driver.OracleDriver").newInstance();
}
catch(ClassNotFoundException e) {
  System.out.println("Oops! Can't find class oracle.jdbc.driver.OracleDriver");
  System.exit(1);
}
catch(IllegalAccessException e) {
  System.out.println("Uh Oh! You can't load oracle.jdbc.driver.OracleDriver");
  System.exit(2);
}
catch(InstantiationException e) {
  System.out.println("Geez! Can't instantiate oracle.jdbc.driver.OracleDriver");
  System.exit(3);
}
```

Formulating a Database URL

After you've loaded the driver, you can establish a connection using the DriverManager.getConnection( ) method. This method is overloaded and therefore has various forms. However, each form requires a database URL. A database URL is an address that points to your database. Formulating a database URL is where most of the problems associated with establishing a connection occur. For Oracle, the database URL has the following general form:

jdbc:oracle:*driver*:@*database*

database ::= {*host*:*port*:*sid* | *net_service_name* | *connect_descriptor*}

which breaks down as:

driver

Specifies the type of JDBC driver to use for the connection. The following choices are available:

oci7

For the Oracle 7.3.4 OCI driver

oci8

For an Oracle 8.x.x OCI driver

oci

For an Oracle 9.x.x OCI driver

thin

For the Oracle Thin driver

kprb

For the Oracle internal driver

database

> Specifies the database to which you want to connect. You can specify a host, port, and SID; a net service name; or a connect descriptor.

`host:port:sid`

> Used only with the Thin driver and identifies the target database using the following information:

> *host*

>> The TCP/IP address or DNS alias (hostname) for your database server

> *port*

>> The TCP/IP port number of the Oracle listener

> *sid*

>> The System Identifier of your database

`net_service_name`

> Used only with the OCI driver. A *net service name*, or *tnsnames.ora* file entry as it is commonly known, is a short name that resolves to a *connect descriptor*, which is a specially formatted Net8 database address. Net service names are often resolved via a local file named *tnsnames.ora* but may also be resolved using centralized methods such as Oracle Names. The OCI driver depends on the Oracle Client software to be able to resolve a net service name. That's why net service names are used only with the OCI driver.

`connect_descriptor`

> Can be used by either driver and is a Net8 address specification such as that normally found in a *tnsnames.ora* file.

Now that you know the rules of how to formulate a database URL, let's look at several examples as we explore the overloaded forms of the getConnection( ) method.

Using a database URL with a username and password

The most commonly used form of getConnection( ) requires you to pass a database URL, a username, and a password:

```
DriverManager.getConnection(String url, String user, String password)
```

When using the Thin driver, you'll specify a *host:port:sid* value for the *database* portion of the URL. For example, if you have a host at TCP/IP address 192.0.0.1 with a host name of *esales*, and your Oracle listener is configured to listen on port 1521, and your database system identifier is orcl, then the *database* portion of the URL would look like:

```
esales:1521:orcl
```

The corresponding complete database URL would then be:

```
jdbc:oracle:thin:@esales:1521:orcl
```

When you call the getConnection( ) method, it returns a Connection object. For example:

```
Connection conn = DriverManager.getConnection(
  "jdbc:oracle:thin:@esales:1521:orcl", "scott", "tiger" );
```

You'll use this Connection object later to create other objects that will allow you to insert, update, delete, and select data.

When using the OCI driver, you'll specify a net service name for the *database* portion of the URL. For example, if your net service name was *esales*, your call to create a connection would look like:

```
Connection conn = DriverManager.getConnection(
  "jdbc:oracle:oci8:@esales", "scott", "tiger" );
```

 Net service names such as *esales* are often defined in a *tnsnames.ora* file. The typical locations for *tnsnames.ora* are *$Oracle Home\network\ admin* (Windows) and */var/opt/oracle* (Unix). Consult with your DBA if you have any doubts as to how net service names are resolved.

You can also use the rather obscure (that is, to a programmer) Net8 connect descriptor for the *database* portion of the URL. You may be familiar with connect descriptors because they are used in the *tnsnames.ora* file for an OCI client to define the specific address details for a net service name. Using a connect descriptor, our getConnection( ) example would look like:

```
Connection conn = getConnection(
  "jdbc:oracle:thin:@(description=(address=(host=esales)
  (protocol=tcp)(port=1521))(connect_data=(sid=orcl)))",
  "scott", "tiger" );
```

You can use a connect descriptor with either driver, OCI or Thin. More information on Net8 can be found in Oracle's *Net8 Administrator's Guide*, which is available on the OTN web site, or in *Oracle Net8 Configuration and Troubleshooting*, by Hugo Toledo and Jonathan Gennick (O'Reilly).

Using only a database URL

A second form of the DriverManager.getConnection( ) method requires only a database URL:

```
DriverManager.getConnection(String url)
```

However, in this case, the database URL includes the username and password and has the following general form:

```
jdbc:oracle:driver:username/password@database
```

For example, to make the same database connection using the Thin driver, as in the previous section's examples, use the following method call:

```
Connection conn = DriverManager.getConnection(
  "jdbc:oracle:thin:scott/tiger@esales:1521:orcl" );
```

Using a database URL and a Properties object

A third form of the DriverManager.getConnection( ) method requires a database URL and a Properties object:

```
DriverManager.getConnection(String url, Properties info)
```

A Properties object holds a set of keyword-value pairs. It's used to pass driver properties to the driver during a call to the getConnection( ) method. To make the same connection made by the previous examples, use the following code:

```
import java.util.*;

Properties info = new Properties( );
info.put( "user", "scott" );
info.put( "password", "tiger" );

Connection conn = DriverManager.getConnection(
  "jdbc:oracle:thin:@esales:1521:orcl", info );
```

In this example, a new Properties object is created. It is then populated with two properties, user and password. The Properties object, named info in this example, is then passed along with the database URL in the call to the getConnection( ) method.

Besides user and password, there are a number of other properties you can set in a Properties object. Table 2-2 shows the connection properties recognized by the Oracle JDBC drivers. Each property has a full name and may also have a short name. You can use either name with a Properties object's put method.

Table 2-2. Oracle driver properties

Name	Short name	Type	Description
user		String	The Oracle username.
password		String	The Oracle password.
database	server	String	The Oracle database URL.
internal_login		String	A username, such as sysdba, that allows you to log onto the database as "internal". This property applies only to the OCI driver.
defaultRowPrefetch	prefetch	String	The default number of rows to prefetch from the server (default = 10).
remarksReporting	remarks	String	A property that allows you to include database comments in the database's metadata. Oracle lets you add comments to both tables and columns. Set this property to "true" to have the getTables( ) and getColumns( ) methods report remarks (default = "false").

Table 2-2. Oracle driver properties (continued)

Name	Short name	Type	Description
defaultBatchValue	batchvalue	String	The default batch value that triggers an execution request (default = 10).
includeSynonyms	synonyms	String	A property that allows you to include database synonyms in the database's metadata. Set this property to "true" to enable the use of synonyms with a call to DatabaseMetaData.get-Columns( ) (default = "false").

The last six properties in Table 2-2 are Oracle extensions. Normally, only user and password are passed in the Properties object.

Mistakes to watch for

The most common mistake made when establishing a connection is the omission of a colon (:), at-sign (@), or a slash character (/) in the database URL. So double-check your typing of the database URL should you have any connection problems.

If you have Oracle installed on the same machine as your JDBC program, you can specify the default database using just an at-sign with no *database* string. For example, a database URL using the oci8 driver would look like this:

```
jdbc:oracle:oci8:@
```

The following example shows the DriverManager object's getConnection(String url, String user, String password) form of getConnection( ) being used to connect to the default database using scott as the username and tiger as the password:

```
Connection conn = DriverManager.getConnection (
  "jdbc:oracle:thin:@", "scott", "tiger" );
```

Note that there's one exception to Oracle's standard implementation of the JDBC driver. The Oracle JDBC driver does not implement the setLoginTimeout( ) method, which allows your login attempt to time-out after a specified length of time.

Application Examples

In this section, I show simple examples of programs that connect to an Oracle database. These programs are terse to ensure that when you run them, there is no possible problem with the program itself. Any errors that occur should only be as a result of your connection parameters. The programs don't include any exception handling code. Instead, they let the JVM handle any exceptions that occur by printing a stack trace. I'll cover exceptions shortly in the section "Handling Exceptions."

As you read over these examples, keep in mind that when you use the DriverManager object's getConnection( ) method with the oracle.jdbc.driver.OracleDriver object, what the method actually returns is an OracleConnection object. A JDBC Connection is an interface that defines a set of methods that must be implemented by any class that states it. The class oracle.jdbc.driver.OracleConnection implements java.sql. Connection, providing you with all the standard JDBC methods plus the Oracle extensions.

An OCI driver example

Example 2-1 tests the OCI driver. Typically, in a client/server application, the user logs into the database when the application is first launched and then logs out when the application is terminated. This example follows that model. First, the program imports the JDBC library java.sql.*. Next, it uses the Class.forName( ) method to load and register the Oracle driver. Then, it establishes a connection using the getConnection(String url, String user, String password) method. Finally, just to prove that the connection has been established, the program creates a SQL statement and executes it. It does this using the Statement and ResultSet objects, which I'll discuss in detail beginning in Chapter 9.

Example 2-1. A test of the OCI driver for an application

```
import java.sql.*;

class TestOCIApp {

  public static void main(String args[])
   throws ClassNotFoundException, SQLException {

    Class.forName("oracle.jdbc.driver.OracleDriver");
    // or you can use:
    // DriverManager.registerDriver(new oracle.jdbc.driver.OracleDriver( ));

    Connection conn = DriverManager.getConnection(
      "jdbc:oracle:oci8:@dssora01.dss","scott","tiger");

    Statement stmt = conn.createStatement( );
    ResultSet rset = stmt.executeQuery(
      "select 'Hello OCI driver tester '||USER||'!' result from dual");
    while(rset.next( ))
      System.out.println(rset.getString(1));
    rset.close( );
    stmt.close( );
    conn.close( );
  }
}
```

For this example to work, the following conditions must be met:

- You must have the Oracle8*i* client installed.
- The Oracle *classes12.zip* file must be listed in your CLASSPATH.
- You must have JDK 1.2.x or higher installed.
- You must have access to an Oracle8*i* (or higher) database.

To compile the program, type the code into a file named *TestOCIApp.java* (remember, Java is case-sensitive). Be sure to change the database, username, and password to values that will work in your environment. Then, to compile and execute the program, type the commands shown in the following example:

```
c:\> javac TestOCIApp.java
c:\> java TestOCIApp
Hello OCI driver tester SCOTT!
```

You should get the short message shown in the example as your output. However, there are a couple of things that can go wrong that will result in an error message and stack trace being displayed instead. For example, you might get an error message such as the following:

```
Exception in thread "main" java.lang.ClassNotFoundException: oracle.jdbc.driver.
OracleDriver
        at java.net.URLClassLoader$1.run(URLClassLoader.java:202)
        at java.security.AccessController.doPrivileged(Native Method)
        at java.net.URLClassLoader.findClass(URLClassLoader.java:191)
        at java.lang.ClassLoader.loadClass(ClassLoader.java:290)
        at sun.misc.Launcher$AppClassLoader.loadClass(Launcher.java:286)
        at java.lang.ClassLoader.loadClass(ClassLoader.java:247)
        at java.lang.Class.forName0(Native Method)
        at java.lang.Class.forName(Class.java:124)
        at TestOCIApp.main(TestOCIApp.java, Compiled Code)
```

This error message indicates that your CLASSPATH setting is probably missing the Oracle JDBC classes file. When looking at a stack trace such as this, you can usually identify the problem by looking at the error message in the first line. In this case, note the ClassNotFoundException and the associated reference to oracle.jdbc.driver.OracleDriver. The rest of the output is a backtrace that shows Java method calls in reverse order. See "Handling Exceptions" later in this chapter for information on reading stack traces.

You can correct the problem with the CLASSPATH setting by adding your Oracle JDBC classes file to your CLASSPATH environment variable. For example, if your Oracle JDBC classes file is located in *c:\oracle\ora81\jdbc\lib\classes12.zip*, then your CLASSPATH environment variable should look something like this:

```
CLASSPATH=c:\oracle\ora81\jdbc\lib\classes12.zip;
```

Even worse than the CLASSPATH error is the one indicated by the following message:

```
Exception in thread "main" java.lang.UnsatisfiedLinkError:  C:\Oracle\Ora81\BIN\
ocijdbc8.dll: One of the library files needed to run this application cannot be found
        at java.lang.ClassLoader$NativeLibrary.load(Native Method)
        at java.lang.ClassLoader.loadLibrary0(ClassLoader.java:1319)
        at java.lang.ClassLoader.loadLibrary(ClassLoader.java:1243)
        at java.lang.Runtime.loadLibrary0(Runtime.java:470)
        at java.lang.System.loadLibrary(System.java:778)
        at oracle.jdbc.oci8.OCIDBAccess.logon(OCIDBAccess.java:208)
        at oracle.jdbc.driver.OracleConnection.<init>(OracleConnection.java:198)
        at oracle.jdbc.driver.OracleDriver.getConnectionInstance
        (OracleDriver.java:251)
```

```
        at oracle.jdbc.driver.OracleDriver.connect(OracleDriver.java:224)
        at java.sql.DriverManager.getConnection(DriverManager.java:457)
        at java.sql.DriverManager.getConnection(DriverManager.java:137)
        at TestOCIApp.main(TestOCIApp.java, Compiled Code)
```

This error indicates that you have a mismatch between your JDBC classes file and your Oracle client version. The giveaway here is the message stating that a needed library file cannot be found. For example, you may be using a *classes12.zip* file from Oracle Version 8.1.6 with a Version 8.1.5 Oracle client. The *classeXXXs.zip* file and Oracle client software versions must match.

Note that my example programs explicitly close the `ResultSet`, `Statement`, and `Connection` objects. That's because the Oracle implementation of JDBC does not have `finalizer` methods. If you don't explicitly close your Oracle JDBC resources, you will run out of database connections, cursors, and/or memory. So remember to always close your Oracle JDBC resources! This is contrary to what you may read about other implementations of JDBC.

A Thin driver example

The second example program, Example 2-2, is just like the first except that it tests the Thin driver. You'll notice that the only significant changes are the use of the word thin in the database URL instead of oci8 and the use of the host:port:sid syntax instead of a net service name.

Example 2-2. A test of the Thin driver for an application

```java
import java.sql.*;

class TestThinApp {

  public static void main (String args[])
   throws ClassNotFoundException, SQLException {

    Class.forName("oracle.jdbc.driver.OracleDriver");
    // or you can use:
    // DriverManager.registerDriver(new oracle.jdbc.driver.OracleDriver());

    Connection conn = DriverManager.getConnection(
      "jdbc:oracle:thin:@dssnt01:1521:dssora01","scott","tiger");

    Statement stmt = conn.createStatement();
    ResultSet rset = stmt.executeQuery(
      "select 'Hello Thin driver tester '||USER||'!' result from dual");
    while(rset.next())
      System.out.println(rset.getString(1));
    rset.close();
    stmt.close();
    conn.close();
  }
}
```

For this example to work, the following conditions must be met:

- You must have the Oracle *classes12.zip* file listed in your CLASSPATH.
- You must have JDK 1.2.x or higher installed.
- You must have access to an Oracle8*i* (or higher) database.

To compile the program, type the code into a file named *TestThinApp.java*. Change the database, in the form *host:port:sid*, the username, and the password to appropriate values for your environment. Then type the commands shown in the following example to compile and run the program:

```
C:\> javac TestThinApp.java
C:\> java TestThinApp
Hello Thin driver tester SCOTT!
```

If you did everything correctly, you should get the "Hello" message shown here when you run the program. Did you also notice that it takes less time for the Thin driver to establish a connection to the database than was required for the OCI driver? I'll talk about why that is in Chapter 19.

If you entered an invalid username or password, you may have received output such as the following when you ran the program:

```
Exception in thread "main" java.sql.SQLException: ORA-01017: invalid
username/password; logon denied
        at oracle.jdbc.ttc7.TTIoer.processError(TTIoer.java)
        at oracle.jdbc.ttc7.O3log.receive2nd(O3log.java, Compiled Code)
        at oracle.jdbc.ttc7.TTC7Protocol.logon(TTC7Protocol.java)
        at oracle.jdbc.driver.OracleConnection.<init>(OracleConnection.java)
        at oracle.jdbc.driver.OracleDriver.getConnectionInstance
        (OracleDriver.java)
        at oracle.jdbc.driver.OracleDriver.connect(OracleDriver.java)
        at java.sql.DriverManager.getConnection(DriverManager.java:457)
        at java.sql.DriverManager.getConnection(DriverManager.java:137)
        at TestThinApp.main(TestThinApp.java, Compiled Code)
```

By examining this exception, specifically the first line, you can see that the error was indeed caused by specifying an invalid username or password. Seeing that it is highly probable that a user will make a mistake entering his username or password, you'll want to catch this error and react appropriately, possibly giving him another chance to enter his username and password. To do that, you'll need to know how to handle exceptions.

Handling Exceptions

If you're a PL/SQL programmer, then the concept of exceptions will not be all that new to you. If you're new to Java and have not previously used a programming language that uses exception handling, then this material may get confusing. Hang in there! By the time we're done, you should have a fairly good idea of what exceptions are and how to deal with them in your JDBC programs.

Java Exception Handling

In Java, exception handling allows you to handle exceptional conditions such as program-defined errors in a controlled fashion. When an exception condition occurs, an exception is thrown. The term *thrown* means that current program execution stops, and control is redirected to the nearest applicable catch clause. If no applicable catch clause exists, then the program's execution ends.

Try blocks

Both the JVM and you—explicitly in your own code—can throw an exception. Java uses a try-catch-finally control block similar to PL/SQL's BEGIN-EXCEPTION-END block. The try statement encloses a block of code that is "risky"—in other words, which can throw an exception—and that you wish to handle in such a way as to maintain control of the program in the event that an exception is thrown. Exceptions thrown in a try block are handled by a catch clause coded to catch an exception of its type or one of its ancestors. For example, when using JDBC, the exception type thrown is usually a SQLException.

A try statement can have any number of catch clauses necessary to handle the different types of exceptions that can occur within the try block. A try block can also have a finally clause. The finally clause is always executed before control leaves the try block but after the first applicable catch clause. Here is the general form of a try block:

```
try {
 // Your risky code goes between these curly braces!!!
}
catch(Exception e) {
 // Your exception handling code goes between these curly braces,
 // similar to the exception clause in a PL/SQL block.
}
finally {
 // Your must-always-be-executed code goes between these curly braces.
}
```

You need to have at least a catch or a finally clause, or both, after a try statement.

An Exception object, or Throwable, is passed in the catch clause. By using this Exception object, or a subclass of it, you can find out additional information about what caused the exception to occur and deal with it appropriately. For example, if you use an object variable that is null (i.e., it does not hold an object reference), your program will throw a NullPointerException. By utilizing a try block, you can capture this error, communicate the problem to the program user in a meaningful way, and exit your program gracefully. If you don't capture the exception, the exception will cause a stack trace to print, and the program will abort.

Try block nesting behavior

Just as PL/SQL blocks can be nested, so can try blocks. This means that if your nested try block does not handle a particular exception, that exception will propagate to the next level. If an exception is not handled at all, then the JVM handles it by printing a stack trace and aborting the program. Look, for example, at the following code:

```
Date        startDate = null;
Long        personId  = null;
Statement stmt1       = null;
Statement stmt2       = null;
String      firstName = null;
String      lastName  = null;
ResultSet rset1       = null;
ResultSet rset2       = null;

try { // try block level 1
  stmt1 = conn.createStatement( );
  rset1 = stmt1.executeQuery(
   "select person_id, last_name, first_name " +
   "from    person");
  while(rset1.next( )) {
    personId  = new Long(rset1.getLong(1));
    lastName  = rset1.getString(2);
    firstName = rset1.getString(3);
  }
  try { // try block level 2
    stmt2 = conn.createStatement( );
    rset2 = stmt2.executeQuery(
     "select p.start_date, p.end_date, l.name " +
     "from    person_location p, location l " +
     "where   p.location_id = l.location_id " +
     "and     p.person_id   = " + personId.toString( ));
    while(rset2.next( )) {
      startDate = rset2.getDate(1);
      endDate   = rset2.getDate(2);
      name      = rset2.getString(3);
      if (new SimpleDateFormat("yyyy").format(endDate).equals("2000")) {
        // ... output some data
      }
    }
    rset2.close( );
    rset2 = null;
    stmt2.close( );
    stmt2 = null;
  }
  catch(SQLException e2) {
    System.err.println("SQLException in the inner loop!");
  } // end of try block 2
```

```
    rset1.close( );
    rset1 = null;
    stmt1.close( );
    stmt1 = null;
  }
  catch(SQLException e1) {
    System.err.println("SQLException in the outer loop!");
  } // part of try block 1
  catch(NullPointerException) {
    System.err.println("NullPointerException in outer loop!");
  } // end of try block 1
  finally {
    if (rset2 != null)
      try {rset2.close( );} catch(SQLException ignore) {}
    if (stmt2 != null)
      try {stmt2.close( );} catch(SQLException ignore) {}
    if (rset1 != null)
      try {rset1.close( );} catch(SQLException ignore) {}
    if (stmt1 != null)
      try {stmt1.close( );} catch(SQLException ignore) {}
  }
```

When the `if` statement in the second, nested `try` block tests to see if the end date for a location assignment was in the year 2000, and it encounters an end date that is NULL in the database, it throws a `NullPointerException`. The second `try` block does not handle this exception, so the exception will propagate outwards to the first `try` block. A `catch` clause in the first `try` block does handle the exception, so it won't propagate any further than that. After the exception is handled by the first `try` block, that block's `finally` clause will be executed, and the program will then terminate normally.

SQLException Methods

For JDBC, the most common exception you'll deal with is `java.sql.SQLException`. A `SQLException` can occur both in the driver and the database. When such an exception occurs, an object of type `SQLException` will be passed to the catch clause. The passed `SQLException` object has the following methods available for retrieving additional information about the exception:

`getErrorCode( )`
    Gets the Oracle error number associated with the exception.

`getMessage( )`
    Gets the JDBC driver's error message for an error handled by the driver or gets the Oracle error number and message for a database error.

`getSQLState( )`
    Gets the XOPEN SQLstate string. For a JDBC driver error, no useful information is returned from this method. For a database error, the five-digit XOPEN SQLstate code is returned. This method can return `null`, so you should program accordingly.

`getNextException( )`

    Gets the next `Exception` object in the exception chain.

`printStackTrace( )`

    Prints the current exception, or throwable, and its backtrace to a standard error stream.

`printStackTrace(PrintStream s)`

    Prints this throwable and its backtrace to the print stream you specify.

`printStackTrace(PrintWriter w)`

    Prints this throwable and its backtrace to the print writer you specify.

By utilizing the information available from the `Exception` object, you can catch an exception and continue your program appropriately. Take, for example, our problem with the invalid username or password. If `getErrorCode( )` returns 1017, you know that the problem is an invalid username or password and can modify your program to ask the user to respecify her username and password. It is important for you to know how to handle exceptions because sometimes they are the only means of program control, as is the case with our previous example. You can find a complete listing of Oracle8i database error codes, messages, and a diagnostic in the *Oracle8i Error Messages* manual available at OTN.

Now that we have covered the basics of establishing a connection to an Oracle database, let's examine issues specific to connecting to a database from an applet.

CHAPTER 3

Applet Database Connections

In this chapter, we'll explore issues that are specific to using JDBC with applets. We'll begin by asking the question: "What type of JDBC driver supports an applet, and for which versions of the JDK?" Then we'll talk about other things you need to know, such as the life cycle of an applet, when to open and close a database connection, how to package an applet that uses Oracle JDBC classes, how to deal with the restrictions placed on JDBC connections by the secure environment of your browser's JVM, and how to connect through a firewall.

Oracle Drivers and JDK Versions

For applets, you have only one driver choice: the client-side Thin driver. Since it's a 100% pure Java driver, you can package it with your applet's archive so it's downloaded by the browser along with your applet. I'll discuss how to package the Thin driver with your applet later in this chapter. For now, just keep in mind as we go along that you'll need to package the appropriate *classesXXX.zip* file with your applet, and you'll be using the Thin database URL syntax discussed in Chapter 2.

As of Oracle8*i* Version 8.1.6, JDK 1.0.x is no longer supported by Oracle. Instead, Oracle8*i* now supports only JDK Versions 1.1.x and 1.2.x. Table 3-1 lists the support files you need to package with your applet to support each of these versions.

Table 3-1. JDBC support files

JDK version	JDBC classes	National Language Support classes
JDK 1.1.x	classes111.zip	nls_charset11.zip
JDK 1.2.x	classes12.zip	nls_charset12.zip

In addition to matching up your applet with the correct support files for the JDK version with which you are developing, you must also make sure that the browser you're targeting (i.e., on which you intend to run your applet) supports the same JDK that you are using to develop the applet. Currently, you either need to use JDK 1.1.x or need to depend on your end users having the Java 2 browser plug-in installed in their browsers. Without that plug-in, the currently predominant versions of both Internet Explorer and Netscape Navigator support only JDK 1.1.x. The newest versions of these browsers, such as Netscape Navigator 6 and other browsers programmed using Java, support JDK 1.2.x or later.

Now that you know which JDBC driver and Oracle JDBC classes to use, let's continue by discussing the implications that the life cycle of an applet has on your JDBC program.

It's an Applet's Life

From a programmer's perspective, an applet has four stages to its life cycle. They are defined by the following four methods that are called by the browser as the applet is loaded and run:

init( )
> This is called just after an applet is created and before the applet is displayed in the browser. It is normally used to perform any initialization that should take place only once in the life cycle of the applet. This includes the creation of a thread to run the applet.

start( )
> This is called when the applet becomes visible in your browser and is used to start the thread that runs the applet.

stop( )
> This is called when the applet is no longer visible. When this method is called, a well behaved applet will put its thread to sleep, or stop the thread entirely, in order to conserve computer resources.

destroy( )
> This is called when the applet is purged from your browser's memory cache. It is used to stop the applet's thread and to release any other computer resources the applet may be using.

The choice of which of these methods you use to open and close a database connection is not straightforward. You must consider how you will use the connection within your applet. If your applet will open a database connection, retrieve some data, then close the connection, and do this only once, you may wish to perform these functions in init( ), as part of start( ), or in a method you create that is in turn run by the thread you start in the start( ) method. If your applet will continue to use its connection throughout its life cycle, you will need to consider whether to use init( ) and destroy( ) or start( ) and stop( ) to open and close the connection.

If you use init( ) and destroy( ) to open and close an applet's connection, you will minimize your cost, because the connection will remain open as long as the applet is in the browser's cache. Opening and closing a database connection is very costly in time and resources, so this can be a good thing. Remember, however, that your database connection will not be closed until the browser flushes the applet from its cache or until the applet closes the connection itself. Balance this behavior against the results of using start( ) and stop( ). Using start( ) and stop( ) will require your applet to open and close the database connection each time the applet appears and disappears from your browser's screen. You risk incurring greater overhead because of the additional open and close activity. However, you reduce the number of simultaneous connections to your database, because the connection will not remain open while the applet is off the screen, even when it is still in the browser's cache.

Example 3-1 shows the code for a simple applet that demonstrates just what we have been discussing. Following that is an HTML file in Example 3-2 that invokes the sample applet. To run the example, follow these steps:

1. Modify the database URL in Example 3-1, changing the username, password, host, port number, and SID to values appropriate for your installation.

2. Compile the applet.

3. Make a copy of your Oracle *classesXXX.zip* file, giving it the same name as the applet but retaining the *.zip* suffix. In the case of Example 3-1, you should name your new file *TestApplet.zip*.

4. Add the applet's class file to your new zip file. According to Oracle's documentation, the zip file must be uncompressed.

5. Copy the *TestApplet.zip* and *TestApplet.html* files to an appropriate directory on a web server.

6. Open the HTML file in your browser.

7. Turn on your browser's Java Console.

Example 3-1. A test life cycle applet

```
import java.applet.Applet;
import java.awt.*;
import java.sql.*;

public class TestApplet extends Applet {
  private Connection conn;
  private Timestamp created = new Timestamp(System.currentTimeMillis( ));

  public void init( ) {
    try {
      System.out.println(
        "init( ): loading OracleDriver for applet created at " +
        created.toString( ));

      Class.forName("oracle.jdbc.driver.OracleDriver");
      System.out.println("init( ): getting connection");
      conn = DriverManager.getConnection(
        "jdbc:oracle:thin:@dssw2k01:1521:orcl","scott","tiger");
    }
    catch (ClassNotFoundException e) {
      System.err.println("init(): ClassNotFoundException: " + e.getMessage( ));
```

Example 3-1. A test life cycle applet (continued)

```
    }
    catch (SQLException e) {
      System.err.println("init(): SQLException: " + e.getMessage());
    }
  }

  public void start() {
    System.out.println("start(): ");
  }

  public void stop() {
    System.out.println("stop(): ");
  }

  public void paint(Graphics g) {
    System.out.println("paint(): querying the database");
    try {
      Statement stmt = conn.createStatement();
      ResultSet rset = stmt.executeQuery(
        "select 'Hello '||initcap(USER) result from dual");
      while(rset.next())
        g.drawString(rset.getString(1),10,10);
      rset.close();
      stmt.close();
    }
    catch (SQLException e) {
      System.err.println("paint(): SQLException: " + e.getMessage());
    }
  }

  public void destroy() {
    System.out.println(
      "destroy(): closing connection for applet created at " +
      created.toString());
    try {
      conn.close();
    }
    catch (SQLException e) {
      System.err.println("destroy: SQLException: " + e.getMessage());
    }
  }
}
```

Example 3-2. A Test Life Cycle Applet's HTML File

```
<html>
<head>
</head>
<body>
<applet code=TestApplet archive=TestApplet.zip width=100 height=25></applet>
</body>
</html>
```

When you execute the applet, you'll see different behavior depending on your browser. If you're using Internet Explorer 4, the applet will be downloaded and cached. Then it will be created, triggering the init( ) method followed by the start( ) method. Now you should see "Hello Scott" or whatever username you used in the applet. If you go to another URL, the stop( ) method is called, followed by the destroy( ) method. If you have the applet on screen and click on the Reload button, you'll see the stop( ) and destroy( ) methods again followed by init( ) and start( ).

If you're using Netscape Navigator 4, you'll see different behavior more closely following my previous explanation about an applet's life cycle. First, the applet will be downloaded and cached. Next, the init( ) method will be called followed by the start( ) method. This time, when you go to another URL, only the stop( ) method is called. When you return to the applet's URL, the start( ) method is called. It's not until you click on Reload or the browser runs out of memory cache that the destroy( ) method is called.

If you're ambitious, you can change one of the System.out.println( ) messages in the applet, rebuild it, put it into the web server's directory while you still have your browser open, and then click on Reload. Guess what? Neither browser actually reloads the applet from the server. You won't see your new applet version until you close and reopen your browser.

Now that you have a better idea of the life cycle of an applet, and how it varies depending on the browser, you may appreciate what I stated earlier: knowing when to open and close a database connection is not straightforward. You must determine which model to use based on how the applet will be used by the end user. Once you've decided on the best strategy for opening and closing your database connection, then you may be faced with restrictions that the browser environment places on an applet's ability to make a connection. But before we discuss that issue, let's move on to the next section and talk a little about packaging your applets.

Packaging Your Applet

After you have written your applet, you'll want to combine its class files with those from the appropriate Oracle *classesXXX.zip* file into a single zip or jar file as you did for Example 3-1. This step is necessary because an applet using JDBC is naturally quite complex and contains many classes. Getting to just one file makes things easier to manage. It is also simpler and more efficient to specify just one file in the HTML APPLET tag rather than specify multiple archive files.

 For simplicity's sake, this discussion on packaging focuses on the use of JDK 1.2. If you are using JDK 1.1, the syntax for using the jar tool to create the jar file will be slightly different. If you use WinZip, the procedure will be the same as it is for JDK 1.2.

A Development Packaging Cycle

During the development stage for an applet, you can begin your packaging effort by simply making a copy of the Oracle *classes12.zip* file. Give it the name of your archive file but retain the *.zip* extension. Then add your applet's class files, uncompressed, to the zip file that you just copied and renamed. Why uncompressed? I actually don't know. This is an Oracle recommendation. I have used them as compressed class files when I have created a jar file, but I have never done so using a zip file. For example, if you're going to create a zip file for an applet named TestAppletPolicy, you should follow these steps:

1. Copy the file *classes12.zip* to *TestAppletPolicy.zip*. On a Windows system, you can do this by executing a command such as:

   ```
   copy c:\windows\ora81\jdbc\lib\classes12.zip TestAppletPolicy.zip
   ```

2. Add your applet's class files to *TestAppletPolicy.zip* using your favorite zip utility. With WinZip, you can right-click on the *TestAppletPolicy.class* file and select Add to Zip. Then just select *TestAppletPolicy.zip* as your destination zip file.

3. As you make changes to your applet, you can continue reading, or refreshing, your applet's files to the *TestAppletPolicy.zip* file. Any time you create a new version of your applet, repeat step 2 to add it to the zip file, overwriting the previous version.

In order to run your applet within a browser, create an HTML file with an APPLET tag, and specify the name of your archive file in the APPLET tag's ARCHIVE parameter. Then, load that HTML file into your browser window.

Production Packaging Cycles

When it comes time to put your highly polished applet into production, you can use the same method as you did for development or the JDK's jar utility to build a new jar file. Regardless, you can reduce the size of your archive by eliminating the *OracleDatabaseMetaData.class* file if it is not needed. The *OracleDatabaseMetaData.class* file allows you to query the database for the names of tables, stored procedures, and so forth. This file is 42 KB in size and a waste of network bandwidth if it is not needed.

To create a zip file, follow the steps outlined for a development packaging cycle in the previous section. To create a jar file for an applet, follow these steps:

1. Create a temporary directory to hold all the class files that you want to place into your new archive. For example, use the command md jar to create a temporary packaging directory named *jar*.

2. Make the temporary directory that you just created your current working directory. Use the command cd jar to do this.

3. Unzip the JDBC support classes into your temporary directory, preserving the directory structure. To unzip the *classes12.zip* file, for example, execute the following command:

```
jar xf c:\oracle\ora81\jdbc\lib\classes12.zip
```

The *jar* utility will then unzip the Oracle *classes12.zip* file into your current working directory. The directory structure of the classes in the zip file will be preserved with subdirectories being created as necessary.

4. Copy your applet's class file to your temporary directory. For example, copy the file *TestAppletPolicy.class* to your *jar* directory by executing the command:

```
copy ..\TestAppletPolicy.class
```

5. If your application never makes a call to Connection.getMetaData( ), delete the *OracleDatabaseMetaData.class* file by executing the command:

```
del oracle\jdbc\driver\OracleDatabaseMetaData.class
```

6. Create a compressed jar file containing all the files in your temporary directory and in subdirectories underneath it. For example, to create a compressed jar file for the TestAppletPolicy applet, execute:

```
jar cf TestAppletPolicy.jar *
```

If you want to create an uncompressed jar, as Oracle suggests, you can do so by executing:

```
jar c0f TestAppletPolicy.jar *
```

Oracle NLS Support

What if you use Oracle's National Language Support (NLS) in your applet? In this case, you'll have to include the necessary NLS files in your jar file. To do that, follow these steps:

1. Unzip the *nls_charset12.zip* file into a temporary directory separate from the one you are using to package your applet. You'll get an *nls\oracle\sql\converter* directory structure as a result.

2. Identify the NLS class file(s) you need.

3. Create an *nls\oracle\sql\converter* directory structure underneath your temporary packaging directory.

4. Copy the NLS class file(s) you need into your *nls\oracle\sql\converter* directory.

You can identify the NLS class files you need by looking in Table 3-2 to find the Oracle character set IDs for the character sets your applet uses. These character set IDs are four-digit numbers that are part of the filenames of the NLS language files. The naming convention is:

```
CharacterConverterOracle_character_set_id.class
```

For example, if you needed to support character set US8PC437, create the directory structure *nls\oracle\sql\converter* in your temporary packaging directory and copy the file *CharacterConverter0004.class* from the *nls\oracle\sql\converter* directory in which you unzipped the NLS classes to the *nls\oracle\sql\converter* directory in your temporary packaging directory.

Table 3-2. Oracle character converter classes and the NLS character sets they support

Oracle character set ID	NLS_CHARSET_NAME	Oracle character set ID	NLS_CHARSET_NAME
0003	WE8HP	002d	VN8MSWIN1258
0004	US8PC437	0032	WE8NEXTSTEP
0005	WE8EBCDIC37	003d	AR8ASMO708PLUS
0006	WE8EBCDIC500	0046	AR8EBCDICX
0008	WE8EBCDIC285	0048	AR8XBASIC
000a	WE8PC850	0051	EL8DEC
000b	D7DEC	0052	TR8DEC
000c	F7DEC	005a	WE8EBCDIC37C
000d	S7DEC	005b	WE8EBCDIC500C
000e	E7DEC	005c	IW8EBCDIC424
000f	SF7ASCII	005d	TR8EBCDIC1026
0010	NDK7DEC	005e	WE8EBCDIC871
0011	I7DEC	005f	WF8EBCDIC284
0012	NL7DEC	0060	WE8EBCDIC1047
0013	CH7DEC	006e	EEC8EUROASCI
0014	YUG7ASCII	0071	EEC8EUROPA3
0015	SF7DEC	0072	LA8PASSPORT
0016	TR7DEC	008c	BG8PC437S
0017	IW7IS960	0096	EE8PC852
0019	IN8ISCII	0098	RU8PC866
0020	EE8ISO8859P2	0099	RU8BESTA
0021	SE8ISO8859P3	009a	IW8PC1507
0022	NEE8ISO8859P4	009b	RU8PC855
0023	CL8ISO8859P5	009c	TR8PC857
0024	AR8ISO8859P6	009e	CL8MACCYRILLIC
0025	FI8ISO8859P7	009f	CL8MACCYRILLICS
0026	IW8ISO8859P8	00a0	WE8PC860
0027	WE8ISO8859P9	00a1	IS8PC861
0028	NE8ISO8859P10	00a2	EE8MACCES
0029	TH8TISASCII	00a3	EE8MACCROATIANS
002a	TH8TISEBCDIC	00a4	TR8MACTURKISHS
002b	BN8BSCII	00a5	IS8MACICELANDICS
002c	VN8VN3	00a6	EL8MACGREEKS

Oracle character set ID	NLS_CHARSET_NAME	Oracle character set ID	NLS_CHARSET_NAME
00a7	IW8MACHEBREWS	00d3	EL8GCOS7
00aa	EE8MSWIN1250	00dd	US8BS2000
00ab	CL8MSWIN1251	00de	D8BS2000
00ac	ET8MSWIN923	00df	F8BS2000
00ad	BG8MSWIN	00e0	E8BS2000
00ae	EL8MSWIN1253	00e1	DK8BS2000
00af	IW8MSWIN1255	00e2	S8BS2000
00b0	LT8MSWIN921	00e7	WE8BS2000
00b1	TR8MSWIN1254	00eb	CL8BS2000
00b2	WE8MSWIN1252	00ef	WE8BS2000L5
00b3	BLT8MSWIN1257	00f1	WE8DG
00b4	D8EBCDIC273	00fb	WE8NCR4970
00b5	I8EBCDIC280	0105	WE8ROMAN8
00b6	DK8EBCDIC277	0106	EE8MACCE
00b7	S8EBCDIC278	0107	EE8MACCROATIAN
00b8	EE8EBCDIC870	0108	TR8MACTURKISH
00b9	CL8EBCDIC1025	0109	IS8MACICELANDIC
00ba	F8EBCDIC297	010a	EL8MACGREEK
00bb	IW8EBCDIC1086	010b	IW8MACHEBREW
00bc	CL8EBCDIC1025X	0115	US8ICL
00be	N8PC865	0116	WE8ICL
00bf	BLT8CP921	0117	WE8ISOICLUK
00c0	LV8PC1117	015f	WE8MACROMAN8
00c1	LV8PC8LR	0160	WE8MACROMAN8S
00c2	BLT8EBCDIC1112	0161	TH8MACTHAI
00c3	LV8RST104090	0162	TH8MACTHAIS
00c4	CL8KOI8R	0170	HU8CWI2
00c5	BLT8PC775	017c	EL8PC437S
00c9	F7SIEMENS9780X	017d	EL8EBCDIC875
00ca	E7SIEMENS9780X	017e	EL8PC737
00cb	S7SIEMENS9780X	017f	LT8PC772
00cc	DK7SIEMENS9780X	0180	LT8PC774
00cd	N7SIEMENS9780X	0181	EL8PC869
00ce	I7SIEMENS9780X	0182	EL8PC851
00cf	D7SIEMENS9780X	0186	CDN8PC863
00d2	WE8GCOS7	0191	HU8ABMOD

Table 3-2. Oracle character converter classes and the NLS character sets they support (continued)

Oracle character set ID	NLS_CHARSET_NAME	Oracle character set ID	NLS_CHARSET_NAME
01f4	AR8ASMO08X	0344	JA16MACSJIS
01f8	AR8NAFITHA711T	0348	KO16KSC5601
01f9	AR8SAKHR707T	034a	KO16DBCS
01fa	AR8MUSSAD768T	034d	KO16KSCCS
01fb	AR8ADOS710T	034e	KO16MSWIN949
01fc	AR8ADOS720T	0352	ZHS16CGB231280
01fd	AR8APTEC715T	0353	ZHS16MACCGB231280
01ff	AR8NAFITHA721T	0354	ZHS16GBK
0202	AR8HPARABIC8T	0355	ZHS16DBCS
022a	AR8NAFITHA711	035c	ZHT32EUC
022b	AR8SAKHR707	035d	ZHT32SOPS
022c	AR8MUSSAD768	035e	ZHT16DBT
022d	AR8ADOS710	035f	ZHT32TRIS
022e	AR8ADOS720	0360	ZHT16DBCS
022f	AR8APTEC715	0361	ZHT16BIG5
0230	AR8MSAWIN	0362	ZHT16CCDC
0231	AR8NAFITHA721	0363	ZHT16MSWIN950
0233	AR8SAKHR706	03e4	KO16TSTSET
0235	AR8ARABICMAC	03e6	JA16TSTSET
0236	AR8ARABICMACS	0726	JA16EUCFIXED
0237	AR8ARABICMACT	0728	JA16SJISFIXED
024e	LA8ISO6937	0729	JA16DBCSFIXED
031d	US8NOOP	0730	KO16KSC5601FIXED
031e	WE8DECTST	0732	KO16DBCSFIXED
033d	JA16VMS	073a	ZHS16CGB231280FIXED
033e	JA16EUC	073c	ZHS16GBKFIXED
033f	JA16EUCYEN	073d	ZHS16DBCSFIXED
0340	JA16SJIS	0744	ZHT32EUCFIXED
0341	JA16DBCS	0747	ZHT32TRISFIXED
0342	JA16SJISYEN	0748	ZHT16DBCSFIXED
0343	JA16EBCDIC930	0749	ZHT16BIG5FIXED

The Oracle character set IDs shown in Table 3-2 and used in the CharacterConverter class files are the hexadecimal values for the character set IDs. For more information on using NLS, see the Oracle8i *National Language Support Guide*, which is available on the Oracle Technology Network (OTN).

Now that you understand how to gather your applet's files into an archive, we can begin our discussion about the restrictions a browser places on an applet's ability to make a database connection and the options available to work around these restrictions.

Getting Around the Sandbox

Applets run in a JVM in your browser. For security reasons, applets, by default, run with restricted access to your computer's local resources. This restricted access to your computer's local resources, or "sandbox" as it is affectionately (sometimes not-so-affectionately) called, limits an applet's ability to contact other computers over the network. The rule is that applets are limited to opening *sockets*, or network connections, only to the host from which they are downloaded. In effect, this limits any applet to connecting to a database only on the same host from which it was downloaded. If your database is installed on the same host as your web server, then this does not pose a problem, but often, databases reside on a host of their own. When the latter is the case, there are two ways you can work around this limitation using JDBC. The first is to use Oracle's Connection Manager. The second is to get socket permissions for your applet.

If you try to connect to a database on a host other than the source of the applet, you'll get a security exception. For example, the following is a security exception received from Internet Explorer while running the applet named TestApplet:

```
init(): loading OracleDriver for applet created at 2000-09-30 19:20:21.606
init(): getting connection
com.ms.security.SecurityExceptionEx[TestAppletInitDestroy.init]: cannot connect to
"dssnt01"
```

Here is the same exception obtained from Netscape Navigator:

```
init(): loading OracleDriver for applet created at 2000-09-30 19:22:33.576
init(): getting connection
netscape.security.AppletSecurityException: security.Couldn't connect to 'dssnt01'
with origin from 'dssw2k01'.
```

Let's continue our discussion by looking at how to get around this restriction by using Oracle's Connection Manager.

Using Connection Manager

Connection Manager is a lightweight, highly scalable, middle-tier program that receives and forwards Net8 packets from one source to another. When Connection Manager resides on the same host as a web server, an applet can get around the network connection restriction of the sandbox by making a connection to Connection Manager, which will in turn forward any Net8 requests on to the appropriate database listener. As I stated in Chapter 2, you can classify the combined use of Oracle's Thin driver together with Connection Manager as a Type 3 driver. To use Connection Manager, you must install it on the same host as your applet's web server. Then you must use a special form of database URL. And you thought we had covered every possible type didn't you? First, let's cover Connection Manager's installation.

Installing Connection Manager

Installing Connection Manager is a simple process involving the following steps:

1. Install Connection Manager from the Oracle Enterprise Edition original distribution CD.
2. Create a configuration file.
3. Start Connection Manager by executing cmctl start.

Follow your operating system's specific instructions to run the Oracle Universal Installer from the original distribution CD. You must choose Install and then select a Custom Install. Next, browse through the uninstalled products list until you find Oracle Connection Manager. Select it and then proceed through the installation following the instructions on the screen.

After you're done installing Connection Manager, look in your *$ORACLE_HOME\ network\admin\sample* directory for a file named *cman.ora*. That file will be a template of a Connection Manager configuration file. Copy the *cman.ora* file to *$ORACLE_HOME\network\admin*. This will give you a default configuration for Connection Manager that uses TCP/IP port 1630 for your JDBC connection. Port 1830 will be used for Connection Manager's administrator program, which is named *cmctl*. The default configuration file contains a large number of comment lines. Example 3-3 shows only the uncommented lines so you can easily see the port number assignments.

Example 3-3. The default Connection Manager configuration file

```
cman = (ADDRESS_LIST=
          (ADDRESS=(PROTOCOL=tcp)(HOST=)(PORT=1630)(QUEUESIZE=32))
      )

cman_admin = (ADDRESS=(PROTOCOL=tcp)(HOST=)(PORT=1830))
cman_profile = (parameter_list=
                 (MAXIMUM_RELAYS=1024)
                 (LOG_LEVEL=1)
                 (TRACING=yes)
                 (TRACE_DIRECTORY=C:\Oracle\Ora81\Network\Log)
                 (RELAY_STATISTICS=yes)
                 (SHOW_TNS_INFO=yes)
                 (USE_ASYNC_CALL=yes)
                 (AUTHENTICATION_LEVEL=0)
                 (REMOTE_ADMIN=FALSE)
               )
```

If you need to reconfigure Connection Manager to use a different set of ports, modify the PORT= item for the cman and cman_admin listening addresses in your *cman.ora* file. Remember to use your new cman port setting in your JDBC database URL.

Finally, to start Connection Manager, execute the command cmctl start. Now, your last step in utilizing Connection Manager is to formulate a database URL.

Formulating a database URL for Connection Manager

When you formulate a database URL for Connection Manager, you're essentially combining an address to Connection Manager with an address to a database. You will use Oracle's Net8 Transparent Network Substrate (TNS) keyword-value syntax to pass two addresses to the Thin driver—the Net8 keyword-value syntax is the only means of specifying more than one address in a URL. The first address will be for the web server host. The second will be for your target database. Since the second address is for a database, it will also specify an Oracle SID. Formulating a database URL for Connection Manager is where most of the problems using Connection Manager occur. For the most part, a URL for Connection Manager has the same general format as you saw in Chapter 2:

```
jdbc:oracle:thin:@database
```

When you're connecting through Connection Manager, the *database* portion of the URL takes on the following form:

```
(description=(address_list=
(address=(protocol=tcp)(host=webhost)(port=1630))
(address=(protocol=tcp)(host=orahost)(port=1521)))
(source_route=yes)(connect_data=(sid=orasid)))
```

which breaks down as:

webhost
> The TCP/IP address, or DNS alias, for your web server's host.

1630
> The Connection Manager port number specified in *cman.ora*. 1630 is the default value.

orahost
> The TCP/IP address, or DNS alias, for your target database's host.

1521
> The Net8 listener port number as specified in the *listener.ora* file on your database server. 1521 is the default listener port.

orasid
> The Oracle SID for your target database.

For example, if your web server's alias is *dssw2k01*, your database server's alias is *dssnt01*, and your database SID is *dssora01*, then you should use the following Connection Manager URL:

```
jdbc:oracle:thin:@
(description=(address_list=
(address=(protocol=tcp)(host=dssw2k01)(port=1630))
(address=(protocol=tcp)(host=dssnt01)(port=1521)))
(source_route=yes)(connect_data=(sid=dssora01)))
```

Modify the connection statement of `TestApplet` from Example 3-1 to incorporate this new URL, and the resulting statement will look like this:

```
conn = DriverManager.getConnection(
  "jdbc:oracle:thin:" +
  "@(description=(address_list=" +
  "(address=(protocol=tcp)(host=dssw2k01)(port=1630))" +
  "(address=(protocol=tcp)(host=dssnt01)(port=1521)))" +
  "(source_route=yes)" +
  "(connect_data=(sid=dssora01)))","scott","tiger");
```

Connection Manager can also be used as a connection concentrator or as a firewall. Multiple Connection Manager addresses can be specified prior to your database server address and SID to create a chain of Connection Manager connections. In other words, you can route a connection through any number of Connection Manager instances. For more information on Connection Manager installation, configuration, and use, see Oracle's *Net8 Administrator's Guide*, which is available on the OTN, or *Oracle Net8 Configuration and Troubleshooting*, by Hugo Toledo and Jonathan Gennick (O'Reilly).

If you think using Connection Manager sounds like a lot of work, wait until you learn about the other workaround option: getting socket permissions.

Getting Socket Permissions

In Java, a socket is the object used to make a TCP/IP connection. Therefore, when a JDBC driver makes a connection to a database it uses a socket object. Since an applet's permissions to operating system resources are typically restricted, using a socket on a host other than the one from which the applet was downloaded is not allowed. Some arrangement must be made to remove this restriction in order to make a remote database connection. Often, documentation on this subject states that all you need to do is sign your applet to get socket permissions. That's an oversimplification. In JDK 1.1, the idea was that a signed applet would run with all the same privileges as an application. However, the implementation didn't strictly follow that idea. Instead, in Netscape Navigator you had to use the `Netscape.security` package and enable `UniversalConnect`. Enabling `UniversalConnect` caused the browser to prompt the user to accept the extended privileges required to use Java sockets. Unfortunately, even if you did go through all the work of adding the `Netscape. security` code to your applet, you soon found that it didn't work, because there's a bug in the package that prevents an applet from getting socket permissions. With Internet Explorer, you could set privileges under View → Internet Options for both unsigned and signed applets. That worked, but then you had a single browser solution. So how do you get socket permissions to work for a larger browser audience? The solution is to use the Java 1.2 (or higher) browser plug-in, a little JavaScript, and a security policy entry for socket permissions. And no, you don't have to sign your applet.

Signing your applet will provide your applet's user with the peace of mind of knowing that it's from you and has not been tampered with. Signing can be used as a basis for setting up a security policy, but the actual policy is what will determine whether your applet will be able to make a connection to a database that resides on a host other than the host from which your applet was downloaded.

Java 2 security policies

The Java 2 platform allows you to set up a security policy by *code base*, which is the URL from which your applet is downloaded; by *signed by*, which is the certificate alias in your key store database in conjunction with signing your applet; or by both. If you set up a policy for a particular code base, you have the following options to control the scope of that policy:

- You can name a specific class, zip, or jar file in your code base URL.
- You can end your code base URL with an asterisk (*) and thus apply the policy to any applet file in the specified directory.
- You can end your code base URL with a dash (-) and thus apply the policy to any applet file in the specified directory or in any directory underneath the specified directory.

If instead you set up a policy for a particular certificate alias, then the policy will hold for any file signed with that certificate. Finally, if you use both methods, then not only does the file need to be signed using the specified certificate, but it also has to reside at the specified code base.

Setting up a SocketPermissions policy

In this section, I show you how to add a code base policy for SocketPermission, for a target of the database's host and port combination, and for a connection.

To add a new policy you have one of two choices. You can create a new policy file and add it to the list of policy files for your plug-in by modifying the policy file URLs list in the file *java.security*, which is typically located in the *c:\Program Files\Javasoft\JRE\1.2\ lib\security* directory. Alternatively, you can add a policy to your *user.home/.java.policy* policy file. Table 3-3 lists the locations of the latter. Modify *java.security* if you want the changes to affect all users on a multiuser system; modify the *.java.policy* file to affect only a single user.

Table 3-3. Java user policy file directories

Operating system	User policy file directory
Window 95	*c:\Windows*
Window 98	*c:\Windows*
Windows NT	*c:\WINNT\Profiles\username*
Windows 2000	*c:\Documents and Settings\username*

You can use a text editor to add the security policy to your policy file, but this requires you to know the policy file's command syntax. You can find the command syntax in the API documentation for the object in question—in our case, a SocketPermission. Rather than use a text editor, you can use the Java 2 policy maintenance program: Policy Tool, a GUI-based application that greatly simplifies specifying a security policy.

Now that you have an overview of how to set up a policy, let's take a look at what is required for opening a database connection on a host other than the web server from which you downloaded your applet.

Your applet will need socket permissions in order to establish a *remote database connection*—a term I use to refer to connections made by an applet to a database on a host other than the one from which the applet was downloaded. To add a socket permissions policy for your applet, start the Policy Tool by executing the *policytool* command at the command line. If you have an existing user policy file, the Policy Tool program will open that file by default when it starts. If you do not have an existing policy file, don't worry; you'll still be able to make a policy entry, which you can then save to a new user policy file. When the Policy Tool application starts, it displays the Policy Tool screen shown in Figure 3-1.

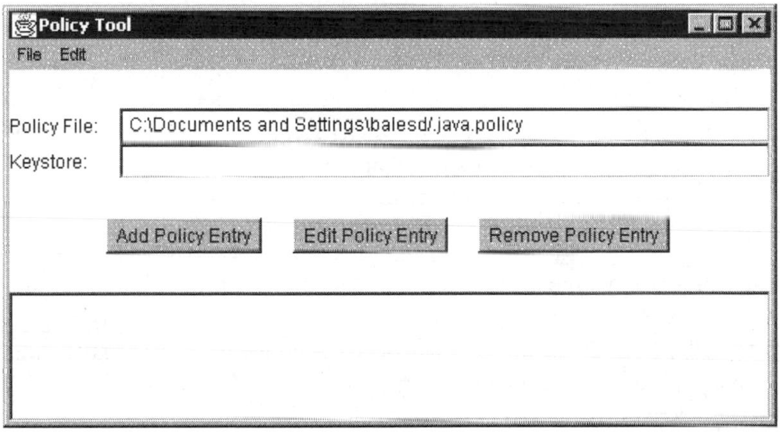

Figure 3-1. The Policy Tool's main screen

Click the Add Policy Entry button, and you will be taken to a screen titled Policy Entry, which is shown in Figure 3-2.

Enter the URL pointing to where your applet resides on the web server into the Code-Base field. You have three choices as to how you can specify your entry. First, you can type the entire URL, including the name of the class file, or archive file, containing the applet. This will limit the policy to only the specified applet or its archive. For example,

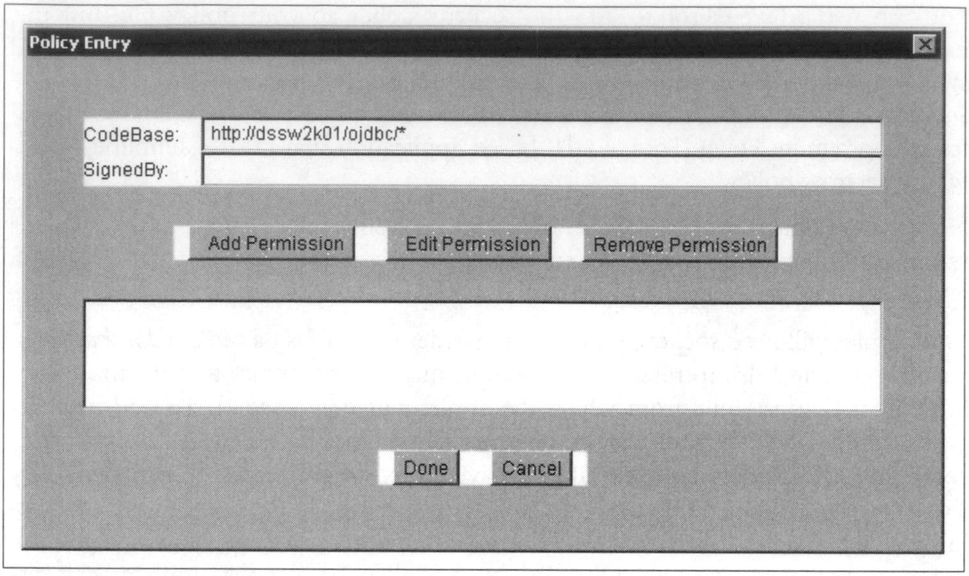

Figure 3-2. The Policy Entry screen

if you have an applet in an archive file named *TestAppletPolicy.zip*, as specified in the applet tag's archive parameter, you can specify a URL such as the following:

```
http://dssw2k01/ojdbc/TestAppletPolicy.zip
```

Your second choice is to specify the policy for any applet located in the last directory of the URL. Do this by typing an asterisk instead of the applet's name or the archive's filename. For example, to specify any applet that resides in the *ojdbc* directory on your web server, you can specify the following:

```
http://dssw2k01/ojdbc/*
```

Finally, you can specify that the policy applies to any applet that exists in the last directory of the URL, or in any directory subordinate to it, by typing a hyphen instead of the filename. For example, to specify any applet in the *ojdbc* directory, or in any directory underneath *ojdbc*, you can specify:

```
http://dssw2k01/ojdbc/-
```

You can see in Figure 3-2 that I specified the second choice, using an asterisk after the directory, so that I can run any applet I create during the development cycle without having to make multiple policy entries.

After you specify the value for CodeBase, click on the Add Permission button. This will take you to the screen titled Permissions (shown in Figure 3-3). Click on the Permission drop-down list box, scroll down, and select SocketPermission. Next, tab to the text field to the right of Target Name. Here you will enter the DNS Alias, or TCP/IP address, for the database server's host followed by a colon character and the port number for which you wish to grant socket permissions. Port 1521 is the typical value for an Oracle database listener. You should just be able to specify 1521, but this does not work on Windows 2000. Instead, you need to specify 1024- as a workaround, as I've done in Figure 3-3. The 1024- syntax opens up ports 1024 and higher.

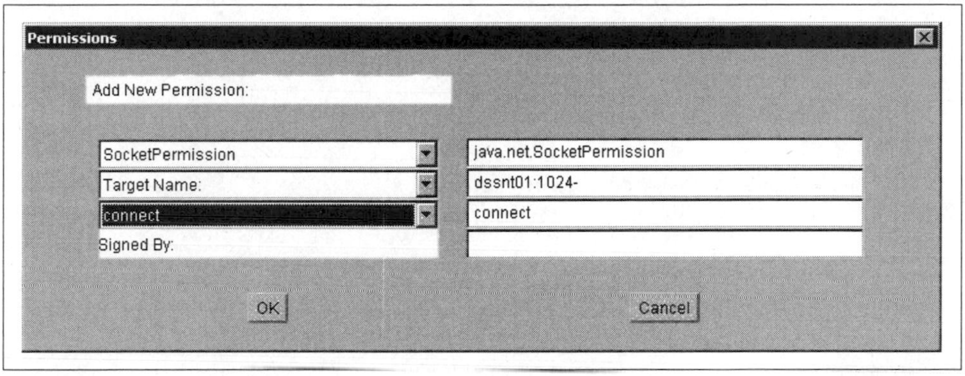

Figure 3-3. The Permissions screen

Next, click on the Action drop-down list box, scroll down, and select connect. Finally, click on the OK button to return to the Policy Entry window (Figure 3-2). From there, click on the Done button. This will bring you back to the Policy Tool window (Figure 3-1). From the Policy Tool window, select File → Save As from the menu to get a save dialog. Save the file as *.java.policy* in the appropriate user policy directory as specified in Table 3-3. For more detail on the specifications for SocketPermission, consult the JDK 1.2 API Javadoc for the SocketPermission class.

At this point, you know how to set up a policy to allow your applet to perform a remote database connection. You can find more information about Java 2 platform security at *http://java.sun.com/security/index.html* or in *Java Security* by Scott Oaks (O'Reilly). Now let's see what we can do to make the Java 2 plug-in load for a wide audience of browsers.

An adaptive applet tag

If the browser your audience will use can load the Java 2 plug-in, they'll be able to use your applet to access a remote database. But how do you code your HTML to activate the Java 2 plug-in? You do so with a rather complex, but effective, use of JavaScript in your HTML file. The following code was originally taken from *http://java.sun.com/products/plugin/1.2/docs/tags.html* with some minor modifications. I suggest you visit the page at this URL for an explanation of how this JavaScript code works, including all the gory details.

First, you need to add some JavaScript to the top of your HTML file's body that will determine whether the browser is Netscape, Internet Explorer, or something else. Here's the code to use:

```
<!-- The following code is specified at the beginning of the <BODY> tag. -->
<SCRIPT LANGUAGE="JavaScript">
```

```
<!--
 var _info = navigator.userAgent;
 var _ns   = false;
 var _ie   = (_info.indexOf("MSIE") > 0
  && _info.indexOf("Win") > 0
  && _info.indexOf("Windows 3.1") < 0);
//-->
</SCRIPT>
<COMMENT>
<SCRIPT LANGUAGE="JavaScript1.1">
<!--
 var _ns = (navigator.appName.indexOf("Netscape") >= 0
  && ((_info.indexOf("Win") > 0
  && _info.indexOf("Win16") < 0
  && java.lang.System.getProperty("os.version").indexOf("3.5") < 0)
  || _info.indexOf("Sun") > 0));
//-->
</SCRIPT>
</COMMENT>
```

Then, for each applet, use the following code. In both the <EMBED> and <APPLET> tags, replace *code*, *codebase*, and *archive* with values appropriate for the applet you are running.

```
<!-- The following code is repeated for each APPLET tag -->
<SCRIPT LANGUAGE="JavaScript">
<!--
 if (_ie == true) document.writeln(
'<OBJECT ' +
' classid="clsid:8AD9C840-044E-11D1-B3E9-00805F499D93" ' +
' codebase="http://java.sun.com/products/plugin/1.2.2/jinstall-1_2_2-win.
cab#Version=1,2,2,0" ' +
' align="baseline" ' +
' height="200" ' +
' width="200" ' +
' ><NOEMBED><XMP>');
 else if (_ns == true) document.writeln(
'<EMBED ' +
' type="application/x-java-applet;version=1.2.2" ' +
' pluginspage="http://java.sun.com/products/plugin/1.2/plugin-install.html" ' +
' code="code.class" ' +
' codebase="codebase" ' +
' archive="archive" ' +
' align="baseline" ' +
' height="200" ' +
' width="200" ' +
' otherparams="Add other parameters here" ' +
' ><NOEMBED><XMP>');
//-->
</SCRIPT>
<APPLET
 code="code.class"
 codebase="codebase"
 archive="archive"
 align="baseline"
```

```
 height="200"
 width="200"
 >
</XMP>
<PARAM NAME="java_code"     VALUE="code.class">
<PARAM NAME="java_codebase" VALUE="codebase">
<PARAM NAME="java_archive"  VALUE="archive">
<PARAM NAME="type"          VALUE="application/x-java-applet;version=1.2.2">
<PARAM NAME="scriptable"    VALUE="true">
<PARAM NAME="otherparams"   VALUE="Add other parameters here">
No JDK 1.2 support for APPLET!!
</APPLET>
</NOEMBED>
</EMBED>
</OBJECT>
```

This JavaScript/HTML code launches the Java 2 plug-in using the <EMBED> tag for
Netscape and the <OBJECT> tag for Internet Explorer. The <APPLET> tag is used for any
other browser, so long as that browser supports Java 2 (Opera, for example).

An applet to test our SocketPermissions policy

We could use TestApplet, introduced earlier in the chapter, to test our applet's security policy, but instead, let's use a slightly modified applet, TestAppletPolicy, along
with a slightly modified version of the <APPLET> tag we just covered to help clarify
how the browser is loading the Java 2 plug-in. The applet modification is this: just
after the init( ) method declaration I've added a call to the System.out.println( )
method, passing the applet parameter otherparams:

```
...
public void init() {
 System.out.println(getParameter("otherparams"));
 try {
 ...
```

We'll use the following HTML document to test our applet policy. In the HTML I've
added a snippet of Javascript to conditionally specify the value of the otherparams
parameter:

```
<html>
<head>
<title>Test an Applet's access to Sockets using Java 2 Policies</title>
</head>
<body>

<!-- The following code is specified at the beginning of the <BODY> tag. -->
<SCRIPT LANGUAGE="JavaScript">
<!--
 var _info = navigator.userAgent;
 var _ns  = false;
 var _ie  = (_info.indexOf("MSIE") > 0
  && _info.indexOf("Win") > 0
  && _info.indexOf("Windows 3.1") < 0);
//-->
```

```
</SCRIPT>
<COMMENT>
<SCRIPT LANGUAGE="JavaScript1.1">
<!--
 var _ns = (navigator.appName.indexOf("Netscape") >= 0
   && ((_info.indexOf("Win") > 0
   && _info.indexOf("Win16") < 0
   && java.lang.System.getProperty("os.version").indexOf("3.5") < 0)
   || _info.indexOf("Sun") > 0));
//-->
</SCRIPT>
</COMMENT>

<!-- The following code is repeated for each APPLET tag -->
<SCRIPT LANGUAGE="JavaScript">
<!--
 if (_ie == true) document.writeln(
'<OBJECT ' +
' classid="clsid:8AD9C840-044E-11D1-B3E9-00805F499D93" ' +
' codebase="http://java.sun.com/products/plugin/1.2.2/jinstall-1_2_2-win.
cab#Version=1,2,2,0" ' +
' align="baseline" ' +
' height="20" ' +
' width="750" ' +
' ><NOEMBED><XMP>' +
' <PARAM NAME="otherparams"   VALUE="Applet launched with OBJECT">');
else if (_ns == true) document.writeln(
'<EMBED ' +
' type="application/x-java-applet;version=1.2.2" ' +
' pluginspage="http://java.sun.com/products/plugin/1.2/plugin-install.html" ' +
' code="TestAppletPolicy.class" ' +
' codebase="." ' +
' archive="TestAppletPolicy.zip" ' +
' align="baseline" ' +
' height="20" ' +
' width="750" ' +
' otherparams="Applet launched with EMBED" ' +
' ><NOEMBED><XMP>');
//-->
</SCRIPT>
<APPLET
 code="TestAppletPolicy.class"
 codebase="."
 archive="TestAppletPolicy.zip"
 align="baseline"
 height="20"
 width="750"
 >
</XMP>
<PARAM NAME="java_code"     VALUE="TestAppletPolicy.class">
<PARAM NAME="java_codebase" VALUE=".">
<PARAM NAME="java_archive"  VALUE="TestAppletPolicy.zip">
<PARAM NAME="type"          VALUE="application/x-java-applet;version=1.2.2">
<PARAM NAME="scriptable"    VALUE="true">
```

```
if (_ie == true) document.writeln(
'<PARAM NAME="otherparams"   VALUE="Applet launched with OBJECT">');
else
document.writeln(
'<PARAM NAME="otherparams"   VALUE="Applet launched with APPLET">');
No JDK 1.2 support for APPLET!!
</APPLET>
</NOEMBED>
</EMBED>
</OBJECT>

</body>
</html>
```

To run TestPolicyApplet and test your security policy, follow these steps:

1. Compile TestPolicyApplet.

2. Add *TestAppletPolicy.class* to a copy of the *classes12.zip* file renamed *TestPolicyApplet.zip*.

3. Place the HTML code in the same directory as the applet archive.

4. Create a policy as previously outlined but use the URL for your web server.

Now open the URL in your browser and you should get a message like this:

```
Hello Scott
```

If you're using Netscape Navigator or Internet Explorer and have the plug-in set to show the Java console, the Java 2 Plug-in console will have opened, and you should be able to see a line such as one of the following:

```
"Applet launched with OBJECT" (Internet Explorer)
"Applet launched with EMBED" (Navigator)
"Applet launched with APPLET" (Java 2 compatible browsers, e.g, Opera)
```

If the Java console didn't show for Navigator or Internet Explorer, run the Java 2 Plug-in Control Panel, select Show Java Console, close and reopen your browser, and try again. If you're using Opera, select the Window → Special Window → Java Console menu item to open the Java Console. There are several valuable pieces of information available from the Java Console. First, Netscape Navigator and Internet Explorer's Java 2 Plug-in console reports the user home directory. You can use this information to verify that you put the policy in the correct file. Second, you can see the name of the class or archive file that was opened. This helps you troubleshoot the value you specify for CodeBase in the policy file.

You can find a complete online reference for the Java 2 plug-in at *http://java.sun.com/products/plugin/1.2/docs/index.docs.html*.

As I've discussed, Java's implementation of the sandbox prevents your applet from opening a socket to make a database connection on a remote database. In the next section, we will see another security device, a firewall, that may also prevent your Java applet from establishing a database connection.

Establishing a Connection Through a Firewall

Another constraint that you may have to deal with when accessing a remote database is the use of firewalls. Firewalls allow only desirable connections between networks. This means that under normal circumstances, a firewall will prevent your applet from connecting to a database located on the other side of the firewall. The solution to this problem is to use a firewall that supports Net8. Additionally, you need to use yet another special form of the Net8 connection string.

Configuring a Firewall for Net8

Firewalls use a set of rules to determine which clients can connect through them. These rules are based on a client's hostname, DNS alias, or IP address. A firewall goes through several steps to determine whether to allow an applet to connect and compare a client's hostname against its set of rules. If a match is not found, the firewall extracts the IP address of a client and compares it with the rules. Since an applet has restricted access to the local system, the JDBC Thin driver cannot get the name of its host to pass in its connection request. You must, therefore, configure a firewall to allow connections from the applet's IP address.

 You must also never allow the hostname __jdbc__ to be used in a firewall's set of rules. This literal has been coded into Net8-compatible firewalls to force the lookup of the IP address. If you inadvertently add this hostname to a firewall's set of rules, any Oracle JDBC Thin driver will be able to pass through the firewall.

You must also take into consideration that your applet may have to use a security policy to access a remote firewall just as it needed a security policy to enable access to a remote database. The only difference is the port you specify when you set up your socket permissions. If the firewall resides on the same host as your web server, you'll have no problem making a connection. If it does not, you'll have to use a security policy to give it socket permissions to access the port on the firewall's server.

Formulating a Firewall Database URL

Similar to how you had to include an address for Connection Manager in the Net8 address string when formulating a database URL to pass through Connection Manager, you'll need to include an address string for your firewall host when making a connection through a firewall. Once again, you will use Oracle's Net8 TNS keyword-value syntax to pass two addresses to the Thin driver. This time, the first address will be for the firewall host; the second will be for your target database. Since the second address is for a database, it will also have an Oracle SID. The resulting database URL still has the same format we have been using all along:

```
jdbc:oracle:thin:@database
```

When you're connecting through a Net8 compliant firewall, the *database* portion of the URL takes on the following form:

```
(description=(address_list=
(address=(protocol=tcp)(host=firewallhost)(port=1610))
(address=(protocol=tcp)(host=orahost)(port=1521)))
(source_route-yes)(conncct_data=(sid-orasid)))
```

which breaks down as:

firewallhost
> The TCP/IP address, or DNS alias, for your firewall server

orahost
> The TCP/IP address, or DNS alias, for your target database server

orasid
> The Oracle SID for your target database

For example, if your firewall server's alias is *dssw2k01*, your database server's alias is *dssnt01*, and your Oracle SID is *dssora01*, then your firewall URL would look like this:

```
jdbc:oracle:thin:@
(description=(address_list=
(address=(protocol=tcp)(host=dssw2k01)(port-1610))
(address=(protocol=tcp)(host=dssnt01)(port=1521)))
(source_route=yes)(connect_data=(sid=dssora01)))
```

For more information on formulating a firewall database URL, see Oracle's *Net8 Administrator's Guide* or *Oracle Net8 Configuration and Troubleshooting*, by Hugo Toledo and Jonathan Gennick (O'Reilly).

Net8-Compliant Firewalls

Net8 is supported by several firewall vendors. To save you some time, I've compiled a list of firewall vendors who state in their documentation that they support Net8. This list includes only vendors whose documentation is available on the Internet. The list is shown in Table 3-4 and consists of the vendor's name, the name of their firewall product, and one or more URLs at which you can find additional information. In addition, the *Firewall Report* is an excellent source of information. It's available for a subscription fee at *http://www.outlink.com/* and contains detailed information on almost every firewall product available.

Table 3-4. Firewall vendors that support Net8

Vendor	Product	URL
Cisco Systems	Cisco PIX Firewall	*http://www.cisco.com/univercd/cc/td/doc/product/iaabu/pix/index.htm*
	Cisco IOS Firewall	*http://www.cisco.com/univercd/cc/td/doc/product/software/index.htm*
Check Point	Firewall-1	*http://www.checkpoint.com/products/firewall-1/index.html*
		http://www.checkpoint.com/products/technology/supported.html
BorderWare Technologies	BorderWare	*http://www.borderware.com/products/fwserver.html*
WatchGuard Technologies	WatchGuard	*http://www.watchguard.com/support/interopapps.asp*
Lucent Technologies	VPN Firewall	*http://www.lucent.com/ins/library/pdf/datasheets/VPN_Firewall_ Family_Datasheet.pdf*
	Lucent Managed Firewall Services	*http://www.lucent-networkcare.com/consulting/services/datasheets/ managed_firewall_serv.asp*
SLM (formerly Milky-Way Networks)	SecurIT	*http://www.milkyway.com/prod.html*
Sun Microsystems	SunScreen Secure Net	*http://www.sun.com/software/white-papers/wp-security-securenettech/*

Guidelines for Choosing a Workaround

Now that you understand the connection restrictions that JDBC applets face, let's discuss the best time to use each solution.

For an intranet-based application, Connection Manager is your easiest solution. If an applet will be used solely on your internal network, common sense dictates that there is probably no need to go through the additional work of signing your applets to establish trust, for you know who has created them, and you implicitly trust the individuals that work for your organization. In addition, and for the same reason, there is no need to set up a security policy to restrict the applet's access to a specified resource. By using Connection Manager, you do not need to go through either of these steps to establish a remote connection, thereby saving you the costs of signing your applets and administering local policy on each user's desktop.

On the other hand, for an Internet-based application, you will want the signed applet to verify a trust chain and to force the use of a security policy to restrict the applet's access to local resources. As an end user of an Internet-based applet, you'll want to verify that the applet is from the source you trust and prevent the applet from accessing any restricted resources. In addition, you may be required to pass through a firewall to access a remote database, in which case the applet's signer will need to use the firewall URL syntax to establish a remote database connection through your firewall and the signer's firewall.

Now that you are aware of the special considerations of establishing a connection in an applet, let's move on to those for servlets in Chapter 4.

Servlet Database Connections

In this chapter, we'll explore issues that are specific to using JDBC with servlets. Unlike applets, servlets can use the OCI driver as well as the Thin driver. Like applets, servlets have a distinct life cycle that will impact your selection of a connection strategy. Let's begin our exploration by examining your driver choices when developing servlets.

Oracle Driver Selection

With servlets, you can use either the OCI driver or the Thin driver. As is the case when developing applications, I recommend you use the Thin driver unless one of the following considerations applies to your work:

- You make heavy use of stored procedures.
- You have the ability to make a Bequeath connection to the database.

For most practical purposes, the Thin driver is just as fast as the OCI driver. One exception is when you execute stored procedures. When stored procedures are invoked, the Thin driver can take up to twice as long as the OCI driver to execute a call. What does this mean in terms of response time? If it typically takes half a second for the OCI driver to make a stored-procedure call, then it will take the Thin driver one second. That's not much of a problem if you make only one stored-procedure call for each call you make to your servlet. The situation changes, however, if you make multiple stored-procedure calls for each call to your servlet. In such a case, your response time can deteriorate quickly. In our scenario, three stored-procedure calls will lead to a three-second delay. So if your servlets typically make several calls to stored procedures, you should consider using the OCI driver.

The other reason to use the OCI driver is to allow your servlet to make a Bequeath connection to the database. Using the *Bequeath* protocol results in a direct connection to a dedicated server process that allows your servlet to communicate directly with the Oracle8i database. You bypass the Net8 listener process and eliminate the layer of software associated with TCP/IP. Consequently, a Bequeath connection can result in a significant gain in response time as opposed to a TCP/IP connection. Bequeath connections, however, can be made only in one situation—your servlet container and your database must reside on the same host.

Now that you understand your options for selecting an Oracle driver for servlet development, let's examine the life cycle of a servlet to see how it will affect your strategy for making a connection.

Servlet Connection Strategies

From a programmer's perspective, a servlet has three stages to its life cycle. They are defined by the following three methods, or types of methods:

init( )

> This method is normally used to perform any initialization that should take place only once in the lifetime of the servlet. The init( ) method is invoked automatically before any of the servlet's doXXX( ) methods can be called.

doXXX( )

> The various *do methods*—doGet( ), doDelete( ), doPost( ), and doPut( )—are called as needed by web users to satisfy their dynamic content and form processing needs.

destroy( )

> This method is called just before the servlet container removes the servlet from memory, which typically happens when the servlet container itself is shutting down.

Given the life cycle described here, you have four strategies for making a database connection. The differences between these strategies hinge on when the connection is made and on whether connections are shared between servlets. The four strategies are:

Per-transaction connection

> You load the Oracle JDBC driver in the servlet's init( ) method, open a connection at the beginning of each doXXX( ) method, and close that connection at the end of each doXXX( ) method.

Dedicated connection

> You use a combination of the init( ) and destroy( ) methods, whereby you load the driver and open a connection in the init( ) method, and then close that connection in the destroy( ) method. As a result, the servlet uses one connection that remains open during the servlet's entire lifetime and is shared by all users of the servlet.

Session connection

> You load the Oracle JDBC driver in the init( ) method, but you don't open a connection until the beginning of the first doXXX( ) method. You then store that

connection in an HTTP Session object, from which it can be retrieved and used by other doXXX( ) method calls invoked by the same user session.

Cached connection

You use a connection pool to minimize the total number of connections that are open at any one time. At the beginning of each doXXX( ) method, you allocate a connection from the connection pool for use while the method executes then return that connection to the pool at the end of the doXXX( ) method.

Let's start a more detailed examination of these methods by looking first at the per-transaction connection strategy.

A Per-Transaction Connection

The *per-transaction connection* strategy is the kind of connection that most CGI programs use, and it's the least efficient of the four strategies. The Oracle JDBC driver is loaded once in the init( ) method. While the servlet is in operation, a new database connection is created at the beginning of each doXXX( ) method and is closed at the end of each doXXX( ) method. This model for managing connections is inefficient, because database connections are costly to create in terms of both response time and system resources. As a result, connecting to a database is a time-consuming process for the servlet. In addition, because connection creation is a costly process for the database, frequent connecting and disconnecting will impact the response time of other database users. Regardless of all this, there may be cases where such an approach is justified. Example 4-1 shows a servlet that uses a per-transaction connection.

Example 4-1. A one-connection-per-transaction servlet

```
import java.io.*;
import java.sql.*;
import javax.servlet.*;
import javax.servlet.http.*;

public class TransactionConnectionServlet extends HttpServlet {

  public void init(ServletConfig config)
    throws ServletException {
    super.init(config);
    try {
      // Load the driver
      Class.forName("oracle.jdbc.driver.OracleDriver").newInstance();
    }
    catch (ClassNotFoundException e) {
      throw new UnavailableException(
        "TransactionConnection.init( ) ClassNotFoundException: " +
        e.getMessage());
    }
    catch (IllegalAccessException e) {
      throw new UnavailableException(
        "TransactionConnection.init( ) IllegalAccessException: " +
```

Example 4-1. A one-connection-per-transaction servlet (continued)

```
      e.getMessage( ));
  }
  catch (InstantiationException e) {
    throw new UnavailableException(
     "TransactionConnection.init( ) InstantiationException: " +
     e.getMessage( ));
  }
}

public void doGet(
 HttpServletRequest request, HttpServletResponse response)
 throws IOException, ServletException {

  response.setContentType("text/html");
  PrintWriter out = response.getWriter( );
  out.println("<html>");
  out.println("<head>");
  out.println("<title>A Per Transaction Connection</title>");
  out.println("</head>");
  out.println("<body>");

  Connection connection = null;
  try {
    // Establish a connection
    connection = DriverManager.getConnection(
     "jdbc:oracle:thin:@dssw2k01:1521:orcl", "scott", "tiger");
  }
  catch (SQLException e) {
    throw new UnavailableException(
     "TransactionConnection.init( ) SQLException: " +
     e.getMessage( ));
  }

  Statement  statement = null;
  ResultSet  resultSet = null;
  String     userName  = null;
  try {
    // Test the connection
    statement = connection.createStatement( );
    resultSet = statement.executeQuery(
     "select initcap(user) from sys.dual");
    if (resultSet.next( ))
      userName = resultSet.getString(1);
  }
  catch (SQLException e) {
    out.println(
     "TransactionConnection.doGet( ) SQLException: " +
     e.getMessage( ) + "<p>");
  }
  finally {
```

Example 4-1. A one-connection-per-transaction servlet (continued)

```
      if (resultSet != null)
        try { resultSet.close( ); } catch (SQLException ignore) { }
      if (statement != null)
        try { statement.close( ); } catch (SQLException ignore) { }
    }

    if (connection != null) {
      // Close the connection
      try { connection.close( ); } catch (SQLException ignore) { }
    }

    out.println("Hello " + userName + "!<p>");
    out.println("You're using a per transaction connection!<p>");
    out.println("</body>");
    out.println("</html>");
  }

  public void doPost(
   HttpServletRequest request, HttpServletResponse response)
   throws IOException, ServletException {
   doGet(request, response);
  }
}
```

When the servlet shown in Example 4-1 is loaded into a servlet container, the init( ) method is called before any of the doXXX( ) method requests are processed. This is standard behavior for any servlet. In this servlet, TransactionConnectionServlet, the init( ) method first passes the config object on to its parent class. Next, it loads the Oracle driver using the Class.forName().newInstance( ) method. Using this form of the Class.forName( ) method guarantees you compatibility with noncompliant JVMs but at the cost of having to catch two additional exception types: IllegalAccessException and InstantiationException. As the servlet operates, whenever a doGet( ) or doPost( ) method is called, a new database connection is opened, the database is queried as needed, and the connection is closed. This is simple, and often effective, but can be an inefficient method for managing connections.

Our next method, a dedicated connection, is somewhat more efficient, so let's take a look at it.

A Dedicated Connection

Of the four strategies, the *dedicated connection* is the most costly in terms of the number of simultaneous database connections. Remember that a dedicated connection is opened when a servlet is initialized and closed when the servlet is destroyed. A dedicated connection remains open during the entire lifetime of a servlet and is dedicated to just that one servlet.

There are three drawbacks to a dedicated connection:

- You need a database connection for every JDBC servlet instance that is active in your servlet container. This may not really be that much of a drawback, because Oracle claims that its database is very efficient at handling many simultaneous connections.

- Since the connection will be shared with every user of the servlet, a transaction cannot span multiple calls to the servlet's doXXX( ) methods. This means that you cannot provide a user with several forms in a row, using several servlets, and commit all the user's database changes after the last of those forms has been filled out. You instead have to commit a user's input for each form as it is submitted.

- Because the Oracle Connection class's methods are synchronized, only one invocation of any given method is allowed at any one time. You will experience a processing bottleneck when multiple invocations of the doXXX( ) methods attempt to use the connection at the same time. The doXXX( ) methods will have to wait their turn for access to the Connection class's synchronized methods.

Example 4-2 shows a sample servlet that uses a dedicated connection.

Example 4-2. A dedicated connection servlet

```
import java.io.*;
import java.sql.*;
import javax.servlet.*;
import javax.servlet.http.*;

public class DedicatedConnectionServlet extends HttpServlet {
  Connection connection;
  long        connected;

  public void init(ServletConfig config)
   throws ServletException {
    super.init(config);
    try {
      // Load the driver
      Class.forName("oracle.jdbc.driver.OracleDriver").newInstance( );
    }
    catch (ClassNotFoundException e) {
      throw new UnavailableException(
       "DedicatedConnection.init( ) ClassNotFoundException: " +
       e.getMessage());
    }
    catch (IllegalAccessException e) {
      throw new UnavailableException(
       "DedicatedConnection.init( ) IllegalAccessException: " +
       e.getMessage());
    }
    catch (InstantiationException e) {
      throw new UnavailableException(
       "DedicatedConnection.init( ) InstantiationException: " +
```

Example 4-2. A dedicated connection servlet (continued)

```
      e.getMessage( ));
  }

  try {
    // Establish a connection
    connection = DriverManager.getConnection(
      "jdbc:oracle:thin:@dssw2k01:1521:orcl", "scott", "tiger");
    connected = System.currentTimeMillis( );
  }
  catch (SQLException e) {
    throw new UnavailableException(
      "DedicatedConnection.init( ) SQLException: " +
      e.getMessage( ));
  }
}

public void doGet(
 HttpServletRequest request, HttpServletResponse response)
 throws IOException, ServletException {

  response.setContentType("text/html");
  PrintWriter out = response.getWriter( );
  out.println("<html>");
  out.println("<head>");
  out.println("<title>A Dedicated Connection</title>");
  out.println("</head>");
  out.println("<body>");

  Statement statement = null;
  ResultSet resultSet = null;
  String    userName  = null;
  try {
    // test the connection
    statement = connection.createStatement( );
    resultSet = statement.executeQuery(
      "select initcap(user) from sys.dual");
    if (resultSet.next( ))
      userName = resultSet.getString(1);
  }
  catch (SQLException e) {
   out.println(
     "DedicatedConnection.doGet( ) SQLException: " +
     e.getMessage( ) + "<p>");
  }
  finally {
    if (resultSet != null)
      try { resultSet.close( ); } catch (SQLException ignore) { }
    if (statement != null)
      try { statement.close( ); } catch (SQLException ignore) { }
  }
  out.println("Hello " + userName + "!<p>");
  out.println(
   "This Servlet's database connection was created on " +
```

Example 4-2. A dedicated connection servlet (continued)

```
    new java.util.Date(connected) + "<p>");
  out.println("</body>");
  out.println("</html>");
}

public void doPost(
 HttpServletRequest request, HttpServletResponse response)
 throws IOException, ServletException {
  doGet(request, response);
}

public void destroy( ) {
  // Close the connection
  if (connection != null)
    try { connection.close( ); } catch (SQLException ignore) { }
}
}
```

When the servlet shown in Example 4-2 is loaded into a servlet container, the init( ) method is invoked. The init( ) method then loads the Oracle JDBC driver. All this occurs before any doXXX( ) method requests are processed. So far, this sequence of events is the same as that for the servlet named TransactionServlet in Example 4-1. In this case, though, the init( ) method also attempts to connect to the database. If the init( ) method cannot load the Oracle JDBC driver and establish a connection, it will throw an UnavailableException. This will manifest itself as a 503 error in the user's browser.

The doGet( ) method shown in Example 4-2 uses the database connection to retrieve the login user's username from the database. It then displays that username in the user's browser along with the date and time that the connection was established. The database connection will persist and can be used by other doXXX( ) methods until the servlet is destroyed. You can verify this by executing the servlet, waiting several minutes, and then executing it again. You'll notice that the servlet displays the same initial connection time no matter how many times you execute it. This connection time indicates how long the connection has been open.

When the servlet is unloaded from the servlet container, the destroy( ) method is invoked. The destroy( ) method in turn closes the dedicated connection.

The dedicated connection strategy yields an improvement in response time efficiency over the per-transaction connection strategy because the connection is already open, but it requires many more simultaneous database connections. This is because you must have a dedicated connection for every servlet that accesses the database. In even a small application, this can be hundreds of connections.

The next strategy we will discuss—the session connection strategy—improves response time by removing the bottleneck of a single connection object. It also resolves the transaction boundary problem. However, all this is still at the cost of many simultaneous database connections.

A Session Connection

If your servlet is part of a larger application that calls for a connection that is dedicated to a particular user, then a *session connection* is your best option. The session connection strategy is similar to that used for an application client—the connection is opened at the beginning of the program and closed when the application is closed. In the case of servlets, a connection is established the first time a particular user calls a servlet requiring a connection. The connection then remains open until the user's session expires.

For example, suppose you are writing a servlet that is part of a human resources application. Due to the highly confidential nature of HR data, and because you need to keep an audit trail of who makes changes to the data, you may decide that you cannot use a dedicated connection as we did in the previous section. Remember that a dedicated connection is shared by all users of a servlet. In this case, to ensure that each session gets its own connection, you can open a connection for a given username and store that connection in an HTTP session object. The session object itself will be available from one HTTP transaction to the next, because a reference to it will be stored and retrieved by your browser using cookies. This functionality is handled automatically by the HttpServlet class as per the servlet API specification. Since the reference for the database connection will be stored in the user's session object, the connection will be available to all servlets invoked by the user's session. Example 4-3 demonstrates one way to implement a session connection strategy.

Example 4-3. A session connection servlet

```
import java.io.*;
import java.sql.*;
import javax.servlet.*;
import javax.servlet.http.*;

public class Login extends HttpServlet {

  public void init(ServletConfig config)
   throws ServletException {
    super.init(config);
    try {
      // Load the driver
      Class.forName("oracle.jdbc.driver.OracleDriver").newInstance( );
    }
    catch (ClassNotFoundException e) {
      throw new UnavailableException(
        "Login init() ClassNotFoundException: " + e.getMessage( ));
    }
    catch (IllegalAccessException e) {
      throw new UnavailableException(
        "Login init() IllegalAccessException: " + e.getMessage( ));
    }
    catch (InstantiationException e) {
      throw new UnavailableException(
        "Login init() InstantiationException: " + e.getMessage( ));
```

Example 4-3. A session connection servlet (continued)

```
    }
  }

  public void doGet(
   HttpServletRequest request, HttpServletResponse response)
   throws IOException, ServletException {

    response.setContentType("text/html");
    PrintWriter out = response.getWriter( );
    out.println("<html>");
    out.println("<head>");
    out.println("<title>Login</title>");
    out.println("</head>");
    out.println("<body>");

    HttpSession session = request.getSession( );
    Connection connection =
     (Connection)session.getAttribute("connection");
    if (connection == null) {
      String userName = request.getParameter("username");
      String password = request.getParameter("password");
      if (userName == null || password == null) {
        // Prompt the user for her username and password
        out.println("<form method=\"get\" action=\"Login\">");
        out.println("Please specify the following to log in:<p>");
        out.println("Username: <input type=\"text\" " +
          "name=\"username\" size=\"30\"><p>");
        out.println("Password: <input type=\"password\" " +
          "name=\"password\" size=\"30\"><p>");
        out.println("<input type=\"submit\" value=\"Login\">");
        out.println("</form>");
      }
      else {
        // Create the connection
        try {
          connection = DriverManager.getConnection(
            "jdbc:oracle:thin:@dssw2k01:1521:orcl", userName, password);
        }
        catch (SQLException e) {
          out.println("Login doGet() " + e.getMessage( ));
        }
        if (connection != null) {
          // Store the connection
          session.setAttribute("connection", connection);
          response.sendRedirect("Login");
          return;
        }
      }
    }
    else {
      String logout = request.getParameter("logout");
      if (logout == null) {
        // Test the connection
```

Example 4-3. A session connection servlet (continued)

```
          Statement statement = null;
          ResultSet resultSet = null;
          String    userName  = null;
          try {
            statement = connection.createStatement();
            resultSet = statement.executeQuery(
            "select initcap(user) from sys.dual");
            if (resultSet.next())
              userName = resultSet.getString(1);
          }
          catch (SQLException e) {
            out.println("Login doGet() SQLException: " + e.getMessage() + "<p>");
          }
          finally {
            if (resultSet != null)
              try { resultSet.close(); } catch (SQLException ignore) { }
            if (statement != null)
              try { statement.close(); } catch (SQLException ignore) { }
          }
          out.println("Hello " + userName + "!<p>");
          out.println("Your session ID is " + session.getId() + "<p>");
          out.println("It was created on " +
           new java.util.Date(session.getCreationTime()) + "<p>");
          out.println("It was last accessed on " +
           new java.util.Date(session.getLastAccessedTime()) + "<p>");
          out.println("<form method=\"get\" action=\"Login\">");
          out.println("<input type=\"submit\" name=\"logout\" " +
           "value=\"Logout\">");
          out.println("</form>");
        }
        else {
          // Close the connection and remove it from the session
          try { connection.close(); } catch (SQLException ignore) { }
          session.removeAttribute("connection");
          out.println("You have been logged out.");
        }
      }
    out.println("</body>");
    out.println("</html>");
  }

  public void doPost(
   HttpServletRequest request, HttpServletResponse response)
   throws IOException, ServletException {
   doGet(request, response);
  }
}
```

As in the previous examples, the init( ) method is called before any of the doXXX( )
method requests are processed. In this servlet, the init( ) method loads the Oracle
JDBC driver using the Class.forName().newInstance( ) method. If the Login servlet
cannot load the Oracle JDBC driver, it throws an UnavailableException.

When a user executes the servlet's doGet( ) method, the following sequence of events occurs:

1. A request object is implicitly passed as part of the HttpServlet class's normal functionality.

2. The doGet( ) method then uses the HttpServletRequest object's getSession( ) method to get the current HttpSession object. If no current HttpSession object exists, the getSession( ) method automatically creates a new one.

3. The doGet( ) method invokes the HttpSession object's getAttribute( ) method in order to get the Connection object for the session. If no Connection object exists, getAttribute( ) returns a null. If a Connection object does exist, control goes to step 7.

4. If the doGet( ) method sees that the Connection object is null, it will then check to see whether the user has passed a username and password as parameters of an HTML form.

5. If username and password values are found, the doGet( ) method uses those passed values to log into the database and create a new database connection. Because this is a sample program, control is then redirected back to the Login servlet to show the user its HttpSession information.

6. If no username and password parameters are found, the doGet( ) method creates an HTML form to prompt the user for that information. When the user enters the username and password into the form and then submits it, the Login servlet is called once again.

7. If a Connection object does exist for the session, the doGet( ) method tests to see if the user has passed a parameter named logout as part of an HTML form.

8. If a logout parameter has been passed, the doGet( ) method closes the database connection, removes the reference to that connection from the session object, and displays a logged out verification message.

9. If a connection exists, and no logout parameter has been passed, the doGet( ) method uses the connection to retrieve the database username from the database. It then displays information about the user's session.

If you were to code a doPost( ) method for the Login servlet, you'd have to add the same session connection code to that method as I've implemented for the doGet( ) method. For that matter, any doXXX( ) method that requires database access would require this session connection code.

Creating a session-bound wrapper for connections

With the servlet shown in Example 4-3, a user's database connection remains open until that user submits a form containing a parameter named logout to the servlet. That's all well and good, but what happens when the user forgets to log out before closing her browser? Or when the session times out? The answer, unfortunately, is that the connection will not be closed. It will remain open until the Oracle process monitor recognizes that the session is gone, at which point the Oracle process monitor closes the connection. This is terribly inefficient! Fortunately, there is an elegant solution to this problem. By using the HttpSessionBinding interface, you can wrap a connection object in a session-bound object that is notified when the session expires. The session-bound object can then in turn close the connection. Example 4-4 shows a wrapper class for a connection. This wrapper class is named SessionConnection.

Example 4-4. A session-bound wrapper class for a connection

```java
import java.sql.*;
import javax.servlet.http.*;

public class SessionConnection
 implements HttpSessionBindingListener {

  Connection connection;

  public SessionConnection() {
    connection = null;
  }

  public SessionConnection(Connection connection) {
    this.connection = connection;
  }

  public Connection getConnection() {
    return connection;
  }

  public void setConnection(Connection connection) {
    this.connection = connection;
  }

  public void valueBound(HttpSessionBindingEvent event) {
    if (connection != null) {
      System.out.println("Binding a valid connection");
    }
    else {
      System.out.println("Binding a null connection");
    }
  }

  public void valueUnbound(HttpSessionBindingEvent event) {
    if (connection != null) {
      System.out.println(
      "Closing the bound connection as the session expires");
      try { connection.close(); } catch (SQLException ignore) { }
    }
  }
}
```

The SessionConnection class shown in Example 4-4 holds a connection and implements the HttpSessionBindingListener interface. When you create a new Connection object, you also need to create a new SessionConnection object. You then store your new Connection object in that SessionConnection object. Then, when a session expires, the HttpSession object notifies the SessionConnection object that it is about to be unbound. This notification happens because the SessionConnection class implements the HttpSessionBindingListener interface. In turn, the SessionConnection object closes the database connection so it's not left hanging in an open state after the session has ended.

Using the session bound wrapper class

Creating the SessionConnection class is not enough. You also need to code your servlet to use that class when managing connections. Example 4-5 shows a modified version of the Login servlet shown earlier. It can now use the SessionConnection class. The servlet has been renamed SessionLogin and uses a SessionConnection object to manage connections.

Example 4-5. An HttpSessionBindingListener session connection servlet

```
import java.io.*;
import java.sql.*;
import javax.servlet.*;
import javax.servlet.http.*;

public class SessionLogin extends HttpServlet {

  public void init(ServletConfig config)
   throws ServletException {
   super.init(config);
   try {
     // Load the driver
     Class.forName("oracle.jdbc.driver.OracleDriver").newInstance( );
   }
   catch (ClassNotFoundException e) {
     throw new UnavailableException(
       "Login init() ClassNotFoundException: " + e.getMessage( ));
   }
   catch (IllegalAccessException e) {
     throw new UnavailableException(
       "Login init() IllegalAccessException: " + e.getMessage( ));
   }
   catch (InstantiationException e) {
     throw new UnavailableException(
       "Login init() InstantiationException: " + e.getMessage( ));
   }
  }

  public void doGet(
   HttpServletRequest request, HttpServletResponse response)
   throws IOException, ServletException {

   response.setContentType("text/html");
   PrintWriter out = response.getWriter( );
```

```java
    out.println("<html>");
    out.println("<head>");
    out.println("<title>Login</title>");
    out.println("</head>");
    out.println("<body>");

    HttpSession session = request.getSession();
    SessionConnection sessionConnection =
     (SessionConnection)session.getAttribute("sessionconnection");
    Connection connection = null;
    if (sessionConnection != null) {
      connection = sessionConnection.getConnection();
    }
    if (connection == null) {
      String userName = request.getParameter("username");
      String password = request.getParameter("password");
      if (userName == null || password == null) {
        // Prompt the user for her username and password
        out.println("<form method=\"get\" action=\"SessionLogin\">");
        out.println("Please specify the following to log in:<p>");
        out.println("Username: <input type=\"text\" " +
          "name=\"username\" size=\"30\"><p>");
        out.println("Password: <input type=\"password\" " +
          "name=\"password\" size=\"30\"><p>");
        out.println("<input type=\"submit\" value=\"Login\">");
        out.println("</form>");
      }
      else {
        // Create the connection
        try {
          connection = DriverManager.getConnection(
            "jdbc:oracle:thin:@dssw2k01.1521:orcl", userName, password);
        }
        catch (SQLException e) {
          out.println("Login doGet() " + e.getMessage());
        }
        if (connection != null) {
          // Store the connection
          sessionConnection = new SessionConnection();
          sessionConnection.setConnection(connection);
          session.setAttribute("sessionconnection", sessionConnection);
          response.sendRedirect("SessionLogin");
          return;
        }
      }
    }
    else {
      String logout = request.getParameter("logout");
      if (logout == null) {
        // Test the connection
        Statement statement = null;
        ResultSet resultSet = null;
        String    userName = null;
```

```
      try {
        statement = connection.createStatement( );
        resultSet = statement.executeQuery(
          "select initcap(user) from sys.dual");
        if (resultSet.next( ))
          userName = resultSet.getString(1);
      }
      catch (SQLException e) {
        out.println("Login doGet() SQLException: " + e.getMessage( ) + "<p>");
      }
      finally {
        if (resultSet != null)
          try { resultSet.close( ); } catch (SQLException ignore) { }
        if (statement != null)
          try { statement.close( ); } catch (SQLException ignore) { }
      }
      out.println("Hello " + userName + "!<p>");
      out.println("Your session ID is " + session.getId( ) + "<p>");
      out.println("It was created on " +
        new java.util.Date(session.getCreationTime( )) + "<p>");
      out.println("It was last accessed on " +
        new java.util.Date(session.getLastAccessedTime( )) + "<p>");
      out.println("<form method=\"get\" action=\"SessionLogin\">");
      out.println("<input type=\"submit\" name=\"logout\" " +
        "value=\"Logout\">");
      out.println("</form>");
    }
    else {
      // Close the connection and remove it from the session
      try { connection.close( ); } catch (SQLException ignore) { }
      session.removeAttribute("sessionconnection");
      out.println("You have been logged out.");
    }
  }
  out.println("</body>");
  out.println("</html>");
}

public void doPost(
 HttpServletRequest request, HttpServletResponse response)
 throws IOException, ServletException {
  doGet(request, response);
 }
}
```

The first notable change in this servlet, with respect to the Login servlet shown in Example 4-3, is that it uses a SessionConnection object as an attribute of the HttpSession object. You can see in the doGet( ) method that instead of getting a Connection object directly from an HttpSession object, this servlet gets a SessionConnection object from an HttpSession object. If the SessionConnection object is valid (i.e., it is not initialized to null), an attempt is then made using that object's getConnection( ) method to get a connection object. If no connection object exists, the doGet( ) method creates one. It then creates a new SessionConnection object in which to store the newly created Connection object. The SessionConnection object in turn is stored in the HttpSession object.

The SessionConnection class shown in Example 4-4 contains several System.out. println( ) method calls you can use for debugging purposes. If you compile the *SessionConnection.java* and *SessionLogin.java* files, place them into service on your servlet container, and set your servlet container's session timeout to a reasonably small period—such as two minutes—you can see the HttpSessionBindingListener interface in action.

As you can see from these last few examples, using the session connection strategy can add a significant amount of code to your servlet. If you don't need a connection dedicated to a user, then you are better off using a cached connection. Let's talk about that next.

A Cached Connection

A *cached connection*, or *pooled connection* as it is sometimes called, is the most efficient connection strategy. A separate Connection Manager object is created in the servlet container that manages a pool of cached connections (you'll see an example Connection Manager implementation shortly). When your servlet requires a connection, it asks Connection Manager for a connection. Connection Manager then finds an unused connection, or creates a new connection if necessary, and passes that back for the servlet to use. The servlet returns the connection to the cache when it is no longer needed.

Connection Manager allocates connections, which are all made using a pool username and password, as needed by the servlets in the servlet container. Rather than close the connections when they are returned to Connection Manager, they are placed in a cache in an open state until another servlet requires them. There are several connection-caching products on the market for Java. Later, in Chapter 7, I will show Oracle's connection-caching implementation. But since I can't dissect them to help you get a better understanding of how they work, I've put together a connection-caching tool of my own for you to examine. This tool consists of the following components:

- A class to wrap cached connections
- A class to load drivers and create connections
- A class to manage cached connections

The following sections show and describe each of these classes. Following the class descriptions are examples of servlets that use the classes to implement a cached connection strategy.

A class to wrap cached connections

For each connection, my caching tool needs to keep track of not only the Connection object itself, but also the following two pieces of information:

- The time the connection was last used
- Whether the connection is currently in use

To accomplish this objective, I've created a wrapper class named CachedConnection, which is shown in Example 4-6.

Example 4-6. The CachedConnection class to wrap cached connections

```java
import java.sql.*;

public class CachedConnection {
  private boolean    inUse;
  private Connection conn;
  private long       lastUsed;
  private String     baseName;

  public CachedConnection( ) {
    conn    = null;
    inUse   = false;
    lastUsed = System.currentTimeMillis( );
    baseName = "Database";
  }

  public CachedConnection(Connection conn, boolean inUse) {
    this.conn     = conn;
    this.inUse    = inUse;
    this.lastUsed = System.currentTimeMillis( );
    this.baseName = "Database";
  }

  public CachedConnection(Connection conn, boolean inUse, String baseName) {
    this.conn     = conn;
    this.inUse    = inUse;
    this.lastUsed = System.currentTimeMillis( );
    this.baseName = baseName;
  }

  public Connection getConnection( ) {
    return conn;
  }

  public void setConnection(Connection conn) {
    this.conn = conn;
  }

  public boolean getInUse( ) {
    return inUse;
  }
}
```

Example 4-6. The CachedConnection class to wrap cached connections (continued)

```
public boolean isInUse() {
  return inUse;
}

public void setInUse(boolean inUse) {
  if (!inUse)
    lastUsed = System.currentTimeMillis();
  this.inUse = inUse;
}

public String getBaseName() {
  return baseName;
}

public void setBaseName(String baseName) {
  this.baseName = baseName;
}

public long getLastUsed() {
  return lastUsed;
}
}
```

A CachedConnection object has the following four attributes:

inUse

> A boolean that keeps track of whether the connection is in use. A value of true indicates that the connection has been checked out by a servlet. A value of false indicates that the connection is available.

conn

> A JDBC Connection object that is cached in the pool.

lastUsed

> A long that holds the time the connection was last checked out. This is used by the management class to determine when to close and remove from the cache connections that have not been used in a predetermined period of time.

baseName

> A String object that holds the name of the pool to which this connection belongs. This allows you to manage several different connection pools simultaneously.

The CachedConnection class's isInUse() method is a function you can use in a logical statement to check if the connection is in use. The rest of the methods are getter-setter methods for the class.

A class to load drivers and create connections

The next class in my connection caching tool is a class to manage the loading of JDBC drivers and the creation of connections. This class is named Database, and it's shown in Example 4-7.

Example 4-7. The database class to manage driver loading and connection creation

```java
import java.sql.*;
import java.util.*;

public class Database {
  private static boolean verbose  = false;

  public static final Connection getConnection(String baseName) {
    Connection conn = null;
    String driver   = null;
    String url      = null;
    String username = null;
    String password = null;
    try {
      ResourceBundle resb = ResourceBundle.getBundle(baseName);
      driver              = resb.getString("database.driver");
      url                 = resb.getString("database.url");
      username            = resb.getString("database.username");
      password            = resb.getString("database.password");
      Class.forName(driver);
    }
    catch(MissingResourceException e) {
      System.err.println("Missing Resource: " + e.getMessage());
      return conn;
    }
    catch(ClassNotFoundException e) {
      System.err.println("Class not found: " + e.getMessage());
      return conn;
    }
    try {
      if (verbose) {
        System.out.println("baseName=" + baseName);
        System.out.println("driver=" + driver);
        System.out.println("url=" + url);
        System.out.println("username=" + username);
        System.out.println("password=" + password);
      }

      conn = DriverManager.getConnection(url, username, password);
    }
    catch(SQLException e) {
      System.err.println(e.getMessage());
      System.err.println("in Database.getConnection");
      System.err.println("on getConnection");
      conn = null;
    }
    finally {
      return conn;
    }
  }
}
```

Example 4-7. The database class to manage driver loading and connection creation (continued)

```
  public static void setVerbose(boolean v) {
    verbose = v;
  }
}
```

Database is a utility class that employs the use of a static variable and two static methods that allow you to call the methods without instantiating the class. The attribute verbose is a boolean that controls the output of diagnostics to standard out. The getConnection( ) method takes a String argument named baseName, which identifies a properties file on the local filesystem. This properties file must be generated before invoking the getConnection( ) method, and in it you should place the connection properties that you want each new connection to have. The following is a hypothetical example of a properties file:

```
database.driver=oracle.jdbc.driver.OracleDriver
database.url=jdbc:oracle:thin:@dssw2k01:1521:orcl
database.username=scott
database.password=tiger
```

In my solution, the pool name is used as the properties filename, so each pool can have its own, distinct set of connection properties. All connections in a given pool share the same set of properties.

A class to manage cached connections

The final piece of my connection-caching solution is a class to manage cached connections, doling them out to servlets as they are needed. The CacheConnection class, shown in Example 4-8, does this.

Example 4-8. The CacheConnection class to manage cached connections

```
import java.io.*;
import java.sql.*;
import java.util.Vector;

public class CacheConnection {
  private static boolean verbose          = false;
  private static int       numberConnections = 0;
  private static Vector   cachedConnections = new Vector();
  private static Thread   monitor           = null;
  private static long     MAX_IDLE          = 1000*60*60;

  synchronized public static Connection checkOut( ) {
    return checkOut("Database");
  }

  synchronized public static Connection checkOut(String baseName) {
    boolean          found = false;
    CachedConnection cached = null;
```

```
   if (verbose) {
     System.out.println("There are " +
      Integer.toString(numberConnections) +
      " connections in the cache");
     System.out.println("Searching for a connection not in use...");
   }
   for (int i=0;!found && i<numberConnections;i++) {
     if (verbose) {
       System.out.println("Vector entry " + Integer.toString(i));
     }
     cached = (CachedConnection)cachedConnections.get(i);
     if (!cached.isInUse() && cached.getBaseName().equals(baseName)) {
       if (verbose) {
         System.out.println("found cached entry " +
          Integer.toString(i) +
          " for " + baseName);
       }
       found = true;
     }
   }
   if (found) {
     cached.setInUse(true);
   }
   else {
     if (verbose) {
       System.out.println("Cached entry not found ");
       System.out.println("Allocating new entry for " + baseName);
     }
     cached = new CachedConnection(
      Database.getConnection(baseName), true, baseName);
     cachedConnections.add(cached);
     numberConnections++;
   }

   if (monitor == null) {
     monitor = new Thread(
      new Runnable() {
        public void run() {
          while(numberConnections > 0) {
            runMonitor();
          }
          monitor = null;
          if (verbose) {
            System.out.println("CacheConnection monitor stopped");
          }
        }
      }
     );
     monitor.setDaemon(true);
     monitor.start();
   }
   return cached.getConnection();
 }
```

```java
synchronized public static void checkIn(Connection c) {
  boolean          found  = false;
  boolean          closed = false;
  CachedConnection cached = null;
  Connection       conn   = null;
  int              i      = 0;

  if (verbose) {
    System.out.println("Searching for connection to set not in use...");
  }
  for (i=0;!found && i<numberConnections;i++) {
    if (verbose) {
      System.out.println("Vector entry " + Integer.toString(i));
    }
    cached = (CachedConnection)cachedConnections.get(i);
    conn = cached.getConnection( );
    if (conn == c) {
      if (verbose) {
        System.out.println("found cached entry " + Integer.toString(i));
      }
      found = true;
    }
  }
  if (found) {
    try {
      closed = conn.isClosed( );
    }
    catch(SQLException ignore) {
      closed = true;
    }
    if (!closed)
      cached.setInUse(false);
    else {
      cachedConnections.remove(i);
      numberConnections--;
    }
  }
  else if (verbose) {
    System.out.println("In use Connection not found!!!");
  }
}

synchronized private static void checkUse( ) {
  CachedConnection cached = null;
  Connection       conn   = null;
  int              i      = 0;
  long             now    = System.currentTimeMillis( );
  long             then   = 0;

  for (i=numberConnections-1;i>-1;i--) {
    if (verbose) {
      System.out.println(
        "CacheConnection monitor checking vector entry " +
```

```
          Integer.toString(i) +
          " for use...");
      }
      cached = (CachedConnection)cachedConnections.get(i);
      if (!cached.isInUse( )) {
        then = cached.getLastUsed( );
        if ((now - then) > MAX_IDLE) {
          if (verbose) {
            System.out.println("Cached entry " +
              Integer.toString(i) +
              " idle too long, being destroyed");
          }
          conn = cached.getConnection( );
          try { conn.close( ); } catch (SQLException e) {
          System.err.println("Unable to close connection: " +
           e.getMessage( )); }
          cachedConnections.remove(i);
          numberConnections--;
        }
      }
    }
  }
}

private static void runMonitor( ) {
  checkUse( );
  if (numberConnections > 0) {
    if (verbose) {
      System.out.println("CacheConnection monitor going to sleep");
    }
    try {
      // 1000 milliseconds/second x 60 seconds/minute x 5 minutes
      monitor.sleep(1000*60*5);
    }
    catch (InterruptedException ignore) {
      if (verbose) {
        System.out.println(
          "CacheConnection monitor's sleep was interrupted");
      }
    }
  }
}

public void finalize( ) throws Throwable {
  CachedConnection cached = null;
  for(int i=0;i<numberConnections;i++) {
    cached = (CachedConnection)cachedConnections.get(i);
    if (cached.getConnection( ) != null) {
      if (verbose) {
        System.out.println(
          "Closing connection on Vector entry " +
          Integer.toString(i));
      }
```

```
      try {
        cached.getConnection().close();
      }
      catch(SQLException ignore) {
        System.err.println("Can't close connection!!!");
      }
    }
  }
  numberConnections = 0;
}

public static void setVerbose(boolean v) {
  verbose = v;
}
}
```

This sample caching object is quite lengthy, but I figure you want a working example, and this is what it takes to get one. Let's start dissecting this class. To begin with, notice that the CacheConnection class has several static attributes, and that all the methods are static as well. That's because this utility class, like the Database class in Example 4-7, is never intended to be instantiated in a servlet. The attributes in the class are:

verbose

> A boolean used throughout the class's methods to turn diagnostic output on or off. Diagnostic output is written to the standard output device.

numberConnections

> An integer to keep track of the number of open connections in the cache.

cachedConnections

> A Vector object to contain the actual cache of connections.

monitor

> A Thread object that runs independently of the CacheConnection object to manage the removal of unused connections in the cache.

MAX_IDLE

> A long to hold the maximum time, in milliseconds, that an idle connection should remain in the cache.

Now that you're familiar with the CacheConnection class's attributes, let's look at the class's methods. In the discussion that follows, I'll work my way down from the top of the class listing and discuss each method in turn.

At the top of the listing, you'll find a pair of overloaded checkOut() methods. The first checkOut() method allocates a database connection from a default pool, while the second allocates a connection from a pool specified by name. The default pool name used by the first checkOut() method is "Database". To allocate a connection from that default pool, the first checkOut( ) method simply calls the second checkOut( ) method, passing "Database" as the pool name parameter. The second checkOut( ) method does all the real work. It looks in the cache for a free connection with the corresponding pool name. If such a connection exists, it is flagged as in use, and returned as the method's result. Otherwise, if no connection exists in the specified pool, a new connection is created, placed into the cache, flagged as in use, and returned as the method's result. Before returning any connection, the checkOut( ) method checks if a monitor Thread object exists, creating one if necessary. I'll cover the function of this monitor Thread object shortly.

The next method, checkIn( ), is used by a servlet to return a connection to the cache when it is no longer needed. Besides returning the connection to the cache, checkIn( ) verifies that the connection is still open. This check is performed to allow a servlet to close a connection should a catastrophic error occur. If the connection is no longer open, the CachedConnection object that holds the connection is removed from the cache. By closing a bad connection and then returning it to the cache, a servlet can permanently remove that connection from the cache, thereby preventing another servlet from using it.

The CacheConnection class's checkUse( ) method is called by the runMonitor( ) method, which is in turn called by the monitor thread. The purpose of the checkUse( ) method is to close any connections that have been idle longer than the time period specified by the MAX_IDLE attribute. The MAX_IDLE attribute specifies the maximum idle time in milliseconds. In Example 4-8, I've specified a value that results in a maximum idle time of 60 minutes. If you set the MAX_IDLE attribute to a lower value, such as 1000*60*2, or two minutes, you can easily watch the monitor thread close idle connections.

The runMonitor( ) method invokes checkUse( ) to check the cache for idle connections. The runMonitor( ) method then puts the Thread object to sleep for five minutes. After the sleep interval, the runMonitor( ) method awakens, and the cycle repeats. When there are no connections remaining in the cache, the monitor thread terminates.

The setVerbose( ) method allows you to control the display of debugging output. Calling setVerbose( ) with an argument of true puts the CacheConnection class, as well as all cached CachedConnection objects, into verbose mode. You'll have to activate this from one of your servlets by calling CacheConnection.setVerbose(true). This causes the CacheConnection object to execute the various System.out.println( ) calls coded within its methods. The resulting debug output is written to your servlet container's error log or to your monitor screen, depending on how your servlet container is configured. Call setVerbose( ) with an argument of false to turn verbose mode off.

The final method is finalize( ) (pun intended). When the servlet container is closed, the finalize( ) method sweeps through the cache and closes any open connections.

A servlet that uses cached connections

Now that you understand the mechanics of the connection cache, let's put it to use. Example 4-9 shows a servlet that implements a cached connection strategy using the three classes just described. The servlet's name is CachedConnectionServlet.

As you read through the code for CachedConnectionServlet, note that there are three significant differences between it and the SessionLogin servlet you should look for:

1. The servlet turns on our Connection Manager's verbose output mode with a call to the CacheConnection.setVerbose( ) method.

2. The servlet allocates a cached connection by calling the CacheConnection. checkOut( ) method. Here, the code is quite compact when compared to the lengthy code required to manage a session connection.

3. The servlet returns the checked-out connection by calling the checkIn( ) method.

In many respects, the cached connection strategy is very similar in implementation in the servlet to the per-transaction strategy, except this time, we've reduced the cost of opening and closing connections by reusing them.

Example 4-9. A cached connection servlet

```
import java.io.*;
import java.sql.*;
import javax.servlet.*;
import javax.servlet.http.*;

public class CachedConnectionServlet extends HttpServlet {

  public void doGet(
    HttpServletRequest request, HttpServletResponse response)
    throws IOException, ServletException {

    response.setContentType("text/html");
    PrintWriter out = response.getWriter( );
    out.println("<html>");
    out.println("<head>");
    out.println("<title>Cached Connection Servlet</title>");
    out.println("</head>");
    out.println("<body>");

    // Turn on verbose output
    CacheConnection.setVerbose(true);

    // Get a cached connection
    Connection connection = CacheConnection.checkOut( );

    Statement  statement  = null;
    ResultSet  resultSet  = null;
    String     userName   = null;
    try {
      // Test the connection
```

Example 4-9. A cached connection servlet (continued)

```
      statement = connection.createStatement( );
      resultSet = statement.executeQuery(
        "select initcap(user) from sys.dual");
      if (resultSet.next( ))
        userName = resultSet.getString(1);
    }
    catch (SQLException e) {
      out.println("DedicatedConnection.doGet( ) SQLException: " +
        e.getMessage( ) + "<p>");
    }
    finally {
      if (resultSet != null)
        try { resultSet.close( ); } catch (SQLException ignore) { }
      if (statement != null)
        try { statement.close( ); } catch (SQLException ignore) { }
    }

    // Return the conection
    CacheConnection.checkIn(connection);

    out.println("Hello " + userName + "!<p>");
    out.println("You're using a cached connection!<p>");
    out.println("</body>");
    out.println("</html>");
  }

  public void doPost(
   HttpServletRequest request, HttpServletResponse response)
   throws IOException, ServletException {
     doGet(request, response);
  }
}
```

This last connection strategy provides the response time efficiency of session connections, while at the same time reduces the number of simultaneous database connections to an on-demand minimum. In practice, I've seen a caching implementation like this handle a web site with more than 1,000 hits a day without ever having more than two simultaneous connections open. Now that's a drastic improvement in the number of simultaneous connections used when compared to the other three strategies.

Unfortunately, this strategy does not enable you to create transactions that span more than one doXXX( ) method invocation. The reason you can't create such transactions is that you have no guarantee of getting the same connection object from one doXXX( ) method call to the next.

So of the four connection strategies I've discussed in this chapter, which method should you choose? Let's discuss that next.

Guidelines for Choosing a Connection Strategy

Of the four strategies outlined in this chapter, a cached connection strategy is best suited for dynamic content that does not need to be kept secure—for example, a public web site that produces its content by retrieving information from a database. If you intend to use authentication to limit your connection audience to a select group of users but don't need to keep track of who's making changes to data, the cached connection strategy is still the most efficient. However, you'll need to add a layer of code to your servlets to prompt the user for authentication and to verify their credentials against an application-maintained list of valid users. You'll also need to store the resulting authorization in a cookie or session object in order to maintain it from one servlet call to the next. You can even use a cached connection for a form processing application, but you will need to use an even more elaborate authenticate-and-store methodology. By the time you're done adding all the extra code to your servlets to manage the authentication process, it may just be easier to use a session connection.

If you have an application that requires a high level of security, then a session-based connection is a better fit. One example of such an application is a medical application in which each transaction needs to be logged to an audit trail showing who added or modified data. With a session-based connection, you can have each application user log in using a distinct database username and password. This facilitates audit logging, because you can use the auditing features that come as part of the database itself, rather than writing your own. Using the database's auditing facility also helps prevent any malicious tampering with the audit trail data.

For more information on writing servlets, I suggest you read *Java Servlet Programming* by Jason Hunter and William Crawford (O'Reilly). You can also browse information about the reference implementation servlet container, Tomcat, which I used to test the examples in this chapter, at *http://www.apache.org*.

Now that you have a solid background in servlet connections, lets take a look at connecting our last type of client, an internal client such as a stored procedure or Enterprise JavaBeans, in Chapter 5.

Internal Database Connections

As you probably already know, the Oracle8*i* database engine includes an embedded JVM known as the JServer. In this chapter, we'll explore the issues that are specific to using JDBC to connect objects that reside in Oracle8*i*'s internal JVM to a database. I say *a* database rather than *the* database, because JDBC can be used to connect internally to the local database or externally to another database. As in the other connection chapters, we'll cover the types of Oracle drivers available. We'll also go over lots of examples to show each type of driver in use and talk about the types of Java objects that the internal JVM supports. Let's begin our discussion by looking at the Oracle drivers that are available for an internal client.

Server-Side Driver Types

To support the use of JDBC by Java code running within JServer, Oracle supplies the following two server-side JDBC drivers:

Server-side internal driver
> The server-side internal driver is used by stored procedures, EJB, or any other type of object that resides in Oracle8*i*'s internal JVM to establish a direct connection internally to the local database. The server-side internal driver runs in the same memory space as the database kernel, the SQL engine, and the JServer JVM. Any Java object that uses this driver to connect to the database has the same default session as any PL/SQL stored procedure or SQL object. This driver has all the same APIs as the client-side drivers.

Server-side Thin driver
> The server-side Thin driver can be used by stored procedures, EJB, and other objects to access databases other than the one in which they are running. The server-side Thin driver is, for all practical purposes, exactly the same as the client-side Thin driver, except that it is an internal driver.

Now that you have an overview of what drivers are available, let's take a closer look at the server-side internal driver.

Using the Server-Side Internal Driver

As with the client-side drivers, when using the server-side internal driver you need to formulate an appropriate database URL for use with the `DriverManager.getConnection()` method. With the server-side internal driver you have two choices for a URL:

```
jdbc:oracle:kprb:
jdbc:default:connection:
```

 The last colon characters on these URLs are necessary only if you want them to work. I say this because I spent several nights unsuccessfully trying to make either of these URLs work. The documentation I was reading showed them used without and with the colon. My preference was to leave off the colon, hence my troubles. When I finally broke down and used the colon on the end, the URLs worked. So, as I say: the last colons on these URLs are necessary only if you want them to work.

I recommend you use `jdbc:oracle:kprb:` as the database URL when connecting through the server-side internal driver. It has the same basic format as the rest of the URLs we've used so far, and you can use it with any form of the `getConnection()` method.

When you invoke `getConnection()` to connect through the server-side internal driver, any unneeded parameters will be ignored. For example, if you pass a username and password, they are simply ignored, because you are using a default connection. This default connection was created when you connected to the database to invoke your stored Java program. This means you can take a Java program you've written to load data into Oracle, change the driver type to kprb, load it into the database, add an appropriate Java security policy to the database for file access permissions, and execute the program without any major modifications. Using `getConnection()` in this way is a good programming practice. It means you'll consistently use the same methodology to connect to the database for both internal and external programs. This will make it easier for you, and especially for the next guy or gal, to maintain your code.

The URL `jdbc:oracle:kprb:` is the most portable of internal URL syntaxes. For example, since the driver type strings oci8, kprb, and thin all use the same relative position within the URL, you can build a helper method that takes a driver type argument passed to your Java program and use it to formulate a valid URL. This would be more difficult with the second internal URL syntax: `jdbc:default:connection:`.

As an alternative to using the `getConnection()` method to open a database connection through the server-side internal driver, you can use the `oracle.jdbc.driver.`

`OracleDriver.defaultConnection()` method. This method is recommended by Oracle but is not portable and, oddly enough, is also deprecated (according to Oracle's API documentation). I do not recommend it.

An Internal Driver Example

In order for me to show you an internal driver example, you will have to know how to load a program into the Oracle database and publish it so it can be invoked from SQL or PL/SQL. So we'll cover these procedures in this section. By the time you're done reading this chapter you may be wondering whether it's a chapter on internal connections or on writing stored procedures. Let me assure you up front, this is a chapter about using internal connections, but that topic requires that I show you how to load and publish a Java stored procedure. Accordingly, my explanations for doing so are very terse. You can find detailed information on writing and loading Oracle Java stored procedures in the *Oracle8i Java Stored Procedures Developer's Guide* available on the Oracle Technology Network (OTN) web site.

There are three steps to making a Java program into a stored procedure.

1. Compile Java source into a Java class file.
2. Load the Java class file into the database.
3. Publish the Java class as a stored procedure.

To get a better understanding of this process, begin by taking a look at Example 5-1, which is a sample stored procedure written to test an internal connection.

Example 5-1. A stored procedure to test an internal connection

```
import java.sql.*;

class TestInternalConnection {

  public static String getGreeting()
   throws ClassNotFoundException, SQLException {
    // With 8.1.6 there's no need to load the driver anymore,
    // but it doesn't hurt if you do
    Class.forName("oracle.jdbc.driver.OracleDriver");
    String greeting = null;
    Connection conn = DriverManager.getConnection("jdbc:oracle:kprb:");
    Statement  stmt = conn.createStatement();
    ResultSet  rset = stmt.executeQuery(
      "select 'Hello '||initcap(USER)||'!' result from dual");
    if (rset.next())
      greeting = rset.getString(1);
    rset.close();
    stmt.close();
    conn.close();
    return greeting;
  }
}
```

The first thing you should notice is that there is nothing remarkable about writing a Java stored procedure. It is simply a Java class with one or more static methods. Our stored procedure, TestInternalConnection, has one static method, getGreeting( ), which returns the username of the user executing the stored procedure. Next, notice that even though as of Oracle8i Version 8.1.6, it is no longer necessary to explicitly load the driver, I do it anyway. Why? Because it's good programming practice to be consistent in how you write Java programs, regardless of whether they are internal or external. By always loading the driver, you can move your programs to either environment without any changes except to the database URL. Lastly, notice that I used the jdbc:oracle:kprb: database URL syntax.

Compile this source into a class file so we can move to the next step, which is to load it into the database.

Loading a class file into a database

If you're going to execute a Java program as a stored procedure, then somehow it must get into the database in order to be available from the database. For our examples, we'll use Oracle's *loadjava* utility to accomplish this task. Accordingly, to load a class file into the database, use the *loadjava* utility as follows:

```
loadjava v t user username/password@host:port:sid classfile
```

The -v switch turns on verbose output, the -t switch tells *loadjava* to use the Thin driver, -user *username/password@host:port:sid* identifies the destination database, and the last parameter is the filename of the class to load. For example, to load TestInternalConnection, you'll need to type a command such as the following at your operating system's command prompt:

```
loadjava v t -user scott/tiger@dssw2k01:1521:orcl TestInternalConnection.class
```

Go ahead and try this command yourself. Be sure that you replace the username, password, and other connection information with values that are appropriate for your environment.

Publishing a class

Now that you have TestInternalConnection loaded, you need to publish its getGreeting( ) method so you can call it as a stored procedure. To *publish* a Java stored procedure, you create a SQL call specification to expose its methods to the rest of the database. Since a Java class file is loaded into an Oracle database, it resides in what you could call, for lack of a better term, a Java namespace. SQL objects, such as tables, PL/SQL stored procedures, and the like exist in a SQL namespace. That's why, even though your Java program resides in the database, you still need to use JDBC to manipulate SQL objects. And from the other perspective, you need some means to tell the SQL namespace that an internal Java program exists before you can invoke one of the program's methods as a stored procedure.

In Oracle, you can create a stored procedure as a standalone function, as a standalone procedure, or as a function or procedure that is part of a package. Accordingly, to create a wrapper for a Java method, use the SQL CREATE FUNCTION or CREATE PROCEDURE syntax or the keywords function or procedure in a package definition. You can execute the CREATE command for the SQL call specification by typing the appropriate command in SQL*Plus, but since this is a book about Java, we'll execute the DDL with a Java program instead.

Example 5-2 is a Java application that creates a function call specification named TIC_getGreeting for TestInternalConnection's getGreeting() method. The DDL statement that PublishTestInternalConnection executes is:

```
create or replace function TIC_getGreeting return varchar2
as language java
name 'TestInternalConnection.getGreeting() return java.lang.String';
```

All that PublishTestInternalConnection does is connect to the database and execute the DDL.

Example 5-2. An application to create a stored function call specification

```java
import java.sql.*;

class PublishTestInternalConnection {

  public static void main(String[] argv)
   throws SQLException {
    DriverManager.registerDriver(new oracle.jdbc.driver.OracleDriver());
    String sql = "create or replace function TIC_getGreeting " +
                 "return varchar2 " +
                 "as language java " +
                 "name 'TestInternalConnection.getGreeting() " +
                 "return java.lang.String';";
    Connection conn = DriverManager.getConnection(
      "jdbc:oracle:thin:dssw2k01:1521:orcl", "scott", "tiger");
    Statement  stmt = conn.createStatement();
    long       rslt = stmt.executeUpdate(sql);
    if (rslt==0)
      System.out.println("OK");
    stmt.close();
    conn.close();
  }
}
```

Modify the database URL in Example 5-2 to a value appropriate for your installation. Then compile the program. Next, execute the program from the command line. It will log into the database and execute the SQL statement, creating the function TIC_getGreeting in the login user's schema.

Executing a Java stored procedure

Now that you have your stored procedure ready, you can test it using the application shown in Example 5-3. Once again, before running the example, modify the database URL to an appropriate value for your environment. Next, compile the program and execute it. If all works well, you should see output such as the following:

```
Hello Scott!
```

Impressive, isn't it? When CallTestInternalConnection is executed, it creates a CallableStatement object that executes the SQL function TIC_getGreeting. TIC_getGreeting in turn calls the Java stored procedure TestInternalConnection.getGreeting( ). The getGreeting( ) method retrieves the user's username and returns the greeting to TIC_getGreeting, which returns it to CallTestInternalConnection.

Example 5-3. A test application to call getGreeting()

```java
import java.sql.*;

class CallTestInternalConnection {

  public static void main(String[] argv)
    throws SQLException {
    DriverManager.registerDriver(new oracle.jdbc.driver.OracleDriver( ));
    Connection conn = DriverManager.getConnection(
      "jdbc:oracle:thin:dssw2k01:1521:orcl", "scott", "tiger");
    CallableStatement cstmt = conn.prepareCall(
      "{?= call TIC_getGreeting}");
    cstmt.registerOutParameter(1, Types.CHAR);
    long rslt = cstmt.executeUpdate( );
    if (rslt>0)
      System.out.println(cstmt.getString(1));
    cstmt.close( );
    conn.close( );
  }
}
```

Internal-Connection Considerations

Now that you understand how to establish an internal connection, there are four important considerations to note. I describe these in the following sections. If you keep these considerations in mind when writing both internal and external programs, you'll have no trouble moving those programs into and out of the database.

You have only one connection

Any time you make a call to getConnection( ), or to defaultConnection( ), you are actually getting the same default connection used by every other internal object, but you are returned a new Connection object. Why is this distinction important? It becomes important only if you will be using object-relational database objects and wish to use custom type maps. By using multiple Connection objects, you can use custom type maps in each connection that will in turn allow you to look at the same database object in different ways. I'll cover type maps in Chapter 16. Just keep the fact that you can use different type maps on the same object by opening an internal connection multiple times tucked away in the back of your mind in case you need it someday.

Closing one of your connections closes all of your connections

Since every Connection object really represents the same connection, if you close any one of your connections, you inadvertently close them all! Oracle recommends that you not close your connections to avoid this problem. That bothers me. It sounds like an invitation to a bad habit, so I close my connections at the end of my stored-procedure call. Do whatever you feel is appropriate. I won't be there to say tsk-tsk, but consider the fact that if you make it a habit not to close your connections in stored procedures, they will lose their portability, and you may end up not closing your connections in applications, applets, and servlets simply out of habit.

Auto-commit is not supported

Auto-commit mode is disabled in the server. If you wish to do any transaction management in a Java stored procedure, you will have to do it manually.

Additional methods are available for use in exception handlers

For code that runs in the JServer, there are two additional Oracle methods available with the OracleSQLException object: getNumParameters( ) and getParameters( ). These two methods make the parameters that are normally passed when calling stored procedures available inside the catch clause of an SQLException. These methods provide the following information:

int getNumParameters( )
    Returns the numbers of parameters available

Object[] getParameters( )
    Returns the parameter values

You will need to cast an SQLException object to an OracleSQLException object to use these methods. For example:

```
. . .
catch (SQLException e) {
Int numParms = (OracleSQLException)e.getNumParameters( );
. . .
}
```

Now that we've covered the internal driver, let's take a look at using the server-side Thin driver to connect to an external database.

Using the Server-Side Thin Driver

With the server-side Thin driver you now have two ways to connect to another Oracle database from a Java program in an Oracle database. You can create a database link or use the server-side Thin driver. In my opinion, it's a much better solution to use database links than to use the server-side Thin driver. With database links you get the following advantages:

- Transparent distributed transaction management
- Centralized administration of the database connection
- Centralized database security

To access another database with the Thin driver, you need to use:

- An XAConnection for distributed transaction management
- An appropriate database URL in each Java object

However, you also open the database to security compromises. For example, to access an Oracle database outside of the current database, you need to set up a SocketPermission security policy to allow your Java program to open a socket to the external database. Once that policy is created, any program can use it to open external connections. This also means that external programs can access the current data base without going through its authentication system. That said, there may be times when an external connection using the Thin driver is the right solution to a problem. So let's examine the use of the Thin driver by working through an example.

A Server-Side Thin Driver Example

Example 5-4 contains a stored procedure that makes a connection to an external database using the Thin driver. This stored procedure, TestExternalConnection, uses the same database URL syntax that is used with the client-side Thin driver.

Example 5-4. A stored procedure to test an external connection

```
import java.sql.*;

class TestExternalConnection {

  public static String getGreeting()
   throws ClassNotFoundException, SQLException {
    Class.forName("oracle.jdbc.driver.OracleDriver");
    String greeting = null;
    Connection conn = DriverManager.getConnection(
     "jdbc:oracle:thin:@dssnt01:1521:dssora01", "scott", "tiger");
    Statement  stmt = conn.createStatement();
    ResultSet  rset = stmt.executeQuery(
     "select 'Hello '||initcap(USER)||'!' result from dual");
    if (rset.next())
      greeting = rset.getString(1);
    rset.close();
```

```
    stmt.close();
    conn.close();
    return greeting;
  }
}
```

Compile the program and then load the class file by executing *loadjava*:

```
    loadjava -v -t -user scott/tiger@dssw2k01:1521:orcl TestExternalConnection.class
```

Next, publish the stored procedure by compiling and executing Example 5-5.

Example 5-5. An application to publish TestExternalConnection

```
import java.sql.*;

class PublishTestExternalConnection {

  public static void main(String[] argv)
   throws SQLException {
    DriverManager.registerDriver(new oracle.jdbc.driver.OracleDriver());
    String sql = "create or replace function TEC_getGreeting " +
                 "return varchar2 " +
                 "as language java " +
                 "name 'TestExternalConnection.getGreeting() " +
                 "return java.lang.String';";
    Connection conn = DriverManager.getConnection(
      "jdbc:oracle:thin:dssw2k01:1521:orcl", "scott", "tiger");
    Statement  stmt = conn.createStatement();
    long       rslt = stmt.executeUpdate(sql);
    if (rslt==0)
      System.out.println("OK");
    stmt.close();
    conn.close();
  }
}
```

Compile and execute Example 5-6 to ultimately invoke `TestExternalConnection`'s `getGreeting()` method. Invoking `getGreeting()` in turn tests the stored procedure's ability to make an external connection.

Example 5-6. An application to execute TestExternalConnection

```
import java.sql.*;

class CallTestExternalConnection {

  public static void main(String[] argv)
   throws SQLException {
    DriverManager.registerDriver(new oracle.jdbc.driver.OracleDriver());
    Connection conn = DriverManager.getConnection(
      "jdbc:oracle:thin:dssw2k01:1521:orcl", "scott", "tiger");
    CallableStatement cstmt = conn.prepareCall(
```

Example 5-6. An application to execute TestExternalConnection (continued)

```
    "{?= call TEC_getGreeting}");
  cstmt.registerOutParameter(1, Types.CHAR);
  long rslt = cstmt.executeUpdate( );
  if (rslt>0)
    System.out.println(cstmt.getString(1));
  cstmt.close( );
  conn.close( );
  }
}
```

What happened? You say it didn't work? Did you get output that looks something like the following:

```
Exception in thread "main" java.sql.SQLException: ORA-29532: Java call terminated by
uncaught Java exception: java.security.AccessControlException: the Permission (java.
net.SocketPermission dssnt01 resolve) has not been granted by dbms_java.grant_
permission to SchemaProtectionDomain(SCOTT|PolicyTableProxy(SCOTT))
ORA-06512: at "SCOTT.TEC_GETGREETING", line 0
ORA-06512: at line 1
        at oracle.jdbc.dbaccess.DBError.throwSqlException(DBError.java:114)
        at oracle.jdbc.ttc7.TTIoer.processError(TTIoer.java:208)
        at oracle.jdbc.ttc7.Oall7.receive(Oall7.java, Compiled Code)
        at oracle.jdbc.ttc7.TTC7Protocol.doOall7(TTC7Protocol.java, Compiled Code)
        at oracle.jdbc.ttc7.TTC7Protocol.parseExecuteFetch(TTC7Protocol.java:738)
        at oracle.jdbc.driver.OracleStatement.executeNonQuery(OracleStatement.java,
          Compiled Code)
        at oracle.jdbc.driver.OracleStatement.doExecuteOther(OracleStatement.java:
          1232)
        at oracle.jdbc.driver.OracleStatement.doExecuteWithBatch(OracleStatement.
          java:1353)
        at oracle.jdbc.driver.OracleStatement.doExecute(OracleStatement.java:1760)
        at oracle.jdbc.driver.OracleStatement.doExecuteWithTimeout(OracleStatement.
          java:1805)
        at oracle.jdbc.driver.OraclePreparedStatement.
          executeUpdate(OraclePreparedStatement.java:322)
        at CallTestExternalConnection.main(CallTestExternalConnection.java:12)
```

It didn't work because, just like applets, internal clients run in a secure JVM, or "sand box," in which they are not allowed access to operating-system resources without previously set up policy entries that allow them to do so. And as with our remote connection applet from Chapter 2, you need to add a SocketPermission policy for our stored procedure to work.

Database SocketPermission Policies

One way you can add a SocketPermission security policy to the database is to use the packaged procedure SYS.DBMS_JAVA.GRANT_PERMISSION. GRANT_PERMIS-SION has the following signature:

```
GRANT_PERMISSION( username, permission, target_name, actions )
```

which breaks down as:

username
> The owner or schema for which to grant the permission

permission
> The Java permission to grant

target_name
> The permission's first parameter, or target name

actions
> The permission's second parameter, commonly a comma-delimited list of applicable actions

You can find more detailed information about Java permissions in the JDK API documentation. Now that you have an idea of how GRANT_PERMISSION works, let's proceed by creating a `SocketPermissions` policy entry. To do this, we'll use yet another Java application. Example 5-7 is our policy creation program. In `PolicyTestExternalConnection` we grant the same permission we set up for an applet in Chapter 3 to allow the user SCOTT to access a remote database.

Example 5-7. An application to create socket permissions

```java
import java.sql.*;

class PolicyTestExternalConnection {

  public static void main(String[] argv)
   throws SQLException {
   DriverManager.registerDriver(new oracle.jdbc.driver.OracleDriver());
   Connection conn = DriverManager.getConnection(
     "jdbc:oracle:thin:dssw2k01:1521:orcl", "scott", "tiger");
   CallableStatement cstmt = conn.prepareCall(
     "{call sys.dbms_java.grant_permission" +
     "('SCOTT','java.net.SocketPermission'," +
     "'dssnt01:1024-','connect,resolve')}");
   long rslt = cstmt.executeUpdate();
   if (rslt==0)
     System.out.println("OK");
   cstmt.close();
   conn.close();
  }
}
```

Modify the database URL, username, and password as is appropriate for your environment. Then compile and execute this program. `PolicyTestExternalConnection` uses the SYS.DBMS_JAVA package's GRANT_PERMISSION procedure to add a `SocketPermission` policy allowing schema SCOTT to access host *dssnt01* using ports 1024 and higher.

Now try executing `CallTestExternalConnection` (Example 5-7) again. This time, it works! If you think about it, accessing external resources through Java in a database opens up unlimited possibilities for expanding the capabilities of the database. You can even go so far as accessing another vendor's database. All you need to do is load the vendor's Type 4 driver and its support files, and you can establish a connection.

 `Cancel( )` and `setQueryTimeout( )` are not supported by the server-side Thin driver.

Now that you have an understanding of the issues involved with using the server-side Thin driver, let's finish this chapter with a discussion of the types of Java programs JServer can support.

JServer Program Support

Oracle states that you can run any Java program in JServer. This is not a false statement, but since JServer does not support servlets in Version 8.1.6, you have to consider the usefulness of what can be run.* You are really limited to two types of objects:

Stored procedures
> These refer to any Java object with a static method that can be wrapped with a SQL function, procedure, or package.

Enterprise JavaBeans (EJB)
> These use JDBC but are not executed using JDBC. Instead, they are executed using the IIOP protocol.

Since the use of JDBC by stored procedures and EJB is the same, I see no point in covering EJB here. One thing worth noting about internal Java programs is what happens when you make calls to `System.out.println( )` and `System.err.println( )`. Where does this output go?

By default, any calls to the methods `System.out.println( )` and `System.err.println( )` goes into a trace file. That's not very useful, but you can make the output go to the SQL*Plus screen buffer. The SQL*Plus screen buffer is the buffer that the SYS. DBMS_OUTPUT.PUT_LINE stored procedure uses. To send Java output to the SQL*Plus screen buffer, call the SYS.DBMS_JAVA.SET_OUTPUT() stored procedure from within your Java stored procedure. The syntax for doing that is:

```
SYS.DBMS_JAVA.SET_OUTPUT(BUFFER_SIZE IN NUMBER)
```

BUFFER_SIZE is an optional parameter. The default buffer size is 2,000 bytes, and the maximum value is 1,000,000 bytes. Of course, the SQL*Plus buffer is useful only while using SQL*Plus. But the buffer output when using SQL*Plus can be an invaluable troubleshooting tool during development.

---

* Servlets are supposedly supported in Version 8.1.7.

Example 5-8 is a stored procedure to test the use of SET_OUTPUT. TestDbmsJavaSetOutput connects to the database using the driver type specified on the command line. Since the static method main( ) is utilized for this stored procedure, you can pass it a driver type at runtime. This allows you to test the procedure both externally and internally. Next, the program uses a SELECT statement to retrieve the user's name. It turns on the redirection of the System.out.println( ) method, which normally goes to stdout, by executing the stored procedure SYS.DBMS_JAVA.SET_OUTPUT and passing it a buffer size of 10,000 bytes. Then, after closing the database connection, it calls the System.out.println( ) method, passing it a greeting using the user's name.

Example 5-8. A test of DBMS_JAVA.SET_OUTPUT

```
import java.sql.*;

class TestDbmsJavaSetOutput {

  public static void main(String[] args)
   throws ClassNotFoundException, SQLException {
    Class.forName("oracle.jdbc.driver.OracleDriver");
    String greeting = null;
    Connection conn = DriverManager.getConnection(
     "jdbc:oracle:" + args[0] + ":", "scott", "tiger");
    Statement   stmt = conn.createStatement();
    ResultSet   rset = stmt.executeQuery(
     "select 'Hello '||initcap(USER)||'!' result from dual");
    if (rset.next())
     greeting = rset.getString(1);
    rset.close();
    stmt.close();
    CallableStatement cstmt = conn.prepareCall(
     "{ call SYS.DBMS_JAVA.SET_OUTPUT( 10000 ) }");
    cstmt.execute();
    cstmt.close();
    conn.close();
    System.out.println(greeting);
  }
}
```

Compile the program and load its class file into the database by executing *loadjava* as follows:

```
loadjava -v -t -user scott/tiger@dssw2k01:1521:orcl TestDbmsJavaSetOutput.class
```

This time, we'll publish the Java stored procedure using SQL*Plus. So log into the database using SQL*Plus and execute the following SQL statement to publish TestDbmsJavaSetOutput:

```
create or replace procedure TDJSO_main(driver_type varchar2)
as language java
name 'TestDbmsJavaSetOutput.main(java.lang.String[])';
```

This SQL statement creates a procedure: TDJSO_main(driver_type varchar2). Next, turn on the SYS.DBMS_OUTPUT.PUT_LINE buffer for SQL*Plus by executing the following command:

```
SQL> set serveroutput on size 10000;
```

Then execute TDJSO_main, passing it the string kprb in order to specify the internal driver type by executing the following command at the SQL*Plus prompt:

```
SQL> execute TDJSO_main('kprb');
Hello Scott!

PL/SQL procedure successfully completed.
```

You can find more information about Java stored procedures in the *Java Stored Procedures Developer's Guide* available on the OTN. You can find additional information about EJB in the *Enterprise JavaBeans and CORBA Developer's Guide*, also available on the OTN, or in *Enterprise JavaBeans* by Richard Monson-Haefel (O'Reilly).

Now that you know how to connect internal objects to the database using JDBC, let's move on to the next chapter where we'll examine advanced security issues such as authentication, data encryption, and data integrity.

CHAPTER 6

Oracle Advanced Security

So far, we have been discussing how to make connections to an Oracle database from applications, applets, servlets, and internal objects . All these connections have had something in common: they were all unsecured connections. With unsecured connections, someone intent on malicious activity can intercept the information being passed between your client and server and even modify it while in transit. Practically speaking, if you're using your application on a corporate intranet, this should not be much of a concern. However, if you're using JDBC to connect to a database over the Internet, the Oracle Advanced Security (ASO) option can protect your data's privacy and integrity.

Oracle Advanced Security is a set of advanced security options, some of which are packaged with Oracle Enterprise Edition, and some of which are purchased from a third party. They allow you to create a secured connection to a database or use a more secure authentication scheme. Oracle Advanced Security provides five security enhancements to JDBC connections:

- Improved authentication using third-party authentication
- Single sign-on using third-party authentication
- Data privacy using encryption
- Data integrity using message digests
- Improved authorization using the Distributed Computing Environment (DCE)

When using the OCI driver, all five of these enhancements are enabled by configuration settings in the Oracle Client software. However, with the Thin driver, none of the authentication and authorization enhancements are available. As for data privacy and integrity, the configuration settings for these are sent to the Thin driver by using a properties object with getConnection( ). So of the five security enhancements, only data privacy and integrity with the use of the Thin driver are a concern for a programmer. Even so, let's start our discussion with authentication.

Authentication

The most common form of *authentication*, that is, proving that you are who you say you are, is *passwords*. The OCI and Thin drivers implement the Oracle O3LOGON challenge-response protocol. This requires a username and password. The OCI driver also supports third-party authentication protocols such as Kerberos, RADIUS, or SecurID. However, the Thin driver supports only O3LOGON. Nonetheless, it may be helpful to understand why third-party authentication is needed in the first place. So let's take a look at the weaknesses of using passwords.

The level of authentication security for a given username is equal to the effort involved in guessing the user's password. Keeping that in mind, let's consider how people typically approach password management.

Most people use easy-to-remember passwords, something they are familiar with, such as a family member's name or a significant date or number. All of these are available to someone with malicious intent, given a little effort. So all of these are easy-to-guess passwords, which provide a low level of security.

To improve security, a person may decide to use a more complex password. But in doing so, he may also make one of two related decisions that compromise security. First, he may decide to use the same password everywhere. This exposes him to the risk that if the password is guessed, a malicious user may use it to get access to all of his systems.

Another related problem is when someone in the password management facility at one site uses another user's password stored at his site to gain access to that user's resources at another site. From this second scenario, you can see that using the same password at every site is a significant security risk.

A third problem with passwords is that, to improve security, a user may decide to use a different complex password at every site. But he may then defeat that decision by writing them down to remember them.

The third-party authentication services provided by Oracle Advanced Security addresses these password weaknesses in various ways. If your Java program, such as an application or servlet, can utilize the OCI driver, you can use third-party authentication to improve your system's security. If you're using the Thin driver, you should remain hopeful, as I am, that the third-party authentication services will be available in a future release of the product.

Data Encryption

Simply stated, *data encryption* equates to data privacy. A malicious user can use a network sniffer to eavesdrop on network traffic. Without encryption, she can collect the network data in a readable form as it is transmitted. If the data is encrypted using the RSA or DES cryptographic algorithms, it can still be collected, but it will be unreadable. Data encryption must be enabled, or requested, by both the client and the server for it to be used when a new connection is created.

Enabling Encryption on a Server

To enable data encryption on the server, you need to set the SQLNET. ENCRYPTION_SERVER and SQLNET.ENCRYPTION_TYPES_SERVER parameters in your server's *sqlnet.ora* file. The syntax for setting these parameters is:

```
SQLNET.ENCRYPTION_SERVER = [REJECTED | ACCEPTED | REQUESTED | REQUIRED]
SQLNET.ENCRYPTION_TYPES_SERVER = (type[,type...])

type ::= [DES40 | RC4_40 | DES | RC4_56 | RC4_128]
```

which breaks down as:

SQLNET.ENCRYPTION_SERVER

> Specifies the server's preference for whether encryption is used when new connections are made. The following are valid values:

> *REJECTED*

>> The server does not support encryption. Connections from clients requesting encryption will be refused.

> *ACCEPTED*

>> The server will accept a request from the client to support encryption.

> *REQUESTED*

>> The server will request encryption from the client.

> *REQUIRED*

>> The server requires encryption. If the client cannot support encryption, then the connection will be refused.

SQLNET.ENCRYPTION_TYPES_SERVER

> Specifies the type, or types, of encryption that the server supports. Since you can specify more than one value for this parameter, a value on the left takes precedence to a value on the right during connection negotiation. You can choose from among one or more of the following:

> *DES40*

>> Provides 40-bit DES encryption.

> *RC4_40*

>> Provides 40-bit RSA encryption.

> *DES*

>> Provides 56-bit DES encryption.

RC4_56

Provides 40-bit RSA encryption.

RC4_128

Provides 128-bit RSA encryption. This is not available in Oracle software exported outside the U.S.

For example, if you wish to require the use of encryption for all connections to your server and support RC4_128 and RC4_56, place the following two lines in your server's *sqlnet.ora* file:

```
SQLNET.ENCRYPTION_SERVER = REQUIRED
SQLNET.ENCRYPTION_TYPES_SERVER = (RC4_128,RC4_56)
```

Enabling Encryption on a Client

How you enable encryption from the client depends on whether you are using the OCI driver or the Thin driver. If you are using the OCI driver, the following properties must be set in the *sqlnet.ora* file on the client:

```
SQLNET.ENCRYPTION_CLIENT = [REJECTED | ACCEPTED | REQUESTED | REQUIRED]
SQLNET.ENCRYPTION_TYPES_CLIENT = (type[,type...])

type := [DES40 | RC4_40 | DES | RC4_56 | RC4_128]
```

The meanings of these parameters and their settings are the same as they are for the corresponding server-side parameters. If you are using the Thin driver and want to use encryption, set the following properties in a Java Properties object passed to getConnection():

oracle.net.encryption_client

Specifies the client's encryption preference and can take on one of the following values:

REJECTED
ACCEPTED
REQUESTED
REQUIRED

oracle.net.encryption_types_client

Specifies the type of encryption requested and can take on one or more of the following values in a comma-delimited list. The list must be enclosed within parentheses. The possible values are:

DES40C

Provides 40-bit DES encryption

RC4_40

Provides 40-bit RSA encryption

DES56C
> Provides 56-bit DES encryption

RC4_56
> Provides 56-bit RSA encryption

The next two sections talk in more detail about the process of negotiating both the use of encryption and the type of encryption to be used. In addition, you'll find a detailed example later in this chapter in the section "A Data Encryption and Integrity Example."

Negotiating the Use of Encryption

During the process of establishing a connection between a client and a server, the server negotiates with the client to establish whether to activate encryption. The combination of the client-side and server-side encryption settings determines the outcome of the negotiation during a connection. Table 6-1 shows the outcome of the various combinations. For example, if a client's setting is REQUESTED, and the server's is ACCEPTED, then a secured connection will be created. However, if a client's setting is ACCEPTED and so is the server's, then the connection will be successful, but the encryption will be off. At least one side must request encryption while the other at least accepts it in order for encryption to be activated.

Table 6-1. Connection settings for encryption and integrity

	Server			
Client	**REJECTED**	**ACCEPTED**	**REQUESTED**	**REQUIRED**
REJECTED	Off	Off	Off	Fails
ACCEPTED	Off	Off	On	On
REQUESTED	Off	On	On	On
REQUIRED	Fails	On	On	On

Negotiating the Type of Encryption

Assuming that a request for a secured connection is accepted, a second set of properties must be set to allow the type of encryption to be negotiated. On the server side, SQLNET.ENCRYPTION_TYPES_SERVER must be set to include one or more encryption types. Accordingly, on the client side, and if you are using the OCI driver, SQLNET.ENCRYPTION_TYPES_CLIENT must be set. If you are using the Thin driver on the client side, you must set the property oracle.net.encryption_types_client in a Java Properties object. You must then pass that Properties object to the Thin driver during a call to the getConnection( ) method.

The values for the ENCRYPTION_TYPES properties specified in the *sqlnet.ora* file on both client and server consist of a list of one or more encryption types separated by commas and enclosed within parentheses. For example:

```
SQLNET.ENCRYPTION_TYPES_SERVER = (RC4_128,RC4_56)
```

The priority of which algorithm to use is determined from left to right in the list. So you should specify the most desirable algorithm first, and then the second most desirable, and so on. During the negotiation process, the server will select the most desirable match between the client and server encryption types lists.

The Thin driver property oracle.net.encryption_types_client also requires that you enclose the encryption algorithm within parentheses but supports only the selection of one algorithm at this time. The parentheses exist for compatibility with a future release that will allow you to specify more than one encryption algorithm. In addition, due to export regulations, the Thin driver, which is the same set of class files for both import and export editions of the software, does not support RC4_128 (128-bit) encryption. Also, note that the literal value for specifying DES is different for the Thin driver than for its OCI counterpart. Don't make the mistake of specifying "DES40" or "DES" instead of "DES40C" or "DES56C" and then pull your hair out because it doesn't work.

As an example of how the type of encryption is negotiated, consider the case in which a server's setting is:

```
SQLNET.ENCRYPTION_TYPES_SERVER = (RC4_128,RC4_56)
```

Then assume a client is using the Thin driver with these settings:

```
Properties prop = new Properties();
prop.setProperty("user", "scott");
prop.setProperty("password", "tiger");
prop.setProperty("oracle.net.encryption_client", "REQUESTED");
prop.setProperty("oracle.net.encryption_types_client", "( RC4_56 )");
```

The server will start the negotiation by requesting RC4_128 encryption. The client will in turn respond that it cannot support RC4_128, so the server will then try the next type in the list, which is RC4_56. The client will respond that it can support RC4_56 encryption, and a connection will be established.

Next, we'll take a look at the second line of defense, data integrity.

Data Integrity

Data integrity ensures that a data packet from one end of a connection reaches the other end unchanged. This prevents two additional types of malicious attacks: data tampering and replay. *Data tampering* occurs when part of a data packet's contents are modified in transit. *Replay* is the process of transmitting a valid transaction multiple times.

Data integrity is ensured using MD5 cryptographic checksums.* When you use Oracle Advanced Security's data integrity facilities, a cryptographically secure message digest is created for, and passed with, each data packet sent across the network. This message digest is a checksum value that changes if any of the data in a data packet changes.

Enabling Data Integrity on a Server

To enable data integrity on a server, you need to set the SQLNET.CRYPTO_ CHECKSUM_SERVER and SQLNET.CRYPTO_CHECKSUM_TYPES_SERVER parameters in your server's *sqlnet.ora* file. The syntax for setting these parameters is:

```
SQLNET.CRYPTO_CHECKSUM_SERVER=[REJECTED | ACCEPTED | REQUESTED | REQUIRED]
SQLNET.CRYPTO_CHECKSUM_TYPES_SERVER=(MD5)
```

which breaks down as:

SQLNET.CRYPTO_CHECKSUM_SERVER

Specifies the server's preference for whether data integrity is used when new connections are made. The following are valid values:

REJECTED

The server does not support data integrity. Connections from clients requesting data integrity will be refused.

ACCEPTED

The server will accept a request from the client to support data integrity.

REQUESTED

The server will request data integrity from the client.

REQUIRED

The server requires data integrity. If the client cannot support data integrity, then the connection will fail.

SQLNET.CRYPTO_CHECKSUM_TYPES_SERVER

Specifies the type of checksum algorithm to use. This is a parenthesis list because more than one algorithm may be supported in the future. However, only MD5 is supported at this time.

Enabling Data Integrity on a Client

As with encryption, to enable data integrity on the client, the appropriate properties must be set in the client's *sqlnet.ora* file if the OCI driver is used, or in a Java Properties object that is passed to the getConnection( ) method if the Thin driver is used.

---

* With Oracle Advanced Security, the term *checksum* is synonymous with the term *integrity*.

If you're using the OCI driver, use the following syntax in your *sqlnet.ora* file to specify data integrity options:

```
SQLNET.CRYPTO_CHECKSUM_CLIENT=[REJECTED | ACCEPTED | REQUESTED | REQUIRED]
SQLNET.CRYPTO_CHECKSUM_TYPES_CLIENT=(MD5)
```

The definitions for these parameters are the same as those for the server. If you're using the Thin driver and you want to enable data integrity, set the following properties in a Java `Properties` object that you pass to getConnection( ):

`oracle.net.crypto_checksum_client`
> Specifies the client's data integrity preference. It can be one of the following values:
>> REJECTED
>> ACCEPTED
>> REQUESTED
>> REQUIRED

`oracle.net.crypto_checksum_types_client`
> Specifies the checksum algorithm preference for the client, of which the only current valid value is MD5.

Negotiating the Use of Data Integrity

During the process of establishing a connection, the server negotiates with the client to determine whether to enable data integrity by using the same process as that used for encryption (which I covered earlier in this chapter). There is only one cryptographic algorithm available at this time, MD5. Still, it is necessary to surround the CRYPTO_CHECKSUM_TYPES_CLIENT parameter's value with parentheses.

A Data Encryption and Integrity Example

Now that we've discussed both data encryption and integrity, let's see them in action. Example 6-1 is a sample application that uses the Thin driver to establish a secure database connection.

First, the program loads the Oracle Thin driver using the DriverManager. registerDriver( ) method. This method is chosen because the use of encryption and integrity is definitely an Oracle extension, and therefore not portable. So why be concerned about using the Class.forName( ) method, along with the extra coding that it requires, when portability is no longer a concern?

Second, the program creates a Properties object named prop and then adds the required properties. It adds the user and password properties because the form of getConnection( ) used with a Properties object does not take them as separate parameters. The program then adds the oracle.net.encryption_client and oracle.net. encryption_types_client properties to require 40-bit encryption. Next, the program adds oracle.net.crypto_checksum_client and oracle.net.crypto_checksum_types_ client properties to require that MD5 message digests be added to each packet.

Third, the program calls the getConnection(String url, Properties info) form of the getConnection( ) method. Then it finishes up in a manner similar to our previous connection examples by querying the database. This is the kind of secured connection you would most likely make for an applet. Alternatively, if you use an application or servlet, you would most likely use the OCI driver, in which case, all these settings would be transparent to the program because they would be set in the Oracle Client's *sqlnet.ora* file.

Example 6-1. A secure database connection application

```
import java.sql.*;
import java.util.*;

public class TestDataEncryptionIntegrity {

 public static void main(String[] argv)
  throws Exception {

  DriverManager.registerDriver(new oracle.jdbc.driver.OracleDriver( ));

  Properties prop = new Properties( );
  prop.setProperty("user", "scott");
  prop.setProperty("password", "tiger");
  prop.setProperty("oracle.net.encryption_client", "REQUIRED");
  prop.setProperty("oracle.net.encryption_types_client", "( RC4_40 )");
  prop.setProperty("oracle.net.crypto_checksum_client", "REQUIRED");
  prop.setProperty("oracle.net.crypto_checksum_types_client", "( MD5 )");

  Connection conn = DriverManager.getConnection(
   "jdbc:oracle:thin:@dssw2k01:1521:orcl", prop);
  Statement stmt = conn.createStatement( );
  ResultSet rset = stmt.executeQuery(
   "select 'Hello Thin driver Encryption & Integrity " +
   "tester '||USER||'!' result from dual");
  while(rset.next( ))
   System.out.println(rset.getString(1));
  rset.close( );
  stmt.close( );
  conn.close( );
 }
}
```

Now that you know how to secure your connection's privacy and integrity, let's examine another data encryption and integrity solution available to the OCI driver, the Secure Sockets Layer.

Secure Sockets Layer

Secure Sockets Layer (SSL) is an industry-standard protocol for secure authentication, data encryption, and data integrity. With Version 8.1.6, SSL is supported only by the OCI driver. So when you configure the Oracle Client and the Server's listener software to use SSL, data encryption and integrity are transparently enabled, that is, as far as your Java programs are concerned. It's just a matter of specifying a net service name configured to use SSL in your database URL. Since the Thin driver does not yet support SSL, and may never support SSL because of export laws, there's no need for a programmer to specify any properties, and therefore, no need to show you an example. Nonetheless, it may be helpful to understand the steps involved in configuring the Oracle Client and Server to use SSL. For testing purposes, here's an outline of the activities required to configure your server for SSL:

1. Use Oracle Wallet Manager to create a new Oracle wallet, which is an abstraction for a X.509 certificate database.

2. In Wallet Manager, create a certificate request using the fully qualified domain name of your server's host as the common name.

3. Export your certificate request and send it to a certificate authority along with the required information to acquire a trusted certificate. For testing purposes, send your request to VeriSign, which you can do at *http://digitalid.verisign.com/server/trial/index.htm*. After VeriSign sends you your certificate via email, install the corresponding test root certificate in Internet Explorer by going to *https://digitalid.verisign.com/server/trial/trialStep4.htm*. The test root certificate is distinct from the one you received via email. You'll want to use Internet Explorer to receive the test root certificate from VeriSign, because you can then export the root certificate by selecting Tools → Internet Options → Content → Certificates → Trusted Roots, scrolling to "Issued To: for VeriSign Authorized testing only," and then selecting Export. The result is an operating-system file. The reason you need to export the test root certification is to make it available to Wallet Manager. At this point you have two certificates: a user certificate in an email and a test root certificate in an operating-system file.

4. After you get your root certificate and your trusted user certificate for the certificate request you created earlier, import them into your wallet using Wallet Manager. Import the root certificate first and then the user certificate.

5. Use Oracle Net8 Assistant to add the necessary parameters for SSL to your profile by clicking on Local, then Profile from the hierarchy tree, then selecting Oracle Advanced Security from the drop-down list box, and finally clicking on the SSL tab. You'll want to specify the same Oracle Wallet directory you used when you created your wallet.

6. Next, add an SSL listener on port 2484 to your listener by clicking on Local, then Listeners, then LISTENER, then selecting Listening Locations from the

drop-down list box, and finally clicking on Add Address. Specify the protocol TCP with SSL, your fully qualified hostname for host, and port 2484.

7. Now for the client-side configuration. Run Oracle Net8 Assistant on your client. Add an SSL net service name using port 2484 to your client by clicking on Local, then Service Naming, then clicking on the Edit/Create menu item. Specify a service name, a protocol of TCP/IP with SSL, your fully qualified hostname for the host, and port 2484.

8. Last, and this is important on Windows NT or Windows 2000, go to the Services Administrator, right click on the Oracle database service (which will be named OracleServiceORCL or something similar), select properties, click on the Log On tab, click on This Account, and specify the name of the user that owns the Oracle Wallet.

Once you have followed these steps, you can use an SSL database connection with the OCI driver. There are no necessary changes to your Java programs, but, as I stated earlier, you are limited for the time being to OCI driver support. SSL cannot be used from the Thin driver.

For all the gory details about Oracle Advanced Security, see the *Oracle Advanced Security Administrator's Guide* available on the OTN.

Now that you can create secured connections, we'll take a look at our last connection topic, Oracle's implementation of DataSources.

CHAPTER 7

JNDI and Connection Pooling

An object-oriented programming language derives its strength from two areas. First, you have the constructs of the programming language itself that allow you to write well-structured objects to extend that language. Second, you have the extensive libraries of APIs that have been written to provide standard functionality. Think for a moment about how APIs are created. A software engineer does not just wake up one morning and have an entire API worked out in every detail. Instead, an API's design is based on the experiences of professionals like you, who, over time, have gained insight through problem solving as to what is needed in an API to make it a useful part of developing an application. Accordingly, over time, an API evolves through this community process to better fit the needs of the programming community.

When it comes to the JDBC API, specifically the DriverManager facility, there is an evolution taking place. In Chapter 4, we needed to put a significant amount of code around DriverManager to implement a sharable connection facility. It took even more work to make our sharable connections cacheable. With the Java 2 Enterprise Edition (J2EE), a framework has been defined for sharing and caching connections. This framework is the JDBC 2.0 Extension API. In this chapter, we'll cover the JDBC 2.0 Extension API, which is a another set of JDBC interfaces, along with Oracle's implementation of these interfaces. We'll also look at a functional caching object using Oracle's connection caching implementation. Let's begin our journey through the new API with a look at the generic source for database connections, the DataSource class.

DataSources

A DataSource object is a factory for database connections. Oracle's implementations of data sources are database connection objects that encapsulate the registration of the appropriate database driver and the creation of a connection using predetermined parameters. DataSource objects are typically bound with the Java Naming and

Directory Interface (JNDI), so they can be allocated using a logical name at a centrally managed facility such as an LDAP directory.

OracleDataSources

Oracle implements the DataSource interface with class OracleDataSource. Table 7-1 lists the standard properties implemented by a DataSource object.

Table 7-1. Standard DataSource properties

Property	Data type	Description
databaseName	String	Oracle SID
dataSourceName	String	Name of the underlying DataSource class
description	String	Description of the DataSource
networkProtocol	String	For OCI driver, determines the protocol used
password	String	Oracle password
portNumber	int	Oracle listener port number
serverName	String	DNS alias or TCP/IP address of the host
user	String	Oracle username

DataSource properties follow the JavaBeans design pattern, and therefore, the following getter/setter methods are in a DataSource object:

```
public synchronized void    setDatabaseName(String databseName)
public synchronized String getDatabaseName()
public synchronized void    setDataSourceName(String dataSourceName)
public synchronized String getDataSourceName()
public synchronized void    setDescription(String description)
public synchronized String getDescription()
public synchronized void    setNetworkProtocol(String networkProtocol)
public synchronized String getNetworkProtocol()
public synchronized void    setPassword(String password)
public synchronized void    setPortNumber(int portNumber)
public synchronized int     getPortNumber()
public synchronized void    setServerName(String ServerName)
public synchronized String getServerName()
public synchronized void    setUser(String user)
public synchronized String getUser()
```

The OracleDataSource class has an additional set of proprietary attributes. These are listed in Table 7-2.

Table 7-2. *OracleDataSource properties*

Property	Data type	Description
driverType	String	kprb for server-side internal connections
		oci8 for client-side OCI driver
		thin for client- or server-side Thin driver
url	String	A convenience property incorporating properties, such as PortNumber, user, and password, that make up a database URL
tnsEntryName	String	TNS names address for use with the OCI driver

And these are the OracleDataSource property getter/setter methods:

```
public synchronized void   setDriverType(String dt)
public synchronized String getDriverType( )
public synchronized void   setURL(String url)
public synchronized String getURL( )
public synchronized void   setTNSEntryName(String tns)
public synchronized String getTNSEntryName( )
```

Common sense prevails with these settings. For example, there is no getPassword( ) method, because that would create a security problem. In addition, the properties have a specific precedence. If you specify a url property, then any properties specified in the url override those that you specify by any of the other setter methods. If you do not set the url property but instead specify the tnsEntryName property, then any related setter methods are overridden by the values in the TNS entry name's definition. Likewise, if you are using the OCI driver and specify a network protocol of IPC, then any communication properties are ignored because the IPC protocol establishes a direct connection to the database. Finally, a username and password passed in the getConnection( ) method override those specified in any other way. Note that you must always specify a username and password with whatever means you choose.

Getting a Connection from a DataSource

To get a connection from a DataSource use one of the two available getConnection( ) methods:

```
public Connection getConnection( )
  throws SQLException
public Connection getConnection(String username, String password)
  throws SQLException
```

The first method creates a new Connection object with the username and password settings from the DataSource. The second method overrides the username and password in the DataSource.

Now that you have an understanding of data sources, let's look at Example 7-1, which is an application to test the Thin driver using a DataSource.

Example 7-1. An application using a DataSource to connect

```
import java.sql.*;
import oracle.jdbc.pool.*;

class TestThinDSApp {

 public static void main (String args[])
  throws ClassNotFoundException, SQLException {

  // These settings are typically configured in JNDI,
  // so they are implementation-specific
  OracleDataSource ds = new OracleDataSource-();
  ds.setDriverType("thin");
  ds.setServerName("dssw2k01");
  ds.setPortNumber(1521);
  ds.setDatabaseName("orcl"); // sid
  ds.setUser("scott");
  ds.setPassword("tiger");

  Connection conn = ds.getConnection();

  Statement stmt = conn.createStatement();
  ResultSet rset = stmt.executeQuery(
    "select 'Hello Thin driver data source tester '||" +
    "initcap(USER)||'!' result from dual");
  if (rset.next())
   System.out.println(rset.getString(1));
  rset.close();
  stmt.close();
  conn.close();
 }
}
```

First, our test application, TestThinDSApp, creates a new OracleDataSource object and then initializes its properties that are relevant to the Thin driver. The OracleDataSource object implements the DataSource interface, so OracleDataSource is also considered to be a DataSource object. Next, the program gets a connection from the DataSource using the getConnection() method. Finally, just to prove everything is working OK, the application queries the database, and closes the connection.

So what have we accomplished using an OracleDataSource object? Recall that in Chapter 4 we established a connection using the following code:

```
Class.forName("oracle.jdbc.driver.OracleDriver");

Connection conn =
 DriverManager.getConnection(
  "jdbc:oracle:thin:@dssw2k01:1521:orcl","scott","tiger");
```

Now, using an OracleDataSource object, our code to establish a connection looks like:

```
OracleDataSource ds = new OracleDataSource();
ds.setDriverType("thin");
ds.setServerName("dssw2k01");
ds.setPortNumber(1521);
ds.setDatabaseName("orcl"); // sid
ds.setUser("scott");
ds.setPassword("tiger");

Connection conn = ds.getConnection();
```

What's going on here? Our code is actually longer, which doesn't seem to improve things much, does it? But from another perspective, using a DataSource does represent an improvement, because a DataSource implements the Serializable interface, which means it can be bound using JNDI to a directory service. What does that mean? It means we can define our connection parameters once, in one place, and use a logical name to get our connection from JNDI. How does this help us? Let's say, for example, that we have 1,000 programs that use the specific connection parameters shown in Example 7-1. Let's further assume that we now have to move our database to another host. If you wrote your programs using the DriverManager facility, you'll need to modify and compile all 1,000 programs. However, if you used a DataSource bound to a directory using JNDI, then you need to change only one entry in the directory, and all the programs will use the new information.

Using a JNDI DataSource

Let's take a look at a couple of sample applications that illustrate the power and utility of using data sources that are accessed via JNDI. The examples use Sun's file-based JNDI implementation. You can download the class files for Sun's JNDI filesystem implementation at *http//:java.sun.com/products/jndi/index.html*.

First, the program in Example 7-2, TestDSBind, creates a logical entry in a JNDI directory to store our DataSource. It uses Sun's JNDI filesystem implementation as the directory. After that, we'll look at another program that uses the DataSource created by the first.

My DataSource bind program, TestDSBind, starts by creating a Context variable named ctx. Next, it creates a Properties object to use in initializing an initial context. In layman's terms, that means it creates a reference to the point in the local filesystem where our program should store its bindings. The program proceeds by creating an initial Context and storing its reference in ctx. Next, it creates an OracleDataSource and initializes its properties. Why an OracleDataSource and not a DataSource? You can't really use a DataSource for binding; you have to use an OracleDataSource, because the setter/getter methods for the properties are implementation- or vendor-specific and are not part of the DataSource interface. Last, the program binds our `OracleDataSource` with the name joe by calling the `Context.bind()` method.

Example 7-2. An application that binds a JNDI DataSource

```java
import java.sql.*;
import java.util.*;
import javax.naming.*;
import oracle.jdbc.pool.*;

public class TestDSBind {

 public static void main (String args [])
  throws SQLException, NamingException {

  // For this to work you need to create the
  // directory /JNDI/JDBC on your filesystem first
  Context ctx = null;
  try {
   Properties prop = new Properties();
    prop.setProperty(
     Context.INITIAL_CONTEXT_FACTORY,
     "com.sun.jndi.fscontext.RefFSContextFactory");
    prop.setProperty(
     Context.PROVIDER_URL,
     "file:/JNDI/JDBC");
   ctx = new InitialContext(prop);
  }
  catch (NamingException ne) {
   System.err.println(ne.getMessage());
  }

  OracleDataSource ds = new OracleDataSource();
  ds.setDriverType("thin");
  ds.setServerName("dssw2k01");
  ds.setPortNumber(1521);
  ds.setDatabaseName("orcl");
  ds.setUser("scott");
  ds.setPassword("tiger");

  ctx.bind("joe", ds);
 }
}
```

Create a directory, JNDI, on your hard drive, and then create a subdirectory, JDBC, in your JNDI directory. Compile Example 7-2 and execute it. Assuming you get no error messages, you should find a bindings file in your new JDBC subdirectory. This file holds the values for a serialized form of your `DataSource` logically named joe. This means that we can later retrieve a new connection by referencing a resource named joe.

Now that we have a directory entry, let's test it with our next program, TestDSLookup, in Example 7-3. First, TestDSLookUp creates an initial context just like TestDSBind did. Next, it uses the Context.lookup( ) method to look up and instantiate a new DataSource from our serialized version of joe. Finally, the program queries the database and closes the connection. Pretty cool huh? When using DriverManager, you typically must specify the JDBC driver and database URL in your source code. By using a DataSource together with JNDI, you can write code that is independent of a JDBC driver and of a database URL.

Example 7-3. An application that uses a JNDI DataSource

```
import java.sql.*;
import javax.sql.*;
import javax.naming.*;
import java.util.*;

public class TestDSLookUp {

 public static void main (String[] args)
  throws SQLException, NamingException {

  Context ctx = null;
  try {
   Properties prop = new Properties( );
   prop.setProperty(
    Context.INITIAL_CONTEXT_FACTORY,
    "com.sun.jndi.fscontext.RefFSContextFactory");
   prop.setProperty(
    Context.PROVIDER_URI,
    "file:/JNDI/JDBC");
   ctx = new InitialContext(prop);
  }
  catch (NamingException ne) {
   System.err.println(ne.getMessage( ));
  }

  DataSource ds = (DataSource)ctx.lookup("joe");
  Connection conn = ds.getConnection( );
  Statement  stmt = conn.createStatement( );
  ResultSet  rset = stmt.executeQuery(
   "select 'Hello Thin driver data source tester '||" +
    "initcap(USER)||'!' result from dual");
  if (rset.next( ))
   System.out.println(rset.getString(1));
  rset.close( );
  stmt.close( );
  conn.close( );
 }
}
```

Caveats

I hope you can appreciate the long-term gain of using DataSources with JNDI rather than embedding connections in your code:

- It makes your code independent of a JDBC driver.
- It makes your code independent of a database URL.
- It allows you to look up the driver and URL in one operation from anywhere on the network.

DataSource objects do, however, have a few drawbacks. One is that you can't use Oracle Advanced Security with the Thin driver, because there is no way to set the oracle.net properties for data encryption and integrity. This is because oracle.net properties are not a part of the standard, nor are they part of Oracle's implementation-specific set of DataSource properties. Another drawback to using DataSources is that you have to make the investment in an LDAP directory to truly leverage the use of JNDI, and that can be quite costly.

In addition to the drawbacks I've mentioned, there are a few DataSource behaviors you should be aware of. One concerns the logging feature. There are two methods you can use to set and get the log writer for a DataSource. A log writer is a PrintWriter object used by the driver to write its activities to a log file. They are:

```
public synchronized void setLogWriter(PrintWriter pw)
  throws SQLException
public synchronized PrintWriter getLogWriter()
  throws SQLException
```

As with the DriverManager facility, logging is disabled by default. You will always need to call the setLogWriter() method after a DataSource has been instantiated, even if you set the log writer before you bind it to a directory. Why? Because the PrintWriter you specify in the setLogWriter() method is transient and therefore cannot be serialized. A second behavior you should be aware of is that when DataSource logging is enabled, it bypasses DriverManager's logging facility.

There are also two methods you can use to set and get the login timeout, which is the amount of time that an idle connection should be kept open. The methods are:

```
public synchronized void setLoginTimeout(int seconds)
  throws SQLException
public synchronized int  getLoginTimeout()
  throws SQLException
```

Now that you have a firm grasp of how and when to use a DataSource object, let's continue our investigation of the JDBC 2.0 Extension API with a look at the connection pooling interface ConnectionPoolDataSource.

Oracle's Connection Cache

Recall that in Chapter 4 we talked about a cached pool of connections used by servlets. When a servlet needed a connection, it drew one from the pool. The servlet did its work, and when it was done, it returned the connection back to the pool. The benefit of using cached connections is that a servlet does not need to go through the resource-intensive task of opening a new database connection each time the servlet is invoked. Also in Chapter 4, I showed a rudimentary connection caching tool. Rudimentary as it was, it still required a fair bit of rather complex code to implement. As part of the JDBC 2.0 Extension API, Oracle provides a ready-made connection cache interface along with a sample implementation. Instead of wasting your precious time doing something that has already been done for you, you can use Oracle's connection cache immediately and in turn concentrate on the business problem at hand.

At the heart of Oracle's connection caching framework is the connection pool data source. It's important you understand what that is and how it works before getting into the details of the connection cache framework itself.

ConnectionPoolDataSources

A `ConnectionPoolDataSource` is a `DataSource` that can be pooled. Instead of returning a `Connection` object as a `DataSource` object does, a `ConnectionPoolDataSource` returns a `PooledConnection` object. A `PooledConnection` object itself holds a physical database connection that is pooled. In turn, a `PooledConnection` returns a `Connection` object. This single layer of indirection allows a `ConnectionPoolDataSource` to manage `PooledConnection` objects.

You can use a `PooledConnection` to add or remove `ConnectionEventListeners`. A `ConnectionEventListener` is any Java program thread that wishes to be notified whenever a connection is opened or closed. When a `Connection` is received from or returned to a `PooledConnection`, the appropriate `ConnectEvent` event is triggered to close or return the `Connection` object to its associated pool. In this case, the `Connection` object is not the same implementation of the `Connection` interface utilized by `DriverManager`. Instead, it's a logical implementation managed by the `PooledConnection` object.

The `ConnectionPoolDataSource` interface is implemented by the class `OracleConnectionPoolDataSource`, which extends `OracleDataSource`. This means that all the methods from the `OracleDataSource` class and `ConnectionPoolDataSource` interface are available in an `OracleConnectionPoolDataSource`.

The `OraclePooledConnection` class implements the `PooledConnection` interface and also provides the following five constructors:

```
public OraclePooledConnection( )
  throws SQLException
```

```
public OraclePooledConnection(String url)
  throws SQLException
public OraclePooledConnection(String url, String user, String password)
  throws SQLException
public OraclePooledConnection(Connection pc)
public OraclePooledConnection(Connection pc, boolean autoCommit)
```

The `OracleConnectionEventListener` class implements the `ConnectionEventListener` interface. It also provides the following two constructors and one additional method:

```
public OracleConnectionEventListener( )
public OracleConnectionEventListener(DataSource ds)
public void setDataSource(DataSource ds)
```

Collectively, these JDBC classes and interfaces, along with Oracle's implementation of them, provide a framework for connection caching. However, the topic of how they can be used to build a connection cache is well beyond the scope of this book. Besides, Oracle already provides a connection cache interface and sample implementation. Let's look at how you can leverage those in your programs.

Connection Cache Implementation

Let's start our discussion of Oracle's connection cache implementation by defining a few important terms:

Connection pool
A pool of one or more `Connections` that use the same properties to establish a physical connection to a database. By "properties," I mean things such as `databaseName`, `serverName`, `portNumber`, etc.

Connection cache
A cache of one or more physical connections to one or more databases.

Pooled connection cache
A cache of one or more connections to the same database for the same username.

Oracle's connection cache interface is named `OracleConnectionCache`. Together, the interface and its implementation provide a cache of physical connections to a particular database for a specified username.

The OracleConnectionCache interface

Oracle's `OracleConnectionCache` interface defines the following three methods to aid you in managing a connection pool cache:

```
public void close( )
  throws SQLException
public void closePooledConnection(PooledConnection pc)
  throws SQLException
public void reusePooledConnection(PooledConnection pc)
  throws SQLException
```

These methods perform the following functions:

close( )
> Used to close a logical connection to the database obtained from a Pooled-Connection. A logical connection is a connection that has been allocated from a pool. When a logical connection is closed, the connection is simply returned to the pool. It may physically remain open but is logically no longer in use.

closePooledConnection( )
> Used to remove the associated PooledConnection from a connection pool.

reusePooledConnection( )
> Used to return a PooledConnection to a connection pool.

The OracleConnectionCacheImpl class

The OracleConnectionCacheImpl class extends OracleDataSource and implements the OracleConnectionCache interface. Beyond what OracleConnectionCacheImpl inherits from OracleDataSource and the methods it implements from the OracleConnectionCache interface, the OracleConnectionCacheImpl class provides the following constants, constructors, and methods:

```
public final int DYNAMIC_SCHEME
public final int FIXED_RETURN_NULL_SCHEME
public final int FIXED_WAIT_SCHEME
public OracleConnectionCacheImpl( )
 throws SQLException
public OracleConnectionCacheImpl(ConnectionPoolDataSource cpds)
 throws SQLException
public int  getActiveSize( )
public int  getCacheSize( )
public void setCacheScheme(int cacheScheme);
public int  getCacheScheme( )
public void setConnectionPoolDataSource(ConnectionPoolDataSource cpds)
 throws SQLException
public void setMinLimit(int minCacheSize)
public int  getMinLimit( )
public void setMaxLimit(int maxCacheSize)
public int  getMaxLimit( )
```

The first three constants are used with the setCacheScheme( ) method to specify the caching scheme to be used by a given connection cache implementation. Caches usually employ a minimum and maximum number of connections as part of a resource strategy. The minimum value keeps a minimum number of connections on hand to speed up the connection process. A cache uses the maximum value to limit the amount of operating-system resources utilized. This prevents the cache from growing beyond its host's ability to provide resources. The setCacheScheme( ) method's constants control the behavior of the cache when the specified maximum connection limit has been exceeded. The values are defined as follows:

DYNAMIC_SCHEME
> The cache will create connections above the specified maximum limit when necessary but will in turn close connections as they are returned to the cache until the number of connections is within the maximum limit. Connections will never be cached above the maximum limit. This is the default setting.

FIXED_RETURN_NULL_SCHEME
> The cache will return a null connection once the maximum connection limit has been exceeded.

FIXED_WAIT_SCHEME
> The cache will wait until there is a connection available and will then return it to the calling application.

The `OracleConnectionCacheImpl` class implements two constructor methods, and there are three ways that you can use them to initialize a cache:

1. You can use the default constructor and set the connection properties individually after you've instantiated an object of the class.

2. You can use the default constructor to instantiate an object of the class. Then you can create a `ConnectionPoolDataSource` object, initialize it, and pass it as a parameter to the `setConnectionPoolDataSource( )` method.

3. You can create and initialize a `ConnectionPoolDataSource` object and then pass it as a parameter to the second form of the `OracleConnectionCacheImpl` constructor.

The other methods implemented by the `OracleConnectionCacheImpl` class are straightforward getter and setter methods. They do exactly what their names indicate.

A Connection Caching Example

Now that you have an idea of what an `OracleConnectionCacheImpl` object can do, let's rewrite our caching object from Chapter 4 using Oracle's caching implementation. We'll build a new caching object named `OCCIConnection` that will use the `OracleConnectionCacheImpl` class to create a modular caching module. The overall development process that we'll follow for this example is:

1. We'll create a program that allows us to create a connection pool data source and bind it to our JNDI directory.

2. We'll create a class to implement and manage connection caches.

3. We'll test the connection cache using one servlet that retrieves and uses connections and another that displays the current status of the cache.

Creating and binding a ConnectionPoolDataSource

In my opinion, there's no advantage to using a DataSource unless you also utilize JNDI, so our examples here will once again use Sun's filesystem implementation of JNDI. First, we'll create a program named OCCIBind, shown in Example 7-4, to bind a ConnectionPoolDataSource to our JNDI directory. OCCIBind is similar to the TestDSBind program shown in Example 7-2, but this time, we bind an OraclePoolConnectionSource.

Example 7-4. An application that binds a ConnectionPoolDataSource

```
import java.sql.*;
import java.util.*;
import javax.naming.*;
import oracle.jdbc.pool.*;

public class OCCIBind {

 public static void main (String args [])
  throws SQLException, NamingException {

  Context context = null;
  try {
   Properties properties = new Properties();
    properties.setProperty(
     Context.INITIAL_CONTEXT_FACTORY,
     "com.sun.jndi.fscontext.RefFSContextFactory");
    properties.setProperty(
     Context.PROVIDER_URI,
     "file:/JNDI/JDBC");
   context = new InitialContext(properties);
  }
  catch (NamingException ne) {
   System.err.println(ne.getMessage());
  }

  OracleConnectionPoolDataSource ocpds =
   new OracleConnectionPoolDataSource();
  ocpds.setDescription("Database");
  ocpds.setDriverType("thin");
  ocpds.setServerName("dssw2k01");
  ocpds.setPortNumber(1521);
  ocpds.setDatabaseName("orcl");
  ocpds.setUser("scott");
  ocpds.setPassword("tiger");

  context.bind(ocpds.getDescription(), ocpds);
 }
}
```

Make sure that the JDBC subdirectory exists under the JNDI directory on your hard drive. Then compile and execute the program. Once again, you can find the serialized values of our newly bound OracleConnectionPoolDataSource in a file named *.bindings* in the JDBC subdirectory.

Creating the connection manager

Next, we'll create the OCCIConnection class in Example 7-5. This class uses static methods so it can perform its functionality without being instantiated. It instantiates a OracleConnectionCacheImpl object to manage the connection pools. When a connection is requested, any existing pools are searched first. If a matching connection pool cannot be found, then a new OracleConnectionCacheImpl is created to hold connections for the new pool.

Example 7-5. An OracleConnectionCacheImpl caching implementation

```
import java.io.*;
import java.sql.*;
import java.util.*;
import javax.naming.*;
import javax.sql.*;
import oracle.jdbc.pool.*;

public class OCCIConnection {
 private static boolean verbose              = false;
 private static int      numberImplementations = 0;
 private static Vector  cachedImplementations = new Vector();

 public synchronized static Connection checkOut() {
  return checkOut("Database");
 }

 public synchronized static Connection checkOut(String baseName) {
  boolean                    found      = false;
  OracleConnectionCacheImpl cached     = null;
  Connection                connection = null;
  if (verbose) {
   System.out.println("There are " +
    Integer.toString(numberImplementations) +
    " connections in the cache");
   System.out.println("Searching for a matching implementation...");
  }
  for (int i=0;!found && i<numberImplementations;i++) {
   if (verbose) {
    System.out.println("Vector entry " + Integer.toString(i));
   }
   cached = (OracleConnectionCacheImpl)cachedImplementations.get(i);
   if (cached.getDescription().equals(baseName)) {
    if (verbose) {
     System.out.println("found cached entry " +
      Integer.toString(i) +
      " for " + baseName);
    }
    found = true;
   }
```

```
    }
    if (!found) {
     if (verbose) {
      System.out.println("Cached entry not found ");
      System.out.println("Allocating new entry for " + baseName);
     }
     try {
      cached = new OracleConnectionCacheImpl(
       getConnectionPoolDataSource(baseName));
      cached.setDescription(baseName);
      cachedImplementations.add(cached);
      numberImplementations++;
     }
     catch (SQLException e) {
      System.err.println(e.getMessage( ) +
       " creating a new implementation for " + baseName);
     }
    }
    if (cached != null) {
     try {
      connection = cached.getConnection( );
     }
     catch (SQLException e) {
      System.err.println(e.getMessage( ) +
       " getting connection for " + baseName);
     }
    }
    return connection;
   }

   public static ConnectionPoolDataSource
    getConnectionPoolDataSource(String baseName) {
    Context                    context = null;
    ConnectionPoolDataSource cpds     = null;
    try {
     Properties properties = new Properties( );
     properties.setProperty(
      Context.INITIAL_CONTEXT_FACTORY,
      "com.sun.jndi.fscontext.RefFSContextFactory");
     properties.setProperty(
      Context.PROVIDER_URL,
      "file:/JNDI/JDBC");
     context = new InitialContext(properties);
     cpds    = (ConnectionPoolDataSource)context.lookup(baseName);
    }
    catch (NamingException e) {
     System.err.println(e.getMessage( ) +
      " creating JNDI context for " + baseName);
    }
    return cpds;
   }

   protected static synchronized void checkIn(Connection c) {
    try {
```

```
  c.close( );
 }
 catch (SQLException e) {
  System.err.println(e.getMessage( ) +
   " closing connection");
 }
}

public static String[] getReport( ) {
 int line = 0;
 String[] lines = new String[numberImplementations * 7];
 OracleConnectionCacheImpl cached = null;

 for (int i=0;i < numberImplementations;i++) {
  cached = (OracleConnectionCacheImpl)cachedImplementations.get(i);
  lines[line++] = cached.getDescription( ) + ":";
  switch (cached.getCacheScheme( )) {
   case OracleConnectionCacheImpl.DYNAMIC_SCHEME:
    lines[line++] = "Cache Scheme  = DYNAMIC_SCHEME";
    break;
   case OracleConnectionCacheImpl.FIXED_RETURN_NULL_SCHEME:
    lines[line++] = "Cache Scheme  = FIXED_RETURN_NULL_SCHEME";
    break;
   case OracleConnectionCacheImpl.FIXED_WAIT_SCHEME:
    lines[line++] = "Cache Scheme  = FIXED_WAIT_SCHEME";
    break;
  }
  lines[line++] = "Minimum Limit = " +
   Integer.toString(cached.getMinLimit( ));
  lines[line++] = "Maximum Limit = " +
   Integer.toString(cached.getMaxLimit( ));
  lines[line++] = "Cache Size    = " +
   Integer.toString(cached.getCacheSize( ));
  lines[line++] = "Active Size   = " +
   Integer.toString(cached.getActiveSize( ));
  lines[line++] = " ";
 }
 return lines;
}

public static void setVerbose(boolean v) {
 verbose = v;
}

}
```

Our caching object, OCCIConnection, has an overloaded checkOut( ) method. The first form of the method takes no argument. It uses the default logical name of "Database", passing it to the second form to allocate from or create an OracleConnectionCacheImpl object. The second form of the checkOut( ) method scans through a Vector of implementations looking for a match. If one is found, it returns a connection from the

---

OracleConnectionCacheImpl object. If a matching implementation, i.e., Oracle-ConnectionCacheImpl object, is not found, then the method creates a new one, stores its reference in the implementation Vector object, and returns a Connection. When the application calls the checkIn() method, the OracleConnectionCacheImpl returns the connection to the cache. The getReport() method returns a String array that contains a report on the current status of each implementation. The last method, setVerbose(), allows the developer to send diagnostics to standard out. I've written this object to get a ConnectionPoolDataSource from a directory when an implementation is not found in the Vector, but we could have set it up to get an OracleConnectionCacheImpl object instead.

Testing our connection cache

OCCIConnectionServlet, shown in Example 7-6, tests the cache by requesting a default connection. This servlet, similar to its counterpart in Chapter 4, checks out a connection, queries the database, and checks in the connection. However, notice that we've added a pair of tight for loops to delay the servlet's completion. This is so you can click on your browser's Reload button several times to force the cache to open multiple connections. Compile this servlet and place it in an appropriate classes directory on your servlet container. Compile the OCCIConnection object from Example 7-5 and place it in the same directory.

Example 7-6. A servlet that tests the caching implementation

```
import java.io.*;
import java.sql.*;
import javax.servlet.*;
import javax.servlet.http.*;

public class OCCIConnectionServlet extends HttpServlet {

  public void doGet(
    HttpServletRequest request,
    HttpServletResponse response)
    throws IOException, ServletException {

    response.setContentType("text/html");
    PrintWriter out = response.getWriter();
    out.println("<html>");
    out.println("<head>");
    out.println(
      "<title>Oracle Cached Connection Implementation Servlet</title>");
    out.println("</head>");
    out.println("<body>");

    // Turn on verbose output
    OCCIConnection.setVerbose(true);
    // Get a cached connection
    Connection connection = OCCIConnection.checkOut();
```

Example 7-6. A servlet that tests the caching implementation (continued)

```
Statement  statement  = null;
ResultSet  resultSet  = null;
String     userName   = null;
try {
 // Test the connection
 statement = connection.createStatement( );
 resultSet = statement.executeQuery(
   "select initcap(user) from sys.dual");
 if (resultSet.next( ))
   userName = resultSet.getString(1);
}
catch (SQLException e) {
 out.println("DedicatedConnection.doGet( ) SQLException: " +
   e.getMessage( ) + "<p>");
}
finally {
 if (resultSet != null)
   try { resultSet.close( ); } catch (SQLException ignore) { }
 if (statement != null)
   try { statement.close( ); } catch (SQLException ignore) { }
}

// Add a little delay to force
// multiple connections in the connection cache
for (int o=0;o < 3;o++) {
 for (int i=0;i < 2147483647;i++) {}
}

// Return the conection
OCCIConnection.checkIn(connection);

out.println("Hello " + userName + "!<p>");
out.println("You're using an Oracle Cached " +
  "Connection Implementation connection!<p>");
out.println("</body>");
out.println("</html>");
}

public void doPost(
 HttpServletRequest request,
 HttpServletResponse response)
 throws IOException, ServletException {
 doGet(request, response);
}
}
```

Our second servlet, OCCIConnectionReportServlet, is shown in Example 7-7. OCCIConnectionReportServlet displays the current status of the connection cache implementations, queries the caching object OCCIConnection using its getReport( ) method, and displays the result of the report in your browser. Compile this servlet and place the resulting class file in the directory with the *OCCIConnection.class* and *OCCIConnectionServlet.class* files.

Example 7-7. A servlet that reports on the caching implementation

```java
import java.io.*;
import java.sql.*;
import javax.servlet.*;
import javax.servlet.http.*;

public class OCCIConnectionReportServlet extends HttpServlet {

  public void doGet(
    HttpServletRequest request,
    HttpServletResponse response)
    throws IOException, ServletException {

    response.setContentType("text/html");
    PrintWriter out = response.getWriter();
    out.println("<html>");
    out.println("<head>");
    out.println("<title>Oracle Cached Connection Implementation " +
      "Report Servlet</title>");
    out.println("</head>");
    out.println("<body>");
    out.println("<h1>Oracle Cached Connection Implementations</h1>");
    out.println("<pre>");
    String[] lines = OCCIConnection.getReport();
    if (lines != null && lines.length > 0) {
      for (int i=0;i < lines.length;i++) {
        out.println(lines[i]);
      }
    }
    else
      out.println("No caches implemented!");
    out.println("</pre>");
    out.println("</body>");
    out.println("</html>");
  }

  public void doPost(
    HttpServletRequest request,
    HttpServletResponse response)
    throws IOException, ServletException {
    doGet(request, response);
  }
}
```

Now execute the report servlet first. You'll notice it reports no implementations of OracleConnectionCacheImpl. Next, open a second browser window, execute the OCCIConnectionServlet, and return to the report servlet and reload it. You should see one connection in the "Database" implementation. Next, return to the test servlet window and click on the Reload button quickly several times in a row. Once again, return to the report servlet window and click on Reload. You'll see several connections in the cache, and perhaps several will still be active.

This concludes Part II: our discussions of establishing a connection to a database. We'll touch on connections one more time when we cover distributed transactions much later. But now it's time to move on to the second part of the book, a discussion of JDBC's use with relational SQL.

Relational SQL

In Part III, we'll discuss the use of JDBC with relational SQL. Why the term *relational* SQL? With Oracle, you have three options as to how you use the database:

- Use the database strictly as a relational database storing information in tables.
- Use tables to store your data and use object views and INSTEAD OF triggers to provide an object-oriented presentation.
- Create relational objects to store and present your information.

So which option is the right choice? That's a matter of argument we won't cover in this book, but I will describe how to use JDBC with all three. To that end, this part of this book covers option one, relational SQL.

CHAPTER 8

A Relational SQL Example

Before starting down the path on how to use JDBC with Data Definition Language (DDL) to create database objects such as tables, sequences, and indexes, and on how to use Data Manipulation Language (DML) to insert, update, delete, or select information from tables, let's take a chapter to develop a hypothetical relational SQL example to use in the chapters that follow. In order to have a context in which to work, we'll formulate a relational solution to part of a common business problem, Human Resource (HR) management.

An HR management system is more than just a means of generating payroll and tax withholding. Large organizations must also comply with safety and environmental regulations. Consequently, their HR systems must keep track of the physical locations in which people perform their work, along with the actual type of work they are performing. For management reasons, HR systems also need to keep track of whom a person reports to and in which department of the organization a person performs work. HR systems also need to track the legal status of their workers to know whether they are employees or contractors. All this information changes. An HR system not only needs to maintain this information for the current point in time, but also for any past point in time.

Since there are many books written on the subject of database analysis and design, I'd like to emphasize here that I will not follow any particular methodology, nor will my analysis and design be all that rigorous. Instead, I'm just going to walk you through my thinking process for this example database. I considered using the Universal Modeling Language (UML) to document my design, but the use of UML is still not widespread enough to address the whole audience of this book. Instead, I use as common a terminology as possible.

Relational Database Analysis

Relational database analysis is a process whereby you identify and classify into groups the information you need to store in a database. In addition, you identify the data items that can be used to uniquely identify data that is grouped together, and you identify the relationships between the different groups of information. An analysis commonly consists of the following major steps:

1. Identify the things for which you need to capture information.
2. Identify the data you need to capture for each thing.
3. Determine the relationships between the different things you identified.

The common term for a "thing" in step 1 is "entity." An *entity* represents a class of a thing about which you want to track information. The actual bits of data that you capture for each entity (step 2) are called *attributes*. The outcome of step 3 is a set of *relations* between entities.

Identifying Entities

If you paid close attention to my discussion of HR systems, you may have noticed that I mentioned the following five entities:

- A person
- A location
- A position or job
- An organization
- A status

When I take the time to consider that a particular person will most likely work in different locations, perform different jobs, work for different organizations, and work as an employee or a contractor at different times, I realize that I'll need to keep track of the times that person is assigned to work at a location, perform a job, and so forth. That means I'll need four more entities to act as intersections:

- A history of the locations where the person has worked
- A history of the jobs the person has performed
- A history of the organizations for which the person has worked
- A history of the person's employment status

Why do I call these intersections? Let's answer this question by examining the first intersection, a person's history of locations. If I have a particular person's information stored in an entity called PERSON, and all the possible locations where they could have worked are stored in an entity called LOCATION, then I need to have a place to store a reference to both the person and a location along with the time period when the person worked at that particular location. This place ends up being an entity in its own right and is called an *intersection* because its attribute values have meaning only in the context of the intersection of two other entities.

Identifying Primary Keys

So far, I've identified nine entities and alluded to the relationships between some of the entities. My next step is to identify data about each entity that can uniquely identify an individual occurrence of the entity. This is called the *primary key*. In addition, I'll also identify any other data, or attributes as they are commonly called, that are needed. I'll start by figuring out how I can uniquely identify a person. What do I know about people that would allow them to be uniquely identified? They have:

- A name
- A birth date
- Parents
- A unique identification number such as a Social Security Number

I could probably use the combination of a person's name, birth date, and parents' names and never run into a nonunique combination of those values. However, a nonunique combination of those values is still possible. I could use a unique identifier, such as a Social Security Number (SSN), assigned by some authority, but what do I do if this is a global application? An SSN exists only in the United States. In other countries they don't use an SSN. For example, in Canada a person may have a Social Insurance Number (SIN), and in the United Kingdom, a person may have a National Identifier (NI). Therefore, calling an attribute to be used as a primary key an SSN will result in geographic limitations for my application.

Since none of the PERSON attributes I've described so far can guarantee a unique ID value, I'll create a generic attribute called ID that can hold any kind of unique identifier (possibly an SSN) and a second attribute, ID TYPE, that can identify the type of identifier in the ID attribute. Thus, I might identify a U.S. citizen as follows:

```
ID = 123-45-6789
ID TYPE = SSN
```

Now that I've identified the PERSON entity, its primary key, and other possible attributes, it's time to represent it with some form of notation. The following notation, or something similar to it, is commonly used to show an entity and its attributes:

PERSON
*ID
*ID_TYPE
LAST_NAME
FIRST_NAME
BIRTH_DATE
MOTHERS_MAIDEN_NAME

The first line is the entity name, which I've shown in bold. The remaining lines list the entity's attributes. The asterisk before an attribute denotes that it is part of the entity's primary key.

The other entities in our HR system are LOCATION, POSITION, ORGANIZA-TION, and STATUS. Over time, individual entries in these entities will go in and out of use. Accordingly, I'll give each entity the following attributes:

- A short description, or code
- A long description, or name
- A start and end date to keep track of when they come into and go out of use

I'll uniquely identify these entities by their code and start date. Both LOCATION and ORGANIZATION can be hierarchical. That is, a high-level organization, such as a company, can have several divisions that belong to it. In turn, each division can have several departments that belong to it. So I'll also give these entities attributes to point to themselves as parents. Here, for example, is the definition of the location entity:

LOCATION
*CODE
*START_DATE
PARENT_CODE
PARENT_START_DATE
NAME
END_DATE

And here is the definition of the person location intersection entity:

PERSON_LOCATION
*ID
*ID_TYPE
CODE
LOCATION_START_DATE
*START_DATE
END_DATE

The first two attributes in the PERSON_LOCATION entity, ID and ID_TYPE, represent the primary key of the person table. The next two attributes, CODE and LOCATION_START_DATE, represent the primary key of the location entity. These attributes are called *foreign keys*, because they point to the primary key of other entities. The primary key of the PERSON_LOCATION entity consists of the primary key from the person entity plus an additional START_DATE (see the fifth column). It is not necessary to include the location entity's primary key in the primary key definition for the intersection, because the person's ID and type, along with the start date of the assignment, make each intersection entry unique. Also, not including the location's primary key enforces a business rule, which prevents a person from being represented as working in more than one place at a time.

Determining Relationships Between Entities

Although I've not talked about them directly, I've been thinking about the relationships between the entities all along. It's hard not to. In the introductory paragraph, I stated that a person works at a location, in a job, for an organization, and is either an employee or contractor. This statement defined four relationships. When I thought more about it, I decided I needed four intersection entities, one each between the PERSON entity and the other four entities: LOCATION, POSITION, ORGANIZA-TION, and STATUS. This is because I will keep a history, not just the current value, of each relationship. Each intersection entity actually represents two relationships, for a total of eight. There are also the 2 hierarchical relationships, so at this point I'm aware of the following 10 relationships:

- PERSON to PERSON_LOCATION
- LOCATION to PERSON_LOCATION
- PERSON to PERSON_POSITION
- POSITION to PERSON_POSITION
- PERSON to PERSON_ORGANIZATION
- ORGANIZATION to PERSON_ORGANIZATION
- PERSON to PERSON_STATUS
- STATUS to PERSON_STATUS
- ORGANIZATION to ORGANIZATION
- LOCATION to LOCATION

All that's left to consider is what is called cardinality. *Cardinality* refers to the number of occurrences of any one entity that can point to occurrences of another, related, entity. For example, zero or more persons can have zero or more person location assignments. And zero or more locations can be assigned to zero or more person location assignments. Cardinality is important because it refines primary key definitions and defines business rules.

In practice, you may end up determining relationships before you identify attributes and primary keys, but analysis is an iterative process, so which comes first is not that important. What is important is that you test your analysis against examples of real-world data so you can uncover any flaws before you start creating any DDL.

Refining the Analysis

The use of real-world information in the primary key, as we just covered, is what I call a smart key solution. A *smart key* is a key composed of real-world data values. This is how most entity-relationship analysis was done in the 1980s. We, the programming community at the time, identified a set of entities that organized and described how information was used and how it related to the real world. We used real-world data values as the primary keys for our tables. But this technique of using real-world information to uniquely identify entries was flawed. As with all things, analysts gained experience over time, and with hard-earned experience, learned a better way to define an entity's primary key.

Defining Dumb Primary Keys

Here's what we learned. We discovered two flaws when using real-world information in a primary key. First, over time, the users of the applications we built no longer wanted to uniquely identify an entry by the real-world information that had been used. Second, they sometimes wanted to rename the real-world values used in a primary key. Since real-world information was used in primary keys, and therefore was referenced in foreign keys, it was not possible to change this real-world information without a major migration of the data in the database. If we changed a primary key in a row of one table, we had to change it in all the rows in related tables. Sometimes, this also led to major modifications to our applications.

The solution to this problem was to use dumb primary keys. *Dumb primary keys* consist of just a single numeric attribute. This attribute is assigned a unique value by the database whenever a new entry is created for an entity. With Oracle, a type of schema element known as a *sequence* can generate unique primary keys for primary entities such as PERSON and LOCATION. Dumb primary keys are then used to establish the relationship between entities, while a unique index is created against the former smart primary key attributes to create a unique key against real-world information. In effect, I end up with both internal (dumb) and external (smart) primary keys.

Employing this technique of using dumb keys, reworking our person entity, and adding a dumb key attribute called PERSON_ID, I get the following new definition for the person entity:

PERSON
*PERSON_ID
ID
ID_TYPE
LAST_NAME
FIRST_NAME

BIRTH_DATE
MOTHERS_MAIDEN_NAME

Now the person entity has one attribute that defines an entry's uniqueness. This attribute is PERSON_ID, and it will be populated with a number generated by an Oracle sequence. For the four other primary entities, I will also add a dumb primary key attribute. I'll name the attribute using a combination of the entity's name and an _ID suffix. These dumb primary key attributes will also hold an Oracle sequence number. For example, for the location entity, our definition changes as follows:

LOCATION
*LOCATION_ID
PARENT_LOCATION_ID
CODE
START_DATE
NAME
END_DATE

And here is the person location intersection entity:

PERSON_LOCATION
*PERSON_ID
LOCATION_ID
*START_DATE
END_DATE

Not only does this new tactic allow us to change the descriptive external primary key at a latter date without destroying relationships, it also simplifies the process of identifying the primary keys and gets rid of the annoying problem of renaming colliding column names (such as location start date in our previous person location intersection) in the intersection entities. Now the intersection entities are more compact. This results in better performance by the SQL engine during joins. However, experience once again has taught us that we can improve on this design.

Reanalysis of the Person Entity

In practice, a person may have several common identifiers used to identify him. For example, he may have a badge number used for a security system, an employee ID used by the HR department, a Social Security Number or Social Insurance Number, and perhaps a phone number or email address. Clearly, it would be better if a system could handle multiple identifiers rather than just one. To that end, I'll add a secondary, or child, entity named PERSON_IDENTIFIER and relate it back to the PERSON entity. Here's the new entity's definition:

PERSON_IDENTIFIER
*PERSON_ID

*ID
*ID_TYPE

Now that I have a separate entity to hold as many ID values as desired for a given person, I modify the PERSON entity as follows:

PERSON
*PERSON_ID
LAST_NAME
FIRST_NAME
BIRTH_DATE
MOTHERS_MAIDEN_NAME

I've taken the ID and ID_TYPE attributes out of the PERSON entity and placed them in the new entity named PERSON_IDENTIFIER. The PERSON_IDENTIFIER entity uses the PERSON_ID, ID, and ID_TYPE attributes as its primary key. This means that the PERSON_IDENTIFIER can hold an unlimited number of unique IDs for each person.

One last change is in order. To maintain data integrity, I'll add a codes entity, named PERSON_IDENTIFIER_TYPE, which will hold valid values for the PERSON_IDEN-TIFIER entity's ID_TYPE attribute. Here's the definition for that entity:

PERSON_IDENTIFIER_TYPE
*ID_TYPE
INACTIVE_DATE

Figure 8-1 is an Entity Relationship Diagram (ERD) for my finished analysis. I'll use this as a context as I cover JDBC in the following chapters. Now that we have the analysis completed, let's move on to the design.

Relational Database Design

At this point, we have a theoretical analysis of the HR database. Before we create a physical implementation, we need to consider how it will be implemented. This is the step in which we decide which data types we will use for the attributes, determine how to constrain those data types, and define external primary keys, among other things. Let's start by deciding which data types to use.

Selecting Data Types

One of the beautiful things about Oracle is that it does not have presentation data types. There is no money type, for example. Not having presentation data types keeps things simple. The number of data types you need to work with is kept to a

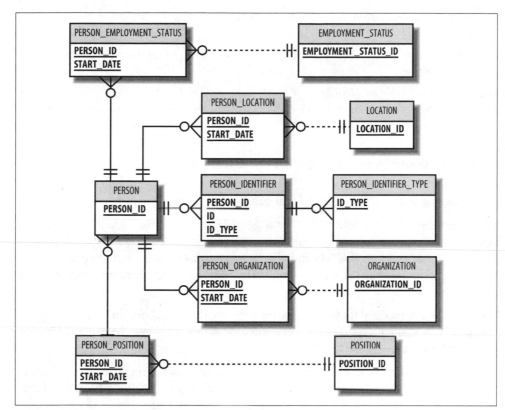

Figure 8-1. Entity relationship diagram for the sample HR database

bare minimum. With Oracle, you get a small number of data types that allow you to work with the following four basic types of data:

- Binary
- Character
- Date
- Numeric

For binary data, you have the following Oracle data types to work with:

RAW
    A varying-length binary type that can hold up to 2 KB

LONG RAW
    A varying-length binary type that can hold up to 2 GB

BLOB
    A varying-length binary type that can hold up to 4 GB

BFILE
    An external file that can hold up to 4 GB

For character data, you have the following types at your disposal:

CHAR (or NCHAR)
A fixed-length character type right-padded with space characters up to its constraining size

VARCHAR2 (or NVARCHAR2)
A varying-length character type that can hold as many characters as will fit within its constraining size

LONG
A varying-length character type that can hold up to 2 GB

CLOB
A varying-length character type that can hold up to 4 GB

When dealing with character data, it's a good idea not to use CHAR, because the side effects of its fixed length require you to right-pad VARCHAR2 data values in order to do comparisons. LONG and CLOB are very specialized and are needed only in rare occasions. That leaves us with VARCHAR2 as the character data type of choice.

The other two types of data you will work with are dates and numbers. For date values, you have the data type DATE. For numeric data, you have the NUMBER type with up to 38 digits of precision.

A VARCHAR2 data type must be constrained with a maximum size, while NUMBER can be constrained or unconstrained as desired. If you are going to use a multi-byte character set in the database, then you need to make the VARCHAR2 or NVARCHAR2 columns larger to hold the same amount of data. On that thought, I suggest you be liberal in the amount of storage you give your VARCHAR2 data types.

When it comes to constraining the size of numbers, I don't. Why should I specify a maximum size when I don't have to? It seems to me that constraining numbers is an old habit from a time when it was necessary to do so for storage management. Since Oracle uses only the number of bytes required to represent something to store it, i.e., varying-length storage, there is no point in constraining numbers, which builds in obsolescence.

So all this discussion has led up to using three data types:

- DATE
- NUMBER
- VARCHAR2

Things couldn't get much simpler. Before I write the actual DDL statements to create tables for the HR application, let's talk about DDL coding conventions.

DDL Coding Conventions

Whether you call them conventions or standards, when everyone on a development team plays by the same rules, it's more efficient and just plain easier. I say conventions rather than standards, because I never found a standard I didn't need to break occasionally in order for things to make sense. Here are my suggested conventions for writing DDL:

1. Make table names singular. For example: PERSON, not PERSONS.

2. Make a primary entity's primary key a sequence-generated number named using the table's name suffixed with _ID. For example: PERSON_ID.

3. Create a sequence for each primary entity's table using the table's name suffixed with _ID. For example: PERSON_ID.

4. Create an index for each primary entity's table using the table's name suffixed with _PK. For example: PERSON_PK.

5. Create any required unique indexes for external primary keys using the table's name suffixed with _UK#. For example, PERSON_UK1.

6. Do not use a parent table's primary key constraint (PKC) as part of the definition for a child table's PKC.

7. Use one of the following two methods to create the PKCs for code tables. First, use the code value as the PKC of the code table. Second, create a dumb key just as you do for primary entities. These two methods are equally valid and fraught with complications. Using code values makes decision support queries easier to write but introduces the problem of lost relationships that the primary entities suffered from in our first analysis.

8. Always create foreign key constraints, even if you must leave them disabled because they are conditional. This helps to document your database. You can always implement a conditional constraint with a database trigger.

If you use these conventions, it will be easy for you to identify the PKCs and unique keys for a given table, transfer system knowledge to other team members, and simplify your documentation process.

Writing the DDL

Now that we have an application context to work from, and some DDL coding conventions to work with, it's time to write some DDL for our HR database. Writing the code for the DDL is a process by which we take our logical model—the entities, attributes, internal and external primary keys, and relationships—and transform them into SQL code to create the physical implementation: tables, columns, PKCs and unique indexes, and foreign key constraints.

We'll start with the PERSON entity. First, here's the table definition:

```
create table PERSON (
person_id           number        not null,
last_name           varchar2(30)  not null,
first_name          varchar2(30)  not null,
middle_name         varchar2(30),
birth_date          date          not null,
mothers_maiden_name varchar2(30)  not null )
tablespace USERS pctfree 20
storage (initial 100 K next 100 K pctincrease 0)
```

Next, here's the PKC:

```
alter  table PERSON add
constraint   PERSON_PK
primary key ( person_id )
using index
tablespace USERS pctfree 20
storage (initial 10 K next 10 K pctincrease 0)
```

Here's our external unique constraint:

```
create unique index PERSON_UK1
on                  PERSON (
last_name,
first_name,
birth_date,
mothers_maiden_name )
tablespace USERS pctfree 20
storage (initial 100 K next 100 K pctincrease 0)
```

And finally, here's our sequence:

```
create sequence PERSON_ID
start with 1
order
```

That takes care of PERSON. Now let's do the same for LOCATION:

```
create table LOCATION (
location_id         number  not null,
parent_location_id  number,
code                varchar2(30)  not null,
name                varchar2(80)  not null,
start_date          date          not null,
end_date            date )
tablespace USERS pctfree 20
storage (initial 100 K next 100 K pctincrease 0)

alter  table LOCATION add
constraint   LOCATION_PK
primary key ( location_id )
using index
tablespace USERS pctfree 20
storage (initial 10 K next 10 K pctincrease 0)
```

```
create unique index LOCATION_UK1
on                 LOCATION (
code,
start_date,
parent_location_id )
tablespace USERS pctfree 20
storage (initial 100 K next 100 K pctincrease 0)

create sequence LOCATION_ID
start with 1
order
```

Here's the PERSON_LOCATION intersection:

```
create table PERSON_LOCATION (
person_id      number  not null,
location_id    number  not null,
start_date     date    not null,
end_date       date )
tablespace USERS pctfree 20
storage (initial 100 K next 100 K pctincrease 0)

alter  table PERSON_LOCATION add
constraint   PERSON_LOCATION_PK
primary key ( person_id, start_date )
using index
tablespace USERS pctfree 20
storage (initial 10 K next 10 K pctincrease 0)
```

and the PERSON_IDENTIFIER entity:

```
create table PERSON_IDENTIFIER (
person_id    number       not null,
id           varchar2(30)  not null,
id_type      varchar2(30)  not null )
tablespace USERS pctfree 20
storage (initial 100 K next 100 K pctincrease 0)

alter  table PERSON_IDENTIFIER add
constraint   PERSON_IDENTIFIER_PK
primary key ( person_id, id, id_type )
using index
tablespace USERS pctfree 20
storage (initial 100 K next 100 K pctincrease 0)
```

and finally, the PERSON_IDENTIFIER_TYPE entity:

```
create table PERSON_IDENTIFIER_TYPE (
code            varchar2(30)  not null,
description     varchar2(80)  not null,
inactive_date   date )
tablespace USERS pctfree 20
storage (initial 100 K next 100 K pctincrease 0)

alter  table PERSON_IDENTIFIER_TYPE add
constraint   PERSON_IDENTIFIER_TYPE_PK
```

```
primary key ( code )
using index
tablespace USERS pctfree 20
storage (initial 100 K next 100 K pctincrease 0)
```

Now that we have some of our needed table definitions, let's create the DDL for foreign key constraints. The person table has no foreign key constraints, so we'll start with the LOCATION table:

```
alter  table LOCATION add
constraint   LOCATION_FK1
foreign key          ( parent_location_id )
references   LOCATION ( location_id )
```

Next, we have PERSON_LOCATION:

```
alter  table PERSON_LOCATION add
constraint   PERSON_LOCATION_FK1
foreign key          ( person_id )
references   PERSON ( person_id )


alter  table PERSON_LOCATION add
constraint   PERSON_LOCATION_FK2
foreign key          ( location_id )
references  LOCATION ( location_id )
```

and then PERSON_IDENTIFIER:

```
alter  table PERSON_IDENTIFIER add
constraint   PERSON_IDENTIFIER_FK1
foreign key          ( person_id )
references   PERSON ( person_id )


alter  table PERSON_LOCATION add
constraint   PERSON_LOCATION_FK2
foreign key                          ( id_type )
references   PERSON_IDENTIFIER_TYPE ( code )
```

Now that we have our DDL, we can move on to the next step in our process, which is to actually create the database objects. Normally, you'd use Oracle's SQL*Plus to accomplish this task. However, since this is a book about JDBC, I'll show you how to use JDBC to execute the DDL instead. In Chapter 9, we'll cover the execution of DDL and DML. Among other things, you'll see how to execute the DDL to create the HR tables.

Statements

Now that you have a firm understanding of how to create a Connection object for each of the four types of clients outlined in Chapter 1, and you have the DDL to create the example HR database to use as a context for the chapters on relational SQL, we're ready to change our focus from the Connection object to the Statement object. The Statement object, which you'll create using a Connection object, allows you to execute both Data Definition Language (DDL) and Data Manipulation Language (DML) statements. The Statement object is the most dynamic of the JDBC objects, because you can use its execute( ) method to execute any valid SQL statement. If you use the execute( ) method, you can use its return value at runtime to determine whether there is a result set and then use the Statement object's getResultSet( ) method to retrieve the result set, or you can use the Statement object's getUpdateCount( ) method at runtime to determine the number of rows affected by your statement. For most situations, however, you won't need that much flexibility. Instead, you'll need to insert rows into a table, update or delete rows in a table, or select rows from a table. To that end, you'll most often use one of the Statement object's other two execute methods, executeUpdate( ) and executeQuery( ).

In this chapter, we'll start by covering how to create a Statement object from a Connection object. Then we'll see how to use the execute( ) method to execute the DDL from Chapter 8. We'll continue by using the executeUpdate( ) method to insert rows into our new tables. Finally, we'll use the executeQuery( ) method to query data in the database.

Creating a Statement Object

Before you can use a Statement object to execute a SQL statement, you need to create one using the Connection object's createStatement( ) method, as in the following example:

```
Statement stmt = null;
try {
```

```
    stmt = conn.createStatement( )
    . . .
}
catch (SQLException e) {
    . . .
}
finally {
    . . .
}
```

In this example, we assume that a Connection object named conn already exists. In a
try block, call the Connection object's createStatement( ) method to create a new
Statement object. If an error occurs during the call, a SQLException is thrown.

Once you've created a Statement object, you can then use it to execute a SQL statement with one of its three execute methods. Select the execute method that best suits
your needs:

boolean execute(String SQL)
> Returns a boolean value of true if a ResultSet object can be retrieved; otherwise,
> it returns false. Use this method to execute SQL DDL statements or when you
> need to use truly dynamic SQL.

int executeUpdate(String SQL)
> Returns the numbers of rows affected by the execution of the SQL statement. Use
> this method to execute SQL statements for which you expect to get a number of
> rows affected—for example, an INSERT, UPDATE, or DELETE statement.

ResultSet executeQuery(String SQL)
> Returns a ResultSet object. Use this method when you expect to get a result set,
> as you would with a SELECT statement.

In the sections that follow, we'll examine the use of these three methods in detail. So
let's start with the execute( ) method.

The execute( ) Method

The execute( ) method is the most generic method you can use to execute a SQL
statement in JDBC. To execute a SQL statement with the execute method, call it by
passing it a valid SQL statement as a String object, or as a string literal, as shown in
the following example:

```
boolean isResultSet = false;
Statement stmt = null;
try {
  stmt = conn.createStatement( );
  isResultSet = stmt.execute("select 'Hello '||USER from dual");
  . . .
}
```

In this example, we assume that Connection object conn already exists. First, a boolean variable named isResultSet is created to hold the return value from the call to the execute( ) method. Next, a variable named stmt is created to hold a reference to the Statement object. In the try block, the Statement object is created with a call to the Connection object's createStatement( ) method. Then, the Statement object's execute( ) method is called passing a SQL SELECT statement. Since this is a SELECT statement, the execute( ) method returns a boolean true to indicate that a result set is available. You can then call the Statement object's getResultSet( ) method to retrieve the ResultSet object that contains the data from the database. For example:

```
boolean isResultSet = false;
Statement stmt = null;
ResultSet rslt = null;
try {
  stmt = conn.createStatement( );
  isResultSet = stmt.execute("select 'Hello '||USER from dual");
  if (isResultSet) {
    rslt = stmt.getResultSet( );
  }
  . . .
}
```

We'll cover result sets in great detail in Chapter 10.

If an INSERT, UPDATE, or DELETE SQL statement is passed to execute( ), the method will return a boolean false, indicating that no result set is available. In that case, call the Statement object's getUpdateCount( ) method to retrieve the number of rows that were affected by the SQL statement. For example:

```
boolean isResultSet = false;
int rslt = null;
Statement stmt = null;
try {
 stmt = conn.createStatement( );
 isResultSet = stmt.execute("delete person");
 if (!isResultSet) {
 rslt = stmt.getUpdateCount( );
 }
 . . .
}
```

If a DDL statement had been passed to the execute( ) method, it too would have returned false. However, since no result set was created, nor were any rows affected by DDL, there is nothing more to do after the execute( ) method is called.

If an error occurs during a call to the execute( ) method, a SQLException is thrown. This means that each call to a method from the Statement object requires you to use a try block or declare that the method from which you are calling a Statement object's method throws a SQLException.

Now that you have the necessary background to use the Statement object's execute( ) method, let's use it to execute the DDL we created in Chapter 8.

Executing DDL

In Chapter 8, we documented the DDL statements required to create the objects for our HR database. We will now execute those statements via JDBC. To do this, we need to choose an appropriate execute method. A DDL statement to create a database object does not affect any rows, nor does it return a result set. Consequently, the execute( ) method is the best candidate for executing our DDL.

Example 9-1 shows a sample program that reads and executes SQL statements contained in a text file. Specify the name of the SQL command file on the command line when you run the program. The program allows each SQL statement in the file to span one or more lines and expects each SQL statement to be terminated with a forward slash character (/) on a separate line following the statement.

Example 9-1. An application that executes DDL statements from a file

```
import java.io.*;
import java.sql.*;

public class ExecuteDDL {
  Connection conn;
  public ExecuteDDL( ) {
    try {
      DriverManager.registerDriver(new oracle.jdbc.driver.OracleDriver( ));
      conn = DriverManager.getConnection(
        "jdbc:oracle:thin:@dssw2k01:1521:orcl", "scott", "tiger");
    }
    catch (SQLException e) {
      System.err.println(e.getMessage( ));
      e.printStackTrace( );
    }
  }

  public static void main(String[] args)
   throws Exception, IOException {
    if (args.length < 1) {
      System.err.println("Usage: java ExecuteDDL <dml file>");
      System.exit(1);
    }
    new ExecuteDDL( ).process(args[0]);
  }

  public void process(String fileName) throws IOException, SQLException {
    boolean       rslt = false;
    BufferedReader in   = new BufferedReader(new FileReader(fileName));
    Statement      stmt = null;
    StringBuffer   sql  = new StringBuffer(1024);
    String         line = null;
```

Example 9-1. An application that executes DDL statements from a file (continued)

```
    while ((line = in.readLine()) != null) {
      System.out.println(line);
      if (line.length() == 1 && line.indexOf("/") > -1) {
        try {
          stmt = conn.createStatement();
          rslt = stmt.execute(sql.toString());
          System.out.println("OK");
          System.out.println(" ");
        }
        catch (SQLException e) {
          System.err.println(e.getMessage());
        }
        finally {
          if (stmt != null)
            try { stmt.close(); } catch (SQLException ignore) { }
        }
        sql = new StringBuffer(1024);
      }
      else {
        sql.append(line);
        sql.append(" ");
      }
    }
    System.out.println(sql);
    in.close();
  }

  protected void finalize()
   throws Throwable {
    if (conn != null)
      try { conn.close(); } catch (SQLException ignore) { }
    super.finalize();
  }
}
```

Our DDL execution program is named ExecuteDDL. In its main( ) method, it first verifies that a parameter has been passed on the command line. Then it creates an anonymous instance of itself and executes that instance's process method. The filename parameter is passed to the process( ) method, which then parses and executes the DDL contained in the specified file. A database connection is made when the ExecuteDDL( ) object instantiates itself. Its default constructor, ExecuteDDL( ), loads the Oracle driver and then connects to the database using the DriverManager. getConnection( ) method.

The process( ) method begins by allocating five variables:

rslt

 A boolean to receive the return value from the execute( ) method

in

 A BufferedReader object used to read the contents of a SQL command file

---

stmt
    A Statement object to execute the DDL

sql
    A StringBuffer object used to hold a SQL statement read from the SQL command file

line
    A String to hold the results of the BufferedReader.readLine() method

The process() method continues by entering a while loop in which lines are read from the specified SQL command file until the end of the file has been reached. Inside the while loop, the method performs the following steps:

1. The current SQL statement is echoed to the screen.

2. An if statement tests to see if the line has a length of 1 and contains a forward-slash (/) character. If these conditions are met, the current statement in the buffer is executed.

3. If the conditions in step 2 are not met, the current input line is appended to the StringBuffer object named sql.

If step 2 indicates that a complete SQL statement has been read into the buffer, the if statement will execute a try block. Inside the try block, the following steps are taken to execute the SQL statement contained in the buffer:

1. A Statement object is created using the Connection object's createStatement() method.

2. The SQL statement is executed using the Statement object's execute() method. The current contents of the StringBuffer object named sql are passed as a String parameter to that method.

3. To give the user of the program a warm fuzzy feeling that everything is working as expected, the word "OK" followed by a blank line is displayed.

If an error occurs inside the try block, execution branches immediately to the catch clause following the try block. There, the code prints the current error message to the screen. Upon completion of the try block, regardless of whether an exception occurs, the finally clause closes the Statement object if it exists (an error could occur prior to the instantiation of the Statement object). The sql buffer is then reinitialized to hold another SQL statement.

When there are no more SQL statement lines to read, the while loop ends. Any partial, unexecuted SQL statement still in the buffer is displayed, and the BufferedReader object is then closed. The program terminates after calling the finalize() method, which closes the database connection.

There are some very important points to note about the code in Example 9-1. First, in the process() method, the Statement variable stmt is declared outside the try block. This is done so that the stmt variable is accessible in the finally clause. Had it been declared inside the try block, it would be out of the scope of the catch and finally clauses. Second, the finally clause guarantees that any open Statement object is closed regardless of whether the statement executed correctly or failed and threw an exception.

 With Oracle's JDBC implementation, you must always explicitly close a Statement object; otherwise, you will leak memory and lose database cursors.

Creating the HR Tables

You can use the program in Example 9-1 to create the tables for the HR example schema used in this book. Begin by entering the commands to create the HR database tables from Chapter 8 into separate text files. Then, if you have any errors in your SQL, it won't be so hard to correct them. Use one file per table and place a CREATE TABLE statement with all related ALTER TABLE, CREATE INDEX, and CREATE SEQUENCE statements into each file. End each command with a forward-slash character (/) on a separate line. Then compile the program in Example 9-1 and execute it for each file using the following syntax:

```
java ExecuteDDL filename
```

If you have any syntax errors in your command files, you will get a fairly informative SQL diagnostic message from the database. Make any necessary corrections and re-execute the files. Continue that process until you have no SQL creation errors. I say creation errors, because you may encounter "object already exists" errors when you reexecute your SQL after making corrections. You can safely ignore any "object already exists" errors.

The executeUpdate( ) Method

Now that we've created some tables using the execute( ) method, we can continue by using the executeUpdate( ) method to insert, update, and delete rows in those tables. The executeUpdate( ) method works just like the execute( ) method, except that it returns an integer value that reports the number of rows affected by the SQL statement. The executeUpdate( ) method effectively combines the execute( ) and getUpdateCount( ) methods into one call:

```
int       rslt = 0;
Statement stmt = null;
try {
  stmt = conn.createStatement( );
  rslt = stmt.executeUpdate("delete person");
  . . .
}
```

In this example, we once again assume that a Connection object named conn already exists. The example starts by declaring the int variable rslt to hold the number of rows affected by the SQL statement. Next, it declares a Statement variable, stmt, to hold the reference to a Statement object. In the try block, the Statement object is created using the Connection object's createdStatement( ) method, and a reference to it is stored in stmt. Then, the Statement object's executeUpdate( ) method is called to execute the SQL DELETE statement, returning the number of rows affected into rslt. Now that you have the general idea, let's see the executeUpdate( ) method in action.

Executing an INSERT, UPDATE, or DELETE Statement

Example 9-2, shows an insert, update, and delete program which uses the executeUpdate( ) method.

Example 9-2. An application to execute, insert, update, or delete DML

```
import java.io.*;
import java.sql.*;

public class ExecuteIUD {
  Connection conn;
  public ExecuteIUD( ) {
    try {
      DriverManager.registerDriver(new oracle.jdbc.driver.OracleDriver( ));
      conn = DriverManager.getConnection(
        "jdbc:oracle:thin:@dssw2k01:1521:orcl", "scott", "tiger");
    }
    catch (SQLException e) {
     System.err.println(e.getMessage( ));
     e.printStackTrace( );
    }
  }

  public static void main(String[] args)
   throws Exception, IOException {
    ExecuteIUD iud = new ExecuteIUD( );

    iud.executeIUD(
     "insert into PERSON_IDENTIFIER_TYPE " +
     "(code, description, inactive_date) " +
     "values ('EID', 'Employee ID', NULL)");

    iud.executeIUD(
     "insert into PERSON_IDENTIFIER_TYPE " +
     "(code, description, inactive_date) " +
     "values ('PHONE', 'Phone Number', NULL)");

    iud.executeIUD(
     "insert into PERSON_IDENTIFIER_TYPE " +
```

```
      "(code, description, inactive_date) " +
      "values ('SSN', 'Social Socurity Number', NULL)");

    iud.executeIUD(
      "update PERSON_IDENTIFIER_TYPE " +
      "set description = 'Social Security Number' " +
      "where code = 'SSN'");

    iud.executeIUD(
      "delete PERSON_IDENTIFIER_TYPE " +
      "where  code = 'PHONE'");
  }

  public void executeIUD(String sql) throws IOException, SQLException {
    int        rslt = 0;
    Statement stmt = null;

    System.out.println(sql);
    try {
      stmt = conn.createStatement( );
      rslt = stmt.executeUpdate(sql);
      System.out.println(Integer.toString(rslt) + " rows affected");
      System.out.println(" ");
    }
    catch (SQLException e) {
      System.err.println(e.getMessage( ));
    }
    finally {
      if (stmt != null)
        try { stmt.close( ); } catch (SQLException ignore) { }
    }
  }

  protected void finalize( )
    throws Throwable {
    if (conn != null)
      try { conn.close( ); } catch (SQLException ignore) { }
    super.finalize( );
  }
}
```

Our insert, update, and delete program, ExecuteIUD, starts out in its main( ) method by instantiating a copy of itself. Then it calls the executeIUD( ) method three times to insert three identifier type codes into the PERSON_IDENTIFIER_TYPE table. These inserts are followed by an UPDATE statement to change the description for type code SSN. Finally, a DELETE statement is executed to delete the phone type code.

The executeIUD( ) method begins by creating two variables. One is an int named rslt that holds the return value from the executeUpdate( ) method. The other is a Statement object named stmt that is used to execute the SQL statements. The method continues by echoing the passed SQL statement to the screen. It then executes the try block, in which the SQL statement is executed.

Inside the try block, the program creates a Statement object and then proceeds to execute the passed SQL statement by using the Statement object's executeUpdate( ) method. The executeUpdate( ) method returns the number of rows affected by the statement, and the program displays that number followed by a blank line on the screen.

If an error occurs in the try block, program execution immediately branches to the SQLException catch clause where the Oracle SQL diagnostic error message is sent to the screen. Upon completion of the try block, the finally clause closes the Statement object if it is open.

The only notable difference between this example and the last, as if you haven't already heard this enough times already, is that the executeUpdate( ) method returns an integer value that reports the number of rows affected by the SQL statement just executed.

Auto-Commit

When you use executeUpdate( ) to perform your inserts, updates, and deletes, be aware that auto-commit is on by default. This means that as each SQL statement is executed, it is also committed. Effectively, each statement execution becomes its own transaction. If you are executing multiple statements, it is not efficient to commit after each one. In addition, if you are performing complex insertion processes such as those involving both parent and child tables, you probably don't want your parent rows to be inserted without the corresponding child rows also being inserted. So for reasons of both performance and transaction integrity, you may want or need to turn off auto-commit. You can do that using the Connection object's setAutoCommit( ) method, passing it a boolean false:

```
conn.setAutoCommit(false);
```

Once you've turned off auto-commit, you can execute any number of executeUpdate( ) calls, which will all form one transaction. Then, when you are done making all your executeUpdate( ) calls, you'll need to call the Connection object's commit( ) method to make your changes permanent.

Oracle and SQL92 Escape Syntax

Another issue to be concerned about when using Statement.executeUpdate( ) is that it requires you to perform rather complex string concatenations. Because executeUpdate( ) requires a String object as an input parameter, you have to convert any values stored in other data types that are required to build your SQL statements into String objects before concatenating them to build your SQL statement. To accomplish this task, you must write your own helper functions and use either Oracle's built-in database functions or SQL92's escape syntax.

As you convert values in other data types to `Strings` and concatenate them into a larger `String` object to represent a SQL statement, you must consider the following issues:

- You must escape any use of the single quote, or tick character.
- You must convert numeric data types to strings.
- You must convert date and time data types to strings and then wrap them with an appropriate database function to convert the string representation of the date or time values to the database's date type.

The next few sections talk about these and other issues in detail. Keep in mind that in Chapter 11, we'll cover an alternative to the `Statement` object, a `PreparedStatement` object that eliminates the need for handling these issues.

Handling ticks

You must replace any occurrences of a tick character (') within your SQL statement with double ticks (''), so they can be parsed correctly by the database. The double tick is Oracle's escape syntax for the tick character. For example, consider a SQL statement such as the following, in which a value contains a tick character:

```
delete person where last_name = 'O'Reilly'
```

Before trying to execute this statement, you must replace the tick character in `O'Reilly` with a double-tick character:

```
delete person where last_name = 'O''Reilly'
```

 Tick characters are also referred to as single-quote characters.

Converting numbers

You must convert any numeric data types to strings using an appropriate wrapper object's `toString()` method. If your numbers are stored in Java primitive data types such as `long` or `double`, then you must call the primitive wrapper class's static `toString()` method. Table 9-1 lists the different `toString()` methods available for primitive data types.

Table 9-1. Primitive data type to string conversion methods

Primitive data type	Wrapper class method to call
short s	`Short.toString(short s)`
int I	`Integer.toString(int I)`

Table 9-1. Primitive data type to string conversion methods (continued)

Primitive data type	Wrapper class method to call
long l	`Long.toString(long l)`
float f	`Float.toString(float f)`
double d	`Double.toString(double d)`

If your numeric data is already stored in a wrapper, or in some other numeric class, you can simply call that class's toString( ) method to convert your numeric value to a String.

Converting date and time values

You must convert any date, time, or timestamp data type values to strings using an appropriate java.text.DateFormat object. For example, you can use a java.text. SimpleDateFormat object. The SimpleDateFormat class allows you to pass in a date format mask when you instantiate an object of the class. Then, you can use the newly instantiated SimpleDateFormat object to convert a Date, Time, or Timestamp object into a String by calling its format( ) method, as shown in the following example:

```
SimpleDateFormat sdf = new SimpleDateFormat("yyyy-MM-dd hh:mm:ss");
String dateString = sdf.format(date);
```

You can find the complete date format syntax to use with SimpleDateFormat in the JDK API documentation for the SimpleDateFormat class.

After you convert a Java Date, Time, or Timestamp to a String, you're still not finished. Next, you must wrap the string value with the Oracle TO_DATE( ) database function or use the SQL92 escape syntax to convert your string representation into an Oracle DATE value, which is what the database expects. The SQL92 escape syntax provides you with a portable means of specifying a date, time, or timestamp. The escape syntax string is translated into native Oracle syntax on the fly by the JDBC driver.

Using Oracle's built-in TO_DATE( ) function

Oracle's TO_DATE( ) function has the following syntax:

```
TO_DATE( varchar2, 'format' )
```

in which *format* can be any combination of format specifiers found in Table 9-2.

Table 9-2. Oracle TO_DATE() format specifiers

Format	Description
yyyy	Four-digit year
mm	Two-digit month
dd	Two-digit day

Table 9-2. Oracle TO_DATE() format specifiers (continued)

Format	Description
hh24	24 clock, two-digit hour
mi	Two-digit minutes
ss	Two-digit seconds

Many more possibilities for format specifiers can be found in the *Oracle SQL Reference* manual. For example, to convert the string value 19800101000000, which happens to be the character representation of the timestamp for midnight on January 1, 1980, to an Oracle DATE value, code the following in a SQL statement:

```
TO_CHAR( '19800101000000', 'YYYYMMDDHH24MISS' )
```

Using SQL92 syntax with dates

Oracle supports the following three SQL92 escape syntaxes for use with date, time, and timestamp values:

{d 'yyyy-mm-dd'}
    For a date
{t 'hh:mm:ss'}
    For a time
{ts 'yyyy-mm-dd hh:mm:ss'}
    For a timestamp

To use one of these escape syntaxes, replace the format with a value that is appropriately formatted for that mask. For example, to use the ts, or timestamp mask, you must convert a Java Date value to a String using the yyyy-MM-dd hh:mm:ss format. If the date is January 1, 1980, then you must convert the Java Date object to a String object that looks like the following:

```
1980-01-01 00:00:00
```

Then, you must wrap the converted timestamp value with the SQL92 escape syntax. The result looks like this:

```
{ts '1980-01-01 00:00:00'}
```

You then use this character representation of the date in your SQL statement:

```
update location set end_date = {ts '1980-01-01 00:00:00'}
```

An escape syntax example

Example 9-3 demonstrates the replacement of single ticks with double ticks. It also demonstrates the use of both the Oracle TO_DATE() database function and SQL92's escape syntax.

Example 9-3. An application that demonstrates SQL statement formulation

```java
import java.io.*;
import java.sql.*;
import java.text.*;

public class ConcatenatingStringsForIUD {
  Connection conn;
  public ConcatenatingStringsForIUD( ) {
    try {
      DriverManager.registerDriver(new oracle.jdbc.driver.OracleDriver( ));
      conn = DriverManager.getConnection(
        "jdbc:oracle:thin:@dssw2k01:1521:orcl", "scott", "tiger");
    }
    catch (SQLException e) {
     System.err.println(e.getMessage( ));
     e.printStackTrace( );
    }
  }

  public static void main(String[] args)
   throws Exception, IOException {
   ConcatenatingStringsForIUD iud = new ConcatenatingStringsForIUD( );

    String last_name          = "O'Reilly";
    String first_name         = "Tim";
    String middle_name        = null;
    Date   birth_date         = Date.valueOf("1971-03-17");
    String mothers_maiden_name = "Oh! I don't know!";

    iud.executeIUD(
     "delete PERSON " +
     "where   last_name = " +
     iud.formatWithTicks(last_name) + " " +
     "and     first_name = " +
     iud.formatWithTicks(first_name));

    iud.executeIUD(
     "insert into PERSON " +
     "(person_id, last_name, first_name, middle_name, " +
     "birth_date, mothers_maiden_name) values " +
     "(person_id.nextval, " +
     iud.formatWithTicks(last_name) + ", " +
     iud.formatWithTicks(first_name) + ", " +
     iud.formatWithTicks(middle_name) + ", " +
     iud.formatWithOracleDate(birth_date) + ", " +
     iud.formatWithTicks(mothers_maiden_name) + ")");

    birth_date = Date.valueOf("1972-03-17");

    iud.executeIUD(
     "update PERSON " +
     "set     birth_date = " +
     iud.formatWithSql92Date(birth_date) + " " +
     "where   last_name = " +
```

```
        iud.formatWithTicks(last_name) + " " +
        "and    first_name = " +
        iud.formatWithTicks(first_name));
    }

    private String formatWithOracleDate(Date date) {
      if (date != null) {
        SimpleDateFormat sdf = new SimpleDateFormat("yyyy-MM-dd hh:mm:ss");
        return "to_date('" + sdf.format(date) + "','YYYY-MM-DD HH24:MI:SS')";
      }
      else {
        return "NULL";
      }
    }

    private String formatWithSql92Date(Date date) {
      if (date != null) {
        SimpleDateFormat sdf = new SimpleDateFormat("yyyy-MM-dd hh:mm:ss");
        return "{ts '" + sdf.format(date) + "'}";
      }
      else {
        return "NULL";
      }
    }

    private String formatWithTicks(String string) {
      if (string != null) {
        char[]      in  = string.toCharArray();
        StringBuffer out = new StringBuffer((int)(in.length * 1.1));
        if (in.length > 0)
          out.append("'");
        for (int i=0;i < in.length;i++) {
          out.append(in[i]);
          if (in[i] == '\'')
            out.append(in[i]);
        }
        if (in.length > 0)
          out.append("'");
        return out.toString();
      }
      else {
        return "NULL";
      }
    }

    public void executeIUD(String sql)
      throws IOException, SQLException {
      int       rslt = 0;
      Statement stmt = null;
      System.out.println(sql);
      try {
        stmt = conn.createStatement();
        rslt = stmt.executeUpdate(sql);
```

Example 9-3. An application that demonstrates SQL statement formulation (continued)

```
      System.out.println(Integer.toString(rslt) + " rows affected");
      System.out.println(" ");
    }
    catch (SQLException e) {
      System.err.println(e.getMessage());
    }
    finally {
      if (stmt != null)
      try { stmt.close(); } catch (SQLException ignore) { }
    }
  }

  protected void finalize()
    throws Throwable {
    if (conn != null)
      { try { conn.close(); } catch (SQLException ignore) { } }
    super.finalize();
  }
}
```

Our sample SQL statement formulation program, ConcatenatingStringsForIUD, starts in its main( ) method. In the main( ) method, it creates several strings for concatenating values in a SQL statement. The program also creates one Date variable, the value of which will later be converted to a String in order to build the program's SQL statements. The variable last_name contains a last name that uses a tick character. If it is not modified to use the Oracle escape syntax of two ticks, the SQL statement will fail. To solve this problem, I've created a helper function, formatWithTicks( ), which replaces any occurrence of one tick with two ticks. The function also surrounds the string value with ticks, which is the necessary format for a string value in a SQL statement.

The variable birth_date contains a Date value. This needs to be converted to a String value in order to build our SQL statements. To that end, I've created two helper functions, formatWithOracleDate( ) and formatWithSql92Date( ), which convert Date values into properly formatted String values for use in a SQL statement.

You should compile and run the program shown in Example 9-3, because running the program will do more to clarify what it does than just looking at the code. When you run it, the program displays each newly formatted SQL statement on the screen right before the statement is executed. It'll be easy to see the effects of the helper functions.

More on SQL92 Escape Syntax

It would be wonderful if Oracle had complete support for SQL92 escape syntax, but it doesn't. In this section, we'll take the time to look at other forms of SQL92 escape syntax that Oracle does support and highlight the more useful forms it does not support. We'll finish up with a sample program you can use to test your SQL92 escape syntax.

SQL92 LIKE escape syntax

There is a seldom used SQL92 escape syntax for the LIKE keyword in a WHERE clause. The LIKE keyword allows you to find strings that match a given pattern. It recognizes the percent (%) and underscore characters (_) as pattern match operators. If you want to actually search for pattern match characters in a string, you need a way to distinguish between when to use them as pattern match characters and when to use them as regular characters. You do this using an escape character, which is defined with the following syntax:

```
{ESCAPE 'escape character'}
```

If you wish to find all the tables you have access to that have an underscore character as a middle character, then you might try a query such as:

```
select table_name
from   all_tables
where  table_name like '%_%'
```

But this query doesn't work as you suspect. Instead, you get all the tables you have access to, not just the ones with an underscore in the middle. In order for the underscore character to be interpreted as a character to search for, not a pattern match operator, you have to escape it:

```
select table_name
from   all_tables
where  table_name like '%/_%' {escape '/'}
```

Note the use of the escape character before the underscore.

If you use the backslash character (\) as the escape character, you also have to use two backslash characters in your Java String literal, because the backslash is also a Java escape character. For example:

```
select table_name
from   all_tables
where  table_name like '%\\_%' {escape '\\'}
```

When using the ESCAPE keyword, you don't need to escape all the pattern match characters in your search string. You only need to escape those that you aren't using as pattern match characters.

Outer join escape syntax

As of Version 8.1.6, Oracle does not support the SQL92 escape syntax for outer joins. For outer joins you have to use the Oracle (+) syntax.

Function escape syntax

Oracle does not support the SQL92 escape syntax for functions. Nor does Oracle support all the scalar database functions. You can use the following four Connection methods to ascertain which scalar functions the driver supports:

```
DatabaseMetaData.getNumericFunctions( )
DatabaseMetaData.getStringFunctions( )
DatabaseMetaData.getSystemFunctions( )
DatabaseMetaData.getTimeDateFunctions( )
```

Unsupported SQL92 syntax

If you use any unsupported SQL92 escape syntax, you will get the following error message in the subsequent SQLException: "Non supported SQL92 token at position xx."

You can test your SQL92 escape syntax by preparsing the SQL statement using the oracle.jdbc.driver.OracleSql.parse( ) method. Example 9-4 takes a SQL92 string at the prompt and converts it into Oracle syntax using the OracleSql.parse( ) method.

Example 9-4. An application that Preparses SQL92 syntax

```
import java.io.*;
import java.sql.*;

public class TestSQL92Syntax {

  public static void main(String[] args)
   throws Exception {
   new TestSQL92Syntax().process( );
  }

  private void process( ) {
    BufferedReader in   = null;
    String         line = null;
    try {
      in = new BufferedReader(new InputStreamReader(System.in));
      System.out.println(" ");
      System.out.print("SQL92> ");
      while (!(line = in.readLine()).equals("")) {
        System.out.println("line = \"" + line + "\"");
        try {
          System.out.println(
            new oracle.jdbc.driver.OracleSql( ).parse(line));
        }
        catch (SQLException e) {
          System.out.println(e.getMessage( ));
        }
        finally {
          System.out.println(" ");
          System.out.print("SQL92> ");
        }
```

Example 9-4. An application that Preparses SQL92 syntax (continued)

```
      }
    }
    catch (IOException e) {
      System.out.println(e.getMessage());
    }
    finally {
      if (in != null)
        try { in.close(); } catch (IOException ignore) { }
    }
  }
}
```

If you execute the program by typing java `TestSQL92Syntax`, you'll get a SQL92 prompt. You can then type your SQL92 escape syntax after the prompt and press Enter to see how it is converted to Oracle syntax. For example, here we test {d '1900-01-01'}:

```
SQL92> {d '1900-01-01'}
line = "{d '1900-01-01'}"
TO_DATE ('1900-01-01', 'YYYY-MM-DD')
SQL92>
```

If we try a SQL statement with a SQL92 outer join, we get a "Non supported SQL92 token ..." error.

Batching

Batching allows you to group related SQL statements into a batch. When you send several SQL statements to the database at once, you reduce the amount of protocol dialog overhead, thereby improving performance.

Oracle's JDBC driver does not actually implement batching for the `Statement` object. You can use the `addBatch()` and `executeBatch()` methods, but each statement is executed on each call to `addBatch()`. Therefore, you will see no performance improvement with the use of `Statement` batching. You must use a `PreparedStatement` object to use batching. We'll discuss batching in detail in Chapter 11.

The executeQuery( ) Method

Now that you've learned how to insert, update, and delete data in a table, it's time to learn how to use a SELECT statement to retrieve data. Whereas the execute() and executeUpdate() methods discussed in previous sections return primitive data types—a boolean and int, respectively—the method normally used with a SELECT statement, executeQuery(), returns a ResultSet object. The executeQuery() method effectively combines the execute() and getResultSet() methods into one call:

```
ResultSet rset = null;
Statement stmt = null;
try {
  stmt = conn.createStatement();
```

```
      rset = stmt.executeQuery("select last_name, first_name from person");
      . . .
  }
```

In this example, we once again assume that a Connection object, conn, already exists. The example starts out by declaring a ResultSet variable, rset, to hold the reference to the ResultSet object generated by the SQL statement. Next, it declares a Statement variable, stmt, to hold the reference to a Statement object. In the try block, the Statement object is created and stored in stmt using the Connection object's createdStatement( ) method. Then, the Statement object's executeQuery( ) method is called to execute the SQL SELECT statement, returning a ResultSet into rset.

A ResultSet (which we will cover in great detail in Chapter 10) is an object that has a set of accessor methods that allow you to get to the data returned from the database. These include methods for positioning the cursor, doing in-place updates, and performing a variety of other functions.

Executing a SELECT Statement

To create a result set, we begin by creating a SQL SELECT statement in a fashion similar to how we created INSERT, UPDATE, and DELETE statements. We then call the executeQuery( ) method to execute the statement and get a ResultSet object. Take a look at the program in Example 9-5, which issues a SELECT statement to query the PERSON_IDENTIFIER_TYPE table.

Example 9-5. An application that demonstrates executeQuery()

```java
import java.io.*;
import java.sql.*;
import java.text.*;

public class ExecuteSelect {
  Connection conn;

  public ExecuteSelect( ) {
    try {
      DriverManager.registerDriver(new oracle.jdbc.driver.OracleDriver( ));
      conn = DriverManager.getConnection(
        "jdbc:oracle:thin:@dssw2k01:1521:orcl", "scott", "tiger");
    }
    catch (SQLException e) {
      System.err.println(e.getMessage( ));
      e.printStackTrace( );
    }
  }

  public static void main(String[] args)
    throws Exception, IOException {
    ExecuteSelect s = new ExecuteSelect( );
```

Example 9-5. An application that demonstrates executeQuery() (continued)

```
    s.executeSelect(
     "select code, description, inactive_date " +
     "from   PERSON_IDENTIFIER_TYPE " +
     "order by code");
  }

  public void executeSelect(String sql)
   throws IOException, SQLException {
    Date        inactive_date = null;
    DateFormat df             =
     DateFormat.getDateInstance(DateFormat.SHORT);
    int         rows          = 0;
    ResultSet  rslt          = null;
    Statement  stmt          = null;

    System.out.println(sql);
    try {
      stmt = conn.createStatement();
      rslt = stmt.executeQuery(sql);
      while (rslt.next()) {
        rows++;
        System.out.print(rslt.getString("code") + "  ");
        System.out.print(rslt.getString("description") + "  "),
        inactive_date = rslt.getDate("inactive_date");
        if (inactive_date != null)
          System.out.println(df.format(inactive_date));
        else
          System.out.println("NULL");
      }
      System.out.println(Integer.toString(rows) + " rows selected");
      System.out.println(" ");
    }
    catch (SQLException e) {
      System.err.println(e.getMessage());
    }
    finally {
      if (rslt != null)
        try { rslt.close(); } catch (SQLException ignore) { }
      if (stmt != null)
        try { stmt.close(); } catch (SQLException ignore) { }
    }
  }

protected void finalize()
 throws Throwable {
  if (conn != null)
    try { conn.close(); } catch (SQLException ignore) { }
  super.finalize();
  }
}
```

In main( ), the program instantiates a copy of itself. The main( ) method then calls the executeSelect( ) method, passing the SQL SELECT statement that will be executed as a parameter. In the executeSelect( ) method, the program starts by creating five variables:

inactive_date
> A Date to hold the inactive date from the database for each row as the while loop moves through cursor values

df
> A DateFormat used to convert the inactive date into a formatted String

rows
> An int used to count the number of rows selected from the database

rslt
> A ResultSet to hold the return value from the executeQuery( ) method

stmt
> A Statement used to execute the SELECT statement

After the program creates its local variables, it continues by echoing the SQL statement to the screen and then enters a try block.

In the try block, the program first creates a Statement object by calling the Connection object's createStatement( ) method. Next, the program executes the SELECT statement using the Statement object's executeQuery( ) method. This method returns a ResultSet object that contains all the rows and columns from the database that satisfy the query. The program proceeds by entering a while loop in which the ResultSet is tested for more results. The program determines if there are more rows by calling the ResultSet object's next( ) method. If there are more results, the row count is incremented and the String values of the columns are displayed on the screen.

If an SQLException occurs during the execution of the statements in the try block, the program immediately branches to the catch clause where the Oracle diagnostic error message is displayed on the screen. Upon completion of the try block, execution branches to the finally clause where the ResultSet and Statement objects are closed. After that, the program terminates.

Notice that I have told you nothing about the ResultSet's methods. This is because we will focus on them in Chapter 10. For now, it is important that you understand that the results from the database are accessed through the ResultSet object returned from the executeQuery( ) method.

Defining Columns

In Example 9-5, a program invoked the executeQuery( ) method to execute a query against the database and returned a result set. But what exactly happened when that executeQuery( ) method was called? First, the Oracle driver parsed the SQL statement.

Next, it queried the database to identify the data types for the columns specified in the SELECT statement. Then it submitted the SELECT statement to the database for processing. Upon completion, the database returned the results to the driver, and the driver in turn returned a ResultSet object to the program. In this scenario, for every SELECT statement we execute, the driver must make two round trips to the database: one to get the query's metadata and another to get the query's results. If we could eliminate the first round trip to the database, we would get a 50% improvement in efficiency and response time for a singleton—that is, a one-row result—query. Oracle has a proprietary solution for this problem, called *defining columns*, which allows you to predefine the column data types.

You can specify the column data types for a query before it is executed, thus avoiding the round trip to the database to retrieve column metadata. You specify the data type for a column using the oracle.jdbc.driver.OracleStatement object's define-ColumnType( ) method. This proprietary method has the following signature:

```
defineColumnType(int column_index, int type) throws SQLException
```

which breaks down as:

column_index
> The relative number of the column in the SELECT statement, starting with 1 and increasing from left to right

type
> One of the java.sql.Types constants

In our last example, we used the following query:

```
select code, description, inactive_date
from   PERSON_IDENTIFIER_TYPE
order by code
```

The column code in this example is column index 1, and its database data type is VARCHAR2. An appropriate java.sql.Types constant for an Oracle VARCHAR2 column would be VARCHAR. The second column, description, is column index 2, and it would also be a VARCHAR. The third column, inactive_date, is column index 3, and its database data type is DATE. An appropriate java.sql.Types constant for an Oracle DATE column would be TIMESTAMP.

To use the defineColumnType( ) method, you must use an OracleStatement object instead of a Statement object or cast your Statement object to an OracleStatement, as in Example 9-6. Notice in the example that the calls to defineColumnType( ) precede the creation of the ResultSet.

Example 9-6. An application that predefines columns

```
import java.io.*;
import java.sql.*;
import java.text.*;
import oracle.jdbc.driver.*;
```

Example 9-6. An application that predefines columns (continued)

```java
public class ExecuteDefinedSelect {
  Connection conn;

  public ExecuteDefinedSelect( ) {
    try {
      DriverManager.registerDriver(new oracle.jdbc.driver.OracleDriver( ));
      conn = DriverManager.getConnection(
        "jdbc:oracle:thin:@dssw2k01:1521:orcl", "scott", "tiger");
    }
    catch (SQLException e) {
      System.err.println(e.getMessage( ));
      e.printStackTrace( );
    }
  }

  public static void main(String[] args)
   throws Exception, IOException {
    ExecuteDefinedSelect s = new ExecuteDefinedSelect( );

    s.executeDefinedSelect(
      "select code, description, inactive_date " +
      "from    PERSON_IDENTIFIER_TYPE " +
      "order by code");
  }

  public void executeDefinedSelect(String sql)
   throws IOException, SQLException {
    Date       inactive_date = null;
    DateFormat df            =
     DateFormat.getDateInstance(DateFormat.SHORT);
    int        rows          = 0;
    ResultSet  rslt          = null;
    Statement  stmt          = null;

    System.out.println(sql);
    try {
      stmt = conn.createStatement( );
      ((OracleStatement)stmt).defineColumnType(1, Types.VARCHAR);
      ((OracleStatement)stmt).defineColumnType(2, Types.VARCHAR);
      ((OracleStatement)stmt).defineColumnType(3, Types.TIMESTAMP);
      rslt = stmt.executeQuery(sql);
      while (rslt.next( )) {
        rows++;
        System.out.print(rslt.getString(1) + "  ");
        System.out.print(rslt.getString(2) + "  ");
        inactive_date = rslt.getDate(3);
        if (inactive_date != null)
          System.out.println(df.format(inactive_date));
        else
          System.out.println("NULL");
      }
      System.out.println(Integer.toString(rows) + " rows selected");
```

Example 9-6. An application that predefines columns (continued)

```
      System.out.println(" ");
    }
    catch (SQLException e) {
      System.err.println(e.getMessage( ));
    }
    finally {
      if (rslt != null)
        try { rslt.close( ); } catch (SQLException ignore) { }
      if (stmt != null)
        try { stmt.close( ); } catch (SQLException ignore) { }
    }
  }

  protected void finalize( )
    throws Throwable {
      if (conn != null)
        try { conn.close( ); } catch (SQLException ignore) { }
      super.finalize( );
    }
}
```

The program in Example 9-6, ExecuteDefinedSelect, is similar to that in Example 9-5 but with two differences. First, the column types are predefined. After the Statement object is created using the Connection.createStatement( ) method, and before it is used to execute the SELECT statement with the Statement.executeQuery( ) method, I added three calls to the OracleStatement.defineColumnType( ) method. These calls cast the JDBC 2.0 interface Statement object to Oracle's implementation of the interface, implemented by the OracleStatement class, using the following syntax:

```
(OracleStatement(Statement))
```

The first two calls to defineColumnType( ) set the data types for the result set's code and description columns to VARCHAR. The third call sets the inactive_date column's data type to TIMESTAMP.

The second difference between the two programs is that the use of defineColumnType( ) requires you to reference the columns by number rather than by name when you get the values; otherwise, the driver is forced to query the database for metadata. Hence, in Example 9-6, you see rslt.getString(1) instead of rslt.getString("code"). The same holds true for the other columns as well.

> The OCI driver returns the result set metadata and the first row of data in a single round trip. Therefore, little is gained by predefining your columns if you will use only the OCI driver.

The result of using Oracle's proprietary extension to define column types is that our sample program takes only half the amount of time to query the database as before.

Oracle also has another proprietary extension that improves SELECT statement response time and efficiency. This other extension is known as row prefetch.

Row Prefetch

Oracle's *row prefetch* extension is a proprietary extension to the JDBC standard that allows rows in a result set to be sent across the network from the database to a client in batches, thereby reducing the number of network round trips and increasing performance. According to the JDBC specification, a JDBC driver should retrieve rows from a database one row at a time. With Oracle's row prefetch extension, rows are, by default, retrieved in sets of 10. There's an exception to this default. If the result set includes a large data type such as a BLOB, BFILE, CLOB, LONG RAW, or LONG, the driver resets the row prefetch to 1.

You can set the default row prefetch value yourself in a Connection object. Consequently, all subsequent object creations, such as those for Statement objects, from the Connection object in question will use the new default value. To set the default prefetch value for a Connection object, you must cast your Connection object to an OracleConnection and then call its setDefaultRowPrefetch( ) method, passing it an int value representing the number of rows to prefetch. For example, to set the default prefetch value to 20, you would use code such as the following:

```
Connection conn = DriverManager.getConnection(...);
(OracleConnection(conn)).setDefaultRowPrefetch(20);
```

You can also change the row prefetch value in a Statement object prior to using it to execute a SELECT statement. Do this by casting the Statement object to an OracleStatement and then call its setRowPrefetch( ) method. For example, to change a Statement object's row prefetch value to 20, use the following code:

```
Statement stmt = conn.createStatement( );
(OracleStatement(stmt)).setRowPrefetch(20);
```

Interestingly enough, Oracle recommends the default row prefetch value of 10 for most situations. You should experiment with different settings on small and large rows to determine if another value is optimal for your situation.

OracleStatement Implements Statement

As you've experienced throughout this chapter, the Oracle implementation of Statement has several extensions to the JDBC standard. Let's finish this chapter with a review of those extensions. When you use a Connection object returned by an oracle.jdbc.driver.OracleDriver object to create a Statement object, what is actually returned is an OracleStatement object. The JDBC Statement object is an interface that defines a set of methods that must be implemented by any class that states it implements java.sql.Statement. oracle.jdbc.driver.OracleStatement implements java.

`sql.Statement`, providing you with all the standard JDBC methods; plus, it implements the following `OracleStatement` methods:

```
clearDefines( ) throws SQLException
defineColumnType(int column_index, int type) throws SQLException
defineColumnType(int column_index, int type, int max_size) throws SQLException
defineColumnType(int column_index, int typeCode, String typeName) throws SQLException
String getOriginalSql( ) throws SQLException
String getRevisedSql( ) throws SQLException
int getRowPrefetch( )
int sendBatch( ) throws SQLException
setResultSetCache(OracleResultSetCache cache) throws SQLException
setRowPrefetch(int value) throws SQLException
```

You should now have a good grasp of how to use a `Statement` object to execute a SQL statement. Let's move on to Chapter 10, where we'll cover everything you'd like to know, and perhaps a little more, about `ResultSet`s.

CHAPTER 10

Result Sets

As you saw in Chapter 9, when you execute a SELECT statement, the results are returned as a `java.sql.ResultSet` object. You'll use the functionality of the `ResultSet` object to scroll through the set of results; work with the values returned from the database; and make inserts, updates, and deletes. In this chapter, we'll start by covering the various data types that can be accessed using JDBC, and then we'll take a practical look at their use while considering the data types available with Oracle. Next, we'll discuss the various `ResultSet` accessor methods. We'll continue by discussing how to handle database NULL values in Java and spend much of the second half of the chapter discussing scrollable and updateable result sets. Finally, we'll discuss the Oracle proprietary extensions to the `ResultSet` object.

Basic Cursor Positioning

When you use the `Statement` object's `executeQuery( )` method to query the database with a SQL SELECT statement, the `Statement` object returns a `ResultSet` object. For the sake of brevity, the returned `ResultSet` object contains the results of your query.

In the database, your data is organized as rows of columns in a table. Consequently, the result of a query against the database is a result set that is also organized as rows of columns. A `ResultSet` object provides a set of methods for selecting a specific row in the result set and another set of methods for getting the values of the columns in the selected row.

When a `ResultSet` object is returned from a `Statement` object, its row pointer, or cursor, is initially positioned before the first row of the result set. You then use the `ResultSet` object's `next( )` method to scroll forward through the result set one row at a time. The `next( )` method has the following signature:

```
boolean next( )
```

The next() method returns true if it successfully positions the cursor on the next row; otherwise, it returns false. The next() method is typically used in a while loop:

```
ResultSet rslt = null;
Statement stmt = null;
try {
  stmt = conn.createStatement();
  rslt = stmt.executeQuery("select owner, table_name from all_tables");
  while (rslt.next()) {
    // Get the column values
    . . .
  }
}
```

This example scrolls through the results of the database query one row at a time until the result set is exhausted. Alternatively, if you know you're working with a single-ton SELECT, you may want to use an if statement:

```
ResultSet rslt = null;
Statement stmt = null;
try {
  stmt = conn.createStatement();
  rslt = stmt.executeQuery("select owner, table_name from all_tables");
  if (rslt.next()) {
    // Get the column values
    . . .
  }
}
```

Here, the cursor is scrolled forward to the first row and then discarded under the assumption that only one row was requested by the query. In both of these examples, the next() method has been used to position the cursor to the next row, but no code has been provided to access the column values of that row. How then, do you get the column values? I answer that question in the next two sections. First, we must cover some background about which SQL data types can be stored into which Java data types. We'll then cover how to use the ResultSet objects accessor methods to retrieve the column values returned by a query.

Data Types

Whether you move data between two computers, computer systems, or programs written in different programming languages, you'll need to identify which data types can be moved from one setup to another and how. This problem arises when you retrieve data from an Oracle database in a Java program and store data from a Java program in the database. It's a function of the JDBC driver to know how to move or convert the data as it moves between your Java program and Oracle, but you as the programmer must know what is possible or, more importantly, legal. Table 10-1 lists the Oracle SQL data types and all their valid Java data type mappings.

Table 10-1. Valid Oracle SQL-to-Java data type mappings

Oracle SQL data type	Valid Java data type mappings
BFILE	oracle.sql.BFILE
BLOB	oracle.sql.BLOB
	java.sql.Blob
CHAR, VARCHAR2, LONG	oracle.sql.CHAR
	java.lang.String
	java.sql.Date
	java.sql.Time
	java.sql.Timestamp
	java.lang.Byte
	java.lang.Short
	java.lang.Integer
	java.lang.Long
	java.lang.Float
	java.lang.Double
	java.math.BigDecimal
	byte
	short
	int
	long
	float
	double
CLOB	oracle.sql.CLOB
	java.sql.Clob
DATE	oracle.sql.DATE
	java.sql.Date
	java.sql.Time
	java.sql.Timestamp
	java.lang.String
OBJECT	oracle.sql.STRUCT
	java.sql.Struct
	oracle.sql.CustomDatum
	java.sql.SQLData

Table 10-1. Valid Oracle SQL-to-Java data type mappings (continued)

Oracle SQL data type	Valid Java data type mappings
NUMBER	`oracle.sql.NUMBER`
	`java.lang.Byte`
	`java.lang.Short`
	`java.lang.Integer`
	`java.lang.Long`
	`java.lang.Float`
	`java.lang.Double`
	`java.math.BigDecimal`
	`byte`
	`short`
	`int`
	`long`
	`float`
	`double`
RAW, LONG RAW	`oracle.sql.RAW`
	`byte[]`
REF	`oracle.sql.REF`
	`java.sql.Ref`
ROWID	`oracle.sql.CHAR`
	`oracle.sql.ROWID`
	`java.lang.String`
TABLE (nested), VARRAY	`oracle.sql.ARRAY`
	`java.sql.Array`
Any of the above SQL types	`oracle.sql.CustomDatum`
	`oracle.sql.Datum`

Besides the standard Java data types, Oracle's JDBC implementation also provides a complete set of Oracle Java data types that correspond to the Oracle SQL data types. These classes, which all begin with `oracle.sql`, store Oracle SQL data in byte arrays similar to how it is stored natively in the database.

For now, we will concern ourselves only with the SQL data types that are not streamable and are available with relational SQL. These data types are:

- CHAR
- VARCHAR2
- DATE

- NUMBER
- RAW
- ROWID

We will cover the other data types in the chapters that follow. For the most part, since the CHAR, RAW, and ROWID data types are rarely used, this leaves us with the Oracle SQL data types: VARCHAR2, NUMBER, and DATE. The question is how to map these Oracle SQL types to Java types. Although you can use any of the SQL-to-Java data type mappings in Table 10-1, I suggest you use the following strategies:

- For SQL character values, map VARCHAR2 to java.lang.String.
- For SQL numeric values, map an integer type NUMBER to java.lang.Long or long, and map a floating-point type NUMBER to java.lang.Double or double.
- For SQL date and time values, map a DATE to java.sql.Timestamp.

Why? Well, let's start with the SQL character types. The only feasible mapping for character data, unless you are writing data-processing-type stored procedures, is to use java.lang.String. When designing tables for a database, I recommend you use VARCHAR2 for all character types that are not large objects. As I stated in Chapter 8, there is no good reason to use an Oracle CHAR data type. CHAR values are fixed-length character values right-padded with space characters. Because they are right-padded with spaces, they cause comparison problems when compared with VARCHAR2 values.

For NUMBER values, there are two possible types of values you can encounter. The first is an integer type NUMBER definition such as NUMBER(18) or NUMBER. You can map such integer values to a java.lang.Integer or int, but you'll have only nine significant digits. By using an integer, you constrain your program in such a way that it may require modifications at a later date. It's much easier to use a data type that can hold all possible values now and in the future. For Java, this is java.math.BigDecimal. However, using BigDecimal is inefficient if full precision is not needed, so I recommend using java.lang.Long or long, both of which have 18 significant digits for precision. For floating-point type NUMBER definitions such as NUMBER(16,2) or NUMBER, I suggest you use a java.lang.Double or double, which also have 18 significant digits for precision for the same reason—you don't want to have to modify your program later to handle larger values than you first anticipated. In designing tables for a database, I recommend you don't constrain NUMBER columns unless there is a compelling reason to do so. That means defining both integer and floating-point values as NUMBER.

For DATE values, I suggest you use java.sql.Timestamp instead of java.sql.Date or java.lang.Time for two reasons. First, Timestamp supports the parsing of SQL92 Timestamp escape syntax. Second, it's good programming practice to set times manually to midnight if you are using only the date portion. The fact that Timestamp supports SQL92 escape syntax makes it easier to set the time to midnight.

Remember what I said earlier: "...unless you are writing data-processing-type stored procedures." Since conversions take place whenever an Oracle SQL data type is accessed as a Java data type, it can be more efficient to use the proprietary Oracle Java types such as `oracle.sql.CHAR`, `oracle.sql.DATE`, and `oracle.sql.NUMBER` in some situations. If you are writing a data-intensive program such as a conversion program to read data from one set of tables and write it to another set, then you should consider using the proprietary Oracle data types. To use them, you'll have to cast your `java.sql.ResultSet` to an `oracle.jdbc.driver.OracleResultSet`.

Now that you have a thorough understanding of which data type mappings are possible and a mapping strategy, let's look at the accessor methods you can use to perform the mapping and get the values from a `ResultSet` object.

Accessor Methods

As I alluded to earlier in the section on cursor positioning, the `ResultSet` object has a set of methods that allow you to get access to the column values for a row in a result set. These `ResultSet` accessor methods are affectionately called the getXXX( ) methods. The XXX is a placeholder for one of the Java data types from Table 10-1. Well, almost. When the XXX is replaced with a class name such as Double, which is a wrapper class for the primitive double, the getXXX( ) method returns the primitive data type, not an instance of the class. For example, getString( ) returns a String object, whereas getDouble( ) (Double is the name of a wrapper class for the primitive data type double) returns a double primitive type, not an instance of the wrapper class Double. The getXXX( ) methods have two signatures:

```
dataType getdataType (int columnIndex)
dataType getdataType (String columnName)
```

which breaks down as:

dataType
> One of the Java data types from Table 10-1. For primitive data types that have wrapper classes, the class name is appended to get. For example, the primitive double data type has a wrapper class named Double, so the get method is named getDouble( ), but the primitive data type's value is passed as the second parameter, not as an instance of its wrapper class.

columnIndex
> The position of the column in the select list, from left to right, starting with 1.

columnName
> The name or alias for the column in the select list. This value is not case-sensitive.

Using the columnIndex form of the getXXX( ) methods is more efficient than the columnName form, because the driver does not have to deal with the extra steps of parsing the column name, finding it in the select list, and turning it into a number. In addition, The columnName form does not work if you use the Oracle extension I talked about in Chapter 9 to predefine column types to improve efficiency. I suggest you use the columnIndex form whenever possible.

Let's take a look at Example 10-1, which uses the getXXX( ) methods.

Example 10-1. Using the getXXX() methods

```
import java.io.*;
import java.sql.*;
import java.text.*;

public class GetXXXMethods {
  Connection conn;

  public GetXXXMethods( ) {
    try {
      DriverManager.registerDriver(new oracle.jdbc.driver.OracleDriver( ));
      conn = DriverManager.getConnection(
        "jdbc:oracle:thin:@dssw2k01:1521:orcl", "scott", "tiger");
    }
    catch (SQLException e) {
      System.err.println(e.getMessage( ));
      e.printStackTrace( );
    }
  }

  public static void main(String[] args)
   throws Exception, IOException {
    new GetXXXMethods().process( );
  }

  public void process( ) throws IOException, SQLException {
    double    age       = 0;
    long      person_id = 0;
    String    name      = null;
    Timestamp birth_date = null;
    int       rows      = 0;
    ResultSet rslt      = null;
    Statement stmt      = null;
    try {
      stmt = conn.createStatement( );
      rslt = stmt.executeQuery(
       "select person_id, " +
       "       last_name||', '||first_name name, " +
       "       birth_date, " +
       "       ( months_between( sysdate, birth_date ) / 12 ) age " +
       "from   PERSON " +
       "where  last_name  = 'O''Reilly' " +
       "and    first_name = 'Tim'");
      if (rslt.next( )) {
        rows++;
        person_id  = rslt.getLong(1);
        name       = rslt.getString(2);
        birth_date = rslt.getTimestamp(3);
        age        = rslt.getDouble(4);
```

Example 10-1. Using the getXXX() methods (continued)

```
        System.out.println("person_id  = " +
         new Long(person_id).toString());
        System.out.println("name       = " + name);
        System.out.println("birth_date = " +
         new SimpleDateFormat("MM/dd/yyyy").format(birth_date));
        System.out.println("age        = " +
         new DecimalFormat("##0.#").format(age));
      }

      rslt.close();
      rslt = null;
      stmt.close();
      stmt = null;
    }
    catch (SQLException e) {
      System.err.println(e.getMessage());
    }
    finally {
      if (rslt != null)
        try { rslt.close(); } catch (SQLException ignore) { }
      if (stmt != null)
        try { stmt.close(); } catch (SQLException ignore) { }
    }
  }

  protected void finalize()
    throws Throwable {
    if (conn != null)
      try { conn.close(); } catch (SQLException ignore) { }
    super.finalize();
  }
}
```

Our sample program, GetXXXMethods, exercises four of the getXXX() methods. The first, getLong(), returns the person row's primary key, a NUMBER, as a primitive data type long. The second, getString(), returns the person's concatenated name, a VARCHAR2, as a String. The third, getTimestamp(), returns the person's birth date, a DATE, as a Timestamp, and the last, getDouble(), returns the person's current age, a NUMBER, as a primitive type double.

But what happens when a returned database value is NULL? For example, what would the primitive data type double for age equal had there been no birth date? It would have been 0. That doesn't make much sense, does it? So how do you detect and handle NULL database values?

Handling NULL Values

SQL's use of NULL values and Java's use of null are different concepts. In a database, when a column has a NULL value, that means that the column's value is unknown. In Java, a null means that an object type variable has been initialized with no reference to an instance of an object. The key point here is that a Java variable that can hold an object reference can be null, but a primitive data type cannot. And when a Java variable is null, it does not mean that its value is unknown, but that there is no object reference stored in the variable. So how do you handle SQL NULL values in Java? There are three tactics you can use:

- Avoid using getXXX( ) methods that return primitive data types.
- Use wrapper classes for primitive data types, and use the `ResultSet` object's `wasNull( )` method to test whether the wrapper class variable that received the value returned by the getXXX( ) method should be set to null.
- Use primitive data types and the `ResultSet` object's `wasNull( )` method to test whether the primitive variable that received the value returned by the getXXX( ) method should be set to an acceptable value that you've chosen to represent a NULL.

Avoiding the use of primitive data types

Our first tactic is to not use any of the getXXX( ) methods that return a primitive data type. This works because the getXXX( ) methods that return an object reference return a null object reference when the corresponding column in the database has a NULL value. Primarily, this means that we don't use getInt( ), getDouble( ), and so forth for numeric data types. The SQL DATE and VARCHAR2 data types do not have a Java primitive data type that they can be mapped to, so with those types you are always retrieving object references. Instead, for SQL NUMBER columns, use `java.math.BigDecimal` variables to hold references from the `ResultSet` object's `getBigDecimal( )` method, as shown in Example 10-2.

Example 10-2. Handling NULL values, tactic one

```
import java.io.*;
import java.math.*;
import java.sql.*;
import java.text.*;

public class HandlingNullValues1 {
  Connection conn;

  public HandlingNullValues1( ) {
    try {
      DriverManager.registerDriver(new oracle.jdbc.driver.OracleDriver( ));
      conn = DriverManager.getConnection(
        "jdbc:oracle:thin:@dssw2k01:1521:orcl", "scott", "tiger");
    }
    catch (SQLException e) {
      System.err.println(e.getMessage( ));
      e.printStackTrace( );
    }
  }
}
```

Example 10-2. Handling NULL values, tactic one (continued)

```java
    public static void main(String[] args)
     throws Exception, IOException {
      new HandlingNullValues1().process();
    }

    public void process() throws IOException, SQLException {
      BigDecimal aBigDecimal = null;
      String     aString     = null;
      Timestamp  aTimestamp  = null;
      int        rows        = 0;
      ResultSet  rslt        = null;
      Statement  stmt        = null;
      try {
        stmt = conn.createStatement();
        rslt = stmt.executeQuery(
         "select to_char( NULL ), " +
         "       to_date( NULL ), " +
         "       to_number( NULL ) " +
         "from   sys.dual");
        if (rslt.next()) {
          rows++;
          aString     = rslt.getString(1);
          aTimestamp  = rslt.getTimestamp(2);
          aBigDecimal = rslt.getBigDecimal(3);

          System.out.println("a String     = " + aString);
          System.out.println("a Timestamp  = " + aTimestamp);
          System.out.println("a BigDecimal = " + aBigDecimal);
        }
        rslt.close();
        rslt = null;
        stmt.close();
        stmt = null;
      }
      catch (SQLException e) {
        System.err.println(e.getMessage());
      }
      finally {
        if (rslt != null)
          try { rslt.close(); } catch (SQLException ignore) { }
        if (stmt != null)
          try { stmt.close(); } catch (SQLException ignore) { }
      }
    }

    protected void finalize()
     throws Throwable {
      if (conn != null)
        try { conn.close(); } catch (SQLException ignore) { }
      super.finalize();
    }
}
```

The output of the sample program, `HandlingNullValues1`, is:

```
a String     = null
a Timestamp  = null
a BigDecimal = null
```

Example 10-2 demonstrates that you can use a variable's null reference to track a database's NULL value in your program. There is one drawback to this tactic: the `BigDecimal` object is expensive compared to the primitive numeric data types in terms of both memory consumption and CPU cycles when it comes to computation. A middle-of-the-road solution is to use wrapper classes to store a column's value and the `ResultSet` object's `wasNull( )` method to detect NULL values.

Using wrapper classes

Our second tactic, then, is to use wrapper classes for primitive data types complemented with the `ResultSet` object's `wasNull( )` method. For any database column that normally uses an object variable, such as SQL VARCHAR2 using `String`, it's business as usual. For a SQL NUMBER, use the appropriate wrapper class—for example, use the `Double` wrapper class for a `double` value—and then call the `wasNull( )` method to determine whether the last `getXXX( )` method call's corresponding column had a NULL value. The `wasNull( )` method has the following signature:

```
boolean wasNull( )
```

`wasNull( )` returns true if the last `getXXX( )` method call's underlying column had a NULL value. If the `getXXX( )` method call does reference a column with a NULL value, set the wrapper class variable to null as in the `process( )` method shown in Example 10-3.

Example 10-3. Handling NULL values, tactic two

```java
import java.io.*;
import java.math.*;
import java.sql.*;
import java.text.*;

public class HandlingNullValues2 {
  Connection conn;

  public HandlingNullValues2( ) {
    try {
      DriverManager.registerDriver(new oracle.jdbc.driver.OracleDriver( ));
      conn = DriverManager.getConnection(
        "jdbc:oracle:thin:@dssw2k01:1521:orcl", "scott", "tiger");
    }
    catch (SQLException e) {
      System.err.println(e.getMessage( ));
      e.printStackTrace( );
    }
  }
```

Example 10-3. Handling NULL values, tactic two (continued)

```java
public static void main(String[] args)
 throws Exception, IOException {
   new HandlingNullValues2().process();
}

public void process() throws IOException, SQLException {
   Double      aDouble = null;
   int         rows    = 0;
   ResultSet   rslt    = null;
   Statement   stmt    = null;
   try {
     stmt = conn.createStatement();
     rslt = stmt.executeQuery(
       "select to_number( NULL ) from sys.dual");
     if (rslt.next()) {
       rows++;

       aDouble = new Double(rslt.getDouble(1));

       System.out.println("before wasNull() a Double = " + aDouble);

       if (rslt.wasNull())
         aDouble = null;

       System.out.println("after  wasNull() a Double = " + aDouble);
     }
     rslt.close();
     rslt = null;
     stmt.close();
     stmt = null;
   }
   catch (SQLException e) {
     System.err.println(e.getMessage());
   }
   finally {
     if (rslt != null)
       try { rslt.close(); } catch (SQLException ignore) { }
     if (stmt != null)
       try { stmt.close(); } catch (SQLException ignore) { }
   }
}

protected void finalize()
 throws Throwable {
   if (conn != null)
     try { conn.close(); } catch (SQLException ignore) { }
   super.finalize();
 }
}
```

In our second sample program, HandlingNullValues2, the program creates a wrapper class variable aDouble to hold a Double object initialized by the double value returned from the ResultSet object's getDouble( ) method. After making the call to getDouble( ), the program calls the ResultSet object's wasNull( ) method to check for NULL values. If there are NULL values in the underlying column, then the program sets the aDouble variable to a null reference. Here's the output from the program:

```
before wasNull( ) a Double = 0.0
after  wasNull( ) a Double = null
```

Notice how the getDouble( ) method returns a double value of 0.0? That's because all primitives in Java cannot be null, and therefore, a default value is given to them when they are created. If getting 0.0 back for a column with NULL values is OK, then you don't have to be concerned about handling NULL values at all.

This tactic of using wrapper classes is the most efficient method for handling NULL values, but it still requires extra memory and CPU cycles along with additional programming effort. If your numeric values have the right characteristics, you might try the third tactic, which is to use some agreed upon value to flag NULL values.

Representing NULL with a special value

The third tactic for handling NULL values is to use a primitive data type to hold the data returned from a getXXX( ) method, then use wasNull( ) and a predetermined special value to flag NULL values. For example, in an accounting system report in which you add up different columns to equal a total amount, you may set a Java double to hold a value retrieved from a database to 0 when the value from the database is NULL. Or you may use a numeric value that you know cannot be valid, such as −1.0. Example 10-4 uses −1.0 to represent NULL values.

Example 10-4. Handling NULL values, tactic three

```java
import java.io.*;
import java.math.*;
import java.sql.*;
import java.text.*;

public class HandlingNullValues3 {
  Connection conn;

  public HandlingNullValues3( ) {
    try {
      DriverManager.registerDriver(new oracle.jdbc.driver.OracleDriver( ));
      conn = DriverManager.getConnection(
        "jdbc:oracle:thin:@dssw2k01:1521:orcl", "scott", "tiger");
    }
    catch (SQLException e) {
      System.err.println(e.getMessage( ));
      e.printStackTrace( );
    }
  }

  public static void main(String[] args)
   throws Exception, IOException {
```

Example 10-4. Handling NULL values, tactic three (continued)

```
    new HandlingNullValues3().process();
  }

  public void process() throws IOException, SQLException {
    // dNull is the agreed-upon flag value for a NULL from the database
    double    dNull    = -1.0;
    double    adouble;
    int       rows     = 0;
    ResultSet rslt     = null;
    Statement stmt     = null;
    try {
      stmt = conn.createStatement();
      rslt = stmt.executeQuery(
       "select to_number( NULL ) from sys.dual");
      if (rslt.next()) {
        rows++;

        adouble = rslt.getDouble(1);

        System.out.println("before wasNull() a double = " + adouble);

        if (rslt.wasNull())
          adouble = dNull;

        System.out.println("after  wasNull() a double = " + adouble);
      }
      rslt.close();
      rslt = null;
      stmt.close();
      stmt = null;
    }
    catch (SQLException e) {
      System.err.println(e.getMessage());
    }
    finally {
      if (rslt != null)
        try { rslt.close(); } catch (SQLException ignore) { }
      if (stmt != null)
        try { stmt.close(); } catch (SQLException ignore) { }
    }
  }

  protected void finalize()
   throws Throwable {
    if (conn != null)
      try { conn.close(); } catch (SQLException ignore) { }
    super.finalize();
  }
}
```

In HandlingNullValues3, the program sets the primitive double variable adouble to −1.0 if the underlying column has a NULL value. This assumes that the column will never have negative values, which is quite restrictive. However, if you can use this tactic, or better yet, use a primitive's default value (0.0 for doubles), this is the most efficient means of dealing with NULL values.

Before we move on to another topic, let's not forget to state the obvious. If the column definition in the database includes the NOT NULL constraint, then you do not need to check for null values at all!

Now that you know how to handle NULL values, let's take a look at the truly dynamic features of a ResultSet, namely those implemented by the ResultSetMetaData object.

ResultSetMetaData

Up to this point, we've been using a getXXX( ) method to retrieve a column value, knowing ahead of time the data type that was appropriate for a corresponding database column. But what if you didn't know? Perhaps you want to build a Java query tool to replace SQL*Plus. A tool like that would allow you to enter any query. How would your program know how many columns are in the result set and what their data types are? To answer this question, you can use the methods provided by the ResultSetMetaData object.

Getting the ResultSetMetaData object

After you execute a SELECT statement and retrieve the ResultSet object, you can use the ResultSet object's getMetaData( ) method to retrieve a ResultSetMetaData object that will give you all the details you need to know to dynamically manipulate the ResultSet. The getMetaData( ) method has the following signature:

```
ResultSetMetaData getMetaData( )
```

Getting column information

The ResultSetMetaData object has a set of get and is methods you can use to dynamically determine information about a result set at runtime. The first method in the list that follows, getColumnCount( ), is the only method that is not column-specific. It returns the number of columns in the result set, starting with 1. Following is a list of the get and is methods. For most of the methods in this list, you'll pass the column number as a parameter.

int getColumnCount( )
> Gets the number of columns in the ResultSet.

String getSchemaName(int column)
> Gets a column's table's schema name. Unfortunately, this method does not work for JDBC driver Version 8.1.6.

String getTableName(int column)
> Gets a column's table name. Unfortunately, this method does not work for JDBC driver Version 8.1.6.

```
String getCatalogName(int column)
```
Gets a column's table's catalog name. Since there are no catalogs in Oracle, this method has no use.

```
String getColumnName(int column)
```
Gets a column's name. This should return the column name as it exists in the database, but it returns the alias for a column if an alias was used.

```
String getColumnLabel(int column)
```
Gets the suggested column title for printouts and displays. This method returns the column name or the alias if one was used.

```
String getColumnTypeName(int column)
```
Gets a column's database-specific data type name.

```
int getColumnType(int column)
```
Gets a column's `java.sql.Types` constant.

```
String getColumnClassName(int column)
```
Gets the fully qualified Java class name of the object that will be returned by a call to the `ResultSet.getObject( )` method.

```
int getColumnDisplaySize(int column)
```
Gets the column's normal maximum width in characters.

```
int getPrecision(int column)
```
Gets the number of decimal digits supported by a NUMBER column.

```
int getScale(int column)
```
Gets the number of digits to the right of the decimal point in a NUMBER column.

```
int isNullable(int column)
```
Indicates whether the column is nullable. This method returns one of the following `ResultSetMetaData` constants:

```
static int columnNoNulls
```
The column may not contain NULL.

```
static int columnNullable
```
The column may contain NULL.

```
static int columnNullableUnknown
```
The nullability of the column is unknown.

```
boolean isAutoIncrement(int column)
```
Indicates whether the column is automatically numbered and is thus read-only. There is currently no use for this method with Oracle, because Oracle does not implement auto-incrementing columns.

```
boolean isCaseSensitive(int column)
```
Indicates whether a column's case matters.

```
boolean isCurrency(int column)
```
Indicates whether the column is a cash value. Oracle does not have a money or currency SQL data type, so this method returns true for any numeric SQL data type.

```
boolean isSigned(int column)
```
Indicates whether values in the column are signed numbers.

```
boolean isSearchable(int column)
```
Indicates whether the column can be used in a WHERE clause.

```
boolean isReadOnly(int column)
```
Indicates whether a column is definitely not writeable.

```
boolean isWritable(int column)
```
Indicates whether it is possible for a write on the column to succeed.

```
boolean isDefinitelyWritable(int column)
```
Indicates whether a write on the column will definitely succeed.

Getting column values

When you are retrieving column values from a result set but do not know which data type they are, you can use a special getXXX( ) method, getObject( ), to retrieve a column value as an instance of the Java class Object. Since all Java objects are descendants of the class Object, you can cast the retrieved Object to a specific descendant type. You'll utilize this technique if you use the ResultSetMetaData object. If you combine the getColumnCount( ) method with the getColumnClassName( ) and ResultSet object's getObject( ) method, you can dynamically get the column values of a result set. Here's how it works. The getColumnCount( ) method returns the actual number of columns in the result set. You can use this number in a for loop to retrieve the column values for each column and use the getColumnClassName( ) method to determine the fully qualified Java class name of the object that is returned when you call the getObject( ) method. You can then use the class name to create an appropriate variable to hold the value returned by getObject( ) and perform an appropriate cast. One of the four overloaded getObject( ) method signatures is:

```
Object getObject(int columnIndex)
```

If you call the getColumnClassName( ) method, and it returns java.lang.BigDecimal, then you'll create a BigDecimal variable and cast the results of a call to getObject( ) to a BigDecimal:

```
BigDecimal column1 = (BigDecimal) rslt.getObject(1)
```

A ResultSetMetaData example

Now that we've covered the ResultSetMetaData object's capabilities, let's take a look at Example 10-5, which uses some of the ResultSetMetaData methods to dynamically retrieve the result set data.

In our sample program, TestMetaData, the program uses the Statement object's execute( ) method to enable the program to execute any SQL statement. If the execute( ) method returns true, a ResultSet object is available, and the program proceeds by calling the Statement object's getResultSet( ) method to retrieve the ResultSet object. Otherwise, the program calls the Statement object's getUpdateCount( ) method to get the number of rows affected by the SQL statement just executed.

If a ResultSet object was returned, the program continues by calling the ResultSet object's getMetaData( ) method to retrieve the result set's ResultSetMetaData object. Using that object, the program calls the getColumnCount( ) method to determine the number of columns in the result set. Next, the program enters a while loop where it iterates through the entire result set one row at a time. For the first row, the program calls a helper method, formatHeader( ), passing the values returned by the ResultSetMetaData object's getColumnLabel( ), getColumnClassName( ), and getColumnDisplaySize( ) methods. The formatHeader( ) method creates an appropriate heading for each column. For each row, the program calls a helper method, formatColumn( ), passing the values returned by the ResultSet object's getObject( ) method and the ResultSetMetaData object's getColumnClassName( ) and getColumnDisplaySize( ) methods. Both helper methods work in a similar fashion, so let's just talk about formatColumn( ) in detail.

In formatColumn( ), the program initializes a String value to an empty set. For each possible class name, the program tests to see if the object is a null reference. If it is, formatColumn( ) returns a properly padded blank String object; otherwise, it creates a String representation of the corresponding object and returns it right- or left-padded with spaces.

Example 10-5. Using ResultSetMetaData

```
import java.io.*;
import java.math.*;
import java.sql.*;
import java.text.*;

public class TestMetaData {
  Connection conn;

  public TestMetaData( ) {
    try {
      DriverManager.registerDriver(new oracle.jdbc.driver.OracleDriver( ));
      conn = DriverManager.getConnection(
        "jdbc:oracle:thin:@dssw2k01:1521:orcl", "scott", "tiger");
    }
    catch (SQLException e) {
      System.err.println(e.getMessage( ));
      e.printStackTrace( );
    }
  }
}
```

Example 10-5. Using ResultSetMetaData (continued)

```
public static void main(String[] args)
  throws Exception, IOException {
  TestMetaData tmd = new TestMetaData( );

  tmd.process(
    "select to_char( NULL )  a_char,  " +
    "       to_date( NULL )  a_date,  " +
    "       to_number( NULL ) a_number " +
    "from    sys.dual");

  tmd.process(
    "select 'ABCDEFG' a_char,     " +
    "       sysdate    a_date,     " +
    "       1          an_integer, " +
    "       1.1        a_float     " +
    "from    sys.dual");

  tmd.process(
    "delete PERSON " +
    "where  1 = 0");
}

public void process(String sql) throws IOException, SQLException {
  int             columns = 0;
  int             i       = 0;
  int             rows    = 0;
  ResultSet       rslt    = null;
  ResultSetMetaData meta  = null;
  Statement       stmt    = null;

  try {
    stmt = conn.createStatement( );
    if (stmt.execute(sql)) {
      rslt = stmt.getResultSet( );
      meta = rslt.getMetaData( );
      columns = meta.getColumnCount( );
      while (rslt.next( )) {
        rows++;
        if (rows == 1) {
          for (i = 1;i <= columns;i++) {
            System.out.print(
            formatHeading(
            meta.getColumnLabel(i),
            meta.getColumnClassName(i),
            meta.getColumnDisplaySize(i)));
          }
          System.out.println("");
        }
        for (i = 1;i <= columns;i++) {
          System.out.print(
          formatColumn(
          rslt.getObject(i),
          meta.getColumnClassName(i),
```

Example 10-5. Using ResultSetMetaData (continued)

```
            meta.getColumnDisplaySize(i)));
        }
        System.out.println("");
      }
      System.out.println("");
      rslt.close();
      rslt = null;
      meta = null;
    }
    else {
      rows = stmt.getUpdateCount();
      System.out.println(Integer.toString(rows) + " rows affected");
      System.out.println("");
    }
    stmt.close();
    stmt = null;
  }
  catch (SQLException e) {
    System.err.println(e.getMessage());
  }
  finally {
    if (rslt != null)
      try { rslt.close(); } catch (SQLException ignore) { }
    if (stmt != null)
      try { stmt.close(); } catch (SQLException ignore) { }
  }
}

private String formatColumn(
 Object object, String className, int displaySize) {
  String value  = "";

  if      (className.equals("java.lang.String")) {
    if (object != null) {
      value = rpad((String)object, displaySize, ' ');
    }
    else {
      value = rpad(value, displaySize, ' ');
    }
  }
  else if (className.equals("java.math.BigDecimal")) {
    if (object != null) {
      BigDecimal n = (BigDecimal)object;
      value = lpad(n.toString(), 9, ' ');
    }
    else {
      value = rpad(value, 9, ' ');
    }
  }
  else if (className.equals("java.sql.Timestamp")) {
    if (object != null) {
      Timestamp ts = (Timestamp)object;
      value = rpad(ts.toString(), 21, ' ');
```

Example 10-5. Using ResultSetMetaData (continued)

```
    }
    else {
      value = rpad(value, 21, ' ');
    }
  }
  else {
    System.err.println("Unsupported class name: " + className);
  }
  return value + " ";
}

private String formatHeading(
 String heading, String className, int displaySize) {
  int    length = displaySize;
  String value  = "";

  if (heading != null) {
    value = heading;
    if      (className.equals("java.lang.String")) {
    }
    else if (className.equals("java.math.BigDecimal")) {
      length = 9;
    }
    else if (className.equals("java.sql.Timestamp")) {
      length = 21;
    }
    else {
      System.err.println("Unsupported class name: " + className);
    }
  }
  return rpad(value, length, ' ') + " ";
}

private String rpad(String in, int length, char pad) {
  StringBuffer out   = new StringBuffer(length);
  int          least = in.length();

  if (least > length)
    least = length;
  out.append(in.substring(0, least));
  int          fill  = length - out.length();
  for (int i=0;i < fill;i++) {
    out.append(pad);
  }
  return out.toString();
}

private String lpad(String in, int length, char pad) {
  StringBuffer out   = new StringBuffer(length);
  int          least = in.length();

  if (least > length)
    least = length;
```

Example 10-5. Using ResultSetMetaData (continued)

```
    out.append(in.substring(0, least));
    int         fill = length - out.length();
    for (int i=0;i < fill;i++) {
      out.insert(0, pad);
    }
    return out.toString();
  }

  protected void finalize()
   throws Throwable {
    if (conn != null)
      try { conn.close(); } catch (SQLException ignore) { }
    super.finalize();
   }
}
```

Instead of using the ResultSetMetaData object's getColumnClassName() method, the program can use the Java instanceof operator to determine the class to which an object belongs. For example:

```
    private String formatColumn(Object object, int displaySize) {
      String value = "";
      if      (object instanceof java.lang.String) {
       value = rpad((String)object, displaySize, ' ');
      }
      else if (object instanceof java.math.BigDecimal) {
       BigDecimal n = (BigDecimal)object;
       value = lpad(n.toString(), 9, ' ');
      }
      else if (object instanceof java.sql.Timestamp) {
       Timestamp ts = (Timestamp)object;
       value = rpad(ts.toString(), 21, ' ');
      }
      else if (object == null) {
       value = rpad(value, displaySize, ' ');
      }
      else {
       System.err.println("Unsupported class: " +
        object.getClass().getName());
      }
      return value + " ";
     }
```

One problem with using instanceof is that you can't identify an object's type when the underlying database column is NULL, because getObject() will return a null reference. For this reason, it is better to use the ResultSetMetaData object's getColumnClassName() method to determine the class of an object.

As far as the ResultSetMetaData object is concerned, we have only scratched the surface here, but if you have to work with a SQL statement built dynamically in your program, you'll know that the JDBC API has all the enabling methods you need in the DatabaseMetaData and ResultSetMetaData objects.

Up to this point all we've been talking about is getting the data from a `ResultSet`; we have conveniently skipped any discussion about row positioning capabilities. So let's tackle that topic next.

Scrollable, Updateable Result Sets

With JDBC 1.0, all result sets could scroll only forward and were read-only. With JDBC 2.0, result sets can scroll in both directions and position the cursor randomly. They are also updateable. To implement this functionality, the `Connection` object's `createStatement( )` method was overloaded with the following signature:

```
Statement createStatement(
  int resultSetType,
  int resultSetConcurrency)
```

For `resultSetType`, there are three possible `ResultSet` constants you can use:

`TYPE_FORWARD_ONLY`
A forward-only cursor.

`TYPE_SCROLL_INSENSITIVE`
A scrollable, positionable result set that is not sensitive to changes made to the database while the `ResultSet` object is open. You would have to create a new `ResultSet` object to see changes made to the database.

`TYPE_SCROLL_SENSITIVE`
A scrollable, positionable result set that can see changes made to the database while the `ResultSet` object is open. Changes made at the database level to any of the column values in the result set are visible.

For `resultSetConcurrency`, there are two possible `ResultSet` constants you can use:

`CONCUR_READ_ONLY`
A read-only ResultSet

`CONCUR_UPDATABLE`
An updateable ResultSet

Since scrollability and sensitivity are independent of updateability, we end up with six possible ResultSet categories:

Forward-only/read-only
Forward-only/updateable
Scroll-insensitive/read-only
Scroll-insensitive/updateable
Scroll-sensitive/read-only
Scroll-sensitive/updateable

Oracle implements scrollability by using a client-side memory cache to store the rows from a scrollable result set. Because of this, you should consider carefully which result sets you make scrollable. A large result set could negatively impact the performance, or cause the failure of, your JVM due to excessive memory consumption. To support updateability, Oracle uses the proprietary SQL data type, ROWID, which uniquely identifies each row in the database. The Oracle JDBC driver automatically retrieves the ROWID for each row in a scrollable result set.

 The default createStatement( ) method, with the signature Statement createStatement( ), creates a forward-only/read-only result set.

Eligible SELECT Statement Rules

The SELECT statement you specify determines whether the ResultSet type and concurrency you specified during the creation of a Statement object is what you will get after the execution of the SQL statement. To create a scroll-sensitive ResultSet, you must:

- Select against only one table
- Explicitly specify the columns for the SELECT statement
- Not use an ORDER BY clause

To create an updateable ResultSet, you must:

- Select against only one table
- Explicitly specify columns for the SELECT statement from a table
- Select all nonnullable columns from the table if you plan to insert new rows via the result set
- Not use an ORDER BY clause

If you can add the pseudo-column ROWID to your list of columns in a SELECT statement, then the statement can probably be used to create a scroll-sensitive, updateable ResultSet.

Downgrade rules

If you attempt to create a result set with an unsuitable SELECT statement, the following downgrade rules apply:

- If you specified TYPE_SCROLL_SENSITIVE, but the JDBC driver can't support it, the type is downgraded to TYPE_SCROLL_INSENSTIVE. If that can't be supported, then the type becomes TYPE_FORWARD_ONLY.
- If you specified CONCUR_UPDATABLE, but the JDBC driver cannot support it, the concurrency is downgraded to TYPE_READ_ONLY.

Verifying the ResultSet category

You can call the ResultSet object's getType( ) and getConcurrency( ) methods after a SELECT statement has been executed to verify the category of the returned result set. The method signatures are:

int getType( )
> Returns a ResultSet object's type constant

int getConcurrency( )
> Returns a ResultSet object's concurrency constant

Scrollability

When you execute a SELECT statement with the executeQuery( ) method, you are returned a ResultSet object. Initially, this ResultSet object's row pointer, or cursor, is positioned before the first row. Typically, you'll use a while loop with the ResultSet object's next( ) method, which returns true if there is another row to position to. You saw several examples of this in Chapter 9. Here's a snippet of code from Example 9-5, ExecuteSelect:

```
stmt = conn.createStatement( );
rslt = stmt.executeQuery(sql);
while (rslt.next( )) {
  rows++;
  System.out.print(rslt.getString("code") + "  ");
  System.out.print(rslt.getString("description") + "  ");
  inactive_date = rslt.getDate("inactive_date");
  if (inactive_date != null)
   System.out.println(df.format(inactive_date));
  else
   System.out.println("NULL");
}
```

After the first call to next( ), the cursor points to the first row of the result set. As the while loop executes, the cursor points to each successive row of the result set until all the results have been referenced, at which point the while loop ends.

There are two types of result sets when it comes to scrollability: forward-only and scrollable. The first is identified by the integer constant TYPE_FORWARD_ONLY and, as the constant's name implies, can scroll forward only one row at a time. With this type of a result set, you can use only the following methods:

boolean next( )
> Moves forward one row

boolean isBeforeFirst( )
> Tests to see if the cursor is positioned before the first row

```
boolean isFirst( )
```
Tests to see if the cursor is positioned on the first row

```
boolean isAfterLast( )
```
Tests to see if the cursor is positioned after the last row

The second type, scrollable, is identified by two integer constants: TYPE_SCROLL_INSENSITIVE and TYPE_SCROLL_SENSITIVE. With these two types you can use the prior cursor positioning methods as well as the following:

```
int getFetchDirection( )
```
Gets the current fetch direction. The value returned will be one of these two constants: FETCH_FORWARD or FETCH_REVERSE.

```
int getRow( )
```
Gets the current row number.

```
setFetchDirection(int direction)
```
Sets the fetch direction. You can use the constants FETCH_FORWARD or FETCH_REVERSE.

 Oracle's JDBC driver for 8.1.6 does not support FETCH_REVERSE. If you need to fetch reversed, use the afterlast( ) method to move to the position after the end of the result set and then use the previous( ) method to scroll backwards through the result set.

```
beforeFirst( )
```
Moves the cursor to a position before the first row.

```
boolean first( )
```
Moves the cursor to the first row. This method returns true if it succeeds and false otherwise (i.e., if there are no rows in the result set).

```
boolean absolute(int row)
```
Moves the cursor to the specified row. If the row is a positive value, the position is relative to the beginning of the result set. If the row is a negative value, the position is relative to the end of the result set. If a value for the row places the cursor on an invalid row number (in other words, one that is before the first, or after the last, row), the cursor is moved before the first row or after the last row, respectively.

```
boolean relative(int rows)
```
Moves the cursor to a specified row relative to the current row. The rows parameter may be either positive or negative. A positive value moves the cursor forward, and a negative value moves the cursor backward. If a value for rows represents an invalid row number that is before the first or after the last row, the cursor is moved before the first or after the last row, respectively.

```
boolean previous( )
        Moves the cursor to the previous row.
boolean last( )
        Moves the cursor to the last row.
afterLast( )
        Moves the cursor beyond the last row.
boolean isLast( )
        Tests to see if the cursor is on the last row.
```

Example 10-6 exercises all these positioning methods.

Example 10-6. TestCursorPositioning methods

```java
import java.io.*;
import java.sql.*;
import java.test.*;

public class TestCursorPositioning {
  Connection conn;

  public TestCursorPositioning( )
    try {
      DriverManager.registerDriver(new oracle.jdbc.driver.OracleDriver( ));
      conn = DriverManager.getConnection(
        "jdbc:oracle:thin:@dssw2k01:1521:orcl", "scott", "tiger");
    }
    catch (SQLException e) {
      System.err.println(e.getMessage( ));
      e.printStackTrace( );
    }
  }

  public static void main(String[] args)
   throws Exception, IOException {
    new TestCursorPositioning( ).process( );
  }

  public void process( ) throws IOException, SQLException {
    int        rows = 0;
    ResultSet rslt = null;
    Statement stmt = null'

    try {
      stmt = conn.createStatement( );
      rslt = stmt.executeQuery(
        "select code, " +
        "       description, " +
        "       inactive_date " +
        "from PERSON_IDENTIFIER_TYPE");

      System.out.println("type          = " +
        formatType(stmt.getResultSetType( )));
```

Example 10-6. TestCursorPositioning methods (continued)

```java
    System.out.println("concurrency    = " +
     formatConcurrency(stmt.getResultSetConcurrency( )));

    System.out.println("before first  = " +
     new Boolean(rslt.isBeforeFirst()).toString( ));

    while (rslt.next( )) {
      rows++;
      if (rslt.isFirst( ))
        System.out.println("the first row = " +
          Integer.toString(rows));

      // Contrary to JDBC API doc, but in accordance with Oracle's doc
      //  if (rslt.isLast( ))
      //    System.out.println("the last row  = " +
      //  Integer.toString(rows));
    }
    System.out.println("after last    = " +
     new Boolean(rslt.isAfterLast()).toString( ));

    System.out.println(Integer.toString(rows) + " rows selected");

    System.out.println(" ");
    rslt.close( );
    rslt = null;
    stmt.close( );
    stmt = null;
  }
  catch (SQLException e) {
    System.err.println(e.getMessage( ));
  }
  finally {
    if (rslt != null)
      try { rslt.close( ); } catch (SQLException ignore) { }
    if (stmt != null)
      try { stmt.close( ); } catch (SQLException ignore) { }
  }

  rows = 0;
  try {
    stmt = conn.createStatement(
    ResultSet.TYPE_SCROLL_SENSITIVE, ResultSet.CONCUR_UPDATABLE);
    rslt = stmt.executeQuery(
    "select code, " +
    "       description, " +
    "       inactive_date " +
    "from   PERSON_IDENTIFIER_TYPE");

    System.out.println("type          = " +
     formatType(stmt.getResultSetType( )));

    System.out.println("concurrency   = " +
     formatConcurrency(stmt.getResultSetConcurrency( )));
```

Example 10-6. TestCursorPositioning methods (continued)

```
System.out.println("before first  = " +
 new Boolean(rslt.isBeforeFirst()).toString( ));

while (rslt.next( )) {
  rows++;
  if (rslt.isFirst( ))
    System.out.println("the first row = " +
     Integer.toString(rows));

  if (rslt.isLast( ))
    System.out.println("the last row  = " +
     Integer.toString(rows));
}
System.out.println("after last    = " +
 new Boolean(rslt.isAfterLast()).toString( ));

System.out.println(Integer.toString(rows) +
 " rows selected");

if (rslt.previous( ))
  System.out.println("the prev row  = " +
   Integer.toString(rslt.getRow( )));

if (rslt.relative(-1))
  System.out.println("rel -1 row    = " +
   Integer.toString(rslt.getRow( )));

if (rslt.absolute(2))
  System.out.println("abs 2 row     = " +
   Integer.toString(rslt.getRow( )));

rslt.beforeFirst( );

System.out.println("bef first row = " +
 Integer.toString(rslt.getRow( )));

if (rslt.first( ))
System.out.println("first row     = " +
  Integer.toString(rslt.getRow( )));

if (rslt.last( ))
 System.out.println("last row      = " +
  Integer.toString(rslt.getRow( )));

rslt.afterLast( );

System.out.println("aft last row  = " +
 Integer.toString(rslt.getRow( )));

System.out.println(" ");
rslt.close( );
rslt = null;
stmt.close( );
```

Example 10-6. TestCursorPositioning methods (continued)

```
      stmt = null;
    }
    catch (SQLException e) {
      System.err.println(e.getMessage());
    }
    finally {
      if (rslt != null)
        try { rslt.close(); } catch (SQLException ignore) { }
      if (stmt != null)
        try { stmt.close(); } catch (SQLException ignore) { }
    }
  }

  private String formatType(int type) {
    switch (type) {
      case ResultSet.TYPE_FORWARD_ONLY:
        return "TYPE_FORWARD_ONLY";
      case ResultSet.TYPE_SCROLL_INSENSITIVE:
        return "TYPE_SCROLL_INSENSITIVE";
      case ResultSet.TYPE_SCROLL_SENSITIVE:
        return "TYPE_SCROLL_SENSITIVE";
      default:
        return "TYPE_UNKNOWN";
    }
  }

  private String formatConcurrency(int Concurrency) {
    switch (Concurrency) {
      case ResultSet.CONCUR_READ_ONLY:
        return "CONCUR_READ_ONLY";
      case ResultSet.CONCUR_UPDATABLE:
        return "CONCUR_UPDATABLE";
      default:
        return "CONCUR_UNKNOWN";
    }
  }

  protected void finalize()
   throws Throwable {
    if (conn != null)
      try { conn.close(); } catch (SQLException ignore) { }
    super.finalize();
  }
}
```

Example 10-6 produces the following output:

```
type          = TYPE_FORWARD_ONLY
concurrency   = CONCUR_READ_ONLY
before first  = true
the first row = 1
after last    = true
2 rows selected
```

```
type          = TYPE_SCROLL_SENSITIVE
concurrency   = CONCUR_UPDATABLE
before first  = true
the first row = 1
the last row  = 2
after last    = true
2 rows selected
the prev row  = 2
rel -1 row    = 1
abs 2 row     = 2
bef first row = 0
first row     = 1
last row      = 2
aft last row  = 0
```

Updateability

A ResultSet object created using the CONCUR_UPDATABLE constant can be used not only to select rows from the database but also to insert, update, and delete rows in a table. Most often, CONCUR_UPDATABLE is used in conjunction with TYPE_SCROLL_SENSITIVE to give the programmer total control of the result set. To support updateability, the resulting ResultSet object implements a second set of accessor methods, updateXXX( ) methods, to set column values for an insert or update operation. These updateXXX( ) methods have the following signatures:

```
update*dataType* (int columnIndex, *dataType x*)
update*dataType* (String columnName, *dataType x*)
```

which break down as:

dataType
> One of the Java data types from Table 10-1. For primitive data types that have wrapper classes, the class name is appended to update. For example, the primitive double data type has a wrapper class named Double, so the update method is named updateDouble( ), but the primitive data type's value is passed as the second parameter, not as an instance of its wrapper class.

columnIndex
> The number of the column in the select list, from left to right, starting with 1.

columnName
> The name or alias for the column in the select list.

x
> The new column value.

As with the getXXX( ) methods, the updateXXX( ) methods that use columnIndex are more efficient than those that use columnName.

Inserting a new row into a result set

To perform an insert operation on a ResultSet, first call the ResultSet object's moveToInsertRow( ) method to position the cursor to a blank, insertable row. Next, call one or more of the required updateXXX( ) methods to set the values for each column. The updateXXX( ) methods are used to set column values for updateable result sets in a way similar to the way in which the getXXX( ) methods get values from columns. When inserting a row into a result set, you must set the column values for all NOT NULL columns. It is not necessary to set the values for nullable columns; their unset values will be NULL.

When you are done setting the column values with the updateXXX( ) methods, call the ResultSet object's insertRow( ) method to generate and send the appropriate INSERT statement to the database. You may then return to the row position prior to the call to the moveToInsertRow( ) method by calling the moveToCurrentRow( ) method. Positioning to another row before calling the insertRow( ) method cancels the insert operation.

Keep in mind that any row inserted into the database from a ResultSet object insert is not visible to the current result set. Nor will any row inserted by another user of the database be visible to the current result set. You must recreate the ResultSet object to see any newly inserted rows.

Updating a row in a result set

To perform an update operation, first position the cursor in the desired row using any of the cursor position methods we have discussed that are appropriate for the ResultSet type. Next, use the updateXXX( ) methods as necessary to update the values of columns. If you wish to set a nullable column to NULL, use the ResultSetobject's updateNull( ) method. When you're finished updating the columns in the result set, call the ResultSet object's updateRow( ) method to generate the appropriate UPDATE statement and send it to the database. Positioning to another row or calling the ResultSet object's cancelRowUpdate( ) method before calling updateRow( ) cancels the update, restoring columns to their original values.

Updates made in your ResultSet object will be visible in your result set, while updates made by other database users will be visible to your result set only after a call is made to the ResultSet object's refreshRow( ) method. The refreshRow( ) method refreshes the current row, and possibly others adjacent to it in the result set, depending on the number of rows you have specified for the JDBC driver to prefetch. refreshRow( ) is called implicitly when you update a row (using updateRow( )).You can also call it explicitly whenever you desire.

Deleting a row in a result set

To perform a delete operation, first position the cursor in the desired row. Then call the ResultSet object's deleteRow( ) method to generate the appropriate DELETE statement and send it to the database. Your delete operation will be visible in a scrollable ResultSet object but not in a forward-only one. In a scrollable result set, the preceding row becomes the current row after a delete operation. Deletes performed by other users will not be visible to your ResultSet object. You must recreate the ResultSet object to detect these external deletes.

Update visibility and detection

Visibility and detection are two distinct concepts. *Visibility* is whether your result set can *see* changes performed internally or externally. *Detection* is whether your result set is notified when an external change takes place.

 Oracle ResultSet objects do not have any detection capability, although it appears from the JDBC specification that they should.

Operations that take place in your result set are called internal changes. Internal insert operations are not visible to any of the three ResultSet types: TYPE_FORWARD_ONLY, TYPE_SCROLL_INSENSITIVE, or TYPE_SCROLL_SENSITIVE. Internal update operations are visible for all three. Internal deletes are visible for TYPE_SCROLL_INSENSITIVE and TYPE_SCROLL_SENSITIVE result sets but not for TYPE_FORWARD_ONLY.

Outside changes—those outside the current program's transaction context—are visibly only if they are updates, because an update does an implicit refresh. This is true even for changes performed by a trigger on a table updated as part of the current transaction. External inserts or deletes are never visible.

 Since an Oracle ResultSet object does not have detection capability, its detection methods—rowInserted( ), rowUpdated( ), and rowDeleted( )—always return false.

The following are the nine DatabaseMetaData methods you can call to determine the current support for visibility and detection. They take one of the three ResultSet type constants for an argument, and they all can throw a SQLException.

```
boolean ownInsertsAreVisible(int)
boolean ownUpdatesAreVisible(int)
boolean ownDeletesAreVisible(int)
boolean othersInsertsAreVisible(int)
boolean othersUpdatesAreVisible(int)
boolean othersDeletesAreVisible(int)
boolean insertsAreDetected(int)
boolean updatesAreDetected(int)
boolean deletesAreDetected(int)
```

As mentioned earlier, an updateRow( ) method call for a SCROLL_SENSITIVE ResultSet object makes an implicit refreshRow( ) call for an updated row. What actually happens when this refresh occurs is that the entire prefetch buffer, typically 10 rows of data, is refreshed. Only the prefetch buffer is refreshed, not the whole result set. And even with the refresh, any internal or external inserts and any external deletes do not become visible.

 The Oracle JDBC driver Version 8.1.6 does not automatically enforce write locks or check for update conflicts. You are responsible for managing these issues manually!

Since Oracle uses ROWID to identify the rows in the database for updating, it is almost always appropriate to use a pessimistic locking scheme to ensure you don't overwrite someone else's changes (I cover this issue thoroughly in Chapter 18). To accomplish this, you should use the FOR UPDATE NOWAIT clause with your SELECT statement to lock the rows you retrieve from the database. You must also turn off auto-commit; otherwise, the first insert, update, or delete operation will release the locks. When you use the NOWAIT option with the FOR UPDATE clause, you will get the following error in a SQLException if another user has already locked the resource:

```
ORA-00054: resource busy and acquire with NOWAIT specified
```

Table 10-2 summarizes the effects that the three different ResultSet types have on visibility.

Table 10-2. Summary of visibility

Can see	Forward-only	Scroll-insensitive	Scroll-sensitive
Own inserts	NO	NO	NO
Own updates	YES	YES	YES
Own deletes	NO	YES	YES
Other's inserts	NO	NO	NO
Other's updates	NO	NO	YES
Other's deletes	NO	NO	NO

Example 10-7 demonstrates the use of an updateable result set to insert, update, and delete a row.

Example 10-7. Inserting, updating, and deleting with ResultSet objects

```
import java.io.*;
import java.sql.*;
import java.text.*;

public class TestResultSetUpdates {
  Connection conn;
```

Example 10-7. Inserting, updating, and deleting with ResultSet objects (continued)

```java
public TestResultSetUpdates( ) {
  try {
    DriverManager.registerDriver(new oracle.jdbc.driver.OracleDriver( ));
    conn = DriverManager.getConnection(
      "jdbc:oracle:thin:@dssw2k01:1521:orcl", "scott", "tiger");
  }
  catch (SQLException e) {
    System.err.println(e.getMessage( ));
    e.printStackTrace( );
  }
}

public static void main(String[] args)
 throws Exception, IOException {
  new TestResultSetUpdates().process( );
}

public void process( ) throws IOException, SQLException {
  BufferedReader in   =
   new BufferedReader(new InputStreamReader(System.in));
  int          rows = 0;
  ResultSet    rslt = null;
  Statement    stmt = null;
  String       sql  =
   "select code,         " +
   "       description,  " +
   "       inactive_date " +
   "from   PERSON_IDENTIFIER_TYPE";
   // can't use for update clause because of driver defect

  try {
    conn.setAutoCommit(false);
    stmt = conn.createStatement(
     ResultSet.TYPE_SCROLL_SENSITIVE, ResultSet.CONCUR_UPDATABLE);
    rslt = stmt.executeQuery(sql);
    System.out.println("type        = " +
     formatType(stmt.getResultSetType( )));
    System.out.println("concurrency = " +
     formatConcurrency(stmt.getResultSetConcurrency( )));
    while (rslt.next( )) {
      rows++;
      if (rslt.getString(1).equals("SDL")) {
        rslt.deleteRow( );
        System.out.print("Deleted, press Enter to continue...");
        System.out.println("");
        in.readLine( );
      }
    }
    rslt.moveToInsertRow( );
    rslt.updateString(1, "SDL");
    rslt.updateString(2, "State Drivers License");
    rslt.updateNull(3);
    rslt.insertRow( );
    rslt.moveToCurrentRow( );
```

```java
      System.out.print("Inserted, press Enter to continue...");
      System.out.println("");
      in.readLine();

      stmt.close();
      stmt = null;
      rslt.close();
      rslt = null;
    }
    catch (SQLException e) {
      System.err.println(e.getMessage());
    }
    finally {
      if (rslt != null)
        try { rslt.close(); } catch (SQLException ignore) { }
      if (stmt != null)
        try { stmt.close(); } catch (SQLException ignore) { }
    }

    try {
      stmt = conn.createStatement(
       ResultSet.TYPE_SCROLL_SENSITIVE, ResultSet.CONCUR_UPDATABLE);
      rslt = stmt.executeQuery(sql);
      while (rslt.next()) {
        rows++;
        if (rslt.getString(1).equals("SDL")) {
          rslt.updateString(2, "State Driver's License");
          rslt.updateRow();
          System.out.print("Updated, press Enter to continue...");
          System.out.println("");
          in.readLine();
        }
      }
      conn.commit();
      System.out.print("Committed, press Enter to continue...");
      System.out.println("");
      in.readLine();

      stmt.close();
      stmt = null;
      rslt.close();
      rslt = null;
    }
    catch (SQLException e) {
      System.err.println(e.getMessage());
    }
    finally {
      if (rslt != null)
        try { rslt.close(); } catch (SQLException ignore) { }
      if (stmt != null)
        try { stmt.close(); } catch (SQLException ignore) { }
    }
  }
```

```
  private String formatType(int type) {
    switch (type) {
      case ResultSet.TYPE_FORWARD_ONLY:
        return "TYPE_FORWARD_ONLY";
      case ResultSet.TYPE_SCROLL_INSENSITIVE:
        return "TYPE_SCROLL_INSENSITIVE";
      case ResultSet.TYPE_SCROLL_SENSITIVE:
        return "TYPE_SCROLL_SENSITIVE";
      default:
        return "TYPE_UNKNOWN";
    }
  }

  private String formatConcurrency(int concurrency) {
    switch (concurrency) {
      case ResultSet.CONCUR_READ_ONLY:
        return "CONCUR_READ_ONLY";
      case ResultSet.CONCUR_UPDATABLE:
        return "CONCUR_UPDATABLE";
      default:
        return "CONCUR_UNKNOWN";
    }
  }

  protected void finalize( )
   throws Throwable {
    if (conn != null)
      try { conn.close( ); } catch (SQLException ignore) { }
    super.finalize( );
  }
}
```

Our sample program, TestResultSetUpdates, starts in its main( ) method where it instantiates itself and executes its process( ) method. In the process( ) method, the program wraps standard input with a BufferedReader, so the person executing the program can pause execution at each step to see its effect from another session. Then the program turns off auto-commit and proceeds by creating a scroll-sensitive, updateable Statement object, which in turn is used to create an appropriate ResultSet object. The SELECT statement executed by the Statement object retrieves a list of codes from the PERSON_IDENTIFIER_TYPE table. Next, the program loops through the result set using a while loop with the next( ) method. In the while loop, the program tests for an entry with a code of SDL. If it finds that entry, it deletes it. After the while loop, the program inserts a new row. Since this new row is not visible, and we want to update it, the program continues by recreating the result set. It then updates the code SDL entry's description. After that, the modifications are committed to the database.

Did you notice that, contrary to my own advice, I did not use the FOR UPDATE NOWAIT clause? That's because the 8.1.6 implementation of updateable result sets has a known defect wherein it reports the following error in a SQLException if you attempt to use FOR UPDATE NOWAIT:

```
ORA-00907: missing right parenthesis
```

This brings up a good question. Given the current FOR UPDATE clause defect with Oracle ResultSet objects, what practical uses do they have? Personally, I am not a fan of the current implementation of result sets, partly because I don't like to use pessimistic locking. It is more efficient to use other means to update the database. So let's take a look at reasons not to use updateable ResultSet objects.

Reasons Not to Use Updateable Result Sets

The first type of updateable ResultSet object is a forward-only result set. Using my imagination, I guess that forward-only result sets can be used to batch update one or more of a table's columns. However, an update statement with a simple or complex, single- or multicolumn, subquery can most often accomplish this kind of update. Using a procedural solution for a set problem is one of the mistakes many developers make. We need to use the inherent capabilities of SQL whenever possible.

If the process of determining the updateable data for an update statement is too complex for a subquery, it would be more efficient to use a batched, prepared statement in Java to make the updates than a result set. I discuss batched, prepared statements in Chapter 11.

The second type of updateable ResultSet object is a scroll-insensitive result set. You use this with the FOR UPDATE NOWAIT clause. In this scenario, you would first turn off auto-commit. Then you would perform your query using the FOR UPDATE NOWAIT clause. Using FOR UPDATE NOWAIT in your query causes Oracle to immediately lock all the rows in the table that meet your query's WHERE clause criteria. The exception is if someone else has previously locked one or more of those rows, in which case, you get a SQLException. You can use FOR UPDATE without the NOWAIT option, but then your program may wait indefinitely for access to the desired rows while another user has them locked. You can use a scroll insensitive result set for this type of update, because once your program has locked the desired rows, no one else can change them. Consequently, it's not necessary to see external changes, a capability a scroll-sensitive ResultSet object would give you, because no one else can make any changes to the rows in your pessimistically locked result set. However, as I have already stated, there is currently a defect in the driver that makes this approach impossible to use.

The third and last possibility is to use a scroll-sensitive ResultSet object. It has the same problems as the scroll-insensitive ResultSet plus, since ROWID is all that is used in the WHERE clause of the subsequently generated update statement, you have no guarantee you won't destroy another user's valid changes.

I'm sure, even with the problems I've just discussed, that some of you will find valid reasons to use updateable result sets. In time, I believe updateable ResultSet objects will further evolve into a more useful implementation, but for now, I would use them cautiously.

ResultSet Is an OracleResultSet

The ResultSet class we have been discussing, java.sql.ResultSet, is an interface that is implemented by oracle.jdbc.driver.OracleResultSet. Beyond the standard JDBC 2.0 implementation, OracleResultSet has the following proprietary methods, all of which can throw a SQLException:

```
ARRAY getARRAY(int columnIndex)
ARRAY getARRAY(String columnName)
BFILE getBfile(int columnIndex)
BFILE getBfile(String columnName)
BFILE getBFILE(int columnIndex)
BFILE getBFILE(String columnName)
BLOB getBLOB(int columnIndex)
BLOB getBLOB(String columnName)
CHAR getCHAR(int columnIndex)
CHAR getCHAR(String columnName)
CLOB getCLOB(int columnIndex)
CLOB getCLOB(String columnName)
ResultSet getCursor(int columnIndex)
ResultSet getCURSOR(String columnName)
CustomDatum getCustomDatum(int columnIndex, CustomDatumFactory factory)
CustomDatum getCustomDatum(String columnName, CustomDatumFactory factory)
DATE getDATE(int columnIndex)
DATE getDATE(String columnName)
NUMBER getNUMBER(int columnIndex)
NUMBER getNUMBER(String columnName)
Datum getOracleObject(int columnIndex)
Datum getOracleObject(String columnName)
RAW getRAW(int columnIndex)
RAW getRAW(String columnName)
REF getREF(int columnIndex)
REF getREF(String columnName)
ROWID getROWID(int columnIndex)
ROWID getROWID(String columnName)
STRUCT getSTRUCT(int columnIndex)
STRUCT getSTRUCT(String columnName)

updateArray(int columnIndex, Array x)
updateArray(String columnName, Array x)
updateARRAY(int columnIndex, ARRAY x)
updateARRAY(String columnName, ARRAY x)
updateBfile(int columnIndex, BFILE X)
updateBfile(String columnName, BFILE x)
```

```
updateBFILE(int columnIndex, BFILE x)
updateBFILE(String columnName, BFILE x)
updateBlob(int columnIndex, Blob x)
updateBlob(String columnName, Blob x)
updateBLOB(int columnIndex, BLOB x)
updateBLOB(String columnName, BLOB x)
updateCHAR(int columnIndex, CHAR x)
updateCHAR(String columnName, CHAR x)
updateClob(int columnIndex, Clob x)
updateClob(String columnName, Clob x)
updateCLOB(int columnIndex, CLOB x)
updateCLOB(String columnName, CLOB x)
updateCustomDatum(int columnIndex, CustomDatum x)
updateCustomDatum(String columnName, CustomDatum x)
updateDATE(int columnIndex, DATE x)
updateDATE(String columnName, DATE x)
updateNUMBER(int columnIndex, NUMBER x)
updateNUMBER(String columnName, NUMBER x)
updateOracleObject(int columnIndex, Datum x)
updateOracleObject(String columnName, Datum x)
updateRAW(int columnIndex, RAW x)
updateRAW(String columnName, RAW x)
updateRef(int columnIndex, Ref x)
updateRef(String columnName, Ref x)
updateREF(int columnIndex, REF x)
updateREF(String columnName, REF x)
updateROWID(int columnIndex, ROWID x)
updateROWID(String columnName, ROWID x)
updateSTRUCT(int columnIndex, STRUCT x)
updateSTRUCT(String columnName, STRUCT x)
```

You may have noticed that up to this point, we have not taken a look at large objects (LOBs) or object data types. As I stated earlier, we'll cover objects in Part III. As for large data types, we need to cover another type of statement object, a PreparedStatement, to have a complete discussion about the large object data types: BFILE, BLOB, CLOB, LONG, and LONG RAW. So let's continue our discussion of JDBC with prepared statements in Chapter 11.

Prepared Statements

Similar to their statement counterparts, prepared statements can be used to insert, update, delete, or select data. However, prepared statements are precompiled statements that can be reused to execute identical SQL statements with different values more efficiently. They make only one trip to the database for metadata, whereas statements make a round trip with each execution. In addition, since bind variables are used, the database compiles and caches the prepared SQL statement and reuses it on subsequent executions to improve the database's performance. Prepared statements are also useful because some types of values, such as BLOBs, objects, collections, REFs, etc., are not representable as SQL text. To support this added functionality, you use a question mark as a placeholder within the text of a SQL statement for values that you wish to specify when you execute that statement. You can then replace that question mark with an appropriate value using one of the many available setXXX( ) accessor methods. setXXX( ) methods are available for setting every data type, just as getXXX( ) methods are available for getting the values for any data type from a result set.

In this chapter, we'll discuss the benefits of using a prepared statement versus a statement, how to format SQL statements for use with a PreparedStatement object, how to use the various setXXX( ) methods, String data type limitations when using a PreparedStatement object, and batching. Let's start by discussing the pros and cons of using a prepared statement.

A Prepared Statement Versus a Statement

It's a popular belief that using a PreparedStatement object to execute a SQL statement is faster than using a Statement object. That's because a PreparedStatement object makes only one round trip to the database to get its data type information when it is first prepared, while a Statement object must make an extra round trip to the database to get its metadata each time it is executed. So the simple conclusion is that on the second and subsequent executions of a prepared statement, it is 50% faster than a statement. However, according to my tests in Chapter 19, due to the overhead of using a PreparedStatement object, it takes at least 65 executions before a PreparedStatement object is faster than a Statement object. For a small number of executions, a PreparedStatement object is not faster than a Statement object.

However, that doesn't mean you shouldn't use a PreparedStatement. On the contrary, if you use the batch capabilities of a PreparedStatement object to execute the same SQL statement many times, it is significantly faster than a Statement object. Oracle's implementation of JDBC implements batching only for PreparedStatement objects, not for Statement objects.

Prepared statements are less dynamic than their statement counterparts; you can build a SQL statement dynamically at runtime, but doing so using a prepared statement requires more coding, and the code required is fairly specific to the task. Prepared statements can, however, greatly simplify formulating your SQL statements, because you don't have to worry about date formats, number formats, or tick characters in strings. And prepared statements allow you to insert or update streaming data types.

The advantages of using prepared statements are that they allow you to improve efficiency by batching, utilize the SQL statement cache in the database to increase its efficiency, simplify your coding, and allow you to insert or update streaming data types, which we'll cover in Chapter 12.

Formulating SQL Statements

When you write a prepared statement, you use a question mark character (?) as a placeholder that will later be replaced by a value you specify using a setXXX( ) method. These placeholders can be used only for values that need to be specified in a SQL statement and not in place of SQL keywords; they can't be used to implement a type of macro language. When building SQL statements, you must abide by certain rules. For an INSERT statement, you can use placeholders only in the VALUES list. For example:

```
insert into person_identifier_type
( code, description, inactive_date )
values
( ?, ?, ? )
```

In this example, the first placeholder, or question mark (?), represents the value for the code column; the second represents the description column, and the third represents the inactive_date column.

For an UPDATE statement, you can use placeholders only in the SET VALUES list and in the WHERE clause. For example:

```
update person_identifier_type
set    description = ?
where  code = ?
```

In this example, the first placeholder represents the new value for the description column, while the second represents a value for the code column in the WHERE clause.

For a DELETE statement, you can use the placeholder only in the WHERE clause. For example:

```
delete person_identifier_type
where  code = ?
```

Finally, for a SELECT statement, you can use the placeholder in the SELECT list, WHERE clause, GROUP BY clause, and ORDER BY clause. For example:

```
select ?, code, description
from   person_identifier_type
where code = ?
order by ?
```

 Important! The question-mark placeholder used in the select list represents a value to be supplied, not a column name.

Did you notice that in these examples, there are no ticks around placeholders that represent character columns? That's because the PreparedStatement object takes care of properly formatting the data. It's important for you to understand that the placeholders allow you to provide actual values before you execute a SQL statement, and once a prepared statement is compiled (i.e., prepared), it can be executed repeatedly with different values supplied for each execution.

Now that you can properly formulate a SQL statement for a PreparedStatement, let's look at the setXXX( ) methods used to set the values for the placeholders.

Accessor Methods

There is a setXXX( ) method for each of the Java data types listed in the righthand column of Table 10-1. Of course, as with the getXXX( ) methods, you must use the appropriate setXXX( ) method for a given SQL type.

The setXXX( ) methods generally have the following signature:

```
setdataType (int parameterIndex, dataType x)
```

which breaks down as:

parameterIndex
    The number of the placeholder in the SQL statement, counting from left to right and starting with 1.

dataType
    A class name from Table 10-1, except for data types with both a primitive data type and a wrapper class, in which case the second parameter is the primitive

data type. For example, with setDouble( ), the parameter x would be of type double.

Let's take a look at two examples. In the first, *dataType* is not a wrapper class. If the column last_name in the person table is a VARCHAR2(30) and is the second parameter in a prepared SQL statement, then an appropriate setXXX( ) method would be setString( ):

```
String lastName = "O'Reilly"
pstmt.setString(2, lastName);
```

In this case, the set suffix, String, and the parameter data type, String, are both the class name, i.e., initial letter capitalized. However, if you need to update a numeric database column, say person_id in the person table (person_id is a NUMBER), and you're using a Java long data type, which is a primitive, then an appropriate setXXX( ) method would be setLong( ):

```
long personId = 1;
pstmt.setLong(1, personId);
```

This time, the set suffix, Long, is capitalized like the wrapper class name for a long. The second parameter, however, is a long data type, the Java primitive data type. The general rule is that you pass class types for everything except the Java primitive data types that represent numbers; those are the primitive data types.

SQL type constants

Since JDBC acts as an interface between Java and a particular vendor's database, JDBC has a standard set of SQL type codes that Java and JDBC drivers use to identify SQL data types. These JDBC type codes, which are integer constants defined in the java.sql.Types class, are used by the various PreparedStatement and CallableStatement accessor methods to map the database's SQL data types to Java data types, and vice versa. Table 11-1 lists the standard Oracle SQL type to Java data type mappings, and Table 11-2 lists the proprietary Oracle SQL type to Java type mappings.

Table 11-1. Standard Oracle SQL type to Java data type mappings

Oracle SQL data types	JDBC types constants (java.sql.Types.)	Standard Java data types	Oracle Java data types (oracle.sql.)
CHAR	CHAR	java.lang.String	CHAR
VARCHAR2	VARCHAR	java.lang.String	CHAR
LONG	LONGVARCHAR	java.lang.String	CHAR
NUMBER	NUMERIC	java.math.BigDecimal	NUMBER
NUMBER	DECIMAL	java.math.BigDecimal	NUMBER
NUMBER	BIT	boolean	NUMBER
NUMBER	TINYINT	byte	NUMBER

Table 11-1. *Standard Oracle SQL type to Java data type mappings (continued)*

Oracle SQL data types	JDBC types constants (java.sql.Types.)	Standard Java data types	Oracle Java data types (oracle.sql.)
NUMBER	SMALLINT	short	NUMBER
NUMBER	INTEGER	int	NUMBER
NUMBER	BIGINT	long	NUMBER
NUMBER	REAL	float	NUMBER
NUMBER	FLOAT	double	NUMBER
NUMBER	DOUBLE	double	NUMBER
RAW	BINARY	byte[]	RAW
RAW	VARBINARY	byte[]	RAW
LONG RAW	LONGVARBINARY	byte[]	RAW
DATE	DATE	java.sql.Date	DATE
DATE	TIME	java.sql.Time	DATE
DATE	TIMESTAMP	java.sql.Timestamp	DATE
BLOB	BLOB	java.sql.Blob	BLOB
CLOB	CLOB	java.sql.Clob	CLOB
user-defined object	STRUCT	java.sql.Struct	STRUCT
user-defined reference	REF	java.sql.Ref	REF
user-defined collection	ARRAY	java.sql.Array	ARRAY

The first column in Table 11-1 lists the Oracle SQL data types. The second column lists the `java.sql.Types` constants that can be associated with each type. These are primarily used with the `PreparedStatement` object's `setObject( )` and with the `CallableStatement` object's `registerOutParameter( )` methods to specify data type conversions between Java and SQL. (We'll cover the `CallableStatement` object's `registerOutParameter( )` in Chapter 13.) However, the `setXXX( )` methods are usually self-specifying. For example, when you use the `setLong( )` method to set a Java `long`, you implicitly specify that the Java data type `long` will be converted to a SQL data type NUMBER. The third column in the table lists the corresponding Java data type for a given `java.sql.Types` constant. The fourth column lists the corresponding Oracle Java data type for a given `java.sql.Types` constant.

Table 11-2. *Proprietary Oracle SQL type to Oracle Java data type mappings*

Oracle SQL data types	Oracle types (oracle.jdbc.driver. OracleTypes.)	Standard Java data types	Oracle Java data types
BFILE	BFILE	n/a	oracle.sql.BFILE
ROWID	ROWID	n/a	oracle.sql.ROWID
REF CURSOR	fCURSOR	java.sql.ResultSet	OracleResultSet

Similar to Table 11-1, the first column in Table 11-2 lists Oracle SQL data types, but these data types are proprietary to Oracle. Accordingly, the second column lists the proprietary Oracle `oracle.jdbc.driver.OracleTypes` constants. The third column lists the corresponding Java data types, and the last column lists the proprietary Oracle Java data types.

NULL values

If you wish to set a parameter in a SQL statement to NULL values, then you must use the setNull( ) method with the following signature:

```
setNull(int parameterIndex, int sqlType)
```

which breaks down as:

parameterIndex
> The position of the placeholder in the SQL statement, counting from left to right and starting with 1

sqlType
> A java.lang.Types constant, which you can find in Table 11-1

For example, here I set the middle_name column to NULL values before inserting it into the database:

```
String insert =
 "insert into person " +
 "( person_id, last_name, first_name, " +
 "middle_name, birth_date, mothers_maiden_name ) " +
 "values " +
 "( ?, ?, ?, ?, ?, ? )";
try {
  pstmt = conn.prepareStatement(insert);
  pstmt.setLong(1, 999999999);
  pstmt.setString(2, "Krishnamurti");
  pstmt.setString(3, "Jiddu");
  pstmt.setNull(4, Types.VARCHAR);
  pstmt.setDate(5, Date.valueOf("1895-05-12"));
  pstmt.setString(6, "Unknown");
  rows - pstmt.executeUpdate();
}
```

Dynamic input

Dynamic input refers to formulating and preparing a SQL statement at runtime. Because you don't know the SQL statement when you write your code, you don't know how many parameters it will have, nor do you know their types. Consequently, you don't know which, or how many, setXXX( ) methods to use, and you need a more general method for setting parameter values. In such a case, you can use the setObject( ) method, which works with the default mappings shown in Tables 11-1 and 11-2. setObject( ) has the following three overloaded signatures:

```
setObject(
  int parameterIndex,
  Object x)

setObject(
  int parameterIndex,
  Object x,
  int targetSqlType)

setObject(
  int parameterIndex,
  Object x,
  int targetSqlType,
  int scale)
```

which break down as:

parameterIndex
> The number of the placeholder in the SQL statement, counting from left to right and starting with 1

Object
> A Java object reference

targetSqlType
> A java.lang.Types constant

scale
> The number of digits to the right of the decimal point for numeric SQL data types

All three methods can throw a SQLException. The first form of setObject( ) assumes the standard mappings shown in Tables 11-1 and 11-2. With the second form of setObject( ), use a java.lang.Types constant to specify the SQL type of the parameter you are setting. The third form of setObject( ) is designed for use with numeric input and enables you to truncate the number of significant digits to the right of the decimal point. For the most part, you'll need only the first form. Here's my earlier example rewritten to use setObject( ):

```
String insert =
  "insert into person " +
  "( person_id, last_name, first_name, " +
  "middle_name, birth_date, mothers_maiden_name ) " +
  "values " +
  "( ?, ?, ?, ?, ?, ? )";
try {
  pstmt = conn.prepareStatement(insert);
  pstmt.setObject(1, new Long(999999999));
  pstmt.setObject(2, "Krishnamurti");
  pstmt.setObject(3, "Jiddu");
  pstmt.setNull(4, Types.VARCHAR);
  pstmt.setObject(5, Date.valueOf("1895-05-12"));
```

```
    pstmt.setObject(6, "Unknown");
    rows = pstmt.executeUpdate( );
  }
```

In this case, because I used setObject( ), the driver must take an extra step to deter-mine the data type being passed to it. Consequently, it's more efficient to use the spe-cific setXXX( ) methods whenever possible. Notice how I used new Long(999999999) to specify a value for the person_id column. I did this because you can't pass a Java primitive when using the setObject( ) methods. Instead, you need to use a wrapper class around the Java primitive numeric data types (also called integrals in the JDK API documentation).

Dynamic input using the Oracle data types

If you wish to work with the Oracle data types in oracle.sql.*, then you need to cast your PreparedStatement object to an OraclePreparedStatement object and use its setOracleObject( ) method:

```
String            insert =
 "insert into person " +
 "( person_id, last_name, first_name, " +
 "middle_name, birth_date, mothers_maiden_name ) " +
 "values " +
 "( ?, ?, ?, ?, ?, ? )";
try {
  pstmt = conn.prepareStatement(insert);

  ((OraclePreparedStatement)pstmt).setOracleObject(
   1, new NUMBER(999999999));

  ((OraclePreparedStatement)pstmt).setOracleObject(
   2, new CHAR("Krishnamurti", CHAR.DEFAULT_CHARSET));

  ((OraclePreparedStatement)pstmt).setOracleObject(
   3, new CHAR("Jiddu", CHAR.DEFAULT_CHARSET));

  ((OraclePreparedStatement)pstmt).setNull(
   4, Types.VARCHAR);

  ((OraclePreparedStatement)pstmt).setOracleObject(
   5, new DATE(Date.valueOf("1895-01-01")));

  ((OraclePreparedStatement)pstmt).setOracleObject(
   6, new CHAR("Unknown", CHAR.DEFAULT_CHARSET));

  rows = ((OraclePreparedStatement)pstmt).executeUpdate( );
  }
```

Fixed-length CHAR columns

There is one proprietary setXXX( ) method you need to be aware of. It is the OraclePreparedStatement object's setFixedCHAR( ). You need to use this if the col-umn you are setting in a WHERE clause is an Oracle CHAR data type, which is fixed-length and right-padded with spaces. `setFixedCHAR( )` sets the column's value and adds any right padding as necessary. To use it, you need to cast your `PreparedStatement` object to an `OraclePreparedStatement` object, as in the following example:

```
PreparedStatement pstmt = conn.prepareStatement( );
((OraclePreparedStatement)pstmt).setFixedCHAR(1, code);
```

Of course, as I have already stated several times in this book, I would never use a CHAR database type.

A prepared statement example

Example 11-1 demonstrates the use of placeholders and the setXXX( ) methods for all four types of DML statements.

Example 11-1. Test placeholders and setter methods

```java
import java.io.*;
import java.sql.*;
import java.text.*;

public class TestPlaceHolder {
  Connection conn;

  public TestPlaceHolder( ) {
    try {
      DriverManager.registerDriver(new oracle.jdbc.driver.OracleDriver( ));
      conn = DriverManager.getConnection(
        "jdbc:oracle:thin:@dssw2k01:1521:orcl", "scott", "tiger");
    }
    catch (SQLException e) {
      System.err.println(e.getMessage( ));
      e.printStackTrace( );
    }
  }

  public static void main(String[] args)
   throws Exception, IOException {
    new TestPlaceHolder().process( );
  }

  public void process( ) throws IOException, SQLException {
    int              rows   = 0;
    ResultSet        rslt   = null;
    PreparedStatement pstmt  = null;

    String           insert =
     "insert into person_identifier_type " +
     "( code, description, inactive_date ) " +
     "values " +
     "( ?, ?, ? )";
    String           update =
     "update person_identifier_type " +
```

Example 11-1. Test placeholders and setter methods (continued)

```
  "set    description = ? " +
  "where  code = ?";
String              delete =
  "delete person_identifier_type " +
  "where  code = ?";
String              select =
  "select ?, code, description " +
  "from   person_identifier_type " +
  "where  code = ? " +
  "order by ?";
try {
  System.out.println(insert);
  pstmt = conn.prepareStatement(insert);
  pstmt.setString( 1, "STD" );
  pstmt.setString( 2, "Student Id" );
  pstmt.setNull( 3, Types.TIMESTAMP );
  rows = pstmt.executeUpdate( );
  pstmt.close( );
  pstmt = null;
  System.out.println(rows + " rows inserted");
  System.out.println("");
}
catch (SQLException e) {
  System.err.println(e.getMessage( ));
}
finally {
  if (pstmt != null)
    try { pstmt.close( ); } catch (SQLException ignore) { }
}

try {
  System.out.println(update);
  pstmt = conn.prepareStatement(update);
  pstmt.setString( 1, "Student ID" );
  pstmt.setString( 2, "SID" );
  rows = pstmt.executeUpdate( );
  pstmt.close( );
  pstmt = null;
  System.out.println(rows + " rows updated");
  System.out.println("");
}
catch (SQLException e) {
  System.err.println(e.getMessage( ));
}
finally {
  if (pstmt != null)
    try { pstmt.close( ); } catch (SQLException ignore) { }
}

try {
  System.out.println(select);
  pstmt = conn.prepareStatement(select);
  pstmt.setString( 1, "A CONSTANT" );
```

Example 11-1. Test placeholders and setter methods (continued)

```
      pstmt.setString( 2, "SID" );
      pstmt.setString( 3, "A" );
      rslt = pstmt.executeQuery( );
      rows = 0;
      while (rslt.next( )) {
        rows++;
        System.out.print(rslt.getString(1) + " ");
        System.out.print(rslt.getString(2) + " ");
        System.out.println(rslt.getString(3));
      }
      pstmt.close( );
      pstmt = null;
      System.out.println(rows + " rows selected");
      System.out.println("");
    }
    catch (SQLException e) {
      System.err.println(e.getMessage( ));
    }
    finally {
      if (rslt  != null)
        try { rslt.close( );  } catch (SQLException ignore) { }
      if (pstmt != null)
        try { pstmt.close( ); } catch (SQLException ignore) { }
    }

    try {
      System.out.println(delete);
      pstmt = conn.prepareStatement(delete);
      pstmt.setString( 1, "SID" );
      rows = pstmt.executeUpdate( );
      pstmt.close( );
      pstmt = null;
      System.out.println(rows + " rows deleted");
    }
    catch (SQLException e) {
      System.err.println(e.getMessage( ));
    }
    finally {
      if (pstmt != null)
        try { pstmt.close( ); } catch (SQLException ignore) { }
    }
  }

  protected void finalize( )
   throws Throwable {
    if (conn != null)
      try { conn.close( ); } catch (SQLException ignore) { }
    super.finalize( );
  }
}
```

Our sample program, `TestPlaceHolder`, starts in its `main( )` method by instantiating itself. It then executes its `process( )` method. The `process( )` method first creates a `PreparedStatement` object for an INSERT statement by calling the `Connection` object's `prepareStatement( )` method. The program then makes three `setXXX( )` method calls using the resulting `PreparedStatement` object:

1. The `setString( )` method is invoked twice to set the `code` and `description` column values.

2. The `setNull( )` method is invoked to set `inactive_date` to NULL values.

Once values have been supplied for all the placeholders, the prepared statement is executed using its `executeUpdate( )` method. This method reports the number of rows affected, and the program echoes that number to the screen. The program goes on to perform similar tasks using an UPDATE, a SELECT, and finally, a DELETE statement.

Limits

When using the `setBytes( )` or `setString( )` methods, there are limits to the amount of data you can specify for a placeholder without using a large data type such as a BFILE, BLOB, CLOB, LONG RAW, or LONG. Table 11-3 lists these size limitations.

Table 11-3. Size limitations for binary and character data

Database	Binary data setBytes( )	Character data setString( )
Oracle7	255 bytes	2,000 bytes
Oracle8	2,000 bytes	4,000 bytes
Oracle8i	2,000 bytes	4,000 bytes

Notice that Table 11-3 specifies the size limitations in terms of bytes, not characters. If you use a multibyte character set, the maximum number of characters you can pass to `setString( )` is affected by the number of bytes required for each character. Assuming three bytes per character, which some character sets require, 4,000 bytes would allow you room for only 1,333 characters. Getting around these limitations is why the large, streaming data types exist, and they are the subject of our next chapter.

Defining Parameter Types

Oracle has a proprietary method, `defineParameterType( )`, which is similar to the `defineColumnType( )` method for SELECT statements (`defineColumnType( )` is covered in Chapter 9). The `defineParameterType( )` method can be used to optimize memory consumption by reducing the size of the temporary buffers allocated to hold the values passed by the setXXX( ) methods before binding them to a SQL statement. The defineParamterType( ) method has the following signature:

```
defineParameterType(
  int parameterIndex,
  int type,
  int maximumSize)
```

which breaks down as:

parameterIndex
> The number of the parameter or placeholder in the SQL statement, counting from left to right and starting with 1

type
> One of the java.sql.Types or oracle.sql.OracleTypes constants

maximumSize
> The maximum size in bytes of the passed value

You can use the defineParameterType( ) method to reduce the default buffer size for a String from 4 KB to a smaller number of bytes if that is all that is needed. This reduces the amount of memory consumed for JDBC driver buffers. You must call this method after you create the PreparedStatement and before you call any of the setXXX( ) methods. Example 11-2 uses defineParameterType( ) to specify buffer sizes of 30 and 80 bytes for the code and description columns, respectively.

Example 11-2. Defining parameter types

```java
import java.io.*;
import java.sql.*;
import java.text.*;
import oracle.jdbc.driver.*;

public class TestDefineParameterType {
  Connection conn;

  public TestDefineParameterType( ) {
    try {
      DriverManager.registerDriver(new oracle.jdbc.driver.OracleDriver( ));
      conn = DriverManager.getConnection(
        "jdbc:oracle:thin:@dssw2k01:1521:orcl", "scott", "tiger");
    }
    catch (SQLException e) {
      System.err.println(e.getMessage( ));
      e.printStackTrace( );
    }
  }

  public static void main(String[] args)
   throws Exception, IOException {
    new TestDefineParameterType().process( );
  }
```

Example 11-2. Defining parameter types (continued)

```java
public void process( ) throws IOException, SQLException {
    int             rows  = 0;
    ResultSet       rslt  = null;
    PreparedStatement pstmt = null;
    String          insert =
     "insert into person_identifier_type " +
     "( code, description, inactive_date ) " +
     "values " +
     "( ?, ?, ? )";
    String          delete =
     "delete person_identifier_type " +
     "where  code = ?";

    try {
      System.out.println(insert);
      pstmt = conn.prepareStatement(insert);

      ((OraclePreparedStatement)pstmt).defineParameterType(
        1, Types.VARCHAR, 30);

      ((OraclePreparedStatement)pstmt).defineParameterType(
        2, Types.VARCHAR, 80);

      pstmt.setString( 1, "SID" );
      pstmt.setString( 2, "Student Id" );
      pstmt.setNull( 3, Types.TIMESTAMP );
      rows = pstmt.executeUpdate( );
      System.out.println(rows + " rows inserted");
      System.out.println("");
      pstmt.close( );
      pstmt - null;
    }
    catch (SQLException e) {
      System.err.println(e.getMessage( ));
    }
    finally {
      if (pstmt != null)
        try { pstmt.close( ); } catch (SQLException ignore) { }
    }

    try {
      System.out.println(delete);
      pstmt = conn.prepareStatement(delete);

      ((OraclePreparedStatement)pstmt).defineParameterType(
        1, Types.VARCHAR, 30);

      pstmt.setString( 1, "SID" );
      rows = pstmt.executeUpdate( );
      System.out.println(rows + " rows deleted");
    }
    catch (SQLException e) {
```

Example 11-2. Defining parameter types (continued)

```
      System.err.println(e.getMessage( ));
    }
    finally {
      if (pstmt != null)
        try { pstmt.close( ); } catch (SQLException ignore) { }
    }
  }

  protected void finalize( )
   throws Throwable {
    if (conn != null)
      try { conn.close( ); } catch (SQLException ignore) { }
    super.finalize( );
  }
}
```

Our sample program, TestDefineParameterType, creates a PreparedStatement for an INSERT statement. It then defines the parameter types for the code and description columns, reducing the buffer size for those columns to match the maximum size of each column as specified in the person_identifier_type table definition. Next, the program calls the appropriate setXXX( ) methods to set values for those columns, and the PreparedStatement is executed. This basic process is then repeated for a DELETE statement. Note that, unlike its counterpart defineColumnType( ), the defineParameterType( ) method does not have to be called for every parameter in a SQL statement.

Now that you know how to conserve memory during your inserts, updates, and deletes, let's take a look at how to conserve network bandwidth and improve response time by taking advantage of JDBC's batching features.

Batching

Batching allows you to gather multiple SQL statements for the same PreparedStatement into a batch. The statements in that batch are in turn sent to the database together instead of sent one statement at a time. This reduces the consumption of network bandwidth by eliminating the overhead of redundant packet headers in small packets. Instead, the statements are transmitted in one or more larger packets. Batching also eliminates the extra data required by Oracle to packetize and unpacketize the sent data.

There are two forms of batching available: the JDBC 2.0 standard model and the Oracle proprietary model. You'll want to use the standard implementation if you are concerned with portability, and use Oracle's implementation if you want to get the best performance, but you cannot mix the two batching formats. If you do, you'll get a SQLException.

Oracle supports batching only for prepared statements. Although it does provide the methods for batching statements and callable statements, it does not actually support batching for them. So if you want to receive any benefit from batching, you must use prepared statements.

Standard Batching Implementation

Taking a look at the big picture, standard batching works as follows. First, you turn off auto-commit and create a prepared statement. Next, you set column values as necessary. Then, instead of calling the executeUpdate( ) method to send the SQL statement to the database immediately, call the addBatch( ) method to add a SQL statement to a batch. Repeat the process of setting values and adding to a batch until you are ready to send the SQL statements to the database. Then, when you are ready to send batched SQL statements to the database, call the executeBatch( ) method. The executeBatch( ) method in turn sends the SQL statements in the batch to the database all at once. Finally, commit your database changes by calling Connection.commit( ). Let's start our lesson on batching by looking at adding a SQL statement to a batch in more detail.

Adding rows to a batch

With the standard JDBC 2.0 implementation, you'll use two methods to implement batching. The first, addBatch( ), adds a SQL statement to a batch. It has the following signature:

    void addBatch( )

All the batching methods can throw a SQLException.

To "execute" a statement, call the PreparedStatement object's addBatch( ) method instead of the executeUpdate( ) method. This will add your prepared statement to a batch of SQL statements, which will then be sent to the database for processing when you call the second method, executeBatch( ).

Executing a batch

The second method, executeBatch( ), sends any batched SQL statements to the database for execution all at once. It has the following signature:

    int[] executeBatch( )

Call the executeBatch( ) method when you are ready to send your batched SQL statements to the database for processing. The int array returned by executeBatch( ), sometimes referred to as the *updates array*, contains the number of rows affected by each statement executed as part of the batch. Unfortunately, for prepared statements, it is not possible to know the number of rows affected by each statement, so you'll get only a value of –2 for each successful operation. You can also use the getUpdateCounts( ) method to retrieve the array of update counts for the most recently executed batch. If an error occurs during the execution of a batch, a BatchUpdateException is generated. If you examine the updates array while in a BatchUpdateException, all elements will have a value of –3, which means, not surprisingly, that there was a batch execution error. In such a situation, you should probably roll back your transaction, but that is a matter of application design, not an absolute recommendation on my part. One final point: it is more efficient if you call the executeBatch( ) method after a specified number of adds, rather than when all rows are batched. I recommend doing so after 5–30 operations.

Canceling a batch

If you wish to discard your batched SQL statements, call the clearBatch( ) method, which has the following signature:

```
void clearBatch( )
```

You must call either executeBatch( ) or clearBatch( ) before calling the executeUpdate( ) method or you'll get a SQLException.

Dependencies

Although Oracle's documentation states that the SQL statements in a batch are processed in the order in which they are added to the batch, discussion on the Oracle Technology Network's JDBC forum suggests otherwise. So, if your inserts are dependent on each other (that is, they must be executed in the order that you insert them, as would be the case with a table that references itself), then you won't be able to batch them.

You should also turn off auto-commit if you wish to get the best performance from batching. Otherwise, the database will commit after each batch execution. Remember that you must commit your batch by calling the Connection object's commit( ) method after you call the executeBatch( ) method.

If either of the two batching models encounters a large data type such as BFILE, BLOB, LONG RAW, CLOB, or LONG, batching is disabled.

A standard batching example

Example 11-3 demonstrates the use of standard batching. Briefly, the program has five try blocks. The first turns off auto-commit. The second inserts the number of rows specified by the first command-line argument to the program, using a Statement object. The third does the same, this time using a PreparedStatement object, but does not use any batching features. The fourth try block uses JDBC 2.0 standard batching. Instead of calling executeUpdate( ), each INSERT statement is added to the batch by a call to the addBatch( ) method. Then, after all rows are added to the batch but not yet inserted into the database, the batch is sent to the database by a call to the executeBatch( ) method. Finally, the fifth try block deletes the rows from the table to allow another invocation to start with an empty table.

Example 11-3. Standard batching

```
import java.io.*;
import java.sql.*;
import java.text.*;

public class TestStandardBatching {
  Connection conn;

  public TestStandardBatching( ) {
    try {
      DriverManager.registerDriver(new oracle.jdbc.driver.OracleDriver( ));
      conn = DriverManager.getConnection(
        "jdbc:oracle:thin:@dssw2k01:1521:orcl", "scott", "tiger");
    }
    catch (SQLException e) {
      System.err.println(e.getMessage( ));
      e.printStackTrace( );
    }
  }

  public static void main(String[] args)
    throws Exception, IOException {
    new TestStandardBatching( ).process(args[0]);
  }

  public void process(String iterations) throws IOException, SQLException {
    int             rows   = 0;
    int             last   = new Integer(iterations).intValue( );
    long            start  = 0;
    long            end    = 0;
    Statement       stmt   = null;
    PreparedStatement pstmt = null;
    String          text   =
      "12345678901234567890123456789012345678901234567890" +
      "12345678901234567890123456789012345678901234567890" +
      "12345678901234567890123456789012345678901234567890" +
      "12345678901234567890123456789012345678901234567890" +
      "12345678901234567890123456789012345678901234567890" +
      "12345678901234567890123456789012345678901234567890" +
      "12345678901234567890123456789012345678901234567890" +
      "12345678901234567890123456789012345678901234567890" +
      "12345678901234567890123456789012345678901234567890" +
      "12345678901234567890123456789012345678901234567890" +
```

Example 11-3. Standard batching (continued)

```
      "12345678901234567890123456789012345678901234567890" +
      "12345678901234567890123456789012345678901234567890" +
      "12345678901234567890123456789012345678901234567890" +
      "12345678901234567890123456789012345678901234567890" +
      "12345678901234567890123456789012345678901234567890" +
      "12345678901234567890123456789012345678901234567890" +
      "12345678901234567890123456789012345678901234567890" +
      "12345678901234567890123456789012345678901234567890" +
      "12345678901234567890123456789012345678901234567890" +
      "12345678901234567890123456789012345678901234567890" +
      "12345678901234567890123456789012345678901234567890" +
      "12345678901234567890123456789012345678901234567890" +
      "12345678901234567890123456789012345678901234567890" +
      "12345678901234567890123456789012345678901234567890" +
      "12345678901234567890123456789012345678901234567890" +
      "12345678901234567890123456789012345678901234567890" +
      "12345678901234567890123456789012345678901234567890" +
      "12345678901234567890123456789012345678901234567890" +
      "12345678901234567890123456789012345678901234567890" +
      "12345678901234567890123456789012345678901234567890" +
      "12345678901234567890123456789012345678901234567890" +
      "12345678901234567890123456789012345678901234567890" +
      "12345678901234567890123456789012345678901234567890" +
      "12345678901234567890123456789012345678901234567890" +
      "12345678901234567890123456789012345678901234567890" +
      "12345678901234567890123456789012345678901234567890" +
      "12345678901234567890123456789012345678901234567890" +
      "12345678901234567890123456789012345678901234567890" +
      "12345678901234567890123456789012345678901234567890" +
      "12345678901234567890123456789012345678901234567890";

    // Turn off auto-commit
    try {
      conn.setAutoCommit(false);
      conn.commit( );
    }
    catch (SQLException e) {
      System.err.println(e.getMessage( ));
    }

    // One statement at a time, awfully slow!
    try {
      start = System.currentTimeMillis( );
      stmt = conn.createStatement( );
      for (int i=0;i < last;i++) {
        rows = stmt.executeUpdate(
          "insert into test_batch " +
          "( test_batch_id, text ) " +
          "values " +
          "( test_batch_id.nextval, '" + text + "' )");
      }
      end = System.currentTimeMillis( );
      stmt.close( );
```

Example 11-3. Standard batching (continued)

```
      stmt = null;
      conn.commit( );
      System.out.println(
       last + " inserts using statement:                   " +
       (end - start) + " milliseconds");
    }
    catch (SQLException e) {
      System.err.println(e.getMessage( ));
    }
    finally {
      if (stmt != null)
        try { stmt.close( ); } catch (SQLException ignore) { }
    }

    // One prepared statement at a time, better!
    try {
      pstmt = conn.prepareStatement(
       "insert into test_batch " +
       "( test_batch_id, text ) " +
       "values " +
       "( test_batch_id.nextval, ? )");
      start = System.currentTimeMillis( );
      for (int i=0;i < last;i++) {
        pstmt.setString( 1, text );
        rows = pstmt.executeUpdate( );
      }
      end = System.currentTimeMillis( );
      pstmt.close( );
      pstmt = null;
      conn.commit( );
      System.out.println(
       last + " inserts using prepared statement:        " +
       (end - start) + " milliseconds");
    }
    catch (SQLException e) {
      System.err.println(e.getMessage( ));
    }
    finally {
      if (pstmt != null)
        try { pstmt.close( ); } catch (SQLException ignore) { }
    }

    // But now using standard batching: wow!!!
    try {
      pstmt = conn.prepareStatement(
       "insert into test_batch " +
       "( test_batch_id, text ) " +
       "values " +
       "( test_batch_id.nextval, ? )");
      start = System.currentTimeMillis( );
      for (int i=0;i < last;i++) {
        pstmt.setString( 1, text );
        pstmt.addBatch( );
```

Example 11-3. Standard batching (continued)

```
        }
        int [] rowArray = pstmt.executeBatch();
        end = System.currentTimeMillis();
        pstmt.close();
        pstmt = null;
        conn.commit();
        System.out.println(
          last + " inserts using prepared statement batching: " +
          (end - start) + " milliseconds");
      }
      catch (SQLException e) {
        System.err.println(e.getMessage());
      }
      finally {
        if (pstmt != null)
          try { pstmt.close(); } catch (SQLException ignore) { }
      }

      // Clean up
      try {
        stmt = conn.createStatement();
        rows = stmt.executeUpdate("delete test_batch");
        conn.commit();
        stmt.close();
        stmt = null;
        System.out.println(rows + " rows deleted");
        System.out.println("");
      }
      catch (SQLException e) {
        System.err.println(e.getMessage());
      }
      finally {
        if (stmt != null)
          try { stmt.close(); } catch (SQLException ignore) { }
      }
    }

  protected void finalize()
    throws Throwable {
    if (conn != null)
      try { conn.close(); } catch (SQLException ignore) { }
    super.finalize();
  }
}
```

Notice that the example saves the current system time before and after execution of
the INSERT statements in order to get a relative measurement of performance. Compile the program and run it the first time specifying a command-line parameter of 1.
Then try the program again using values of 2, 10, 20, 30, 100, and 1,000. You'll
notice that for a small number of inserts, say 1–5, the Statement object is faster than
the PreparedStatement object, unbatched or batched. But when the number of inserts
is six or greater, the batched PreparedStatement is always faster by as much as 30%.

The increase in performance that you get from batching varies depending on the type and size of the SQL statement in question, as well as on the network connection you're using.

Now that you have an understanding of standard batching, let's look at Oracle's proprietary solution.

Oracle's Batching Implementation

Oracle's proprietary batching works as follows. First, as you did with standard batching, turn off auto-commit and create a prepared statement. Next, set an *execute* batch size using one of three methods I'll cover shortly. This batch size is used by Oracle batching to determine when to send a batch to the database. When the number of batched SQL statements reaches the specified batch size, the Oracle driver automatically sends the SQL statements to the database. So instead of calling the executeBatch( ) method at an appropriate interval, the driver takes care of sending SQL statements for you. Now all you have to do is set the column values using the appropriate setXXX( ) methods and then call the executeUpdate( ) method, as you would do normally.

To enable Oracle batching, set the Oracle prepared statement's executeBatch value to a value greater than 1 (the default executeBatch value). To do so, use one of three methods:

- Make a call to the OracleConnection object's setDefaultExecuteBatch( ).
- Specify a defaultExecuteBatch property in a Properties object passed to the Connection object's getConnection( ) method.
- Use the PreparedStatement object's setExecuteBatch( ) method to specify a batch size for a specific statement.

The first two methods set a default batch size for all statements created by a connection. The third method sets a batch size for a specific statement.

Setting a default batch size for a connection

You can set the default batch size for all statements created by a connection by casting your Connection object to an OracleConnection object, then calling its setDefaultExecuteBatch( ) method to set the defaultBatchValue in the OracleConnection object. Then, any subsequent calls to the prepareStatement( ) method for that connection will result in PreparedStatement objects with the batch size you specified as the default. The setDefaultExecutionBatch( ) method has the following signature:

```
void setDefaultExecuteBatch(int batchSize)
```

The batchSize parameter represents the number of executeUpdate( ) invocations that will take place before the batch is automatically sent to the database. This is where the two batching implementations differ: Oracle batching takes place at regularly specified intervals instead of all at once, and it's not necessary to manually execute a batch through an invocation of the executeBatch( ) method. The following example shows the default batch size set to 30:

```
((OracleConnection)conn).setDefaultExecuteBatch(30);
```

Another method for setting the default batch size for a connection is to set the property defaultExecuteBatch in a Properties object that you pass to the getConnection( ) method. For example:

```
Properties info = new Properties( );
info.put( "user", "scott" );
info.put( "password", "tiger" );
info.put( "defaultExecuteBatch", "30" );

Connection conn = DriverManager.getConnection(
  "jdbc:oracle:thin:@dssw2k01:1521:orcl", info );
```

However, you set the default value; doing so for a Connection object affects all subsequent PreparedStatement objects.

Setting a batch size for a specific statement

If you want to set a different batch size for each prepared statement, cast your PreparedStatement object to an OraclePreparedStatement object, then call its setExecuteBatch( ) method. The setExecuteBatch( ) method has the following signature:

```
void setExecuteBatch(int batchSize)
```

For example, to set the batch size for a PreparedStatement to 30:

```
((OraclePreparedStatement)pstmt).setExecuteBatch(30);
```

Forcing batch execution

You can force an OraclePreparedStatement to send its current batch to the database by calling the sendBatch( ) method. This method has the following signature:

```
int sendBatch( )
```

Whenever you call the sendBatch( ) method, it returns the total number of rows affected by all the batched SQL statements. Likewise, when you call executeUpdate( ), and it in turn causes a batch to be sent to the database, it also returns the total number of rows affected by all the batched SQL statements. If, on the other hand, a call to executeUpdate( ) does not trigger the sending of the batch, then no rows are affected, and accordingly, the method will return zero.

It's not necessary, however, to call sendBatch( ) at all, because this is done automatically any time there is a call to the Connection or PreparedStatement object's close( ) method or to the Connection object's commit( ) method.

An Oracle batching example

Example 11-4 demonstrates Oracle batching. Briefly, our second batch test program, TestOracleBatching, is almost exactly like its standard batching counterpart, but with the following changes:

- There is an additional import statement: import oracle.jdbc.driver.*, to support the Oracle objects.

- In its fourth try block, the program starts by turning on Oracle batching with a call to the OraclePreparedStatement object's setExecuteBatch( ) method, passing it an appropriate value from 1 to 30.

- Most notably, the example simply uses the standard executeUpdate( ) method to add statements to the batch transparently. When the executeBatch value is reached, the SQL statements are automatically sent to the database.

Example 11-4. Oracle batching

```
import java.io.*;
import java.sql.*;
import java.text.*;
import oracle.jdbc.driver.*;

public class TestOracleBatching {
  Connection conn;

  public TestOracleBatching( ) {
    try {
      DriverManager.registerDriver(new oracle.jdbc.driver.OracleDriver( ));
      conn - DriverManager.getConnection(
        "jdbc:oracle:thin:@dssw2k01:1521:orcl", "scott", "tiger");
    }
    catch (SQLException e) {
      System.err.println(e.getMessage( ));
      e.printStackTrace( );
    }
  }

  public static void main(String[] args)
   throws Exception, IOException {
    new TestOracleBatching( ).process(args[0]);
  }

  public void process(String iterations)
   throws IOException, SQLException {
    int        rows    = 0;
    int        last    = new Integer(iterations).intValue( );
    long       start   = 0;
    long       end     = 0;
    Statement  stmt    = null;
```

Example 11-4. Oracle batching (continued)

```
PreparedStatement pstmt    = null;
String           text  =
 "12345678901234567890123456789012345678901234567890" +
 "12345678901234567890123456789012345678901234567890" +
 "12345678901234567890123456789012345678901234567890" +
 "12345678901234567890123456789012345678901234567890" +
 "12345678901234567890123456789012345678901234567890" +
 "12345678901234567890123456789012345678901234567890" +
 "12345678901234567890123456789012345678901234567890" +
 "12345678901234567890123456789012345678901234567890" +
 "12345678901234567890123456789012345678901234567890" +
 "12345678901234567890123456789012345678901234567890" +
 "12345678901234567890123456789012345678901234567890" +
 "12345678901234567890123456789012345678901234567890" +
 "12345678901234567890123456789012345678901234567890" +
 "12345678901234567890123456789012345678901234567890" +
 "12345678901234567890123456789012345678901234567890" +
 "12345678901234567890123456789012345678901234567890" +
 "12345678901234567890123456789012345678901234567890" +
 "12345678901234567890123456789012345678901234567890" +
 "12345678901234567890123456789012345678901234567890" +
 "12345678901234567890123456789012345678901234567890" +
 "12345678901234567890123456789012345678901234567890" +
 "12345678901234567890123456789012345678901234567890" +
 "12345678901234567890123456789012345678901234567890" +
 "12345678901234567890123456789012345678901234567890" +
 "12345678901234567890123456789012345678901234567890" +
 "12345678901234567890123456789012345678901234567890" +
 "12345678901234567890123456789012345678901234567890" +
 "12345678901234567890123456789012345678901234567890" +
 "12345678901234567890123456789012345678901234567890" +
 "12345678901234567890123456789012345678901234567890" +
 "12345678901234567890123456789012345678901234567890" +
 "12345678901234567890123456789012345678901234567890" +
 "12345678901234567890123456789012345678901234567890" +
 "12345678901234567890123456789012345678901234567890" +
 "12345678901234567890123456789012345678901234567890" +
 "12345678901234567890123456789012345678901234567890" +
 "12345678901234567890123456789012345678901234567890" +
 "12345678901234567890123456789012345678901234567890" +
 "12345678901234567890123456789012345678901234567890";

// Turn off auto-commit
try {
  conn.setAutoCommit(false);
  conn.commit( );
}
catch (SQLException e) {
  System.err.println(e.getMessage( ));
}
```

Example 11-4. Oracle batching (continued)

```
// One statement at a time, awfully slow!
try {
  start = System.currentTimeMillis();
  stmt = conn.createStatement();
  for (int i=0;i < last;i++) {
    rows = stmt.executeUpdate(
     "insert into test_batch " +
     "( test_batch_id, text ) " +
     "values " +
     "( test_batch_id.nextval, '" + text + "' )");
  }
  end = System.currentTimeMillis();
  stmt.close();
  stmt = null;
  conn.commit();
  System.out.println(
    last + " inserts using statement:              " +
    (end - start) + " milliseconds");
}
catch (SQLException e) {
  System.err.println(e.getMessage());
}
finally {
  if (stmt != null)
     try { stmt.close(); } catch (SQLException ignore) { }
}

// One prepared statement at a time, better!
try {
  pstmt = conn.prepareStatement(
   "insert into test_batch " +
   "( test_batch_id, text ) " +
   "values " +
   "( test_batch_id.nextval, ? )");
  start = System.currentTimeMillis();
  for (int i=0;i < last;i++) {
    pstmt.setString( 1, text );
    rows = pstmt.executeUpdate();
  }
  end = System.currentTimeMillis();
  pstmt.close();
  pstmt = null;
  conn.commit();
  System.out.println(
    last + " inserts using prepared statement:           " +
    (end - start) + " milliseconds");
}
catch (SQLException e) {
  System.err.println(e.getMessage());
}
finally {
  if (pstmt != null)
```

Example 11-4. Oracle batching (continued)

```
      try { pstmt.close( ); } catch (SQLException ignore) { }
}

// But now using Oracle batching: wow!!!
try {
  pstmt = conn.prepareStatement(
    "insert into test_batch " +
    "( test_batch_id, text ) " +
    "values " +
    "( test_batch_id.nextval, ? )");
  if (last < 30) {
    ((OraclePreparedStatement)pstmt).setExecuteBatch(last);
  }
  else {
    ((OraclePreparedStatement)pstmt).setExecuteBatch(30);
  }
  start = System.currentTimeMillis( );
  for (int i=0;i < last;i++) {
    pstmt.setString( 1, text );
    rows = pstmt.executeUpdate( );
  }
  end = System.currentTimeMillis( );
  pstmt.close( );
  pstmt = null;
  conn.commit( );
  System.out.println(
    last + " inserts using prepared statement batching: " +
    (end - start) + " milliseconds");
}
catch (SQLException e) {
  System.err.println(e.getMessage( ));
}
finally {
  if (pstmt != null)
    try { pstmt.close( ); } catch (SQLException ignore) { }
}

// Clean up
try {
  stmt = conn.createStatement( );
  rows = stmt.executeUpdate("delete test_batch");
  conn.commit( );
  stmt.close( );
  stmt = null;
  System.out.println(rows + " rows deleted");
  System.out.println("");
}
catch (SQLException e) {
  System.err.println(e.getMessage( ));
}
finally {
```

Example 11-4. Oracle batching (continued)

```
    if (stmt != null)
       try { stmt.close( ); } catch (SQLException ignore) { }
  }
}

protected void finalize( )
 throws Throwable {
  if (conn != null)
     try { conn.close( ); } catch (SQLException ignore) { }
  super.finalize( );
 }
}
```

Compile TestOracleBatching and execute it passing the same parameters you used for TestStandardBatching; you'll find that it's almost always 5 to 10% faster than its standard batching counterpart when the number of SQL statements in a batch is greater than 30.

Now that you've seen both implementations at work, let's move on to our last topic in this chapter, a summary of the relationship between PreparedStatement and OraclePreparedStatement.

PreparedStatement Is an OraclePreparedStatement

The PreparedStatement object is an interface, java.sql.PreparedStatement, implemented by the oracle.jdbc.driver.OraclePreparedStatement class that extends oracle.jdbc.driver.OracleStatement. This means that all of the proprietary methods available in OracleStatement are also available in OraclePreparedStatement. The following are the proprietary methods for an OraclePreparedStatement, all of which can throw a SQLException:

```
defineParameterType(int param_index, int type, int max_size)
int getExecuteBatch( )
int sendBatch( )
setARRAY(int paramIndex, ARRAY arr)
setBFILE(int paramIndex, BFILE file)
setBfile(int paramIndex, BFILE file)
setBLOB(int paramIndex, BLOB lob)
setCHAR(int paramIndex, CHAR ch)
setCLOB(int paramIndex, CLOB lob)
setCursor(int paramIndex, ResultSet rs)
setCustomDatum(int paramIndex, CustomDatum x)
setDATE(int paramIndex, DATE date)
setExecuteBatch(int batchValue)
setFixedCHAR(int paramIndex, String x)
setNUMBER(int paramIndex, NUMBER num)
```

```
setOracleObject(int paramIndex, Datum x)
setRAW(int paramIndex, RAW raw)
setREF(int paramIndex, REF ref)
setRefType(int paramIndex, REF ref)
setROWID(int paramIndex, ROWID rowid)
setSTRUCT(int paramIndex, STRUCT struct)
```

Now that you have an understanding of how to use a PreparedStatement, we can move on to the next chapter on streaming data types.

CHAPTER 12

Streaming Data Types

Most of the time, the 4,000 bytes of storage available with the VARCHAR2 data type under Oracle8 and higher is sufficient for application needs. But occasionally, applications require larger text fields or need to store complex binary data types such as word processing files and photo images in the database. Oracle8's solution to the problem of storing large amounts of data is the binary file (BFILE), binary large object (BLOB), and character large object (CLOB) data types. These large object (LOB) data types ease the storage restriction to 4 GB. The difference between a CLOB and a BLOB is that a CLOB is subject to character set translation as part of Oracle's National Language Support (NLS), whereas a BLOB's data is taken verbatim.

Oracle7's solution to the problem of storing large amounts of data is the LONG and LONG RAW data types. A LONG column can hold up to 2 GB of character data, while a LONG RAW can hold up to 2 GB of binary data. However, the truth of the matter is that LONGs exist in Oracle8 and higher only for the purpose of backward compatibility.

I recommend you use the BLOB and CLOB data types for all new development when you need to store more than 4,000 bytes of data for a column. Collectively, LOBs are normally transferred between your application and the database using streams instead of the get/set accessor methods used for VARCHAR2 and other types. Consequently, LOBs are also referred to as *streaming data types*.

 Throughout this chapter I will refer to large objects, that is both BLOBs and CLOBs, as LOBs. When I use the term LOB, I'm referring to a concept that applies to both types.

There are differences in the way that the two client-side drivers, the OCI driver and the Thin driver, actually manipulate LOB data. The OCI driver uses native code in the driver, while the Thin driver uses Oracle's built-in DBMS_LOB package. From your perspective, this difference is apparent only when an attempt is made to use the PreparedStatement interface's methods to write LOB data. A PreparedStatement can write LOB data only when the OCI driver is used. I'll mention this again when it's applicable.

You may be wondering why there is such a thing as a streaming data type. Why the need for streams? The answer is that when writing large objects, streams are more efficient than the setXXX( ) methods. There's quite a bit of hearsay about the efficiency of using LOBs. It's common to hear someone say: "Using LOBs is really slow!" The truth of the matter is that for all practical purposes, byte-for-byte, using a large object data type is no slower than writing data to a VARCHAR2. What some folks forget is that writing 1 MB of data takes longer than writing 2 KB. If you need to store large objects in a database, then LOBs are the data types of choice.

In this chapter, we'll cover the use of both the streaming methods and the get/set accessor methods for inserting, updating, and selecting the large object, streaming data types. We'll start with a detailed explanation of Oracle8's BLOB data type and then move on to cover the differences involved when using a CLOB. Next, we'll cover the Oracle proprietary type BFILE. Finally, we'll briefly discuss the use of LONG and LONG RAW. Let's begin our journey with a look at binary large objects.

BLOBs

BLOBs can be used to store any type of information you desire, as long as the data is less than 4 GB. Unlike the other data types we have covered so far in this book, BLOB data is accessed using a locator stored in a table. This locator points to the actual data. Since the locator is an internal database pointer, you can't create a locator in your application. Instead, you must create a BLOB locator by either inserting a new row into your database or updating an existing row. Once you create a locator, you then retrieve it using SELECT FOR UPDATE to establish a lock on it.

When a BLOB locator is retrieved from the database, an instance of the java.sql.Blob, or oracle.sql.BLOB, class is used to hold the locator in your Java program. These classes hold the BLOB locator, not the actual data. To get the actual data, you must use one of the Blob, or BLOB, methods to read the data from the database as a stream or to get the data into a byte array.

While the Blob interface supports getting BLOB data from the database, it does not define any methods for inserting or updating that data. Insert and update functionality is JDBC driver-specific. I hope that this inconsistent behavior in the interface for LOBs—of using methods from the locator to get data but not having any defined for storing it—will be corrected in the next version of JDBC. For now, you can use Oracle's proprietary methods to write the contents as a stream, or you can use a set accessor method to set the data as a byte array.

The JDBC 2.0 specification states that the PreparedStatement object's setObject( ) and setBinaryStream( ) methods may be used to set a BLOB's value, thus bypassing the locator. However, this functionality is currently supported only by Version 8.1.6 of the OCI driver to an 8.1.6 database. In this chapter, I'll first show you how to use `oracle.sql.BLOB` to manipulate BLOBs. This approach works for either driver. Then I'll show you how to use `java.sql.PreparedStatement`, which is supported only by the OCI driver.

Let's take a moment to clarify some nomenclature. Since I'm an object-oriented programmer, I believe that using the same name for something in different contexts is a great idea. It helps to autodocument the subject. At the same time, however, it can cause some confusion, as it does when discussing LOBs. For example, in this section, the word "blob" has three definitions:

BLOB
> Refers to the SQL data type for a binary large object

BLOB
> Refers to the `oracle.sql.BLOB` class used to hold a BLOB's locator in your Java program

Blob
> Refers to the `java.sql.Blob` interface, which is implemented by the `oracle.sql.BLOB` class and is used to hold a BLOB's locator in your Java program

Please keep these distinctions in mind as you read through this section, or you may become hopelessly confused. Before we get into an explanation of how to manipulate BLOBs, we first need a table with a BLOB column in it for our examples. So let's proceed by creating a LOB table.

An Example LOB Table

Before you can insert a BLOB, you must have a table containing a BLOB column. For our examples, we'll expand our HR database with a `person_information` table. In this table, we'll use `person_id` as a primary key and as a foreign key that references the person table, a biography column defined as a CLOB to hold a person's biographical information, and a `photo` column defined as a BLOB to hold a picture of the person in question. The following is the DDL for our `person_information` table:

```
drop   table PERSON_INFORMATION
/
create table PERSON_INFORMATION (
person_id  number  not null,
biography  clob,
photo      blob )
tablespace USERS pctfree 20
storage (initial 100 K next 100 K pctincrease 0)
/
alter  table PERSON_INFORMATION add
constraint   PERSON_INFORMATION_PK
primary key ( person_id )
using index
tablespace USERS pctfree 20
storage (initial 10 K next 10 K pctincrease 0)
/
```

Now that we have a table for our examples, we can continue by looking at how you insert a BLOB.

Inserting a BLOB Using oracle.sql.BLOB

In earlier chapters, when we discussed how to insert, update, delete, and select a DATE, NUMBER, or VARCHAR2 data type, it was simply a matter of providing a character representation of the data for a Statement object, or using a setXXX( ) method with a PreparedStatement object, and then executing the SQL statement. However, with LOBs, this one-step process does not work. Instead, when working with a LOB you need a three-step process. That's because with a LOB, a locator object, not the actual data, is stored in a table's column. You need to retrieve the locator to insert or update the actual LOB data. The three-step process is:

1. Create a locator by inserting a row into a table.

2. Retrieve the locator from the inserted row using a SELECT statement with the FOR UPDATE clause to manually lock the row.

3. Use the locator to insert the BLOB data into the database.

Creating a locator

A locator is an object that points to the actual location of the BLOB data in the database. You need a locator to manipulate the BLOB data. Because it points to a location in the database address space, only the database can create a new locator. Therefore, your Java program cannot create a locator. I know that last sentence is redundant, but it's very important that you realize up front that creating a locator is solely the job of the database.

To create a new locator for a BLOB, use the empty_blob( ) database function to generate the BLOB column's value in an INSERT statement. For example, to insert a new row into the person_information table and at the same time create a new BLOB locator, use the empty_blob( ) database function:

```
insert into person_information
    ( person_id, photo      )
values ( 1,        empty_blob( ) )
```

In this example, the number 1 is passed as the person_id value, and the result of the empty_blob( ) function is passed as the photo value. When this statement is executed, the database creates a new locator for the person_information table's photo column and stores that locator in the row being inserted. Initially, the locator points to a location that contains no data, for you have not yet used the locator to store any data. If you don't use the empty_blob( ) database function to generate a locator, you'll get a null reference error when you later attempt to retrieve the locator to insert your BLOB data.

Now that you know how to create a locator, let's look at how to retrieve that locator from the database.

Retrieving a locator

To retrieve a locator, you must execute a SELECT statement for the BLOB column using either a `Statement` or `PreparedStatement` object. You must include the FOR UPDATE clause, or the FOR UPDATE NOWAIT clause, in the SELECT statement to lock the locator; the locator must be manually locked for you to use it to insert or update BLOB data. For example, to retrieve and lock the locator inserted earlier, use the following SQL statement:

```
select photo
from    person_information
where   person_id = 1
for update nowait
```

In your Java program, you get the locator value from a `ResultSet` object using the `getBlob()` accessor method. Alternatively, you can call the `OracleResultSet` object's `getBLOB()` accessor method. The locator is then assigned to an `oracle.sql.BLOB` object in your program. If you use the `ResultSet.getBlob()` method, you'll have to cast the returned `java.sql.Blob` object to an `oracle.sql.BLOB` object. For example, you'll use code similar to the following:

```
ResultSet rslt = stmt.executeQuery(
  "select photo " +
  "from    person_information " +
  "where   person_id = 1 " +
  "for update nowait");
rslt.next();
oracle.sql.BLOB photo = (oracle.sql.BLOB)rslt.getBlob(1);
```

Now that you know how to retrieve a locator, let's see how you can use it to actually insert some BLOB data.

Using the locator to insert BLOB data

Once you've retrieved a valid BLOB locator from the database, you can use it to insert binary data into the database. First, you need to get a binary output stream from the BLOB object using the `getBinaryOutputStream()` method, which has the following signature:

```
OutputStream getBinaryOutputStream()
```

Next, you need to get the optimal buffer size when writing the binary data to the database by calling the `BLOB` object's `getBufferSize()` method, which has the following signature:

```
int getBufferSize()
```

You can use the optimal buffer size to allocate a byte array to act as a buffer when you write binary data using the BLOB object's OutputStream object. At this point, all that's left to do is use the output stream's write( ) method to write the binary data to the database. The OutputStream object's write( ) method has the following signature:

```
write(byte[] buffer, int offset, int length)
```

which breaks down as:

buffer
> A byte array containing the BLOB data you desire to write to the database BLOB column

offset
> The offset from the beginning of the array to the point from which you wish to begin writing data

length
> The number of bytes to write to the BLOB column

After you're done writing the data, you'll need to call the OutputStream object's close( ) method, or your written data will be lost. For example, given that you have someone's picture in a *.gif* file, and you want to load it into the database using the locator photo that we created earlier, you'll use code such as the following:

```
try {
  // Open a gif file for reading
  File binaryFile = new File("picture.gif");
  in = new FileInputStream(binaryFile);

  // Get the BLOB's output stream
  out = photo.getBinaryOutputStream( );

  // Get the optimal buffer size from the BLOB
  int optimalSize = photo.getBufferSize( );

  // Allocate an optimal buffer
  byte[] buffer = new byte[optimalSize];

  // Read the file input stream, in, and
  // write it to the the output stream, out
  // When length = -1, there's no more to read
  int length = 0;
  while ((length = fin.read(buffer)) != -1) {
    out.write(buffer, 0, length);
  }

  // You need to close the output stream before
  // you commit, or the changes are lost!
  out.close( );
  out = null;
  fin.close( );
  fin = null;
  conn.commit( );
}
```

An example that inserts a BLOB using an output stream

Example 12-1 shows a complete, fully functional program that uses the BLOB object's getBinaryOutputStream( ) method to insert a *.gif* file into the person_information table using an output stream.

Example 12-1. Using getBinaryOutputStream() to insert a BLOB

```java
import java.io.*;
import java.sql.*;
import java.text.*;
// Add these imports for access to the required Oracle classes
import oracle.jdbc.driver.*;
import oracle.sql.BLOB;

public class TestBLOBGetBinaryOutputStream {
  Connection conn;

  public TestBLOBGetBinaryOutputStream( ) {
    try {
      DriverManager.registerDriver(new oracle.jdbc.driver.OracleDriver( ));
      conn = DriverManager.getConnection(
        "jdbc:oracle:thin:@dssw2k01:1521:orcl", "scott", "tiger");
    }
    catch (SQLException e) {
      System.err.println(e.getMessage( ));
      e.printStackTrace( );
    }
  }

  public static void main(String[] args)
   throws Exception, IOException {
    new TestBLOBGetBinaryOutputStream().process( );
  }

  public void process( ) throws IOException, SQLException {
    int             rows      = 0;
    FileInputStream fin       = null;
    OutputStream    out       = null;
    ResultSet       rslt      = null;
    Statement       stmt      = null;
    BLOB            photo     = null;  // NOTE: oracle.sql.BLOB!!!
    long            person_id = 0;
    try {
      conn.setAutoCommit(false);

      // Get Tim's person_id
      stmt = conn.createStatement( );
      rslt = stmt.executeQuery(
        "select person_id " +
        "from   person " +
        "where  last_name  = 'O''Reilly' " +
        "and    first_name = 'Tim'");
      while (rslt.next( )) {
        rows++;
```

Example 12-1. Using getBinaryOutputStream( ) to insert a BLOB (continued)

```
        person_id = rslt.getLong(1);
      }
      if (rows > 1) {
        System.err.println("Too many rows!");
        System.exit(1);
      }
      else if (rows == 0) {
        System.err.println("Not found!");
        System.exit(1);
      }
      rslt.close( );
      rslt = null;

      // Check to see if the row already exists
      rows = 0;
      rslt = stmt.executeQuery(
       "select photo " +
       "from    person_information " +
       "where  person_id = " + Long.toString( person_id ) + " " +
       "for update nowait");
      while (rslt.next( )) {
        rows++;
        photo = (BLOB)rslt.getBlob(1);
      }
      rslt.close( );
      rslt = null;

      // If it doesn't exist, then insert
      // a row in the information table
      // This creates the LOB locators
      if (rows == 0) {
        rows = stmt.executeUpdate(
          "insert into person_information " +
          "( person_id, biography, photo ) " +
          "values " +
          "( " + Long.toString(person_id) +
          ", empty_clob(), empty_blob( ))");
        System.out.println(rows + " rows inserted");

        // Retrieve the locator
        rows = 0;
        rslt = stmt.executeQuery(
          "select photo " +
          "from    person_information " +
          "where  person_id = " + Long.toString( person_id ) + " " +
          "for update nowait");
        rslt.next( );
        photo = ((OracleResultSet)rslt).getBLOB(1);
        rslt.close( );
        rslt = null;
      }
```

Example 12-1. Using getBinaryOutputStream( ) to insert a BLOB (continued)

```
      stmt.close( );
      stmt = null;

      // Now that we have the locator,
      // lets store the photo
      File binaryFile = new File("tim.gif");
      fin = new FileInputStream(binaryFile);
      out = photo.getBinaryOutputStream( );
      // Get the optimal buffer size from the BLOB
      byte[] buffer = new byte[photo.getBufferSize( )];
      int length = 0;
      while ((length = fin.read(buffer)) != -1) {
        out.write(buffer, 0, length);
      }
      // You need to close the output stream before
      // you commit, or the changes are lost!
      out.close( );
      out = null;
      fin.close( );
      fin = null;
      conn.commit( );
    }
    catch (SQLException e) {
      System.err.println("SQL Error: " + e.getMessage( ));
    }
    catch (IOException e) {
      System.err.println("IO Error: " + e.getMessage( ));
    }
    finally {
      if (rslt != null)
        try { rslt.close( ); } catch (SQLException ignore) { }
      if (stmt != null)
        try { stmt.close( ); } catch (SQLException ignore) { }
      if (out != null)
        try { out.close( ); } catch (IOException ignore) { }
      if (fin != null)
        try { fin.close( ); } catch (IOException ignore) { }
    }
  }

  protected void finalize( )
    throws Throwable {
    if (conn != null)
      try { conn.close( ); } catch (SQLException ignore) { }
    super.finalize( );
  }
}
```

Since Example 12-1, TestBLOBGetBinaryOutputStream, utilizes Oracle classes, we've added two additional import statements: import oracle.jdbc.driver.* and import oracle.sql.BLOB. The program starts in its main( ) method by instantiating itself and then executes its process( ) method. The process( ) method begins by allocating the following variables:

rows

An int value to hold the number of rows retrieved by a SELECT statement

fin

A FileInputStream used to read a file from the filesystem

out

An OutputStream object used to write the BLOB data into the database

rslt

A ResultSet object used to retrieve a BLOB locator from the database

stmt

A Statement object used to retrieve a BLOB locator from the database and to execute an INSERT statement to create that locator in the first place

photo

A BLOB object to hold a valid locator from the database

person_id

A long to hold the primary key for a person row from the person table

Next, the program enters a try block where it starts by turning off auto-commit. It then executes a SELECT statement against the person table to get the primary key value for Tim O'Reilly. If the program finds Tim O'Reilly in the person table, it continues by executing a SELECT statement that retrieves and locks the photo column locator for Tim. In the while loop for this SELECT statement, I use the java.sql.ResultSet object's getBlob( ) method to retrieve the locator from the result set. Since this method returns a java.sql.Blob, I cast it to an oracle.sql.BLOB in order to assign it to the photo variable.

If the program doesn't find an existing entry for Tim in the person_information table, it proceeds by inserting a new row and uses the empty_blob( ) database function in the INSERT statement to create a new locator. The program then retrieves that newly inserted locator with a lock. In the while loop for this SELECT statement, I take a different approach to the casting problem. Instead of casting the object returned from getBlob( ) to an oracle.sql.BLOB, I cast the ResultSet object, rslt, to an OracleResultSet object and call the OracleResultSet object's getBLOB( ) method.

At this point in the program, photo is a valid locator that can be used to insert BLOB data into the database. The program proceeds by creating a File object for a file named *tim.gif*. It uses the File object as an argument to the constructor of a FileInputStream object. This opens the *tim.gif* file in the local filesystem for reading. Next, the program creates a byte array to act as a buffer, passing to its constructor the optimal buffer size by calling the getBufferSize( ) method of the BLOB object, photo. Now the program has an input stream and an output stream. It enters a while loop where the contents of the input stream are read and then written to the database. The while loop contains the following elements:

`fin.read(buffer)`
> Reads as many bytes of data from the input stream as will fit into the byte array named buffer.

`length = fin.read(buffer)`
> Stores the number of bytes actually read into the variable length. The read( ) method of the input stream returns the number of bytes that are actually read as an int.

`(length = fin.read(buffer))`
> Evaluates to the actual number of bytes read, so that value can be used in the while loop's conditional statement.

`while ((length = fin.read(buffer)) != -1)`
> The conditional phrase for the while loop. When the end of the file is reached for the input stream, the read( ) method returns a value of –1, which ultimately ends the while loop.

`out.write(buffer, 0, length)`
> Calls the OutputStream object's write( ) method, passing it the byte array (buffer), the starting position in the array from which to write data (always 0), and the number of bytes to write. This one statement is the body of the while loop. The write( ) method reads data from the buffer and writes it to the database.

After writing the data to the database using an output stream, effectively inserting the data, the program continues by closing the output stream with a call to its close( ) method. This is a critical step. If you don't close the stream, the data is lost. Also, the output stream must be closed before you commit or, again, the data will be lost. The program finishes up by closing the input stream and committing the data.

Example 12-1 has highlighted a very important point about LOBs. LOB data is streamed to the database in chunks rather than sent all at once. This is done for two reasons. First, the amount of memory consumed by a program is conserved. Without streaming, if you had a *.jpeg* file that was 1 GB, you'd need to consume at least 1 GB of memory to load the *.jpeg* file's data into memory. With streaming, you can read reasonably small chunks of data into memory. Second, it prevents your data transmission from monopolizing the network's available bandwidth. If you sent 1 GB of data in one transmission to the database, everyone else's transmission would have to wait until yours was finished. This might cause network users to think there was something wrong with the network. By streaming the data in chunks, you release access of the network to other users between each chunk.

A nonstreaming alternative for small BLOBs

It's an oxymoron: small binary large objects. But there is nothing to prevent you from using BLOBs to store small amounts of binary data in the database. If your binary data is always under 4,000 bytes, then you might consider using the oracle.sql.BLOB object's putBytes( ) method to send the data to the database. The putBytes( ) method works in a manner similar to the setXXX( ) accessor methods and has the following signature:

```
int putBytes(long position, byte[] bytes)
```

which breaks down as:

position
    The starting position, in bytes, within the BLOB in the database. Data is written into the BLOB starting from this point.

bytes
    A byte array that contains the data to write to the BLOB in the database.

putBytes
    Returns an int value with the number of bytes actually written to the BLOB.

The putBytes( ) method is actually one of several methods that allow you to directly modify a BLOB in the database. In this chapter, I show you how to use it to insert a BLOB value as one chunk of data.

An example that inserts a BLOB using the putBytes( ) method

Example 12-2 inserts a new row into the database, creating a new, empty locator at the same time. In then uses the empty locator stored in the oracle.sql.BLOB object and that BLOB object's putBytes( ) method to update the BLOB.

Example 12-2. Using putBytes() to insert a BLOB

```
import java.io.*;
import java.sql.*;
import java.text.*;

public class TestBLOBPutBytes {
  Connection conn;

  public TestBLOBPutBytes( ) {
    try {
      DriverManager.registerDriver(new oracle.jdbc.driver.OracleDriver( ));
      conn = DriverManager.getConnection(
        "jdbc:oracle:thin:@dssw2k01:1521:orcl", "scott", "tiger");
    }
    catch (SQLException e) {
      System.err.println(e.getMessage( ));
      e.printStackTrace( );
    }
  }
```

Example 12-2. Using putBytes() to insert a BLOB (continued)

```java
public static void main(String[] args)
  throws Exception, IOException {
  new TestBLOBPutBytes().process();
}

public void process() throws IOException, SQLException {
  int             rows      = 0;
  FileInputStream fin       = null;
  ResultSet       rslt      = null;
  Statement       stmt      = null;
  Blob            photo     = null;
  long            person_id = 0;

  try {
    conn.setAutoCommit(false);

    // Get Tim's person_id
    stmt = conn.createStatement();
    rslt = stmt.executeQuery(
      "select person_id " +
      "from    person " +
      "where  last_name  = 'O''Reilly' " +
      "and    first_name = 'Tim'");
    while (rslt.next()) {
      rows++;
      person_id = rslt.getLong(1);
    }
    if (rows > 1) {
      System.err.println("Too many rows!");
      System.exit(1);
    }
    else if (rows == 0) {
      System.err.println("Not found!");
      System.exit(1);
    }
    rslt.close();
    rslt = null;

    // check to see if the row already exists
    rows = 0;
    rslt = stmt.executeQuery(
      "select photo " +
      "from    person_information " +
      "where  person_id = " + Long.toString( person_id ) + " " +
      "for update nowait");
    while (rslt.next()) {
      rows++;
      photo = rslt.getBlob(1);
    }
    rslt.close();
    rslt = null;
```

Example 12-2. Using putBytes() to insert a BLOB (continued)

```
        // If it doesn't exist, then insert
        // a row in the information table
        // This creates the LOB locators
        if (rows == 0) {
          rows = stmt.executeUpdate(
            "insert into person_information " +
            "( person_id, biography, photo ) " +
            "values " +
            "( " + Long.toString( person_id ) +
            ", empty_clob(), empty_blob() )");
          System.out.println(rows + " rows inserted");

          // Retrieve the locator
          rows = 0;
          rslt = stmt.executeQuery(
            "select photo " +
            "from    person_information " +
            "where   person_id = " + Long.toString( person_id ) + " " +
            "for update nowait");
          rslt.next( );
          photo = rslt.getBlob(1);
          rslt.close( );
          rslt = null;
        }
        stmt.close( );
        stmt = null;

        // Copy the entire contents of the file to a buffer
        File binaryFile = new File("tim.gif");
        long fileLength = binaryFile.length( );
        fin = new FileInputStream(binaryFile);
        byte[] buffer = new byte[(int)fileLength];
        fin.read(buffer);
        fin.close( );
        fin = null;

        // Write the buffer all at once
        int bytesWritten = ((oracle.sql.BLOB)photo).putBytes(1, buffer);

        if (bytesWritten == fileLength)
          System.out.println(fileLength + " bytes written");
        else
          System.out.println("only " + bytesWritten + " bytes written");

        conn.commit( );

      }
      catch (SQLException e) {
        System.err.println("SQL Error: " + e.getMessage( ));
      }
      catch (IOException e) {
        System.err.println("IO Error: " + e.getMessage( ));
      }
```

Example 12-2. Using putBytes() to insert a BLOB (continued)

```
    finally {
      if (rslt != null)
        try { rslt.close(); } catch (SQLException ignore) { }
      if (stmt != null)
        try { stmt.close(); } catch (SQLException ignore) { }
      if (fin != null)
        try { fin.close(); } catch (IOException  ignore) { }
    }
  }

  protected void finalize()
   throws Throwable {
    if (conn != null)
      try { conn.close(); } catch (SQLException ignore) { }
    super.finalize();
  }
}
```

Example 12-2, `TestBLOBPutBytes`, works exactly the same as Example 12-1, except for the last section of the try block where it uses the `oracle.sql.BLOB` object's `putBytes()` method to send the data to the database as one chunk instead of as several streamed chunks. The section starts out by creating a `File` object for the *tim.gif* file, just as in the earlier example, but this time, since the data will be sent all at once, the program calls the `File` object's `length()` method to determine the size of the *.gif* file in bytes. The program then uses the file's size as an argument to the constructor of a byte array, named `buffer`, to create an array large enough to hold the entire contents of the *.gif* file. Next, creating a new `FileInputStream` object opens the file. Then, the entire contents of the file are read into the buffer through a call to the input stream's `read()` method.

Now that the program has the file in memory, it casts the `photo` variable from a `java.sql.Blob` to an `oracle.sql.BLOB` and calls its `putBytes()` method to write the data to the database. The first argument to the `putBytes()` method is 1. This is the starting position at which to begin writing data to the database BLOB. Notice that the starting position is a 1 and not a 0. While arrays start at 0 in Java, they start at 1 in the database. The second argument to the method is the byte array, `buffer`, which contains the data to be written.

Did you notice that no SQL statement was required to update the BLOB when we used the locator? All we needed to do was use the locator's `putBytes()` method.

With the BLOB data written, the program commits the changes and unlocks the row by calling the `commit()` method.

Inserting a BLOB Using java.sql.PreparedStatement

As an alternative to using Oracle's `oracle.sql.BLOB` object and its `getBinaryOutput-Stream()` method, you can insert a BLOB using the `PreparedStatement` object's setBinaryStream( ) method, setBytes( ) method, or setObject( ) method. Using a PreparedStatement object even appears to bypass the process of creating and retrieving a locator. Most likely, this part of the process actually occurs but is handled by the driver. Currently, this approach of using PreparedStatement methods works only with the 8.1.6 OCI driver connected to an 8.1.6 database. Let's take a look at how each of these three methods is used. We'll begin with the streaming method, setBinaryStream( ).

Using setBinaryStream( ) to insert a BLOB

Using the setBinaryStream( ) method makes inserting BLOB data into the database a one-step process. Instead of inserting a row using the empty_blob( ) database function to create a locator and then retrieving that row to get the locator, you simply formulate an INSERT statement for a PreparedStatement object and then call that object's setBinaryStream( ) method. When you call the setBinaryStream( ) method, you pass it an input stream. You can use the following INSERT statement, for example, to insert a BLOB into the photo column:

```
insert into person_information
        ( person_id, photo )
values ( ?,          ?    )
```

The first placeholder's value is set using the setLong( ) accessor method, while the second value is set using the setBinaryStream( ) method. The setBinaryStream( ) method has the following signature:

```
setBinaryStream(
  int parameterIndex,
  InputStream inputStream,
  int length)
```

which breaks down as:

parameterIndex
> The position of the placeholder in the SQL statement, counting from left to right and starting with 1

inputStream
> An open InputStream object that points to the BLOB data to load into the database

length
> The length of the binary data in bytes

You may recall that in Example 12-1 you had to code a while loop to send data from the input stream to the database one chunk at a time. When you use the setBinaryStream( ) method, the driver manages that process for you. This means you open an input stream, pass it to the driver with a call to setBinaryStream( ), and the driver takes care of all the gory details for you. Example 12-3 demonstrates this.

Example 12-3. Using setBinaryStream() to insert a BLOB

```java
import java.io.*;
import java.sql.*;
import java.text.*;

public class TestBlobSetBinaryStream {
  Connection conn;

  public TestBlobSetBinaryStream() {
    try {
      DriverManager.registerDriver(new oracle.jdbc.driver.OracleDriver());
      conn = DriverManager.getConnection(
        "jdbc:oracle:oci8:@dssw2k01", "scott", "tiger");
    }
    catch (SQLException e) {
      System.err.println(e.getMessage());
      e.printStackTrace();
    }
  }

  public static void main(String[] args)
   throws Exception, IOException {
    new TestBlobSetBinaryStream().process();
  }

  public void process() throws IOException, SQLException {
    FileInputStream    fin       = null;
    int                rows      = 0;
    long               person_id = 0;
    PreparedStatement  pstmt     = null;
    ResultSet          rslt      = null;
    Statement          stmt      = null;
    try {
      conn.setAutoCommit(false);

      // Get Tim's person_id
      stmt = conn.createStatement();
      rslt = stmt.executeQuery(
       "select person_id " +
       "from   person " +
       "where  last_name  = 'O''Reilly' " +
       "and    first_name = 'Tim'");
      while (rslt.next()) {
        rows++;
        person_id = rslt.getLong(1);
      }
      if (rows > 1) {
        System.err.println("Too many rows!");
        System.exit(1);
      }
      else if (rows == 0) {
```

Example 12-3. Using setBinaryStream() to insert a BLOB (continued)

```
        System.err.println("Not found!");
        System.exit(1);
      }
      rslt.close();
      rslt = null;

      // Delete an existing row
      rows = stmt.executeUpdate(
       "delete person_information " +
       "where  person_id = " + Long.toString( person_id ));

      stmt.close();
      stmt = null;

      // Insert the data bypassing the locator using a stream
      // This works only for oci8 driver 8.1.6 to database 8.1.6
      pstmt = conn.prepareStatement(
       "insert into person_information " +
       "( person_id, biography, photo ) " +
       "values " +
       "( ?, empty_clob(), ? )");

      // Open the input stream
      File binaryFile = new File("tim.gif");
      long fileLength = binaryFile.length();
      fin = new FileInputStream(binaryFile );

      // Set the parameter values
      pstmt.setLong(1, person_id);
      pstmt.setBinaryStream(2, fin, (int)fileLength);
      rows = pstmt.executeUpdate();
      fin.close();
      System.out.println(rows + " rows inserted");

      conn.commit();

      pstmt.close();
      pstmt = null;
    }
    catch (SQLException e) {
      System.err.println("SQL Error: " + e.getMessage());
    }
    catch (IOException e) {
      System.err.println("IO Error: " + e.getMessage());
    }
    finally {
      if (rslt != null)
        try { rslt.close();  } catch (SQLException ignore) { }
      if (stmt != null)
        try { stmt.close();  } catch (SQLException ignore) { }
      if (pstmt != null)
        try { pstmt.close(); } catch (SQLException ignore) { }
```

Example 12-3. Using setBinaryStream( ) to insert a BLOB (continued)

```
    }
  }

  protected void finalize( )
   throws Throwable {
    if (conn != null)
      try { conn.close( ); } catch (SQLException ignore) { }
    super.finalize( );
  }
}
```

Since this sample program, `TestBlobSetBinaryStream`, is similar to the earlier examples, let's skip ahead to where it differs. After the program has created a `PreparedStatement` object for the INSERT statement and a `FileInputStream` object for *tim.gif*, the program proceeds by setting the primary key value using the `setLong( )` method. Next, it calls the `setBinaryStream( )` method passing the input stream, `fin`, and the file's `length`. The program actually writes the data to the database by calling the `executeUpdate( )` method, causing the JDBC driver to read data from the input stream until it reaches the specified number of bytes. Immediately after calling `executeUpdate( )`, the program calls the input stream's `close( )` method.

 You must always close the input stream after the execution of the SQL statement but before you commit to ensure that all the data is written.

Now that you've seen how to use `setBinaryStream( )`, which is a streaming method, let's take a look at the first of the two nonstreaming alternatives.

Using setBytes( ) to insert a BLOB

Using the `PreparedStatement` object's `setBytes( )` method to insert the BLOB data into the database is very similar to using the `oracle.sql.BLOB` object's `putBytes( )` method. You'll use a prepared INSERT statement as you did with `setBinaryStream( )`. However, this time you need all the binary data in memory, and you call the `setBytes( )` accessor method instead of `setBinaryStream( )`. The `setBytes( )` accessor method has the following signature:

```
    setBytes(int parameterIndex, byte[] buffer)
```

which breaks down as:

`parameterIndex`
> The position of the placeholder in the SQL statement, counting from left to right and starting with 1

`buffer`
> A byte array that contains the BLOB data to be written to the database

Example 12-4 uses the PreparedStatement object's setBytes( ) method to insert BLOB data into a database.

Example 12-4. Using setBytes() to insert a BLOB

```java
import java.io.*;
import java.sql.*;
import java.text.*;

public class TestBlobSetBytes {
  Connection conn;
  public TestBlobSetBytes( ) {
    try {
      DriverManager.registerDriver(new oracle.jdbc.driver.OracleDriver( ));
      conn = DriverManager.getConnection(
        "jdbc:oracle:oci8:@dssw2k01", "scott", "tiger");
    }
    catch (SQLException e) {
      System.err.println(e.getMessage( ));
      e.printStackTrace( );
    }
  }

  public static void main(String[] args)
   throws Exception, IOException {
    new TestBlobSetBytes().process( );
  }

  public void process( ) throws IOException, SQLException {
    int                rows      = 0;
    FileInputStream    fin       = null;
    ResultSet          rslt      = null;
    Statement          stmt      = null;
    PreparedStatement pstmt      = null;
    long               person_id = 0;
    try {
      conn.setAutoCommit(false);

      // Get Tim's person_id
      stmt = conn.createStatement( );
      rslt = stmt.executeQuery(
       "select person_id " +
       "from    person " +
       "where   last_name  = 'O''Reilly' " +
       "and     first_name = 'Tim'");
      while (rslt.next( )) {
        rows++;
        person_id = rslt.getLong(1);
      }
      if (rows > 1) {
        System.err.println("Too many rows!");
        System.exit(1);
      }
      else if (rows == 0) {
        System.err.println("Not found!");
```

Example 12-4. Using setBytes() to insert a BLOB (continued)

```
      System.exit(1);
    }
    rslt.close( );
    rslt = null;

    // Delete an existing row
    rows = stmt.executeUpdate(
      "delete person_information " +
      "where  person_id = " + Long.toString( person_id ));

    stmt.close( );
    stmt = null;

    // Read the entire file into a buffer
    File binaryFile = new File("tim.gif");
    long fileLength = binaryFile.length( );
    byte[] buffer = new byte[(int)fileLength];
    fin = new FileInputStream(binaryFile);
    int bytes = fin.read(buffer);
    fin.close( );

    // Insert the data bypassing the locator
    // This works only for oci8 driver 8.1.6 to database 8.1.6
    pstmt = conn.prepareStatement(
      "insert into person_information " +
      "( person_id, biography, photo ) " +
      "values " +
      "( ?, empty_clob( ), ? )");
    pstmt.setLong(1, person_id);
    pstmt.setBytes(2, buffer);
    rows = pstmt.executeUpdate( );
    System.out.println(rows + " rows inserted");

    conn.commit( );

    pstmt.close( );
    pstmt = null;
  }
  catch (SQLException e) {
    System.err.println("SQL Error: " + e.getMessage( ));
  }
  catch (IOException e) {
    System.err.println("IO Error: " + e.getMessage( ));
  }
  finally {
    if (rslt != null)
      try { rslt.close( );  } catch (SQLException ignore) { }
    if (stmt != null)
      try { stmt.close( );  } catch (SQLException ignore) { }
    if (pstmt != null)
      try { pstmt.close( ); } catch (SQLException ignore) { }
  }
}
```

Example 12-4. Using setBytes() to insert a BLOB (continued)

```
  protected void finalize()
   throws Throwable {
    if (conn != null)
      try { conn.close(); } catch (SQLException ignore) { }
    super.finalize();
  }
}
```

In this example, `TestBlobSetBytes`, the process for setting the BLOB column differs from the streaming example, `TestBlobSetBinaryStream`, in two ways. First, this program reads the entire contents of the *tim.gif* file into a byte array (`buffer`), whereas in `TestBlobSetBinaryStream`, an input stream was opened for the file but was read by the JDBC driver. Second, in this program, the value of the BLOB column is set using the `setBytes()` method, passing it the byte array `buffer`. In `TestBlobSetBinaryStream`, the input stream is passed as the input argument, whereupon the driver reads the input stream, and thus the file. While it may appear to be desirable to use the `setBytes()` method, I recommend you do so only for small binary objects. The streaming methods are much more efficient. Now let's take a look at the second, nonstreaming alternative for inserting BLOB data.

Using setObject( ) to insert a BLOB

You can also use the `setObject()` method to insert binary data into a BLOB column in the database. We covered the `setObject()` method in Chapter 11, but just in case you forgot, here's the applicable signature:

```
    setObject(int parameterIndex, Object x)
```

which breaks down as:

parameterIndex
> The position of the placeholder in the SQL statement, counting from left to right and starting with 1

x
> A Java object that you wish to insert into the database

To use this method to insert a BLOB value into the database, use the same approach as in Example 12-4 but call `setObject()` instead of `setBytes()`. Now that you know how to insert a BLOB value into a database, let's look at how to- update it.

Updating a BLOB

Updating a BLOB in the database—in other words, replacing an entire BLOB, not modifying it in place—requires processes similar to those used to insert a BLOB. Once again, the process differs depending on whether you're using an `oracle.sql.BLOB` object or a `PreparedStatement` object. First, let's take a look at the process when using an `oracle.sql.BLOB` object, which works for both the OCI and Thin drivers.

Using oracle.sql.BLOB to update a BLOB

It took three steps to insert BLOB data into the database when using an oracle.sql. BLOB object. It takes only two steps to update a BLOB using an oracle.sql.BLOB object:

1. Retrieve the locator from a row using the SELECT FOR UPDATE syntax to acquire a manual lock.
2. Use the locator to write the new BLOB data into the database.

Essentially, the process for updating a BLOB is the same as inserting a BLOB, except that you don't need to create the locator. In an update, the locator already exists. If you take another look at Example 12-1, you'll see that the program was actually written to update a BLOB if one already existed; otherwise, a new BLOB was inserted. The second SELECT statement in TestBLOBGetBinaryOutput (Example 12-1) attempted to retrieve an existing row in the person_information table. If an existing row could be retrieved, the program skipped the INSERT and SELECT statements that created a new row with an empty locator and proceeded directly to updating the BLOB data using the getBinaryOutputStream( ) method in concert with the input stream for file *tim.gif*.

Updating a BLOB using the putBytes( ) method is also done in much the same manner as inserting a BLOB with putBytes( ). Now let's take a look at using the PreparedStatement object to update a BLOB value.

Using java.sql.PreparedStatement to update a BLOB

Once again, the process for updating a BLOB value using a prepared statement is much like that for inserting a BLOB using a prepared statement. The only difference is the use of a prepared UPDATE statement instead of an INSERT statement. For example, the following SQL statement can be used with a PreparedStatement object to update a BLOB's value:

```
update person_information
set    photo = ?
where  person_id = ?
```

With this statement, you can use the setBinaryStream( ), setBytes( ), or setObject( ) method to set the BLOB value for the first parameter, as we did for the photo column in Examples 12-3 and 12-4.

Deleting a BLOB

Deleting a BLOB is simple enough: just delete the row in which its locator resides, and the BLOB value is deleted, too. But what if you simply want to set the BLOB value to NULL values? If you update a BLOB column, setting it to NULL values, then you end up destroying the locator, which is not desirable. If a Java program retrieves a BLOB column expecting to get a locator, and one doesn't exist (because it's been set to NULL values), then a NullPointerException is thrown. What you really want to do is get the locator to point to nothing, as it did when it was first created. The solution to this problem is to update the BLOB column using the empty_blob( ) database function:

```
update person_information
set    photo = empty_blob( )
where  person_id = ?
```

When this UPDATE statement is executed, a new BLOB locator will replace the existing locator, giving you an empty BLOB, which effectively translates to "no value." This is as close as you can get to setting a BLOB value to NULL values.

Selecting a BLOB

Unlike selecting other data types from a database, to get BLOB data out of the database, you must follow a two-step process.

1. Select a BLOB locator from a table.
2. Use the Blob object's getBinaryStream( ) method, or its getBytes( ) method, to access the binary data.

Just as when you insert or update a BLOB, it's more efficient when selecting a BLOB to use the getBinaryStream( ) streaming method instead of the getBytes( ) method. Unlike inserting and updating a BLOB, you can use only a java.sql.Blob object's methods to get the data out; there are no methods to bypass the locator. As I stated earlier, this makes the current implementation of the java.sql.Blob interface inconsistent, and perhaps this inconsistency will be addressed in the next release of JDBC.

The choice of which method to use—the streaming getBinaryStream( ) or non-streaming getBytes( ) method—will ultimately be determined by your application's use of the binary data once it is retrieved from the database. As I explained earlier when discussing Oracle's getBinaryOutputStream( ) method to insert BLOB data, the use of the streaming methods can significantly reduce the amount of memory consumed by your application and can also reduce your application's impact on other users of the network. If you have a program that can read and then immediately write streamed data, or that can work with chunks of binary data, not requiring all the data to be in memory at once, then you should use the getBinaryStream( ) method to retrieve BLOB data.

Using getBinaryStream( ) to retrieve BLOB data

To get a BLOB locator from the database, you must execute a SQL SELECT statement that includes the BLOB column. For example, to retrieve the locator for the photo column, you may use a prepared SELECT statement such as the following:

```
select photo
from   person_information
where  person_id = ?
```

After you've retrieved the column and thus have a result set, you can use the ResultSet object's getBlob( ) method to store the locator into a local variable:

```
java.sql.Blob photo = rslt.getBlob(1);
```

Once you have a locator, you can use it to get a binary input stream that in turn can be used to retrieve the BLOB data from the database. The getBinaryStream( ) method has the following signature:

```
InputStream getBinaryStream( )
```

Using the locator, you can get an input stream:

```
InputStream in = photo.getBinaryStream( );
```

Next, use a while loop to read the input stream and write to an output stream one buffer (or chunk) of data at a time, as shown in the following example:

```
int bufferSize = 1024;
byte[] buffer = new byte[bufferSize];
while ((length = in.read(buffer)) != -1) {
  out.write(buffer, 0, length);
}
```

There's a lot happening in this example, so let's dissect it one step at a time:

int bufferSize = 1024
: This is an int variable that will be used to specify the buffer's size.

byte[] buffer = new byte[bufferSize]
: This creates a byte array, buffer, to act as the buffer for streaming the data between the input stream and the output stream. In this case, a maximum of 1,024 bytes can be read into the buffer from the input stream and then written from the buffer to the output stream.

in.read(buffer)
: This reads data from the input stream into the buffer, up to the buffer's size.

length = in.read(buffer)
: This statement assigns the return value to the length variable for later use. The call to the read( ) method returns an int value representing the actual number of bytes read.

(length = in.read(buffer))
: This expression evaluates to the number of bytes read from the input stream; it evaluates to −1 when there is no more data to read.

while ((length = in.read(buffer)) != -1)
: This is the conditional statement of the while loop. If there is no more data to be read from the input stream, the while loop ends.

out.write(buffer, 0, length)
: This writes the data in the buffer to the output stream.

An example using getBinaryStream( )

Example 12-5, a servlet named TestBlobServlet, uses the java.sql.Blob object's getBinaryStream( ) method to send a photo to your browser's screen. The servlet is called passing a last name and first name using the following syntax after the servlet's name on your browser's URL address line:

```
?last_name=last name&first_name=first name
```

For example, assuming that you have a servlet container installed on your computer configured for port 8080 and are using ojdbc as the servlet context directory, to open Tim's photo, type the following URL in your browser:

```
http://localhost:8080/ojdbc/servlet/TestBlobServlet?last_name=O'Reilly&first_name=Tim
```

Your browser will then execute the servlet, passing "Tim" for the first_name parameter and "O'Reilly" for the last_name parameter.

Example 12-5. A servlet to view a person's photo

```java
import java.io.*;
import java.sql.*;
import javax.servlet.*;
import javax.servlet.http.*;

public class TestBlobServlet extends HttpServlet {

  public void doGet(
   HttpServletRequest request,
   HttpServletResponse response)
   throws IOException, ServletException {

   ServletOutputStream out = response.getOutputStream( );

   Blob       photo      = null;
   Connection connection = CacheConnection.checkOut( );
   Statement  statement  = null;
   ResultSet  resultSet  = null;
   String     sql        =
    "select photo " +
    "from   person p, person_information i " +
    "where  p.person_id = i.person_id " +
    "and    last_name = " +
      formatWithTicks(request.getParameter("last_name")) + " " +
    "and    first_name = " +
      formatWithTicks(request.getParameter("first_name"));

   try {
     statement = connection.createStatement( );
     resultSet = statement.executeQuery(sql);
     if (resultSet.next( )) {
       photo = resultSet.getBlob(1);
     }
     else {
       response.setContentType("text/html");
```

Example 12-5. A servlet to view a person's photo (continued)

```
        out.println("<html><head><title>Person Photo</title></head>");
        out.println("<body><h1>No data found</h1></body></html>");
        return;
      }
      response.setContentType("image/gif");

      InputStream in = photo.getBinaryStream( );
      System.out.println("after getBinaryStream");

      int length      = (int)photo.length( );
      System.out.println("lenght of the blob is " + length);

      int bufferSize = 1024;
      System.out.println("buffer size is " + bufferSize);

      byte[] buffer = new byte[bufferSize];

      while ((length = in.read(buffer)) != -1) {
        System.out.println("writing " + length + " bytes");
        out.write(buffer, 0, length);
      }

      System.out.println("written");
      in.close( );
      out.flush( );
    }
    catch (SQLException e) {
      System.out.println("TestBlobServlet.doGet( ) SQLException: " +
        e.getMessage( ) + "executing ");
      System.out.println(sql);
    }
    finally {
      if (resultSet != null)
        try { resultSet.close( ); } catch (SQLException ignore) { }
      if (statement != null)
        try { statement.close( ); } catch (SQLException ignore) { }
    }
    // Return the conection
    CacheConnection.checkIn(connection);
  }

public void doPost(
 HttpServletRequest request,
 HttpServletResponse response)
 throws IOException, ServletException {
  doGet(request, response);
}

private String formatWithTicks(String string) {
  if (string != null) {
    char[]        in  = string.toCharArray( );
    StringBuffer out = new StringBuffer((int)(in.length * 1.1));
    if (in.length > 0)
```

Example 12-5. A servlet to view a person's photo (continued)

```
    out.append("'");
  for (int i=0;i < in.length;i++) {
    out.append(in[i]);
    if (in[i] == '\'')
      out.append(in[i]);
  }
  if (in.length > 0)
    out.append("'");
  return out.toString( );
  }
  else {
    return "NULL";
  }
 }
}
```

Using the URL shown earlier, the servlet starts in its doGet( ) method by creating several variables. The first, out, is a ServletOutputStream that will be used to write the binary GIF data to your browser. The second, photo, is a Blob to hold the photo's locator from the database. The last four are JDBC objects you're now familiar with and will be used to retrieve the locator from the database. Next, the program enters a try block in which it queries the database for a photo using the parameters from the URL. After the servlet calls the executeQuery( ) method, it tests for the existence of a photo. If one exists, it retrieves the locator using the ResultSet object's getBlob( ) method. Next, the program sends an image/gif content header. Then it gets the Blob object's input stream by calling its getBinaryStream( ) method. It uses this input stream to find the length of the BLOB and then executes a while loop from which the contents of the BLOB are sent to the browser. Finally, it closes the input stream and flushes the servlet's output stream. You can use this sample program to verify that the insert and update programs shown earlier actually did insert BLOB data into the photo column.

Oracle BLOB Methods

The oracle.sql.BLOB class implements java.sql.Blob. The following are the oracle.sql.BLOB proprietary methods, all of which can throw a SQLException:

```
OutputStream getBinaryOutputStream( )
int getBufferSize( )
int getBytes(long pos, int length, byte buf[])
int getChunkSize( )
OracleConnection getConnection( )
boolean isConvertibleTo(Class jClass)
int putBytes(long pos, byte bytes[])
Object toJdbc( )
```

Now that you can insert, update, delete, and select BLOBs, you have a good foundation for understanding the character-specific implementation of a LOB, which is a character large object, or CLOB.

CLOBs

For the most part, a CLOB behaves just like a BLOB, except it exists specifically for storing character data and is subject to National Language Support (NLS) character conversion. Whereas an `oracle.sql.BLOB` object has methods for handling binary data, an `oracle.sql.CLOB` object has methods for reading and writing both ASCII and Unicode (character) data. If you use the ASCII methods—`getAsciiStream( )`, `setAsciiStream( )`, and `getAsciiOutputStream( )`—the driver translates the client character set of ASCII to and from the database's character set. If you use the character methods—`getCharacterStream( )`, `setCharacterStream( )`, `getCharacterOutputStream( )`, and `putChars( )`—the driver translates the client character set of Unicode to the database's character set. The database will handle the data as ASCII if the database character set is ASCII; otherwise, the database will perform NLS character set translations to maintain the Unicode characters if the database uses, for example, the UTF-8 character set.

You can just as easily store text in a BLOB, so why should you use a CLOB instead of a BLOB? The most compelling reason to use a CLOB is its NLS abilities, that is, its abilities to handle NLS character set conversions. And to access these, you need a database that uses a UTF-8 character set, and you need to use the character methods. The only advantage to using the ASCII methods is that they are more efficient. However, if you code your applications with the character methods, they will work with ASCII data in an ASCII database or with any supported character set for a UTF-8 database.

The use of the word "clob" has three different definitions in this section, so let's take a moment here to clarify some nomenclature:

CLOB
: Refers to the SQL data type for a character large object

CLOB
: Refers to the `oracle.sql.CLOB` class used to hold a CLOB's locator in your Java program

Clob
: Refers to the `java.sql.Clob` interface, which is implemented by the `oracle.sql.CLOB` class and is used to hold a CLOB's locator in your Java program

As with BLOBs, CLOBs have three different classes that provide methods for manipulating the LOB data. To write CLOB data, use the Oracle proprietary methods from class `oracle.sql.CLOB` or the JDBC interface `java.sql.PreparedStatement`. To read CLOB data, use methods from the standard JDBC interface `java.sql.Clob`.

Inserting a CLOB Using oracle.sql.CLOB

Let's start our discussion on inserting CLOBs by noting some significant differences in the nomenclature between BLOBs and CLOBs. When we talk about *binary* data, we refer to data units of 1 byte each. The CLOB equivalent is to talk about *character* data in terms of characters, which may be 1 or more bytes in length. The ASCII CLOB methods represent an exception to this rule: they deal with bytes. A similar nomenclature difference exists with respect to streams. To read and write a BLOB, we use InputStream and OutputStream objects, whereas with a CLOB, we use Reader and Writer objects. Once again, ASCII data is an exception. Other than these nomenclature differences, the mechanics of reading and writing CLOB data parallels those of its BLOB sibling.

When you use an oracle.sql.CLOB object to write data to the database, you need to use the three-step method outlined with the use of an oracle.sql.BLOB. That is, you need to create a locator, retrieve the locator, and then use the locator via an oracle. sql.CLOB object to write the CLOB data. Just as you use the empty_blob( ) database function to create a new locator for a BLOB, you use the empty_clob( ) database function to create a new locator for a CLOB. Once you have a valid locator, you can use one of the following methods from the oracle.sql.CLOB class for writing CLOB data to a database:

OutputStream getAsciiOutputStream( )
> Returns an OutputStream object that can be used to write CLOB data as ASCII characters to the database using streams.

Writer getCharacterOutputStream( )
> Returns an OutputStream object that can be used to write CLOB data as Unicode characters to the database using streams.

int putChars(long position, char[] buffer)
> Writes a char array (buffer) to a CLOB in the database. The writing begins at the specified position within the CLOB in the database. This method returns the actual number of characters written.

int putString(long position, String string)
> Writes a String object (string) to a CLOB in the database. The writing begins at the specified position within the CLOB in the database. This method returns the actual number of characters written.

Using getCharacterOutputStream( ) to insert a CLOB

Example 12-6, TestCLOBGetCharacterOutputStream, is the CLOB version of Example 12-1. The getCharacterOutputStream( ) method works with Unicode, i.e., character data, from a Java program. Since the CLOB example programs are almost the same as their BLOB counterparts, I'll describe only the significant differences following the example.

Example 12-6. Using getCharacterOutputStream( ) to insert a CLOB

```
import java.io.*;
import java.sql.*;
import java.text.*;
```

Example 12-6. Using getCharacterOutputStream() to insert a CLOB (continued)

```java
import oracle.jdbc.driver.*;
import oracle.sql.CLOB;

public class TestCLOBGetCharacterOutputStream {
  Connection conn;

  public TestCLOBGetCharacterOutputStream( ) {
    try {
      DriverManager.registerDriver(new oracle.jdbc.driver.OracleDriver( ));
      conn = DriverManager.getConnection(
        "jdbc:oracle:thin:@dssw2k01:1521:orcl", "scott", "tiger");
    }
    catch (SQLException e) {
      System.err.println(e.getMessage( ));
      e.printStackTrace( );
    }
  }

  public static void main(String[] args)
   throws Exception, IOException {
    new TestCLOBGetCharacterOutputStream().process( );
  }

  public void process( ) throws IOException, SQLException {
    int            rows      = 0;
    FileReader     fin       = null;
    Writer         out       = null;
    ResultSet      rslt      = null;
    Statement      stmt      = null;
    CLOB           biography = null;  // NOTE: oracle.sql.CLOB!!!
    long           person_id = 0;

    try {
      conn.setAutoCommit(false);

      // Get Tim's person_id
      stmt = conn.createStatement( );
      rslt = stmt.executeQuery(
        "select person_id " +
        "from   person " +
        "where  last_name  = 'O''Reilly' " +
        "and    first_name = 'Tim'");
      while (rslt.next( )) {
        rows++;
        person_id = rslt.getLong(1);
      }
      if (rows > 1) {
        System.err.println("Too many rows!");
        System.exit(1);
      }
      else if (rows == 0) {
        System.err.println("Not found!");
        System.exit(1);
```

Example 12-6. Using getCharacterOutputStream( ) to insert a CLOB (continued)

```
    }
    rslt.close( );
    rslt = null;

    // Check to see the row already exists
    rows = 0;
    rslt = stmt.executeQuery(
     "select biography " +
     "from    person_information " +
     "where   person_id = " + Long.toString( person_id ) + " " +
     "for update nowait");
    while (rslt.next( )) {
      rows++;
      biography = (CLOB)rslt.getClob(1);
    }
    rslt.close( );
    rslt = null;

    if (rows == 0) {
      // Insert a row in the information table
      // This creates the LOB locators
      rows = stmt.executeUpdate(
       "insert into person_information " +
       "( person_id, biography, photo ) " +
       "values " +
       "( " + Long.toString( person_id ) +
       ", empty_clob(), empty_blob() )");
      System.out.println(rows + " rows inserted");
      // Retrieve the locator
      rows = 0;
      rslt = stmt.executeQuery(
       "select biography " +
       "from    person_information " +
       "where   person_id = " + Long.toString( person_id ) + " " +
       "for update nowait");
      rslt.next( );
      biography = ((OracleResultSet)rslt).getCLOB(1);
      rslt.close( );
      rslt = null;
    }

    // Now that we have the locator, lets store the biography
    File characterFile = new File("tim.txt");
    fin = new FileReader(characterFile);
    char[] buffer = new char[biography.getBufferSize( )];
    out = biography.getCharacterOutputStream( );
    int length = 0;
    while ((length = fin.read(buffer)) != -1) {
      out.write(buffer, 0, length);
    }
    // You need to close the output stream before
    // you commit, or the changes are lost!
    out.close( );
```

Example 12-6. Using getCharacterOutputStream( ) to insert a CLOB (continued)

```
      out = null;
      fin.close( );
      fin = null;
      conn.commit( );
    }
    catch (SQLException e) {
      System.err.println("SQL Error: " + e.getMessage( ));
    }
    catch (IOException e) {
      System.err.println("IO Error: " + e.getMessage( ));
    }
    finally {
      if (rslt != null)
        try { rslt.close( ); } catch (SQLException ignore) { }
      if (stmt != null)
        try { stmt.close( ); } catch (SQLException ignore) { }
      if (out != null)
        try { out.close( ); } catch (IOException ignore) { }
      if (fin != null)
        try { fin.close( ); } catch (IOException ignore) { }
    }
  }

  protected void finalize( )
    throws Throwable {
    if (conn != null)
      try { conn.close( ); } catch (SQLException ignore) { }
    super.finalize( );
  }
}
```

In Example 12-6, the program stores a CLOB locator into an oracle.sql.CLOB object. Next, it opens a large text file, *tim.txt*, using a Reader object. Then the program creates a character buffer using the optimal buffer size from the locator. Next, the program gets a Writer from the CLOB object by calling its getCharacterOutputStream( ) method. Then the program enters a while loop from which the contents of the text file are streamed into the CLOB in the database.

Next, let's examine how using the ASCII method differs from this example.

Using getAsciiOutputStream( )

If your program does not use Unicode, you can use the getAsciiOutputStream( ) method instead of getCharacterOutputStream( ). Here's a program snippet using the BLOB object's getAsciiOuputStream( ) method:

```
FileInputStream fin        = null;
OutputStream    out        = null;
...
    // Now that we have the locator, lets store the biography
    File asciiFile = new File("tim.txt");
    fin = new FileInputStream(asciiFile);
```

```
byte[] buffer = new byte[biography.getBufferSize()];
out = biography.getAsciiOutputStream();
int length = 0;
while ((length = fin.read(buffer)) != -1) {
  out.write(buffer, 0, length);
}
```

In this program snippet from TestCLOBGetAsciiOutputStream (a program listing you can find in the examples online at this book's web page), all that is different between it and its Unicode sibling, Example 12-6, is:

- The use of an InputStream instead of a Reader
- The use of an OutputStream instead of a Writer
- The use of a byte array instead of a char array

Otherwise, the mechanics of the two programs are the same. Next, let's take a look at an example using the PreparedStatement object.

Inserting a CLOB Using java.sql.PreparedStatement

Once again, when you use a PreparedStatement object, the process of writing CLOB data parallels that of writing BLOB data. Specifically, the PreparedStatement object's methods appear to bypass the use of a locator. At least they do from a programmer's perspective.

The PreparedStatement interface implements three methods that you need to know about. The first is setCharacterStream(), which can be used to write Unicode data to a CLOB in the database using streams. The method signature is:

```
setCharacterStream(
  int parameterIndex,
  Reader reader,
  int length)
```

which breaks down as:

parameterIndex
: The position of the placeholder in the prepared SQL statement, counting from left to right and starting with 1

reader
: A Reader object to be read by the driver

length
: The size, in number of characters, of the data available from the Reader object

The second method is setAsciiStream(), which can be used to write ASCII data to a CLOB in the database using streams. The method signature is:

```
setAsciiStream(
  int parameterIndex,
  InputStream inputStream,
  int length)
```

which breaks down as:

parameterIndex
> The position of the placeholder in the prepared statement, counting from left to right and starting with 1

inputStream
> An InputStream object to be read by the driver

length
> The size, in number of bytes, of the data available from the input stream

The last method is setObject( ), which can be used to write Unicode data to a CLOB in the database from a String object. The method signature is:

```
setObject(int parameterIndex, Object charArray)
```

which breaks down as:

parameterIndex
> The position of the placeholder in the prepared SQL statement, counting from left to right and starting with 1

charArray
> A char array containing the characters to be written to the database

Remember that the use of a PreparedStatement object to insert CLOB data is currently supported using only the Version 8.1.6 OCI driver while connected to a Version 8.1.6 database. Consider this when you decide whether to use the oracle.sql. BLOB object or the PreparedStatement. Regardless, the process for inserting a CLOB using a PreparedStatement object closely parallels its BLOB counterpart. All that really differs is the use of a Reader instead of an InputSteam object. And, as always, writing ASCII data represents the exception. When writing ASCII data, an InputStream object is used. Let's take a look at inserting Unicode data.

Using setCharacterStream( )

Example 12-7 is the CLOB counterpart for Example 12-3 and inserts data into a CLOB using the setCharacterStream( ) method. Except for the use of a Reader instead of an InputStream and the call to the setCharacterStream( ) method instead of setBinaryStream( ), the programs are almost identical.

Example 12-7. Using setCharacterStream to insert a CLOB

```
import java.io.*;
import java.sql.*;
import java.text.*;

public class TestClobSetCharacterStream {
  Connection conn;

  public TestClobSetCharacterStream() {
    try {
```

Example 12-7. Using setCharacterStream to insert a CLOB (continued)

```
      DriverManager.registerDriver(new oracle.jdbc.driver.OracleDriver( ));
      conn = DriverManager.getConnection(
        "jdbc:oracle:oci8:@dssw2k01", "scott", "tiger");
    }
    catch (SQLException e) {
      System.err.println(e.getMessage( ));
      e.printStackTrace( );
    }
  }

  public static void main(String[] args)
   throws Exception, IOException {
    new TestClobSetCharacterStream().process( );
  }

  public void process( ) throws IOException, SQLException {
    FileReader        fin       = null;
    int               rows      = 0;
    long              person_id = 0;
    PreparedStatement pstmt     = null;
    ResultSet         rslt      = null;
    Statement         stmt      = null;

    try {
      conn.setAutoCommit(false);

      // Get Tim's person_id
      stmt = conn.createStatement( );
      rslt = stmt.executeQuery(
        "select person_id " +
        "from    person " +
        "where  last_name  = 'O''Reilly' " +
        "and     first_name = 'Tim'");
      while (rslt.next( )) {
        rows++;
        person_id = rslt.getLong(1);
      }
      if (rows > 1) {
        System.err.println("Too many rows!");
        System.exit(1);
      }
      else if (rows == 0) {
        System.err.println("Not found!");
        System.exit(1);
      }
      rslt.close( );
      rslt = null;

      // Delete an existing row
      rows = stmt.executeUpdate(
        "delete person_information " +
        "where  person_id = " + Long.toString( person_id ));
```

Example 12-7. Using setCharacterStream to insert a CLOB (continued)

```
      stmt.close( );
      stmt = null;

      // Insert the data bypassing the locator using a stream
      // This works only for oci8 driver 8.1.6 to database 8.1.6
      pstmt = conn.prepareStatement(
        "insert into person_information " +
        "( person_id, biography, photo ) " +
        "values " +
        "( ?, ?, empty_blob( ) )");

      File characterFile = new File("tim2.txt");
      long fileLength = characterFile.length( );
      fin = new FileReader(characterFile);

      pstmt.setLong(1, person_id);
      pstmt.setCharacterStream(2, fin, (int)fileLength);
      rows = pstmt.executeUpdate( );
      fin.close( );
      System.out.println(rows + " rows inserted");

      conn.commit( );

      pstmt.close( );
      pstmt = null;
    }
    catch (SQLException e) {
      System.err.println("SQL Error: " + e.getMessage( ));
    }
    catch (IOException e) {
      System.err.println("IO Error: " + e.getMessage( ));
    }
    finally {
      if (rslt != null)
        try { rslt.close( );  } catch (SQLException ignore) { }
      if (stmt != null)
        try { stmt.close( );  } catch (SQLException ignore) { }
      if (pstmt != null)
        try { pstmt.close( ); } catch (SQLException ignore) { }
    }
  }

  protected void finalize( )
   throws Throwable {
    if (conn != null)
      try { conn.close( ); } catch (SQLException ignore) { }
    super.finalize( );
  }
}
```

Using setAsciiStream( )

If you're not going to write Unicode data, you may want to use the setAsciiStream( ) method to insert CLOBs. In the following sample program snippet from TestClobSetAsciiStream (available with the examples you can download from this book's web page), the program uses the setAsciiStream( ) method to bypass the CLOB locator when writing the ASCII data to the database. What's significant here is that it uses an InputStream object to write ASCII, as opposed to Writer.

```
// Insert the data bypassing the locator using a stream
// This works only for oci8 driver 8.1.6 to database 8.1.6
pstmt = conn.prepareStatement(
  "insert into person_information " +
 "( person_id, biography, photo ) " +
  "values " +
  "( ?, ?, empty_blob( ) )");

File asciiFile = new File("tim.txt");
long fileLength = asciiFile.length( );
fin = new FileInputStream(asciiFile);

pstmt.setLong(1, person_id);
pstmt.setAsciiStream(2, fin, (int)fileLength);
rows = pstmt.executeUpdate( );
fin.close( );
System.out.println(rows + " rows inserted");

conn.commit( );
```

Now that you know how to insert a CLOB, you also know how to update one!

Updating a CLOB

The process of updating a CLOB, that is, replacing the entire contents of the CLOB, is very similar to updating a BLOB. The differences lie in the method you invoke and in the use of Reader and Writer objects for streaming Unicode data.

Using oracle.sql.CLOB to update a CLOB

If you're going to use the getCharacterOutputStream( ) or getAsciiOutputStream( ) methods to update a CLOB in the database, then the update process will require the following two steps:

1. Retrieve an existing locator.
2. Use the locator to update the data.

You retrieve a locator the same way you've seen in all the previous examples in this chapter—you select the CLOB column from the database into a ResultSet object. Then you use the ResultSet object's getClob( ) accessor method and cast its returned value to an oracle.sql.CLOB. Alternatively, you can cast the ResultSet object to an

`OracleResultSet` object and use its `getCLOB( )` method to retrieve the `oracle.sql.CLOB` object directly.

Once you have the locator, you can call the `CLOB` object's `getCharacterOutputStream( )` method to get a `Writer` object to use in writing Unicode data. Or, if you wish to write ASCII data, you can call the `getAsciiOutputStream` method to get an `OutputStream`. After you have the appropriate stream object, you can use it in a `while` loop, as I did in the earlier sections on inserting a CLOB, to write the new CLOB data to the database.

Using java.sql.PreparedStatement

The process for using a `PreparedStatement` object's methods to update a CLOB closely parallels the insert process. You just create a prepared UPDATE statement and use the appropriate accessor method. So the difference lies solely in the use of an UPDATE statement instead of an INSERT statement. To update Unicode data, use the `setCharacterStream( )` method, passing it a `Reader` object. To update ASCII data, use `setAsciiStream( )` method, passing it an `InputStream` object.

Deleting a CLOB

Deleting a CLOB is accomplished by deleting the row in the database that contains the CLOB locator, although when you think of deleting a CLOB, you may actually be thinking about how to set the CLOB data to NULL. The easiest way to accomplish the latter is to execute an UPDATE statement and specify the `empty_clob( )` database function as the value for the column that holds the CLOB locator. This replaces the existing locator with a new "empty" locator. This is as close as you can get to a CLOB with NULL values. See the section "Deleting a BLOB" for an example.

Selecting a CLOB

Only the methods in the `java.sql.Clob` interface allow you to retrieve CLOB data from a database. The `java.sql.Clob` interface is implemented by the `oracle.sql.CLOB` class, so the methods listed here can be found in both objects. These methods can be used to read CLOB data from a database:

`InputStream getAsciiStream( )`
> This method returns an `InputStream` object that can read ASCII data from a CLOB in the database using streams.

`Reader getCharacterStream( )`
> This method returns a `Reader` object that can read Unicode data from a CLOB in the database using streams.

`String getSubString(long position, int length)`
> This method can read a substring of data from a CLOB in the database. It returns a `String` object containing the CLOB data. If you set position to 1 and

length to the length of the CLOB in the database, you can return the entire CLOB as a String.

The ResultSet interface provides a getClob( ) method, but it's used to get the locator for a CLOB from a result set, not the CLOB's data. You must, in turn, use the locator to retrieve the actual data. Therefore, selecting a CLOB's value from a database is a two-step process:

1. Select a CLOB locator from a table.
2. Use the java.sql.Clob object's getCharacterStream( ) or getAsciiStream( ) method to access the data.

Selecting a locator from the database is accomplished by selecting a CLOB column in the database. The CLOB column in the database contains a locator, not the actual data. In your program, create a java.sql.Clob variable to hold the locator returned by a call to the result set's getClob( ) accessor method.

Once you have the locator in a Clob object, use the getCharacterStream( ) method to retrieve it as a Unicode data stream or use the getAsciiStream( ) method to retrieve it as an ASCII data stream. Let's take a look at an example using getCharacterStream( ). Example 12-8 is a servlet, as it is in its BLOB counterpart in Example 12-5, except that it displays a person's biography, not their photo, on your browser.

Example 12-8. A servlet to view a person's biography

```
import java.io.*;
import java.sql.*;
import javax.servlet.*;
import javax.servlet.http.*;

public class TestClobCharacterServlet extends HttpServlet {

  public void doGet(
   HttpServletRequest request,
   HttpServletResponse response)
   throws IOException, ServletException {

    PrintWriter out = response.getWriter();

    Clob       biography  = null;
    Connection connection = CacheConnection.checkOut();
    Statement  statement  = null;
    ResultSet  resultSet  = null;
    String     sql        =
     "select biography " +
     "from    person p, person_information i " +
     "where   p.person_id = i.person_id " +
     "and     last_name = " +
     formatWithTicks(request.getParameter("last_name")) + " " +
     "and     first_name = " +
     formatWithTicks(request.getParameter("first_name"));
```

Example 12-8. A servlet to view a person's biography (continued)

```
    try {
      statement = connection.createStatement( );
      resultSet = statement.executeQuery(sql);
      if (resultSet.next( )) {
        biography = resultSet.getClob(1);
      }
      else {
        response.setContentType("text/html");
        out.println("<html><head><title>Person Biography</title></head>");
        out.println("<body><h1>No data found</h1></body></html>");
        return;
      }
      response.setContentType("text/plain");

      Reader in = biography.getCharacterStream( );
      System.out.println("after getCharacterStream");
      int length = (int)biography.length( );
      System.out.println("lenght of the Clob is " + length);
      char[] buffer = new char[1024];
      while ((length = in.read(buffer)) != -1) {
        System.out.println("writing " + length + " chars");
        out.write(buffer, 0, length);
      }
      System.out.println("written");
      in.close( );
      in = null;
      out.flush( );
    }
    catch (SQLException e) {
      System.out.println(
       "TestClobCharacterServlet.doGet( ) SQLException: " +
       e.getMessage( ) + "executing ");
      System.out.println(sql);
    }
    finally {
      if (resultSet != null)
        try { resultSet.close( ); } catch (SQLException ignore) { }
      if (statement != null)
        try { statement.close( ); } catch (SQLException ignore) { }
    }
    // Return the conection
    CacheConnection.checkIn(connection);
  }

  public void doPost(
   HttpServletRequest request,
   HttpServletResponse response)
   throws IOException, ServletException {
    doGet(request, response);
  }

  private String formatWithTicks(String string) {
    if (string != null) {
```

Example 12-8. A servlet to view a person's biography (continued)

```
    char[]       in = string.toCharArray();
    StringBuffer out = new StringBuffer((int)(in.length * 1.1));
    if (in.length > 0)
      out.append("'");
    for (int i=0;i < in.length;i++) {
      out.append(in[i]);
      if (in[i] == '\'')
        out.append(in[i]);
    }
    if (in.length > 0)
      out.append("'");
    return out.toString();
  }
  else {
    return "NULL";
  }
 }
}
```

Example 12-8, `TestClobCharacterServlet`, sets the content type to text/plain and uses a `PrintWriter` for output to the browser. It selects the biography column's locator from the database and then uses it to get a `Reader` object. Using the `Reader` object in a while loop, the contents of the CLOB are read from the database 1,024 characters at a time and are then written to the browser.

Oracle CLOB Methods

The `oracle.sql.CLOB` class implements the `java.sql.Clob` interface. Here are the `oracle.sql.CLOB` proprietary methods, all of which can throw an `SQLException`:

```
    OutputStream getAsciiOutputStream()
    int getBufferSize()
    Writer getCharacterOutputStream()
    int getChars(long pos, int length, char buffer[])
    int getChunkSize()
    OracleConnection getConnection()
    boolean isConvertibleTo(Class jClass)
    int putChars(long pos, char chars[])
    int putString(long pos, String str)
    Object toJdbc()
```

Now that you can manipulate BLOBs and CLOBs, lets take a look at Oracle's read-only binary file extension, BFILE.

BFILEs

There are times when data, such as reference data, is provided by an external vendor on read-only media. You can go through the work of creating a database schema to hold the data, create procedures to load the data into the database as BLOBs, and

---

then repeat those procedures again and again and again, as the reference data is updated, but BFILEs provide a better solution to this problem. BFILEs allow you to simply go through the database and directly access the data on the host's filesystem.

An instance of a `oracle.sql.BFILE` class is used in your Java program to hold a copy of a BFILE's read-only locator from the database. You can then use the `oracle.sql.BFILE` object's methods to retrieve the contents of the external binary file using streams.

To use BFILEs, you must follow these steps:

1. Create a directory on the host's filesystem for your files and store your files there.
2. Create a directory object in the database to store the host filesystem's directory specification using the create directory DDL statement.
3. Create a table to hold BFILE locators for the external binary files.
4. Insert locators for the external binary files into the table.
5. Retrieve the external binary file data using the BFILE locator.

In the earlier section on BLOBs, we stored a photo in the database. In this section, instead of storing a photo in the database, we'll store it in an operating-system file. To do this, create a BFILE directory, *c:\TestBfile*, on your host. Then create a directory object in the database to point to that directory. Store the photo in that directory, create a BFILE locator (in a table) pointing to the photo file, and finally, read the photo from the filesystem using the BFILE locator.

Creating a Directory Object

Your first task is to create a directory on a host's filesystem. For example:

```
mkdir c:\TestBfile
```

Then you have to create a directory object to represent it in the database. To accomplish this, use the CREATE DIRECTORY statement. The CREATE DIRECTORY statement has the following syntax:

```
CREATE DIRECTORY db_dir_name AS 'fs_dir_name'
```

which breaks down as:

db_dir_name
    The logical name you use in the database to refer to the physical directory on the filesystem

fs_dir_name
    The filesystem's name for the directory

To execute the CREATE DIRECTORY command, you need to be logged in with a username that has CREATE DIRECTORY rights. For this example, log in as System, create a directory called `TestBFile`, and grant scott the rights to read it. You can do all this using the following SQL commands:

```
/* You need to be logged-in as System to have rights */
create directory TestBfile as 'c:\TestBfile'
/
grant read on directory TestBfile to scott
/
```

Now that you have a physical directory and a logical name for it in the database, you need to create a table to hold BFILE entries.

Creating a BFILE Table

Creating a table to hold BFILE entries is quite similar to creating one for BLOBs and CLOBS. This time, however, you specify a BFILE as the data type for the column. The following is sample DDL for the `person_picture` table:

```
create table person_picture (
person_id  number  not null,
picture    bfile )
tablespace USERS pctfree 20
storage (initial 100K next 100K pctincrease 0)
/
alter  table person_picture add
constraint    person_picture_pk
primary key (
person_id )
using index
tablespace USERS pctfree 20
storage (initial 10K next 10K pctincrease 0)
/
```

Now that you have a table to hold BFILE locators for person pictures, let's see how you add an entry to the table.

Inserting a BFILE

You can insert a BFILE locator into the table using the `bfilename( )` database function in a manner similar to the use of `empty_blob( )` with BLOBs. It has the following signature:

```
bfilename(varchar2 directory_name, varchar2 file_name)
```

which breaks down as:

directory_name
    The name of a database directory object

file_name
    The filesystem's name for the file

Example 12-9, TestBFILE, demonstrates the use of the bfilename() function to create a BFILE locator in the person_picture table.

Example 12-9. Inserting a BFILE locator

```java
import java.io.*;
import java.sql.*;
import java.text.*;

public class TestBFILE {
  Connection conn;

  public TestBFILE() {
    try {
      DriverManager.registerDriver(new oracle.jdbc.driver.OracleDriver());
      conn = DriverManager.getConnection(
        "jdbc:oracle:thin:@dssw2k01:1521:orcl", "scott", "tiger");
    }
    catch (SQLException e) {
      System.err.println(e.getMessage());
      e.printStackTrace();
    }
  }

  public static void main(String[] args)
   throws Exception, IOException {
    new TestBFILE().process();
  }

  public void process() throws IOException, SQLException {
    int         rows      = 0;
    ResultSet   rslt      = null;
    Statement   stmt      = null;
    long        person_id = 0;

    try {
      conn.setAutoCommit(false);

      // Get Tim's person_id
      stmt = conn.createStatement();
      rslt = stmt.executeQuery(
        "select person_id " +
        "from   person " +
        "where  last_name  = 'O''Reilly' " +
        "and    first_name = 'Tim'");
      while (rslt.next()) {
        rows++;
        person_id = rslt.getLong(1);
      }
      if (rows > 1) {
        System.err.println("Too many rows!");
        System.exit(1);
      }
      else if (rows == 0) {
        System.err.println("Not found!");
```

Example 12-9. Inserting a BFILE locator (continued)

```
        System.exit(1);
      }
      rslt.close();
      rslt = null;

      // Delete an existing row
      rows = stmt.executeUpdate(
        "delete person_picture " +
        "where  person_id = " + Long.toString( person_id ));

      rows = stmt.executeUpdate(
        "insert into person_picture " +
        "( person_id, picture ) " +
        "values " +
        "( " + Long.toString( person_id ) +
        ", bfilename( 'TESTBFILE', 'tim.gif' ) )");

      System.out.println(rows + " rows inserted");

      conn.commit();

      stmt.close();
      stmt = null;
    }
    catch (SQLException e) {
      System.err.println("SQL Error: " + e.getMessage());
    }
    finally {
      if (rslt != null)
        try { rslt.close();  } catch (SQLException ignore) { }
      if (stmt != null)
        try { stmt.close();  } catch (SQLException ignore) { }
    }
  }

  protected void finalize()
   throws Throwable {
    if (conn != null)
      try { conn.close(); } catch (SQLException ignore) { }
    super.finalize();
  }
}
```

The program starts in its main( ) method by instantiating a copy of itself and executing its process( ) method. The process( ) method begins by creating several variables:

rows

> An integer to keep track of the number of rows returned by, or affected by, the various executeXXX( ) methods

rslt

> A ResultSet used to hold the results of your query to get the person_id from the person table

stmt

A Statement to hold the statement object returned by the createStatement( ) method

person_id

A long to hold the primary key for the row that will be inserted

After creating the variables, the program enters a try block in which the bulk of the processing occurs. In the try block, the program first turns off auto-commit. Next, it creates a Statement object and uses it to query the database for the primary key required to insert an entry into the person_picture table. The results of the query are returned as a ResultSet object, which in turn is walked through by the while statement to get the person_id. The program continues by deleting any existing entry for the person_id. Next, the program inserts a row into the database utilizing the database function bfilename( ) to create the BFILE locator for the specified directory object and filename. Finally, the INSERT statement is committed.

As you can see from this example, we did not create the BFILE locator in our Java program. Just like the BLOB and CLOB locators, the BFILE locator can be created only by the database.

Updating a BFILE

There are two ways you can update a BFILE. First, you can use the bfilename( ) database function to recreate the BFILE locator. Second, you can copy a valid BFILE locator from one row or table to another. In the first instance, you would use the same syntax in an UPDATE statement that you just used in the INSERT statement. In the second instance, you would place the BFILE into an oracle.sql.BFILE variable (an oracle.sql.BFILE is a Java class that holds a read-only BFILE locator from the database) from a ResultSet and then use the OraclePreparedStatement object's setBFILE( ) method to update it.

Deleting a BFILE

Deleting a BFILE is simply a process of deleting the row in which the BFILE locator exists. You may consider setting the locator column to NULL to denote that no external file exists. Rather than do that, however, I recommend that you create an empty file in the filesystem and point to that file instead. I make this recommendation because if you try to retrieve and use a BFILE locator where the column is NULL, you'll get a NullPointerException. It's easier to implement a "no value" BFILE by retrieving an empty file.

Selecting BFILEs

Once you have a BFILE locator in a table, you can access the data directly from the filesystem through Oracle by using the BFILE object's openFile( ), getBinaryStream( ), and closeFile( ) methods. Example 12-10, TestBFILEServlet, does just that.

Example 12-10. A servlet to view a person's photo stored as a BFILE

```
import java.io.*;
import java.sql.*;
import javax.servlet.*;
import javax.servlet.http.*;
import oracle.jdbc.driver.*;
import oracle.sql.BFILE;

public class TestBFILEServlet extends HttpServlet {

  public void doGet(
   HttpServletRequest request,
   HttpServletResponse response)
   throws IOException, ServletException {

    ServletOutputStream out = response.getOutputStream( );

    BFILE      photo       = null;
    Connection connection = CacheConnection.checkOut( );
    Statement  statement  = null;
    ResultSet  resultSet  = null;
    String     sql        =
     "select picture " +
     "from    person p, person_picture i " +
     "where   p.person_id = i.person_id " +
     "and     last_name = " +
     formatWithTicks(request.getParameter("last_name")) + " " +
     "and     first_name = " +
     formatWithTicks(request.getParameter("first_name"));

    try {
      statement = connection.createStatement( );
      resultSet = statement.executeQuery(sql);
      if (resultSet.next( )) {
        photo = ((OracleResultSet)resultSet).getBFILE(1);
      }
      else {
        response.setContentType("text/html");
        out.println("<html><head><title>Person Photo</title></head>");
        out.println("<body><h1>No data found</h1></body></html>");
        return;
      }
      response.setContentType("image/gif");
      photo.openFile( );
      InputStream in = photo.getBinaryStream( );
```

```
      System.out.println("after getBinaryStream");
      int length = (int)photo.length();
      System.out.println("lenght of the blob is " + length);
      byte[] buffer = new byte[1024];
      while ((length = in.read(buffer)) != -1) {
        System.out.println("writing " + length + " bytes");
        out.write(buffer, 0, length);
      }
      System.out.println("written");
      in.close();
      in = null;
      photo.closeFile();
      out.flush();
    }
    catch (SQLException e) {
      System.out.println("TestBFILEServlet.doGet() SQLException: " +
        e.getMessage() + "executing ");
      System.out.println(sql);
    }
    finally {
      if (resultSet != null)
        try { resultSet.close(); } catch (SQLException ignore) { }
      if (statement != null)
        try { statement.close(); } catch (SQLException ignore) { }
    }
    // Return the conection
    CacheConnection.checkIn(connection);
  }

  public void doPost(
   HttpServletRequest request,
   HttpServletResponse response)
   throws IOException, ServletException {
    doGet(request, response);
  }

  private String formatWithTicks(String string) {
    if (string != null) {
      char[]      in  = string.toCharArray();
      StringBuffer out = new StringBuffer((int)(in.length * 1.1));
      if (in.length > 0)
        out.append("'");
      for (int i=0;i < in.length;i++) {
        out.append(in[i]);
        if (in[i] == '\'')
          out.append(in[i]);
      }
      if (in.length > 0)
        out.append("'");
      return out.toString();
    }
```

```
  else {
    return "NULL";
  }
 }
}
```

Using the same URL syntax used for `TestBLOBServlet` in Example 12-5, this servlet, `TestBFILEServlet`, retrieves the BFILE locator from the database and then opens the file using `openFile( )`. Next, it enters a `while` loop from which it reads the contents of the file using an `InputStream` object returned by the `getBinaryStream( )` method. In the `while` loop, the servlet writes to the browser all data read from the BFILE. When the `while` loop is complete, the input stream is closed, and the file reference is closed using `closeFile( )`. You can use the `TestBFILEServlet` program to verify that the earlier `TestBFILE` program (Example 12-9) correctly created a BFILE locator.

BFILE Methods

The following is a list of the `oracle.sql.BFILE` methods, all of which can throw an `SQLException`:

```
InputStream asciiStreamValue( )
void closeFile( )
boolean fileExists( )
InputStream getBinaryStream( )
byte[] getBytes(long pos, int length)
int getBytes(long pos, int length, byte buf[])
OracleConnection getConnection( )
String getDirAlias( )
String getName( )
boolean isConvertibleTo(Class jClass)
boolean isFileOpen( )
long length( )
void openFile( )
long position(BFILE pattern, long start)
long position(byte pattern[], long start)
Object toJdbc( )
```

At this point, we've covered the three large data types that Oracle recommends you use. The remaining two, LONG RAW and LONG, collectively known as LONGs, were used with Oracle7. And though they remain only as a means to be backward-compatible, they are still viable, and therefore, we shall cover them briefly.

LONG RAWs

As I stated indirectly at the beginning of the chapter, the BLOB data type has replaced the LONG RAW data type. This does not mean, however, that LONG RAW is no longer useful. There are many applications in which Oracle7 or LONGs are still in

---

use and in which, consequently, LONG RAW is the only option for storing large amounts of binary data. Given this fact, it is valuable for you to understand how this data type can be manipulated.

Unlike the three LOB types, which you access via locators, there is no locator involved when accessing a LONG RAW. When a query selects a LONG RAW column, the data is immediately available using the getXXX() accessor methods. The JDBC driver transfers data for these columns between the database and the client using streams. Even if you get the data as a byte array, the driver streams the data for you.

Creating a Table with a LONG RAW

Of course, to use a LONG RAW data type, you first need to create a table that uses a LONG RAW. As I stated at the beginning of the chapter, LONGs have restrictions that the other large data types do not. One of the most important restrictions is that you can have only one LONG column in a table. When using LOBs, you can combine both the biography and photo columns in one person_information table. However, when using LONGs, you need to create two tables, one for the biography and a second for the photo. Since we're discussing the binary LONG RAW, I'll mention that you can create a person_photo table using the following DDL:

```
drop    table person_photo
/
create table person_photo (
person_id  number  not null,
photo      long raw )
tablespace USERS pctfree 20
storage (initial 100K next 100K pctincrease 0)
/
alter  table person_photo add
constraint   person_photo_pk
primary key (
person_id )
using index
tablespace USERS pctfree 20
storage (initial 10K next 10K pctincrease 0)
/
```

Now that you have your table, let's take a look at how to insert values into a LONG RAW column.

Inserting a LONG RAW

To insert values into a LONG RAW column, use the PreparedStatement object's setBinaryStream() method or setBytes() method. Both methods stream the data just as they do for the locator data types, but the setBinaryStream() method is more efficient because you don't need a buffer large enough to hold all your binary data.

Instead, you can use a fairly small buffer and send the data one small buffer at a time. Example 12-11 demonstrates an insert operation using setBinaryStream( ).

Example 12-11. Inserting a LONG RAW

```java
import java.io.*;
import java.sql.*;

public class TestLongRawSetBinaryStream {
  Connection conn;

  TestLongRawSetBinaryStream( ) {
    try {
      Class.forName("oracle.jdbc.driver.OracleDriver");
      conn = DriverManager.getConnection(
        "jdbc:oracle:thin:@dssw2k01:1521:orcl", "scott", "tiger" );
    }
    catch (ClassNotFoundException e) {
      System.err.println("Class Not Found Error: " + e.getMessage( ));
      System.exit(1);
    }
    catch (SQLException e) {
      System.err.println("SQL Error: " + e.getMessage( ));
      System.exit(1);
    }
  }

  public static void main(String[] args) {
    new TestLongRawSetBinaryStream().process( );
  }

  private void process( ) {
    FileInputStream    fin       = null;
    int                rows      = 0;
    long               person_id = 0;
    PreparedStatement  pstmt     = null;
    Statement          stmt      = null;
    ResultSet          rslt      = null;

    try {
      conn.setAutoCommit(false);

      // Get Tim's person_id
      stmt = conn.createStatement( );
      rslt = stmt.executeQuery(
        "select person_id " +
        "from   person " +
        "where  last_name  = 'O''Reilly' " +
        "and    first_name = 'Tim'");
      while (rslt.next( )) {
        rows++;
        person_id = rslt.getLong(1);
      }
      if (rows > 1) {
        System.err.println("Too many rows!");
```

Example 12-11. Inserting a LONG RAW (continued)

```
            System.exit(1);
          }
          else if (rows == 0) {
            System.err.println("Not found!");
            System.exit(1);
          }
          rslt.close( );
          rslt = null;

          rows = stmt.executeUpdate(
            "delete person_photo " +
            "where  person_id = " + Long.toString(person_id));
          System.out.println(rows + " rows deleted");

          stmt.close( );
          stmt = null;

          pstmt = conn.prepareStatement(
            "insert into person_photo " +
            "( person_id, photo ) " +
            "values " +
            "( ?, ? )");
          pstmt.setLong(1, person_id);

          File fileName = new File("tim.gif");
          long fileLength = fileName.length( );
          fin = new FileInputStream(fileName);
          System.out.println(fileLength + " bytes read");
          pstmt.setBinaryStream(2, fin, (int)fileLength);
          rows = pstmt.executeUpdate( );
          System.out.println(rows + " rows inserted");

          fin.close( );
          fin = null;

          conn.commit( );

          pstmt.close( );
          pstmt = null;
        }
        catch (IOException e) {
          System.out.println("IO Error: " + e.getMessage( ));
          System.exit(1);
        }
        catch (SQLException e) {
          System.out.println("SQL Error: " + e.getMessage( ));
          System.exit(1);
        }
        finally {
          if (rslt != null)
            try { rslt.close( ); } catch (SQLException ignore) { }
          if (stmt != null)
            try { stmt.close( ); } catch (SQLException ignore) { }
```

Example 12-11. Inserting a LONG RAW (continued)

```
    if (fin  != null)
      try { fin.close( );  } catch (IOException ignore) { }
  }
 }

 protected void finalize( ) throws Throwable {
   if (conn != null)
     try { conn.close( ); } catch (SQLException ignore) { }
   super.finalize( );
 }
}
```

For the most part, TestLongRawSetBinaryStream functions the same as our BLOB sample program, TestBlobSetBinaryStream, shown in Example 12-3. The only significant difference is that the program does not bypass a locator to write the binary values, because a LONG RAW data type does not use a locator. Once again, it is worth noting that the FileInputStream needs to be closed after the executeUpdate( ) call but before the commit, to make sure all the data is written to the database.

Updating a LONG RAW

Updating LONG RAW is accomplished using the same methods used to insert the values—namely, setBinaryStream( ) and setBytes( ). Your only concern is to lock the table row by using the SELECT FOR UPDATE syntax as you do when updating the locator data types.

Deleting a LONG RAW

To delete a LONG RAW just delete its row. Unlike the locator data types, you can also set the LONG RAW column to NULL without the adverse effect of later retrieving an invalid locator, because no locator is used with LONG RAW.

Selecting a LONG RAW

Selecting a LONG RAW is done as easily as inserting one but with some important access order rules. To retrieve the data as a stream, use the getBinaryStream( ) method. However, when retrieving the data, you must call the getXXX( ) methods for all the columns in the SELECT statement in the same order as the columns are listed in the SELECT statement, and when you call a streaming data type, you must process the data immediately, that is, before you call any another getXXX( ) method, or the streamed data will no longer be accessible. Any columns following a LONG RAW column are not accessible until you read the contents of the LONG RAW column. If you want to bypass the LONG RAW column, get its stream using getBinaryStream( ) and then immediately call the stream's close( ) method. Once the column is skipped, its data will no longer be accessible. Example 12-12 is a servlet that retrieves and displays a person's photo from the LONG RAW column in the person_photo table.

Example 12-12. A servlet to view a person's photo stored as a LONG RAW

```java
import java.io.*;
import java.sql.*;
import javax.servlet.*;
import javax.servlet.http.*;

public class TestLongRawServlet extends HttpServlet {

  public void doGet(
   HttpServletRequest request,
   HttpServletResponse response)
   throws IOException, ServletException {

    ServletOutputStream out = response.getOutputStream();

    Connection conn = CacheConnection.checkOut();
    Statement  stmt = null;
    ResultSet  rslt = null;

    response.setContentType("image/gif");

    try {
      stmt = conn.createStatement();
      rslt = stmt.executeQuery("select photo from person_photo");
      if (rslt.next()) {
        byte[] buffer = new byte[32];
        int    length = 0;
        InputStream in = rslt.getBinaryStream(1);
        while ((length = in.read(buffer)) != -1) {
          out.write(buffer, 0, length);
        }
      }
      else {
        response.setContentType("text/html");
        out.println("<html><head><title>Person Photo</title></head>");
        out.println("<body><h1>No data found</h1></body></html>");
        return;
      }
      stmt.close();
      stmt = null;
    }
    catch(SQLException e) {
      System.out.println("SQLException cause: " + e.getMessage());
    }
    finally {
      if (rslt != null)
        try { rslt.close(); } catch (SQLException ignored) {}
      if (stmt != null)
        try { stmt.close(); } catch (SQLException ignored) {}
```

```
    }
    CacheConnection.checkIn(conn);
  }
}
```

Just like its BLOB peer, `TestBlobServlet` in Example 12-5, our LONG RAW servlet, `TestLongRawServlet`, retrieves the data as a stream and writes it directly to the browser. However, this time, no special locator method is used. Instead, the `ResultSet` object's `getBinaryStream( )` method is called. The program could also have used the `getBytes( )` method, which would not have returned a stream.

When working with LONG RAW, using the `getBytes( )` or `setBytes( )` methods makes coding simpler than using streams. However, these methods require significantly more memory, so use them cautiously. It is better to use the streaming methods.

You can prevent the JDBC driver from streaming the LONG RAW data by using the `OracleResultSet` object's `defineColumnType( )` method and setting the data type to `Types.VARBINARY`. An important side effect of using LONGs is that any time the JDBC driver encounters a streamed data type such as a LONG RAW, the prefetch buffer and the Oracle batching `executeUpdate` value are both set to 1. This means that row prefetching and batching are effectively disabled whenever you access a table with any streaming data type.

Now that you understand how to manipulate a LONG RAW, let's take a look at the character-specific data type, LONG.

LONGs

Just like the LONG RAW data type, a LONG data type is streamed. And, like a CLOB data type, a LONG is subject to NLS character set conversion. LONG column values can be updated using the `PreparedStatement` object's `setAsciiStream( )`, `setBinary-Stream( )`, and `setCharacterStream( )` streaming methods. Alternatively, LONG values can be updated using the `setBytes( )` and `setString( )` methods. LONG column values are read using the `ResultSet` object's complementary get methods. The streaming get methods are `getAsciiStream( )`, `getBinaryStream( )`, and `getCharacter-Stream( )`; the nonstreaming get methods are `getBytes( )` and `getString( )`.

Inserting or Updating a LONG

Other than the use of the methods just mentioned, when inserting or updating a LONG, there are limitations on the size of a `String` or byte array that you can update using the setString( ) or setBytes( ) methods. These limitations are listed in Table 11-3. When you exceed these limits, you will get the following error message: "Data size bigger than max size for this type: ####." To work around these limitations, you need to use the streaming methods.

Selecting a LONG

To retrieve data in ASCII, use the ResultSet object's getAsciiStream( ) method. You can use the getAsciiStream( ) method only if the underlying database uses the US7ASCII or WE8ISO8859P1 character set. Otherwise, you can use the getCharacterStream( ) method, which returns UCS-2-encoded characters (Unicode) regardless of the underlying database's character set. Even if you get the data as a String, the JDBC driver will stream the data for you.

If you use the getBinaryStream( ) method, one of two possibilities exists. If you are using the OCI driver, and its client character set is not set to US7ASCII or WE8ISO8859P1, then a call to the getBinaryStream( ) method returns data in the UTF-8 character set. If you are using the Thin driver, and the database's character set is not set to US7ASCII or WE8ISO8859P1, then a call to the getBinaryStream( ) method also returns data in the UTF-8 character set. Otherwise, you'll get the data in the US7ASCII character set.

As with the LONG RAW data type, you must call the getXXX( ) methods for each column returned by the SELECT statement in the same order in which those columns are listed in the SELECT statement. Also, when processing a streamed column, you must process the streamed data before calling another getXXX( ) method. Once you move on to another getXXX( ) method, the streamed data is no longer accessible. In addition, you can prevent the JDBC driver from streaming LONG data by using the OracleResultSet object's defineColumnType( ) method, setting the data type of a LONG column to Types.VARCHAR. This may be desirable if there are a small number of characters in the data to be stored.

Now that you are an expert on using streaming data types, let's take a look at how to call stored procedures in Chapter 13.

CHAPTER 13
Callable Statements

`CallableStatement` objects are used to call stored procedures. The stored procedures themselves can be written using PL/SQL or Java. If they are written in Java, they must be published to the RDBMS by creating a SQL call specification. You can see examples of this in Chapter 5. Stored procedures exist to perform data-intensive operations that cannot be accomplished using just SQL, and they perform these operations inside the database where network performance is a moot issue.

For example, let's say you need to access five different tables in order to perform a complex calculation and need to store the result in a sixth table. Let's further assume that the calculation is complex enough that it cannot be performed using just SQL. If you perform the work on a client, then the client will have to retrieve all the data necessary to perform the calculation and send the result back to the database. If the number of rows that need to be retrieved by the client is large, this network transfer of data could consume an inordinate amount of elapsed time. However, if you perform the calculation as a stored procedure, the elapsed time of transmitting data across the network will be eliminated, and the resulting calculation will be much quicker. This example represents the type of situation in which stored procedures excel.

As with all good things, stored procedures are sometimes taken to an extreme and are sometimes used as a panacea. For example, some developers eliminate SQL from their application altogether and use only stored procedures. This is not a good use of Oracle stored procedures, simply because selecting data from a table from your application is faster than calling a stored procedure that selects data from a table and returns it to your application. When you go through a stored procedure, you have two network round trips instead of one.

Enough with my soapbox speeches! Let's get on to some real meat. In this chapter, you'll learn how to identify the parameters for, and formulate, stored procedure calls using both SQL92 and Oracle syntax. You'll learn how to create a `CallableStatement` object to execute stored procedures, how to set and retrieve parameter values, and how to actually execute a stored procedure. Let's get started by looking at how to identify stored procedure names and parameter types.

Understanding Stored Procedures

With Oracle, *stored procedure* actually refers collectively to standalone stored functions, standalone procedures, packaged functions, and procedures. So when I use the term stored procedure in this chapter, please understand that I am referring generally to any of these procedure or function types.

To call a stored procedure, you need to know the procedure name and know about any parameters that will be passed to the procedure. In the case of a function, you also need to know the return type. One way to get this information is to query Oracle's data dictionary views for stored procedure source code and look at the signature for the procedures you wish to use. The next section shows you how to interpret Oracle's stored procedure signatures. Following that is a section that shows you, among other things, how to query the data dictionary for procedure signatures.

Stored Procedure Signatures

It's important to know the differences in the syntax used by stored procedures so you can code your callable statements appropriately. Oracle stored procedures are created using three different syntaxes, one for standalone functions, another for standalone procedures, and a third for functions and procedures that are part of a package.

Standalone functions

The difference between a procedure and function is that a function returns a value, so it can be used as an evaluated item in an expression. The syntax to create a stored function is:

```
CREATE [OR REPLACE] [user.]FUNCTION function_name
 [(parameters)]
 RETURN data_type {AS | IS}
function_body

parameters ::= parameter_declaration [,parameter_declaration...]

parameter_declaration ::- parameter_name [IN | OUT | IN OUT] data_type
```

which breaks down as:

user
> The schema owner of the function.

function_name
> The name of the function.

RETURN *data_type*
> Specifies the SQL data type returned by the function.

parameter_name
> The name of a parameter passed to the function. Zero or more parameters may be passed to a function.

IN | OUT | IN OUT
> Specifies the use of a parameter. An IN parameter can be read, but you cannot write to it. An OUT parameter can be written to but not read. You can both read from and write to an IN OUT parameter.

data_type
> The SQL data type of the parameter.

For example, to create an errorless TO_NUMBER function for user SCOTT, log into Oracle with SQL*Plus as SCOTT/TIGER and execute the following PL/SQL code:

```
create or replace function ToNumberFun (
aiv_varchar2 in varchar2 )
return          number is
begin
 return to_number( aiv_varchar2 );
exception
 when OTHERS then
  return null;
end ToNumberFun;
/
```

Standalone procedures

Use the following syntax to create a standalone stored procedure. A procedure does not return a value. However, both functions and procedures can have OUT or IN OUT variables that return values.

```
CREATE [OR REPLACE] [user.]PROCEDURE procedure_name
 [(parameters)] {AS | IS}
procedure_body
parameters ::= parameter_declaration [,parameter_declaration...]

parameter_declartion ::= parameter name [IN | OUT | IN OUT] data_type
```

See "Standalone functions" for an explanation of the syntax.

Packages

A package is a collection of related functions and procedures. It has a specification that defines which functions, procedures, and variables are publicly accessible. It also has a body that contains the functions and procedures defined in the specification and possibly also contains private functions, private procedures, and private variable declarations. Packages are an improvement over standalone functions and procedures, because the separation between the specification and body reduces stored procedure dependency problems. The syntax for creating a package specification is:

```
CREATE [OR REPLACE] PACKAGE package_name AS
package_specification
```

in which *package_name* is the name of the package. The following syntax is used to create a package body:

```
CREATE [OR REPLACE] PACKAGE BODY package_name AS
package_body
```

Why is this explanation of stored procedure syntax important? Because you need to understand the stored procedure syntax in order to know the name of a stored procedure (or function), which data types you can pass to it, and which data type it returns.

Describing Signatures

If you want to invoke a stored procedure and double-check its name and the parameters you must pass to it, you can take one of several approaches. If you have access to SQL*Plus, you can use one of the following variations on the DESCRIBE command:

```
desc[ribe] [schema.]function_name
desc[ribe] [schema.]procedure_name
desc[ribe] [schema.]package_name
```

The following example shows the DESCRIBE command being used to display information about the ToNumberFun function owned by the user Scott:

```
SQL> desc tonumberfun
FUNCTION tonumberfun RETURNS NUMBER
 Argument Name                      Type                     In/Out Default?
 ---------------------------------- ------------------------ ------ --------
 AIV_VARCHAR2                       VARCHAR2                 IN
```

The JDBC API defines a method, named DatabaseMetaData.getProcedureColumns( ), you can invoke to get stored procedure signature data. In practice, however, the getProcedureColumns( ) method is not all that useful. Oracle stored procedures can be overloaded, and, using getProcedureColumns( ), you can't distinguish between the different overloaded versions of the same stored procedure. So, for Oracle at least, the getProcedureColumns( ) method is useless.

A third way to determine the signature for a standalone function, standalone procedure, or package is to take a peek at the source code. The program named DescribeStoredProcedures, shown in Example 13-1, does this. You pass in the name of a stored procedure on the command line, then the program queries the SYS.DBA_SOURCE view for the source code and displays that source code. If you don't have access to the DBA views, you can change the program to use SYS.ALL_SOURCE.

Example 13-1. Describing a stored procedure

```java
import java.io.*;
import java.sql.*;
import java.text.*;

public class DescribeStoredProcedures {
  Connection conn;

  public DescribeStoredProcedures( ) {
    try {
      DriverManager.registerDriver(new oracle.jdbc.driver.OracleDriver( ));
      conn = DriverManager.getConnection(
        "jdbc:oracle:thin:@dssw2k01:1521:orcl", "scott", "tiger");
    }
    catch (SQLException e) {
      System.err.println(e.getMessage( ));
      e.printStackTrace( );
    }
  }

  public static void main(String[] args)
   throws Exception, IOException {
    String storedProcedureName = null;
    String schemaName         = null;
    if (args.length > 0)
      schemaName          = args[0];
    if (args.length > 1)
      storedProcedureName = args[1];
    new DescribeStoredProcedures( ).process(
      schemaName, storedProcedureName);
  }

  public void process(
   String schemaName,
   String storedProcedureName)
   throws SQLException {

    int rows                  = 0;
    ResultSet rslt            = null;
    Statement stmt            = null;
    String previous           = "~";
    String schemaPattern      = "%";
    String procedureNamePattern = "%";

    try {
      if (schemaName != null && !schemaName.equals(""))
        schemaPattern = schemaName;
      if (storedProcedureName != null && !storedProcedureName.equals(""))
        procedureNamePattern = storedProcedureName;
      stmt = conn.createStatement( );
      rslt = stmt.executeQuery(
       "select type||' '||owner||'.'||name, line, text " +
       "from   sys.dba_source " +
```

Example 13-1. Describing a stored procedure (continued)

```
        "where  type = 'FUNCTION' " +
        "and    owner like '" + schemaPattern + "' " +
        "and    name  like '" + procedureNamePattern + "' " +
        "union all " +
        "select type||' '||owner||'.'||name, line, text " +
        "from   sys.dba_source " +
        "where  type = 'PROCEDURE' " +
        "and    owner like '" + schemaPattern + "' " +
        "and    name  like '" + procedureNamePattern + "' " +
        "union all " +
        "select type||' '||owner||'.'||name, line, text " +
        "from   sys.dba_source " +
        "where  type = 'PACKAGE' " +
        "and    owner like '" + schemaPattern + "' " +
        "and    name  like '" + procedureNamePattern + "' " +
        "union all " +
        "select type||' '||owner||'.'||name, line, text " +
        "from   sys.dba_source " +
        "where  type = 'TYPE' " +
        "and    owner like '" + schemaPattern + "' " +
        "and    name  like '" + procedureNamePattern + "' " +
        "order by 1, 2");
      while (rslt.next()) {
        rows++;
        if (!rslt.getString(1).equals(previous)) {
          if (!previous.equals("~"))
          System.out.println("");
          previous = rslt.getString(1);
        }
        System.out.print(rslt.getString(3));
      }
      if (!previous.equals("~"))
        System.out.println("");
    }
    catch (SQLException e) {
      System.err.println("SQL Error: " + e.getMessage());
    }
    finally {
      if (rslt !- null)
        try { rslt.close();  } catch (SQLException ignore) { }
      if (stmt != null)
        try { stmt.close();  } catch (SQLException ignore) { }
    }
  }

  protected void finalize()
   throws Throwable {
   if (conn != null)
     try { conn.close(); } catch (SQLException ignore) { }
   super.finalize();
  }
}
```

Here are the results of using `DescribeStoredProcedures` to describe the scott. ToNumberFun function:

```
C:\>java DescribeStoredProcedures SCOTT TONUMBERFUN
function ToNumberFun (
aiv_varchar2 in varchar2 )
return         number is
begin
 return to_number( aiv_varchar2 );
exception
 when OTHERS then
  return null;
```

Of course, the best place to get information on stored procedure names and parameters is from written documentation, but we all know that from time to time, written documentation is not available. Consequently, the SQL*Plus DESCRIBE command and the `DescribeStoredProcedures` program can be quite handy.

Once you have the signature for the stored procedure you wish to execute, there is a problem that can arise: the username that will execute the stored procedure may not have the rights to do so.

The SYS.DBA and SYS.V_$ Views

Every developer who plans to work with an Oracle database should have access to the SYS.DBA and SYS.V_$ views. These views show all the objects for all the schemas in a database, even if the current user does not have access to them. At the same time, they do not show any of the actual data in schemas that a developer does not have access to, so they can't be used for malicious activities.

If a developer does have access to these views, she can determine whether a problem with not finding a database object is due to grants (or lack thereof) or due to the fact that an object does not actually exist in the database. She can do this by comparing the output of the SYS.ALL views, which everyone typically has access to, against their SYS. DBA counterparts.

So if you don't have access to the DBA views, request it. It will save you a great deal of time to be able to query the data dictionary views yourself.

Granting Execute Rights

If you've written a stored procedure, how do you determine who has access to it? Initially, only you, the owner of the stored procedure, and anyone who has been granted the EXECUTE ANY PROCEDURE system privilege have access to your new procedure. But how can you tell if another user has EXECUTIVE rights? Examine the SYS.ALL_TAB_PRIVS view and look at the rows from the view that contain the name of the stored procedure in the `table_name` column. The view and column names make doing this a bit confusing, but that's the way things work. For example, to see who has access to user SCOTT's `ToNumberFun` function, execute the following query:

```
select  grantee,
        privilege
from    sys.all_tab_privs
where   table_name   = 'TONUMBERFUN'
and     table_schema = 'SCOTT'
```

This gets results such as the following:

```
GRANTEE                             PRIVILEGE
----------------------------------- -----------------------------------------
SYSTEM                              EXECUTE
```

In this case, because no users are listed in the output, you know that user SCOTT has not yet granted anyone else access to `ToNumberFun`. If you find that a particular username or role needs to be granted access to a stored procedure, you or your DBA can grant those rights using the following form of the GRANT statement:

```
GRANT EXECUTE ON [schema.]stored_procedure TO {user_name | role_name}
```

which breaks down as:

schema
> Optionally used by a DBA to grant someone access to another user's object

stored_procedure
> The name of a standalone function, standalone procedure, or package

user_name | role_name
> The name of the user or role to which you are granting EXECUTE rights

Given the information in this section, you can check whether a stored procedure that does not seem to exist really does not exist or if the EXECUTE privilege has just not been granted to the desired user.

Now that you have some background in Oracle stored procedure signatures and in the granting of EXECUTE privileges, let's take a look at how to formulate a stored procedure call for a callable statement.

Calling Stored Procedures

Calling a stored procedure from your Java program requires a five-step process:

1. Formulate a callable statement.
2. Create a `CallableStatement` object.
3. Register any OUT parameters.
4. Set any IN parameters.
5. Execute the callable statement.

In the sections that follow, I'll describe each of the steps listed here. The function `ToNumberFun`, owned by the user SCOTT, will form the basis for most of the examples.

Formulating a Callable Statement

The first step in the process of calling a stored procedure is to formulate a stored procedure call, that is, properly format a string value that will be passed to a Connection object's prepareCall( ) method in order to create a CallableStatement object. When it comes to formulating a stored procedure call, you have two syntaxes at your disposal: the SQL92 escape syntax and the Oracle syntax. In theory, because it's not vendor-specific, the SQL92 escape syntax gives you better portability. But let's be realistic. Stored procedure capabilities and syntax vary wildly from one database vendor to another. If you choose to invest in stored procedures, I'd say you're not too interested in portability. Nonetheless, let's first take a look at the SQL92 escape syntax.

SQL92 escape syntax

When using the SQL92 escape syntax, the String object or string literal you pass to the Connection object's prepareCall( ) method to create a CallableStatement object takes on one of the following forms:

```
{? = call [schema.][package.]function_name[(?,?,...)]}
```

```
{call [schema.][package.]procedure_name[(?,?,...)]}
```

which breaks down as:

schema
> Refers to the stored procedure's owner's username or schema name

package
> Refers to a package name and applies only when you are not calling a standalone function or procedure

function_name
> Refers to the name of a standalone function or to the name of a function in a package

procedure_name
> Refers to the name of a standalone procedure or to the name of a procedure in a package

?
> A placeholder for an IN, OUT, or IN OUT parameter, or for the return value of a function

 In this syntax diagram, the curly braces ({}) are part of the syntax; they do not, in this case, denote optional choices.

The question mark characters (?) in the procedure or function call mark the locations of parameters that you supply later, after creating the CallableStatement object and before executing the statement. For example, consider the following signature for the ToNumberFun standalone function:

```
create or replace function ToNumberFun (
aiv_varchar2 in varchar2 )
return number;
```

The properly formatted callable statement string for this function would look like:

```
{ ? = call tonumberfun( ? ) }
```

If you are calling a stored procedure rather than a stored function, omit the leading ? = characters. That's because procedures do not return a value as functions do. The following is an example of a standalone procedure:

```
create or replace procedure ToNumberPrc (
aiv_varchar2 in varchar2,
aon_number out number )
begin
 aon_number := to_number( aiv_varchar2 );
exception
 when OTHERS then
  aon_number := null;
end ToNumberPrc;
/
```

A properly formatted callable statement string for the ToNumberPrc procedure would look like:

```
{ call tonumberprc( ?, ? ) }
```

If the procedure or function that you are calling is part of a stored package, then you need to reference the package name when creating your callable statement. The following is a package named chapter_13 that implements a procedure and a function, both of which are named ToNumber:

```
REM  The specification

create or replace package chapter_13 as

function ToNumber (
aiv_varchar2 in varchar2 )
return number;

procedure ToNumber (
aiv_varchar2 in varchar2,
aon_number out number );

end;
/

REM  The body

create or replace package body chapter_13 as
```

```
function ToNumber (
aiv_varchar2 in varchar2 )
return number is
begin
 return to_number( aiv_varchar2 );
exception
 when OTHERS then
   return null;
end ToNumber;

procedure ToNumber (
aiv_varchar2 in varchar2,
aon_number out number ) is
begin
 aon_number := to_number( aiv_varchar2 );
exception
 when OTHERS then
   aon_number := null;
end ToNumber;

end;
/
```

The callable statement strings for the ToNumber function and procedure defined in the chapter_13 package would look like:

```
{ ? = call chapter_13.tonumber( ? ) }
```

```
{ call chapter_13.tonumber( ?, ? ) }
```

Now that you understand the SQL92 escape syntax, let's take a look at Oracle's syntax for callable statements.

Oracle syntax

Oracle's syntax, which is PL/SQL syntax, is very similar to SQL92 syntax:

```
begin ?:=[schema.][package.]function_name[(?,?,...)]; end;
```

```
begin [schema.][package.]procedure_name[(?,?,...)]; end;
```

This breaks down as:

schema
  Refers to the stored procedure owner's username or schema name

package
  Refers to a package name and applies if you are not calling a standalone stored procedure

function_name

Refers to the name of a standalone function or to the name of a function in a package specification

procedure_name

Refers to the name of a standalone procedure or to the name of a procedure in a package specification

?

A placeholder for an IN, OUT, or IN OUT parameter, or for the return value of a function.

The Oracle syntax for callable-statement string literals for the four stored procedure signatures shown in the previous section on SQL92 syntax is described here:

For the standalone function ToNumberFun with a signature of:

```
function ToNumberFun (
aiv_varchar2 in varchar2 )
return number;
```

the callable statement string is:

```
begin ? := tonumberfun( ? ); end;
```

For the standalone procedure ToNumberProc with a signature of:

```
procedure ToNumberPrc (
aiv_varchar2 in varchar2,
aon_number out number )
```

the callable statement string is:

```
begin tonumberprc( ?, ? ); end;
```

For the function and procedure ToNumber in the chapter_13 package with the following signatures:

```
function ToNumber (
aiv_varchar2 in varchar2 )
return number;

procedure ToNumber (
aiv_varchar2 in varchar2,
aon_number out number );
```

the callable statement strings are:

```
begin ? := chapter_13.tonumber( ? ); end;

begin chapter_13.tonumber( ?, ? ); end;
```

Now that you know how to formulate a stored procedure, callable-statement string literal, let's look at how to use these string literals when creating a CallableStatement object.

Creating a CallableStatement

To create a `CallableStatement` object, use the `Connection.prepareCall( )` method. You need to pass it one parameter—a string—describing how the procedure or function is invoked. For example:

```
CallableStatement cstmt = null;
try {
 cstmt = conn.prepareCall("{ ? = call tonumberfun( ? ) }");
 . . .
}
```

In this example, the following string was passed as an argument to `prepareCall( )`:

```
{ ? = call tonumberfun( ? ) }
```

Next, let's look at some possible errors that you might encounter when creating a `CallableStatement` object.

Handling Errors

As with the `Statement` and `PreparedStatement` objects we have already covered, if there is something wrong with your stored procedure, callable-statement syntax, the call to your `Connection` object's `prepareStatement( )` method will throw a `SQLException`. The most common `SQLException` occurs when a procedure or function does not exist:

```
SQL Error: ORA-06550: line 1, column 13:
PLS-00201: identifier 'TONUMBERFUN' must be declared
ORA-06550: line 1, column 7:
PL/SQL: Statement ignored
```

This error may come about because the procedure or function does not actually exist in the database, or it could be that the username you are using when you call the stored procedure does not have EXECUTE rights on the procedure.

After you create a `CallableStatement` object, you need to register any OUT parameters before executing the statement. Next, let's see how you do that.

Registering OUT Parameters

In order to get the results from a stored procedure call, you must register any OUT or IN OUT parameters before executing the `CallableStatement`. To do this, call the `CallableStatement` object's `registerOutParameter( )` method, passing it the position of the placeholder character in the callable-statement string starting at 1 and moving from left to right, just as you do for the other accessor methods, and a `java.sql. Types` constant to specify the SQL data type that will be returned. There are two applicable signatures for the `registerOutParameter( )` method. For VARCHAR2 and DATE parameters, use the following signature:

```
registerOutParameter(
 int parameterIndex,
```

```
int sqlType)
throws SQLException
```

For NUMBER data types, you need to specify the scale of the number being returned, so use the following `registerOutParameter( )` signature:

```
registerOutParameter(
int parameterIndex,
int sqlType,
int scale)
throws SQLException
```

The scale in the second signature allows you to control the number of significant digits to the right of the decimal point that are returned. To set the OUT parameter for our sample function, ToNumberFun, shown earlier in "SQL92 escape syntax," you can specify the following:

```
cstmt.registerOutParameter(1, Types.DOUBLE, 2);
```

You can determine the Types constant to use for a given OUT parameter by referring to Table 10-2. In this case, I used Types.DOUBLE, because it is one of the floating point Java data types. After registering OUT parameters, continue by setting any IN parameters.

Setting IN Parameters

Setting IN or IN OUT parameters is done in a fashion similar to that used in Chapter 11 to set parameters for prepared statements. You use the setXXX( ) accessor methods, passing the position of the placeholder character in the callable-statement string (starting from 1, counting from left to right) along with an appropriate Java data type. When determining the ordinal position of a parameter, start counting with the left-most placeholder and count each placeholder in the statement until you get to the parameter that you are setting. Be sure to count each placeholder, whether it is an IN, OUT, or IN OUT parameter. Let's look at an example. For the ToNumberFun standalone function, the callable-statement string literal was:

```
{ ? = call tonumberfun( ? ) }
```

Therefore, an appropriately coded setXXX( ) method would be:

```
cstmt.setString(2, aString);
```

But what if you need to set a parameter value to NULL? There is a special setXXX( ) method for setting an IN parameter to NULL values.

Handling NULL Values

If you wish to set a parameter value to NULL, then you must use the setNull( ) method, which has the following signature:

```
setNull(int parameterIndex, int sqlType)
```

`sqlType` is the appropriate `java.sql.Types` constant for the SQL data type of the parameter in question. You can determine which `Types` constant to use by referring to Table 10-1.

Executing a Stored Procedure

After a `CallableStatement` has been created, any OUT parameters registered, and any IN parameters set, you can execute the `CallableStatement` using its execute( ) method. For example:

```
cstmt.execute();
```

You can use the `CallableStatement` object's executeUpdate( ) method to execute a stored procedure, but you'll always get back a value of 1, meaning one row was affected, which doesn't make much sense. You can ignore the value, but what is the sense of using a method that returns a nonsensical value? When you execute the stored procedure, JDBC passes any of the IN or IN OUT parameters you set to the database. In turn, the database returns any OUT or IN OUT parameters to you via JDBC.

Getting OUT Parameter Values

To get the values from OUT or IN OUT parameters, use the getXXX( ) accessor methods similar to how they were used with result sets in Chapter 10. This time, however, call the getXXX( ) methods using a reference to the `CallableStatement` object. For example, to get the returned value from the `ToNumberFun` function used in earlier examples, and to get that return value as a `double`, use the following code:

```
double aNumber = cstmt.getDouble(1);
```

Putting It All Together

Now that we have gone through the entire process of executing a stored procedure, from identifying its signature through getting the results, let's take a look at an example. The program `TestStoredProcedures`, shown in Example 13-2, exercises our sample stored procedures—`ToNumberFun`, `ToNumberPrc`, `Chapter_13.ToNumber` (the function), and `Chapter_13.ToNumber` (the procedure)—using both SQL92 escape syntax and Oracle syntax. Before you try this example, make sure you have compiled the four aforementioned stored procedures using the SCOTT user ID.

Example 13-2. Executing stored procedures

```
import java.io.*;
import java.sql.*;
import java.text.*;

public class TestStoredProcedures {
  Connection conn;
```

Example 13-2. Executing stored procedures (continued)

```
public TestStoredProcedures( ) {
  try {
    DriverManager.registerDriver(new oracle.jdbc.driver.OracleDriver( ));
    conn = DriverManager.getConnection(
      "jdbc:oracle:thin:@dssw2k01:1521:orcl", "scott", "tiger");
  }
  catch (SQLException e) {
    System.err.println(e.getMessage( ));
    e.printStackTrace( );
  }
}

public static void main(String[] args)
  throws Exception {
  new TestStoredProcedures().process( );
}

public void process( )
  throws SQLException {
  Double aNumber            = null;
  long    start             = 0;
  long    end               = 0;
  String aString            = "1234567.890";
  CallableStatement cstmt = null;

  try {
    start = System.currentTimeMillis( );

    // *** SQL92 escape syntax ***

    // Create the callable statement
    cstmt = conn.prepareCall(
      "{ ? = call scott.tonumberfun( ? ) }");

    // Register the OUT parameter
    cstmt.registerOutParameter(1, Types.DOUBLE, 2);

    // Set the IN parameter
    cstmt.setString(2, aString);

    // Execute the stored procedure
    // Using executeUpdate( ); it returns a value of 1
    int rows = cstmt.executeUpdate( );
    System.out.println("rows = " + rows);

    // Get the returned value
    aNumber = new Double(cstmt.getDouble(1));

    // Check to see if the returned value was NULL
    if (cstmt.wasNull( )) aNumber = null;

    // Display the returned value
    System.out.println(aString + " converted to a number = " + aNumber);
```

Example 13-2. Executing stored procedures (continued)

```
cstmt = conn.prepareCall(
 "{ call scott.tonumberprc( ?, ? ) }");
cstmt.registerOutParameter(2, Types.DOUBLE);
cstmt.setString(1, aString);
cstmt.execute( );
aNumber = new Double(cstmt.getDouble(2));
if (cstmt.wasNull( )) aNumber = null;
System.out.println(aString + " converted to a number = " + aNumber);

cstmt = conn.prepareCall(
 "{ ? = call scott.chapter_13.tonumber( ? ) }");
cstmt.registerOutParameter(1, Types.DOUBLE);
cstmt.setString(2, aString);
cstmt.execute( );
aNumber = new Double(cstmt.getDouble(1));
if (cstmt.wasNull( )) aNumber = null;
System.out.println(aString + " converted to a number = " + aNumber);

cstmt = conn.prepareCall(
 "{ call scott.chapter_13.tonumber( ?, ? ) }");
cstmt.registerOutParameter(2, Types.DOUBLE);
cstmt.setString(1, aString);
cstmt.execute( );
aNumber = new Double(cstmt.getDouble(2));
if (cstmt.wasNull( )) aNumber = null;
System.out.println(aString + " converted to a number = " + aNumber);

// *** Oracle PL/SQL syntax ***

cstmt = conn.prepareCall(
 "begin ? := scott.tonumberfun( ? ); end;");
cstmt.registerOutParameter(1, Types.DOUBLE);
cstmt.setString(2, aString);
cstmt.execute( );
aNumber = new Double(cstmt.getDouble(1));
if (cstmt.wasNull( )) aNumber = null;
System.out.println(aString + " converted to a number = " + aNumber);

cstmt = conn.prepareCall(
 "begin scott.tonumberprc( ?, ? ); end;");
cstmt.registerOutParameter(2, Types.DOUBLE);
cstmt.setString(1, aString);
cstmt.execute( );
aNumber = new Double(cstmt.getDouble(2));
if (cstmt.wasNull( )) aNumber = null;
System.out.println(aString + " converted to a number = " + aNumber);

cstmt = conn.prepareCall(
 "begin ? := scott.chapter_13.tonumber( ? ); end;");
cstmt.registerOutParameter(1, Types.DOUBLE);
```

Example 13-2. Executing stored procedures (continued)

```
        cstmt.setString(2, aString);
        cstmt.execute( );
        aNumber = new Double(cstmt.getDouble(1));
        if (cstmt.wasNull( )) aNumber = null;
        System.out.println(aString + " converted to a number = " + aNumber);

        cstmt = conn.prepareCall(
          "begin scott.chapter_13.tonumber( ?, ? ); end;");
        cstmt.registerOutParameter(2, Types.DOUBLE);
        cstmt.setString(1, aString);
        cstmt.execute( );
        aNumber = new Double(cstmt.getDouble(2));
        if (cstmt.wasNull( )) aNumber = null;
        System.out.println(aString + " converted to a number = " + aNumber);

        end = System.currentTimeMillis( );
        System.out.println("Average elapsed time = " +
          (end - start)/8 + " milliseconds");
      }
    catch (SQLException e) {
      System.err.println("SQL Error: " + e.getMessage( ));
      }
    finally {
      if (cstmt != null)
        try { cstmt.close( );  } catch (SQLException ignore) { }
      }
    }
  }

  protected void finalize( )
    throws Throwable {
    if (conn != null)
      try { conn.close( ); } catch (SQLException ignore) { }
      super.finalize( );
    }
  }
}
```

Like our earlier examples, TestStoredProcedures, starts in its main( ) method by instantiating a copy of itself and then executes its process( ) method. In the process( ) method, the program first allocates several local variables:

aNumber

A Double to hold the value returned from the stored procedure.

aString

A String to hold the character representation of a number to be converted by the stored procedure.

start

A long to hold the start time, used later to calculate the average execution time of the stored procedures.

end

A second long to hold the completion time after all the stored procedures have been executed. It will be used with start to calculate an average elapsed time in milliseconds for each stored procedure call.

cstmt

A CallableStatement object to execute the stored procedures.

Next, the program enters a try block where it prepares and executes the stored procedures shown earlier using both the SQL92 escape syntax and the Oracle syntax.

Let's study the first stored procedure call in detail. The program creates a CallableStatement object by calling the Connection object's prepareCall() method and passing a properly formatted SQL92 syntax string. Next, it registers the OUT parameter for the stored function using the CallableStatement object's registerOutParameter() method, passing it ordinal position 1 and a java.sql.Types.DOUBLE constant. Then, it sets the second parameter, an IN parameter, using the CallableStatement object's setString() method. Next, it executes the stored procedure by calling the CallableStatement object's executeUpdate() method, capturing the return value of the method, which the program in turn reports to you via a call to System.out.println(). (The program will always report that one row was affected.) The program then proceeds by getting the return value of the stored procedure using the CallableStatement object's getDouble() method. Since the getDouble() method will return 0.0 if the returned value from the stored procedure is NULL, the program then calls the CallableStatement object's wasNull() method to determine whether to set aNumber to null in order to correctly store the return value of the stored procedure. Finally, the program prints the conversion result using the System.out.println() method.

The process of executing a stored procedure is followed seven more times to demonstrate that all eight syntax strings work properly. Finally, the program records the end of the last stored procedure and displays an average execution time on the screen.

Why did we compute an average execution time for the stored procedure calls? Because I want you to be able to compare the performance of the different JDBC drivers with respect to stored procedure calls. If you change the driver type from Thin to OCI, and run the program several times, you'll see that the OCI driver is slightly faster. If the sample stored procedure transferred a larger amount of data in each direction, you'd see an even larger difference in the performance of the two drivers, with the OCI driver being as much as 50% faster.

CallableStatement Is an OracleCallableStatement

The CallableStatement object used in this chapter's examples is an interface. The full interface name is java.sql.CallableStatement. This interface is implemented by oracle.jdbc.driver.OracleCallableStatement, which extends oracle.jdbc.driver.OraclePreparedStatement. This means that all the proprietary methods that are available in OracleStatement and OraclePreparedStatement are also available in Oracle-CallableStatement. The following is a list of the proprietary methods available in OracleCallableStatement, all of which can throw a SQLException:

```
clearParameters( )
ARRAY getARRAY(int parameterIndex)
InputStream getAsciiStream(int parameterIndex)
BFILE getBFILE(int parameterIndex)
InputStream getBinaryStream(int parameterIndex)
BLOB getBLOB(int parameterIndex)
CHAR getCHAR(int parameterIndex)
CLOB getCLOB(int parameterIndex)
ResultSet getCursor(int parameterIndex)
Object getCustomDatum(int parameterIndex, CustomDatumFactory factory)
DATE getDATE(int parameterIndex)
NUMBER getNUMBER(int parameterIndex)
Datum getOracleObject(int parameterIndex)
RAW getRAW(int parameterIndex)
REF getREF(int parameterIndex)
ROWID getROWID(int parameterIndex)
STRUCT getSTRUCT(int parameterIndex)
InputStream getUnicodeStream(int parameterIndex)
registerOutParameter(
  int paramIndex, int sqlType, int scale, int maxLength)
```

Object-Relational SQL

We've now covered everything there is to know about using JDBC with relational SQL. Our second and third options for how to use the database involve object-relational SQL. Object-relational SQL is the application of SQL to Oracle database objects and forms the basis of the object portion of Oracle's object-relational features. In Part IV we'll cover the use of the Statement, ResultSet, PreparedStatement, and CallableStatement Java objects with Oracle database objects. So let's start our journey into object-relational SQL with an overview of Oracle's object-relational technology.

CHAPTER 14

An Object-Relational SQL Example

Oracle documentation refers to Oracle8*i*'s ability to store user-defined data types in the database as object-relational SQL. I think this is quite appropriate. With Oracle you have the choice of creating three different kinds of tables:

- A traditional relational table using native SQL data types such as VARCHAR2, DATE, and NUMBER.
- A relational table with object columns. This type of table is a hybrid, using both native SQL data types and user-defined data types.
- An object table, which is defined solely based on a user-defined data type.

The best part of this architecture is that it's flexible enough to facilitate both relational SQL and object-oriented development tools by providing both a relational view and an object view of the same database. You can create object views against relational tables to create an object face to a relational database or create object tables and access the column attributes as though they are part of relational tables by using the TABLE operator. You can have your cake and eat it too!

In this chapter, we'll discuss the use of JDBC with database objects. We'll start by examining object analysis and design but not from the traditional point of view. Instead, we'll look at how we can transform our relational model from that shown in Chapter 8 into an object model. We'll then look at how we can transform our relational database into an object database by implementing object views on our relational data. We'll finish up by creating object tables to replace our relational tables, and we'll use those object tables for examples in the chapters that follow.

From Relational Tables to Object Views

In Chapter 8, we discussed creating a demographic database for HR data. By the end of the chapter we had gone through several evolutions with our analysis and had presented 11 entities. We then created the DDL for five of the entities:

PERSON
PERSON_IDENTIFIER

```
PERSON_IDENTIFIER_TYPE
PERSON_LOCATION
LOCATION
```

We can now take these five entities and create object views to present our relational database as an object-relational database. Seeing that we are now looking at the data from an object perspective, we have two ways in which to implement an object solution. We can create object views on top of our relational tables or transform our entities into object tables.

Transforming Entities into Objects

Recalling all the entities we identified in Chapter 8, we can first create object tables for EMPLOYMENT STATUS, LOCATION, ORGANIZATION, and POSITION. Then we can create another object table for PERSON, folding into it the following intersection entities as nested tables or varying arrays:

```
PERSON_EMPLOYMENT_STATUS
PERSON_LOCATION
PERSON_ORGANIZATION
PERSON_POSITION
PERSON_IDENTIFIER
```

Nested tables and varying arrays are both referred to as *collections*. Adding the five collections listed here to a person object table would create a rather large person object that would need to retrieve all related person data at one time. This may be desirable for you, the programmer, but it will lead to poor application performance. It is much more advisable to fold only the PERSON_IDENTIFIER entity into the person entity as a collection, creating a new PERSON object table, because it is common to query for persons by their identifiers. This leaves the intersection entities as separate object tables with the end result being that we are left with four objects: PERSON, PERSON_IDENTIFIER_TYPE, PERSON_LOCATION, and LOCATION.

Our next decision is whether to use references, or primary and foreign keys to enforce referential integrity. Since there are some negative performance implications associated with using references in object views, we'll use primary and foreign keys. With these decisions behind us, let's move forward by creating object views for our four new objects.

Creating Object Views

To create an object view, follow these steps:

1. Define an object type in which its attributes correspond to the column types of the associated relational table.

2. Identify a unique value from the underlying relational table to act as a reference value for the rows.

---

3. Create an object view to extract the data.

4. Create INSTEAD OF triggers to make the view updateable.

We'll do this for the PERSON and PERSON_IDENTIFIER tables. As a reminder, the following is the DDL for the PERSON and PERSON_IDENTIFIER tables introduced in Chapter 8:

```
create table PERSON (
person_id               number          not null,
last_name               varchar2(30)    not null,
first_name              varchar2(30)    not null,
middle_name             varchar2(30),
birth_date              date            not null,
mothers_maiden_name     varchar2(30)    not null )

create table PERSON_IDENTIFIER (
person_id   number          not null,
id          varchar2(30)    not null,
id_type     varchar2(30)    not null )
```

Creating user-defined data types

Step 1 is to create a user-defined data type to represent the data from these two tables as an object. We'll start with the PERSON_IDENTIFIER table. Here's the DDL to create a corresponding user-defined data type:

```
create type PERSON_IDENTIFIER_typ as object (
id          varchar2(30),
id_type     varchar2(30) )
```

Notice that we don't have the person_id in the type definition. That's because the person_id will be implicit, because the identifiers are stored in the form of a nested table within the enclosing person object. Next, we need to create a nested table type definition to transform the PERSON_IDENTIFIER table into a collection for the person object. Here's the DDL to do that:

```
create type PERSON_IDENTIFIER_tab as
table of   PERSON_IDENTIFIER_typ
```

Now that we have a collection type for the PERSON_IDENTIFIER table, we can define the person type:

```
create type PERSON_typ as object (
person_id               number,
last_name               varchar2(30),
first_name              varchar2(30),
middle_name             varchar2(30),
birth_date              date,
mothers_maiden_name     varchar2(30),
identifiers             person_identifier_tab,
map member function get_map return varchar2,
member function get_age return number,
member function get_age_on( aid_date in date ) return number,
```

```
    static function get_id  return number );
    /

    create type body PERSON_typ as
    map member function get_map return varchar2 is
    begin
     return rpad( last_name, 30 )||
            rpad( first_name, 30 )||
            rpad( middle_name, 30 )||
            rpad( mothers_maiden_name,30 )||
            to_char( birth_date, 'YYYYMMDDHH24MISS' );
    end get_map;

    member function get_age return number is
    begin
     return trunc( months_between( SYSDATE, birth_date ) / 12 );
    end get_age;

    member function get_age_on( aid_date in date ) return number is
    begin
     return trunc( months_between( aid_date, birth_date ) / 12 );
    end get_age_on;

    static function get_id  return number is
    n_person_id number := 0;
    begin
     select person_seq.nextval into n_person_id from dual;
     return n_person_id;
    end get_id;

    end;
    /
```

We've added one static and three member methods to person_typ. I'll use these in the coming chapters to demonstrate how to call a database object's methods.

Selecting a reference value

Now that we have defined types for the PERSON and PERSON_IDENTIFIER tables, we need to decide which value to use for an object reference. An object reference acts as a unique identifier for an object, just as a primary key acts as a unique identifier for a row in a relational table. Since we're creating object views, and the column person_id is common to both tables, we'll use it for the reference value.

If we were creating an object table, as we will do later in this chapter, we could choose between using a unique value in the attribute of a user-defined data type or a reference. A *reference* is a database-generated global unique identifier (GUID). My preference, even with object tables, is to use an attribute as a primary key instead of a GUID, because you can create foreign key constraints between object tables with a primary key.

Creating an object view

Now that we have all the necessary types defined and have selected a reference value, we can move on to step 3, which is to create a view to extract the data from our two relational tables and cast it to a person type object. Here's the object view:

```
create or replace view person_ov of
person_typ with object identifier( person_id ) as
select person_id,
       last_name,
       first_name,
       middle_name,
       birth_date,
       mothers_maiden_name,
        cast(
         multiset (
          select i.id,
                 i.id_type
           from   person_identifier i
           where  i.person_id = p.person_id ) as
          person_identifier_tab ) as
          identifiers
    from    person p
```

In this object view, we select data from the PERSON table and use the CAST and MULTISET keywords to transform the related values in the PERSON_IDENTIFER table into a person_identifier_tab object. The MULTISET keyword is used because the result of the subquery has multiple rows. The CAST keyword takes the values and creates a person_identifier_typ object for each row, which in turn becomes elements of the person_identifier_tab object. The result of a query against the person_ov object view is a person_typ object for each PERSON row in the database. Each person_typ object includes any related person_identifiers.

Creating INSTEAD OF triggers

At this point, we can retrieve data from the PERSON and PERSON_IDENTIFIER tables in the form of a table of person_ov objects. However, if we need to insert, update, or delete objects, we need to create INSTEAD OF triggers on person_ov. INSTEAD OF triggers encapsulate insert, update, and delete logic for a view in the form of PL/SQL or Java code. Example 14-1 shows the three INSTEAD OF triggers required for the PERSON table, and Example 14-2 shows the three required triggers for the nested PERSON_IDENTIFIER table. All six of these INSTEAD OF triggers are required to make the person_ov object view updateable.

The first three triggers, shown in Example 14-1, are PERSON_OV_IOI, PERSON_OV_IOU, and PERSON_OV_IOD. These triggers intercept inserts, updates, and deletes against the person_ov object view and propagate them to the PERSON table instead.

Example 14-1. person_ov INSTEAD OF triggers for the PERSON table

```
create or replace trigger person_ov_ioi
instead of insert on        person_ov
for each row
declare
t_identifiers  person_identifier_tab;
begin

 insert into person (
         PERSON_ID,
         LAST_NAME,
         FIRST_NAME,
         MIDDLE_NAME,
         BIRTH_DATE,
         MOTHERS_MAIDEN_NAME )
 values (
         :new.PERSON_ID,
         :new.LAST_NAME,
         :new.FIRST_NAME,
         :new.MIDDLE_NAME,
         :new.BIRTH_DATE,
         :new.MOTHERS_MAIDEN_NAME );

 if :new.identifiers is not null then
  t_identifiers := :new.identifiers;
  for i in t_identifiers.first..t_identifiers.last loop
   insert into person_identifier (
          PERSON_ID,
          ID,
          ID_TYPE )
   values (
          :new.PERSON_ID,
          t_identifiers( i ).ID,
          t_identifiers( i ).ID_TYPE );
  end loop;
 end if;

end;
/

create or replace trigger person_ov_iou
instead of update on        person_ov
for each row
declare
t_identifiers  person_identifier_tab;
begin

 update person
 set    PERSON_ID          = :new.PERSON_ID,
        LAST_NAME          = :new.LAST_NAME,
        FIRST_NAME         = :new.FIRST_NAME,
        MIDDLE_NAME        = :new.MIDDLE_NAME,
        BIRTH_DATE         = :new.BIRTH_DATE,
```

```
        MOTHERS_MAIDEN_NAME = :new.MOTHERS_MAIDEN_NAME
  where   PERSON_ID          = :old.PERSON_ID;

  delete person_identifier
  where   PERSON_ID          = :old.PERSON_ID;

  if :new.identifiers is not null then
   t_identifiers := :new.identifiers;
   for i in t_identifiers.first..t_identifiers.last loop
    insert into person_identifier (
           PERSON_ID,
           ID,
           ID_TYPE )
    values (
           :new.PERSON_ID,
           t_identifiers( i ).ID,
           t_identifiers( i ).ID_TYPE );
   end loop;

  end if;

end;
/


create or replace trigger person_ov_iod
instead of delete on      person_ov
for each row
declare
begin

 delete person_identifier
 where   PERSON_ID          = :old.PERSON_ID;

 delete person
 where   PERSON_ID          = :old.PERSON_ID;

end;
/
```

The next three triggers, IDENTIFIERS_OF_PERSON_OV_IOI, IDENTIFIERS_OF_ PERSON_OV_IOU, and IDENTIFIERS_OF_PERSON_OV_IOD (shown in Example 14-2) handle inserts, updates, and deletes against the PERSON_IDENTI- FIER table, respectively, which is represented by the nested table identifiers in person_ov. These are used only when the identifiers attribute of the person_typ is the only attribute modified by a SQL statement.

Example 14-2. person_ov INSTEAD OF triggers for the PERSON_IDENTIFIER table

```
create or replace trigger         identifiers_of_person_ov_ioi
instead of insert on nested table identifiers of person_ov
for each row
```

```
declare
begin

 insert into person_identifier (
       PERSON_ID,
       ID,
       ID_TYPE )
 values (
       :parent.PERSON_ID,
       :new.ID,
       :new.ID_TYPE );

end;
/

create or replace trigger        identifiers_of_person_ov_iou
instead of update on nested table identifiers of person_ov
for each row
declare
begin

 update person_identifier
 set    ID        = :new.ID,
        ID_TYPE   = :new.ID_TYPE
 where  PERSON_ID = :parent.PERSON_ID
 and    ID        = :old.ID
 and    ID_TYPE   = :old.ID_TYPE;

end;
/

create or replace trigger        identifiers_of_person_ov_iod
instead of delete on nested table identifiers of person_ov
for each row
declare
begin

 delete person_identifier
 where  PERSON_ID = :parent.PERSON_ID
 and    ID        = :old.ID
 and    ID_TYPE   = :old.ID_TYPE;

end;
/
```

With our six INSTEAD OF triggers in place, we have a fully updateable object view, named person_ov, for the PERSON and PERSON_IDENTIFIERS table. With the person_ov object view, we can update the underlying tables with relational SQL or treat them as an object. Using object views, you can migrate a legacy relational database to a relational-object database. While creating an object view does not take much effort, writing the INSTEAD OF triggers to make the view updateable takes a great deal of effort. The best solution for a new application is to create object tables directly based on our user-defined data types. Object tables can be modified using either relational SQL or object-relational SQL.

Object Tables

Now that you've seen the object view solution, let's examine the use of object tables. In this section, we'll take the four example entities: person, location, person location, and person identifier type, and create object tables to represent those entities as objects. We'll create the user-defined database types, and the object tables to implement them, in order of the dependence.

To begin, we create an object table corresponding to the person identifier type entity. First, we need to define a type:

```
create type PERSON_IDENTIFIER_TYPE_typ as object (
code            varchar2(30),
description     varchar2(80),
inactive_date   date )
/
```

Now that we have the type definition, we create the person_identifier_type_ot object table using the following DDL:

```
create table PERSON_IDENTIFIER_TYPE_ot of
             PERSON_IDENTIFIER_TYPE_typ
tablespace USERS pctfree 20
storage (initial 100 K next 100 K pctincrease 0)
/
alter  table PERSON_IDENTIFIER_TYPE_ot add
constraint   PERSON_IDENTIFIER_TYPE_ot_PK
primary key (
code )
using index
tablespace USERS pctfree 20
storage (initial 10 K next 10 K pctincrease 0)
/
```

Notice that we also created a primary key constraint on the table using the code attribute.

Next, we define the location type:

```
create type LOCATION_typ as object (
location_id          number,
parent_location_id   number,
code                 varchar2(30),
name                 varchar2(80),
start_date           date,
end_date             date,
map member function get_map return varchar2,
static function get_id  return number );
/
create type body LOCATION_typ as
map member function get_map return varchar2 is
```

```
begin
 return rpad( code, 30 )||
        rpad( name, 80 )||
        to_char( start_date, 'YYYYMMDDHH24MISS' );
end get_map;

static function get_id  return number is
n_location_id number := 0;
begin
 select location_seq.nextval into n_location_id from dual;
 return n_location_id;
end get_id;

end;
/
```

And now that we have the location type, we create the location_ot object table using the following DDL:

```
create table LOCATION_ot of
              LOCATION_typ
tablespace USERS pctfree 20
storage (initial 100 K next 100 K pctincrease 0)
/
alter  table LOCATION_ot add
constraint   LOCATION_ot_PK
primary key ( location_id )
using index
tablespace USERS pctfree 20
storage (initial 10 K next 10 K pctincrease 0)
/

create unique index LOCATION_ot_UK1
on                LOCATION_ot (
code,
name,
start_date )
tablespace USERS pctfree 20
storage (initial 100 K next 100 K pctincrease 0)
/

drop   sequence LOCATION_ID
/
create sequence LOCATION_ID
start with 1
order
/
```

This time we created a sequence to provide unique values for the primary key attribute location_id. We also created a unique "external" key against the code, name, and start_date attributes.

Now we need to create the person_ot object table, but to do so, we first need to define not only the person type, but also the person_identifer type and the person_ identifier collection type. We can reuse the three types we defined for the person_ov object view, so here's the DDL for the person_ot object table:

```
create table PERSON_ot of
              PERSON_typ
nested table identifiers store as PERSON_IDENTIFIER_ot
tablespace USERS pctfree 20
storage (initial 100 K next 100 K pctincrease 0)
/
alter  table PERSON_ot add
constraint   PERSON_ot_PK
primary key ( person_id )
using index
tablespace USERS pctfree 20
storage (initial 10 K next 10 K pctincrease 0)
/

alter  table PERSON_IDENTIFIER_ot add
constraint   PERSON_IDENTIFIER_ot_PK
primary key (
id,
id_type )
using index
tablespace USERS pctfree 20
storage (initial 10 K next 10 K pctincrease 0)
/

create unique index PERSON_ot_UK1
on            PERSON_ot (
last_name,
first_name,
birth_date,
mothers_maiden_name )
tablespace USERS pctfree 20
storage (initial 100 K next 100 K pctincrease 0)
/

drop    sequence PERSON_ID
/
create sequence PERSON_ID
start with 1
order
/
```

Here, we not only created a nested table but also created a primary key constraint on it to prevent duplicate values in the collection. In addition, we created a unique index, person_ot_uk1, on the attributes of the person_ot to prevent duplicate entries based on real-world values.

Now that we have a location_ot object table and a person_ot object table, we can create the intersection entity person location. First, we define a type:

```
create type PERSON_LOCATION_typ as object (
person_id      number,
```

```
location_id    number,
start_date     date,
end_date       date )
/
```

For this type, we used the attributes `person_id` and `location_id` to act as foreign keys to `person_ot` and `location_ot`, respectively. Had we not defined primary keys on `person_ot` and `location_ot`, we could just as well have used object references to link occurrences of `person_location_typ` to `person_ot` and `location_ot` objects. The primary key approach to uniquely identifying an object is actually more loosely coupled than the use of a global unique identifier (GUID) object reference. As a result, the primary key approach is more adaptable for decision support activities such as reporting, because it allows you to continue to use the tables as though they are relational and doesn't force you to follow the object references to establish relationships. In addition, the use of primary keys also allows the use of foreign keys, which prevents dangling references that can occur when using GUID object references.

Finally, here's the DDL for the `person_location_ot` object table:

```
create table PERSON_LOCATION_ot of
            PERSON_LOCATION_typ
tablespace USERS pctfree 20
storage (initial 100 K next 100 K pctincrease 0)
/
alter  table PERSON_LOCATION_ot add
constraint   PERSON_LOCATION_ot_PK
primary key (
person_id,
start_date )
using index
tablespace USERS pctfree 20
storage (initial 10 K next 10 K pctincrease 0)
/
```

Table 14-1 shows the migration from relational tables to object views to the object tables outlined in this chapter. At this point, we've defined four object tables, which we'll use as a basis for our object-relational SQL manipulations using JDBC in the next two chapters. Chapter 15 will cover the use of the weakly typed data types for manipulating object data. Chapter 16 will cover the use of the strongly typed interfaces.

Table 14-1. Relational to object-relational table migration

Relational table(s)	Object table
person	person_ot
person_identifier	
person_identifier_type	person_identifier_type
location	location_ot
person_location	person_location_ot

Weakly Typed Object SQL

Weakly typed object SQL refers to the use of structures, arrays, and references to insert, update, delete, and select SQL objects. A structure refers to a structured SQL data type, which is a user-defined SQL data type synonymous with a Java class. An array refers to a SQL ARRAY, and a reference refers to a SQL REF. These SQL data types are represented in JDBC by the java.sql.Struct, java.sql.Array, and java.sql.Ref interfaces. A Struct is a JDBC object that retrieves a database object. It represents the locator for a structured SQL data type, or database object, in your Java program. After retrieving a database object with a Struct, you retrieve the object's attributes by calling its getAttributes( ) method, which returns a Java Object array. Since the attributes are returned as an Object array, it's up to you, the programmer, to properly cast each object value as it is used. Hence, a Struct is weakly typed. If, in turn, an attribute of the Struct represents another structured SQL data type, or database object, then that attribute must itself be cast to the Struct. Likewise, if the attribute of a Struct is an array of values, such as an Oracle varying array or nested table, then you must cast that attribute to another JDBC object type, an Array.

Similar to a Struct, an Array represents the locator for a SQL ARRAY. It has a method, getArray( ), which returns the database array values as a Java Object array. If an element of the returned Object array is a singleton value, that is, not a structured SQL data type, then the element is cast to a standard Java data type. Otherwise, if an element is a database object, then it must be cast to a Struct. Yes, it can get confusing, but given these two JDBC object types, you can retrieve any type of database object value.

On the other hand, a Ref is used differently. A Ref object allows you to retrieve a unique identifier for a given object from the database. If you decide to use your Oracle database with loosely coupled relationships, you can store a reference from one object table in the attribute of another object table, replacing the need for primary and foreign keys. I call this loosely coupled, because you can't enforce references as you can foreign keys, so you can end up with dangling refs, as they are called, which point to a row that no longer exists. Hmmm, shades of Oracle Version 6? For this reason, I like to use primary and foreign keys. You can also use the Oracle implementation of the Ref interface, REF, to get and set object values.

Now that you have the big picture, we'll take a look at how to use each object type. We'll cover the use of the standard JDBC interfaces, java.sql.Struct, java.sql.Array, and java.sql.Ref, along with the Oracle implementations: oracle.sql.STRUCT and oracle.sql.StructDescriptor, oracle.sql.ARRAY, oracle.sql.ArrayDescriptor, and oracle.sql.REF.

Keep in mind that I am assuming that you've read the earlier chapters, so you're already familiar with the use of the Statement, PreparedStatement, and ResultSet objects. Also, we'll discuss how to insert, select, update, and delete database objects using these interfaces. Before we get started with all that, I'll digress and take a moment to look at another alternative, accessing object tables as relational tables, and the reasons why we will not cover this alternative in any great detail.

Accessing Objects as Relational Tables

Oracle enriches the SQL language to allow you to manipulate object tables as though they are good, old-fashioned relational tables. For example, you can insert an entry into person_ot with the following SQL statement:

```
insert into person_ot values (
person_typ(
 person_id.nextval,
 'Doe',
 'John',
 'W',
 to_date('19800101','YYYYMMDD'),
 'Yew',
 person_identifier_tab(
  person_identifier_typ( 'CA123456789', 'SDL' ),
  person_identifier_typ( '001019999',   'SSN' ) ) ) )
/
```

The only difference between this SQL and the SQL you'd use to insert a row into a relational table is that you need to use the constructors for the database types to create the appropriate objects. But, if you remember our discussion of the Statement object in Chapter 9, building the appropriate SQL statements to dynamically insert object data in this way can be quite complicated and fraught with troubles. Besides, this is really not the kind of update methodology we are trying to accomplish with object SQL. We want to insert, update, and select objects as if we're using object-oriented technology! So, to that end, we won't cover how to update object tables or select data from them using the TABLE keyword, etc. Instead, we will concentrate on a methodology with which we can take a Java object and insert it into the database, update it, or select it from the database. In this chapter, we'll concentrate on the weakly typed solutions for doing this. Let's begin our journey into the weakly typed objects with the Struct object.

Structs

You use a `java.sql.Struct` object to insert object data into the database, update it, or select object data from the database. A `Struct` object represents a database object as a record of `Object` attributes. If the database object consists of objects within objects, then a given attribute that represents another database object type will itself need to be cast to another `Struct` for as many levels as are needed to resolve all the attributes. Let's start our detailed look at using a `Struct` with inserting object values into the database.

Inserting Object Values

There are four steps to inserting an object into the database using a `Struct` object:

1. Create an `oracle.sql.StructDescriptor` object for the database data type.
2. Create a Java `Object` array with the same number of elements as there are attributes in the database data type and populate it with Java objects of the appropriate data type.
3. Create a `Struct` object using the `oracle.sql.STRUCT` constructor, passing the appropriate `StructDescriptor`, `Connection`, and `Object` array of objects.
4. Use a `PreparedStatement` object and its `setObject()` method to insert the data represented by the `Struct` object into the database.

Let's look at these steps in detail.

Creating a StructDescriptor

The `java.sql.Struct` interface, being rather new, supports only selecting objects from a database into a `Struct` object. The interface does not support creating a `Struct` object in a Java program and using it to store the data it in the database. The missing functionality, that is, the ability to create a new `Struct` object to hold a Java object's data and to use that `Struct` object to update the database, is up to the JDBC driver vendor to implement. In Oracle's case, two classes are used to create a `Struct` object. The first is `oracle.sql.StructDescriptor`. You pass a `StructDescriptor` for a particular database type into the constructor for an `oracle.sql.STRUCT` to create a `Struct` object for the desired type. To create a `StructDescriptor` object, call the `StructDescriptor` factory method `createDescriptor()`. Here's the method's signature:

```
StructDescriptor createDescriptor(String databaseType, Connection conn)
```

which breaks down as:

databaseType
> The name of a user-defined data type in the database

conn
> A valid database connection for the database containing the user-defined data type

For example, to create a new descriptor for person_ot, which is based on the type person_typ, use the following code:[*]

```
StructDescriptor personSD =
  StructDescriptor.createDescriptor("SCOTT.PERSON_TYP", conn);
```

 Notice that the database data type, not the table name, is specified when creating the StructDescriptor. I mention this here because using the table name instead of the type name is a common mistake.

Creating an Object array

In creating a Struct object, in addition to a StructDescriptor object, you need to pass the oracle.sql.STRUCT object's constructor a Java Object array. This Object array must be populated with the appropriate Java objects that correspond sequentially with the attributes of the user-defined SQL data type defined by the StructDescriptor object. For example, person_ot, which is based on the user-defined SQL data type, person_typ, has seven attributes. So we create an Object array with seven elements:

```
Object[] attributes = new Object[7];
```

Since Java arrays start with an index of zero, the elements of the Object array attributes map to the attributes of person_typ, as shown in Table 15-1.

Table 15-1. Java Object array to person_typ mappings

Array index	person_typ attribute	SQLtype	Java type
0	person_id	NUMBER	BigDecimal
1	last_name	VARCHAR2	String
2	first_name	VARCHAR2	String
3	middle_name	VARCHAR2	String
4	birth_date	DATE	Timestamp
5	mothers_maiden_name	VARCHAR2	String
6	identifiers	ARRAY	Array

Now that we have an Object array, we populate it with appropriate values:

```
attributes[0] = new BigDecimal(1);
attributes[1] = "O'Reilly";
attributes[2] = "Tim";
attributes[3] = null;
attributes[4] = Timestamp.valueOf("1972-03-17 00:00:00.0");
```

[*] Since you're working with the Oracle classes, you need to add the import statement, import oracle.sql.*;, to your program.

```
attributes[5] = "Idunno";
attributes[6] = null;
```

Notice that an Object array can be populated only with Java objects, not with primary data types. So if you use a primary data type such as long in your program, you have to use the wrapper class Long if you want to add its value to an Object array.

In the example, we've set the identifiers attribute to null for now, because we have yet to discuss the Array object. But don't worry—we'll cover the Array object later in this chapter.

Creating a Struct object

Once you have a StructDescriptor and an Object array with the attributes for the new Struct, you can create a new Struct object for the corresponding type by using the new operator with the oracle.sql.STRUCT constructor, which has the following signature:

```
oracle.sql.STRUCT oracle.sql.STRUCT(
  StructDescriptor structDescriptor,
  Connection connection,
  Object[] attributes)
```

For example, to create a Struct for person_ot, use the following code:

```
oracle.sql.STRUCT person =
  new oracle.sql.STRUCT(personSD, conn, attributes);
```

Inserting a Struct using java.sql.PreparedStatement

Now that we have the Struct named person, we can use the PreparedStatement object and its setObject() method to insert the value into the database:

```
PreparedStatement pstmt =
  conn.prepareStatement("insert into person_ot values ( ? )");
pstmt.setObject(1, person, Types.STRUCT);
int rows = pstmt.executeUpdate();
```

We used the Types constant STRUCT as the third argument to the setObject() method so it would know that we were passing it a Struct object.

Once you have an object stored in the database, you'll most likely want to select or update it. To update an object, you first need to retrieve a copy of the object, so let's cover selecting an object next.

Retrieving Object Values

There are actually two ways you can retrieve object values as objects from a database. You can get an object by using the value() database function or you can get a reference by using the ref() database function and then use the REF object's getValue( ) method. We'll cover the first method here and the second later on when we cover the Ref interface.

Formulating a SELECT statement

To retrieve objects from the database, you need to formulate a SELECT statement that uses the value( ) database function. The value( ) database function has the following signature:

```
value( table_alias in varchar2 )
```

Since the value( ) function requires a table alias, you need to add a table alias after your table list in your SELECT statement. For example, to select an object (the row), not columns, from person_ot, use the SELECT statement:

```
select value(p) from person_ot p
```

The table name alias, p, is passed as a parameter to the value( ) database function to get the object value for a row rather than column values. Some documentation may state that you can use the following SELECT statement:

```
select * from person_ot
```

But it simply will not work. You must use the value( ) database function with a table alias.

 When using object SQL it's important to get into the habit of using table aliases for every table and prefixing every column name with an alias. This is because with object SQL, you use dot notation to reference nested columns, so the SQL parser requires an alias to qualify your column names.

Retrieving an object value as a Struct

When you use the value( ) database function, use the ResultSet object's getObject( ) method and cast the returned object to a Struct:

```
Statement stmt = conn.createStatement( );
ResultSet rslt = stmt.executeQuery(
  "select value(p) from person_ot " +
  "where last_name = 'O''Reilly' and first_name = 'Tim'");
rslt.next( );
Struct person = (Struct)rslt.getObject(1);
```

Then, to get to the attributes of the database object, use the Struct object's getAttributes( ) method, which returns the attributes as a Java Object array.

Casting the returned object attributes

To use the objects returned by getAttributes( ), cast them as needed to the appropriate Java type. Valid SQL to Java type mappings can be found in Table 10-1. For example, to get a person's objects attributes, use the following code:

```
Object[] attributes          = person.getAttributes();
BigDecimal personId          = (BigDecimal)attributes[0];
String     lastName          = (String)attributes[1];
String     firstName         = (String)attributes[2];
String     middleName        = (String)attributes[3];
Timestamp  birthDate         = (Timestamp)attributes[4];
String     mothersMaidenName = (String)attributes[5];
```

At this point, you know how to insert an object and how to retrieve it. Next, let's see how to update it.

Updating Object Values

When it comes to updating object values, there are once again two approaches you can take. The first is to use a Struct object, and the second is to use a Ref object. To update the database using a Struct object, there are five steps you must follow:

1. Retrieve the database object's value into a Struct.

2. Place the Struct object's attributes into an Object array.

3. Modify the desired attributes in the Object array.

4. Get the StructDescriptor object from the original Struct object.

5. Create a new Struct using the StructDescriptor and Object array.

6. Use a PreparedStatement object and its setObject( ) method to update the database.

Since we just performed steps 1 and 2 in the last section, we can move on to step 3, in which you modify the desired attributes. In our example, change Tim O'Reilly's mother's maiden name to "unknown":

```
attributes[5] = "unknown";
```

Next, in step 4, you can either create a StructDescriptor as we did in the section "Inserting Object Values," or get the original Struct object's StructDescriptor using the oracle.sql.STRUCT object's getStructDescriptor( ) method:

```
StructDescriptor personSD = ((STRUCT)person).getStructDescriptor()
```

Then, in step 5, using the retrieved StructDescriptor and modified Object array, create a new Struct object with the modified attributes:

```
person = new oracle.sql.STRUCT(personSD, conn, attributes);
```

Finally, in step 6, use a `PreparedStatement` object to update the value:

```
PreparedStatement pstmt = conn.prepareStatement(
  "update person_ot p set value(p) = ? " +
  "where last_name = 'Doe' and first_name = 'John'");
pstmt.setObject(1, person);
int rows = pstmt.executeUpdate();
```

As you can see, updating an object is a fairly simple process but can be somewhat tedious, because you have to get an object, get its attributes, modify its attributes, recreate the object, and then update the database with it, instead of just updating the attributes in place, as you would if they were columns in a relational table. For example, you could have used the following relational SQL statement:

```
update person_ot
set    mothers_maiden_name = 'unknown'
where  last_name = 'O''Reilly' and first_name = 'Tim'
```

But using this statement would be treating an object table as a relational table, and what we're trying to do here is understand how to manipulate objects. That's the trade-off of using an object database instead of a relational database. When you work with objects, you retrieve, manipulate, and store a complex structure with attributes rather than work with individual columns.

Now that we've inserted, selected, and updated database objects, all that's left is deleting them. And that's as simple as a relational SQL DELETE statement.

Deleting Object Values

There is nothing special about deleting an object from an object table. You just need to identify the desired object row to delete using the appropriate WHERE criteria. For example, to delete Tim O'Reilly's `person_ot` row, use the following DELETE statement:

```
delete person_ot
where  last_name = 'O''Reilly' and first_name = 'Tim'
```

Couple the above statement with a `Statement` object, and the following Java code will delete the desired row:

```
Statement stmt = conn.createStatement();
int rows = stmt.executeUpdate(
  "delete person_ot " +
  "where last_name = 'O''Reilly' and first_name = 'Tim'");
```

Now that you're an expert at using a `Struct`, we can turn our attention to `person_ot` attribute number six, `identifiers`. I've been avoiding it because it is an Oracle collection or, more precisely, a nested table, which requires the use of a `java.sql.Array`. So let's take a look at the `Array` interface.

Arrays

A `java.sql.Array` is used as an object attribute of a Struct to store a Java array in or retrieve one from a SQL ARRAY attribute. This means you'll use an Array object to manipulate Oracle collections: varying arrays (VARRAYs) or nested tables.

An Array can represent an array of a single predefined data type such as String. For example, if you have an array of String objects, you can store them as an Oracle collection. Using the default mapping, Oracle will convert the array of Strings into a collection of VARCHAR2s. An Array can also store an array of objects—for example, a PersonIdentifier object that has two attributes, an id, and an id_type.

If you wish to store an array of Java objects such as PersonIdentifier as a collection of database objects, you first have to convert the Java objects themselves into Struct objects and then create a new Array by passing the array of Struct objects to the constructor of the Array. This is because a database object, whether it's a table row, column, or part of a collection, is represented by a Struct object.

Just like its weakly typed counterpart Struct, java.sql.Array is an interface that defines how to materialize a SQL ARRAY from a database, but it is up to the database vendor to provide the functionality to be able to create new Array objects in a Java program. And, in a similar fashion, you use oracle.sql.ArrayDescriptor to create an Array, just as you used a StructDescriptor to create a Struct. Let's look at how you create a java.sql.Array.

Creating an Array

There are three steps to creating an Array:

1. Create an ArrayDescriptor object for the database collection type.
2. Create a Java Object array to hold the values of an appropriate data type for a database collection type.
3. Create an Array object using the oracle.sql.ARRAY constructor, passing an appropriate ArrayDescriptor object, connection, and Java Object array.

Let's take a look at these steps in detail.

Creating an ArrayDescriptor

The first step in creating an Array object is to create an oracle.sql.ArrayDescriptor object for the Oracle database collection type. The distinction here, that you are creating an ArrayDescriptor object for a collection type, is critical. If you define a person_identifier type as:

```
create type PERSON_IDENTIFIER_typ as object (
id          varchar2(30),
```

```
    id_type      varchar2(30) )
    /
```

you then need to define a collection type as a varying array or nested table to hold an array of this database type. For example, you can define a nested table type as:

```
create type PERSON_IDENTIFIER_tab as
table of   PERSON_IDENTIFIER_typ
    /
```

Then, when you specify the collection type to create the ArrayDescriptor, you must specify the name person_identifier_tab (the collection type), not person_identifier_typ (the object type).

An ArrayDescriptor is created using the oracle.sql.ArrayDescriptor factory method createDescriptor( ), which has the following signature:

```
ArrayDescriptor createDescriptor(
  String databaseCollectionType,
  Connection conn)
```

This breaks down as:

databaseCollectionType
    The user-defined collection type

conn
    A valid connection to a database that contains the specified collection type
    definition

So, to create an ArrayDescriptor object for person_identifier_tab, use the following code:

```
ArrayDescriptor personIdentifierAD =
  ArrayDescriptor.createDescriptor("PERSON_IDENTIFIER_TAB", conn);
```

Creating an Object array

Now that you have an ArrayDescriptor object, you can move on to step 2, which is to create a Java array of the appropriate type. In this example, you need to create an array of Struct objects, because the underlying database type for the collection is an object type, person_identifier_typ. This is where the use of Struct and Array objects can get confusing. So let's take a moment to review the relationships between the person_ot attributes.

person_ot is an object table based on type person_typ. person_typ itself has seven attributes. The first six attributes are built-in SQL data types. The last attribute, identifiers, is an Oracle nested table represented as a SQL ARRAY. The identifiers attribute is based on type person_identifier_tab. This is the type used for the array descriptor. The underlying type for the elements of type person_identifier_tab is type person_identifier_typ. So the Struct objects you create to hold the values for the identifiers must use a structure descriptor based on type person_identifier_typ. For example, to create an Object array for three identifiers, code something like this:

```
// You need a StructDescriptor for the collection's
// underlying database object type
StructDescriptor identifiersSD =
 StructDescriptor.createDescriptor("SCOTT.PERSON_IDENTIFIERS_TYP", conn);

// You need three collection entries
Object[] identifiersStructs = new Object[3];

// two attributes in person_identifier_typ
Object[] identifiersAttributes = new Object[2];

// Populate the identifier attributes
identifiersAttributes[0] = "1000000";
identifiersAttributes[1] = "Employee Id";

// Create a Struct to mirror an identifier entry
// and add it to the Array's object array
identifiersStructs[0] =
new oracle.sql.STRUCT(identifiersSD, conn, identifiersAttributes );

// Add a second identifier
identifiersAttributes[0] = "CA9999999999";
identifiersAttributes[1] = "State Driver's License Number";
identifiersStructs[1] =
 new oracle.sql.STRUCT(identifiersSD, conn, identifiersAttributes );

// Add a third identifier
identifiersAttributes[0] - "001010001";
identifiersAttributes[1] - "Social Security Number";
identifiersStructs[2] =
 new oracle.sql.STRUCT(identifiersSD, conn, identifiersAttributes );
```

At this point, you have the array you need, so you can proceed to step 3, which is to create an Array.

Creating an Array object

The Struct objects created to represent identifiers are then gathered into a Java Object array and passed to the oracle.sql.ARRAY object's constructor along with an ArrayDescriptor object created using the collection type person_identifier_tab. This creates a new Array for the identifiers attribute. You create a new Array by using the new operator with the oracle.sql.ARRAY, which has the following signature:

```
oracle.sql.ARRAY oracle.sql.ARRAY(
 ArrayDescriptor arrayDescriptor,
 Connection conn,
 Object[] objects)
```

This breaks down as:

arrayDescriptor
An ArrayDescriptor object for the desired collection type

conn
A valid connection to a database containing the specified database type

objects
A Java object array containing the values for the collection

Pass the constructor, the appropriate ArrayDescriptor, Connection, and the Java Object array:

```
// now create the Array
Array identifiers =
  new oracle.sql.ARRAY(identifiersAD, conn, identifiersStructs );

// update the person Struct
personAttributes[6] = identifiers;
```

And, as in the previous example, you then use the newly created array as an attribute assignment for a Struct. Now that we've covered the Struct and Array interfaces, it's time to address the Ref interface.

Refs

A java.sql.Ref is an object that holds a reference to a database object. Depending on how you implement your Oracle objects, a Ref may hold a global unique identifier (GUID) or a primary key column, and may also contain a ROWID. But what it contains is moot. It's how you use a Ref that's important. A Ref object is simply an address to a database object. With it, you can retrieve, or materialize, an object value. And with Oracle's implementation, oracle.sql.REF, you can also update a value. But you can't create a new database reference in your Java program. That simply doesn't make any sense. Since a reference points to a location of an object in the database, the database has to create a reference when an object is inserted, and then you must retrieve the newly created object's reference into a Ref object, similar to how we handled a Blob or Clob in Chapter 12.

References can also be stored as attributes in other database objects to establish relationships between objects. In this chapter, we'll cover how to retrieve a reference into a Ref object, how to use it to materialize an object value, and finally, how to use it to update a database object. So let's start with retrieving a reference.

Retrieving a Reference

To retrieve a reference from a database, use the ref( ) database function. Do you remember how you used the value( ) function? Well, you use the ref( ) database function the same way. You use it in a SELECT statement, passing it an alias for a table name. For example, to select a reference to an object row in person_ot, use the following SQL statement:

```
select ref(p) from person_ot p
```

To get a reference to the object row that contains Tim O'Reilly's information, use the following code:

```
Statement stmt = conn.createStatement();
ResultSet rslt = stmt.executeQuery(
  "select ref(p) from person_ot " +
  "where last_name = 'O''Reilly' and first_name = 'Tim'");
rslt.next();
java.sql.Ref personRef = rslt.getRef(1);
```

Notice that there's a specific accessor method for a Ref object, getRef( ). Once you have a Ref object, you can use it in an assignment to another table's row attribute, or you can materialize the object value.

Materializing Object Values Using a Ref

If you have a reference to a database row object in a Ref object, retrieving the database object is simple when using the oracle.sql.REF method getValue( ). All that is required is to cast the java.sql.Ref to an oracle.sql.REF in order to call the function:

```
Struct person = (Struct)((oracle.sql.REF)personRef).getValue();
```

Now you have both a reference to the row object and its value. Using the Struct object you can update one or more of its attributes and save the update to the database. To save the update, use a PreparedStatement object as we did earlier. Or, since you have a Ref object, you can cast that object to oracle.sql.REF and use the resulting REF object to save the update.

Updating Object Values Using a Ref

All you need to do to update a database object once you have a Ref object is to cast it to oracle.sql.REF and then call its setValue( ) method. For example, after modifying and reconstructing a person Struct object, use the following code to save your changes:

```
((oracle.sql.REF)personRef).setValue(person);
```

There's no need for a SQL statement to update an object when you use a reference, because the REF interface uses the reference, which is a locator, to update the object directly. This is similar to how BLOB and CLOB objects can be updated via their locators.

At this point, you've seen how we can select and update an object, but you can also delete a row object using its Ref.

Deleting Object Values Using a Ref

If you have a reference to a row object in the form of a Ref object, then all you have to do to delete the row is to use a PreparedStatement object, passing it the Ref in its WHERE clause. So to delete Tim O'Reilly's row object using the Ref we retrieved earlier, you'd code something like this:

```
PreparedStatement pstmt = conn.prepareStatement(
  "delete person_ot p where ref(p) = ?");
pstmt.setObject(1, personRef);
int rows = pstmt.executeUpdate( );
```

In this example, we use the ref( ) database function to get the reference for the object rows in person_ot and then compare them to the reference we set in the DELETE statement with the setObject( ) method.

Now that you've seen how to insert, select, update, and delete row objects in a detailed, step-by-step fashion using the Struct, Array, and Ref interfaces, let's take a look at how to execute database object methods.

Calling Object Methods

A database object can have two kinds of methods: static or member. The first, static, is just like a static Java method, in that it can be called by using its type name, just as a static Java method is called using its class name. For example, type person_typ, which has a static method get_id( ) that returns the next person_id sequence value, can be called as a stored procedure:

```
person_typ.get_id( )
```

To execute get_id( ), use a callable statement, which we covered in Chapter 13. Although using a callable statement to execute a static method is pretty straightforward, calling member methods presents a new problem.

Member methods—just like their public, nonstatic Java counterparts—must be associated with an instance of the object in order to be executed. But how do you get an instance of the object in the database to execute its member method? Your first guess might be to use a reference, which makes pretty good sense to me, too. But the functionality to execute a member method with a reference doesn't exist yet. Instead, use the object value returned from the database value( ) function or the proprietary oracle.sql.REF object's getValue( ) method. In this case, that object value is a Struct, and you pass that Struct as the first argument of the member function or procedure. Pass it as the first argument even though it is not a visibly defined parameter. The syntax is:

```
user_defined_type.method_name(
  self in user_defined_type
[, parameter_1 IN data_type
 , ...
 , parameter_n IN data_type] )
```

which breaks down as:

user_defined_type
   A database user-defined data type or object

method_name
   The name of a member method for the user-defined data type

self
   An object retrieved from the database—in our case, a Struct object—upon which the member method is executed

parameter_1
   The first parameter for the member method

parameter_n
   The *n*th parameter for the member method

data_type
   A SQL built-in or user-defined data type

For example, type person_typ has a member function get_age( ) that returns a person's current age. The function get_age( ) has the following signature:

```
get_age return number
```

To execute the function, call it as a stored procedure:

```
person_typ.get_age(self)
```

Pass a Struct object that represents the object you retrieved from the database as the person_typ self parameter. For example:

```
Statement stmt = conn.createStatement( );
ResultSet rslt = stmt.executeQuery("select value(p) from person_ot p");
while (rslt.next( )) {
 Struct person = (Struct)rslt.getObject(1);
 rslt.close( );
 rslt = null;
 stmt.close( );
 stmt = null;
 cstmt = conn.prepareCall("{ ? = call PERSON_TYP.get_age( ? ) }");
 cstmt.registerOutParameter(1, Types.NUMERIC);
 // Pass the Struct person as the member SELF variable
 cstmt.setObject(2, person);
 cstmt.execute( );
 System.out.println("age = " + new Long(cstmt.getLong(1)).toString( ));
 cstmt.close( );
 cstmt = null;
}
```

Notice in the previous example that even though the person_typ member method get_age( ) does not have any parameters in its definition, the Struct object, person, is passed as the first argument, self.

Now you have a means to execute database object methods if you decide to use the Struct, Array, and Ref interfaces. Let's put what we now know into a comprehensive example.

Putting It All Together

Example 15-1 puts all the concepts and short examples we've seen in this chapter into one cohesive example. Here's the big picture: the TestStruct program starts by cleaning up any rows left over from a prior execution. Then it adds a person and a location and ties them together with a person_location entry so that there are foreign key constraints on the person and location objects. Next, the program modifies the person object using both the PreparedStatement object's setObject() method and the oracle.sql.REF object's setValue() method. Finally, the program selects the person object and displays its contents. Since the person object has a collection for identifiers, the example exercises not only oracle.sql.STRUCT, but also oracle.sql. ARRAY. Let's continue by examining the TestStruct program in detail.

Example 15-1. Testing weakly typed JDBC object types

```
import java.io.*;
import java.math.*;
import java.sql.*;
import java.text.*;

public class TestStruct {
  Connection conn;

  public TestStruct() {
    try {
      DriverManager.registerDriver(new oracle.jdbc.driver.OracleDriver());
      conn = DriverManager.getConnection(
        "jdbc:oracle:thin:@dssw2k01:1521:orcl", "scott", "tiger");
    }
    catch (SQLException e) {
      System.err.println(e.getMessage());
      e.printStackTrace();
    }
  }

  public static void main(String[] args)
   throws Exception {
    new TestStruct().process();
  }

  public void process() throws SQLException {
    // PERSON_TYP attributes
    final int PT_PERSON_ID       = 0;
    final int PT_LAST_NAME       = 1;
    final int PT_FIRST_NAME      = 2;
    final int PT_MIDDLE_NAME     = 3;
    final int PT_BIRTH_DATE      = 4;
```

Example 15-1. Testing weakly typed JDBC object types (continued)

```
      final int PT_MOTHERS_MAIDEN_NAME = 5;
      final int PT_IDENTIFIERS         = 6;
      // PERSON_IDENTITIFERS_TYP attributes
      final int PIT_ID                 = 0;
      final int PIT_ID_TYPE            = 1;
      // LOCATION_TYP attributes
      final int LT_LOCATION_ID         = 0;
      final int LT_PARENT_LOCATION_ID  = 1;
      final int LT_CODE                = 2;
      final int LT_NAME                = 3;
      final int LT_START_DATE          = 4;
      final int LT_END_DATE            = 5;
      // PERSON_LOCATION_TYP attributes
      final int PLT_PERSON_ID          = 0;
      final int PLT_LOCATION_ID        = 1;
      final int PLT_START_DATE         = 2;
      final int PLT_END_DATE           = 3;

      Array             identifiers   = null;
      CallableStatement cstmt         = null;
      long              location_id   = 0;
      long              person_id     = 0;
      PreparedStatement pstmt         = null;
      Ref               personRef     = null;
      ResultSet         rslt          = null;
      Statement         stmt          = null;
      Struct            location      = null;
      Struct            person        = null;
      Struct            personLocation = null;

      // Clean up a prior execution
      try {
        conn.setAutoCommit(false);

        stmt = conn.createStatement();
        stmt.executeUpdate(
          "delete person_location_ot where person_id = " +
          "( select person_id from person_ot " +
          "where last_name = 'O''Reilly' and first_name = 'Tim' )");
        stmt.executeUpdate(
          "delete location_ot " +
          "where code = 'SEBASTOPOL'");
        stmt.executeUpdate(
          "delete person_ot " +
          "where last_name = 'O''Reilly' and first_name = 'Tim'");
        stmt.close();
        stmt = null;
        conn.commit();
      }
      catch (SQLException e) {
        System.err.println("SQL Error: " + e.getMessage());
      }
      finally {
```

Example 15-1. Testing weakly typed JDBC object types (continued)

```
    if (stmt != null)
      try { stmt.close( ); } catch (SQLException ignore) { }
  }

  // Insert a person
  try {
    // Create an array and the struct descriptors
    // the person and person identifier type
    // not the table name!
    oracle.sql.ArrayDescriptor identifiersArrayDescriptor =
     oracle.sql.ArrayDescriptor.createDescriptor(
       "PERSON_IDENTIFIER_TAB", conn );
    oracle.sql.StructDescriptor identifiersStructDescriptor =
     oracle.sql.StructDescriptor.createDescriptor(
       "PERSON_IDENTIFIER_TYP", conn );
    oracle.sql.StructDescriptor personStructDescriptor =
     oracle.sql.StructDescriptor.createDescriptor(
       "PERSON_TYP", conn );

    Object[] personAttributes = new Object[7];

    cstmt = conn.prepareCall("{ ? = call PERSON_TYP.get_id( ) }");
    cstmt.registerOutParameter(1, Types.NUMERIC);
    cstmt.execute( );
    person_id = cstmt.getLong(1);
    cstmt.close( );
    cstmt = null;

    personAttributes[PT_PERSON_ID] = new BigDecimal(person_id);
    personAttributes[PT_LAST_NAME] = "O'Reilly";
    personAttributes[PT_FIRST_NAME] = "Tim";
    personAttributes[PT_MIDDLE_NAME] = null;
    personAttributes[PT_BIRTH_DATE] =
     Timestamp.valueOf("1972-03-17 00:00:00.0");
    personAttributes[PT_MOTHERS_MAIDEN_NAME] = "Oh! I don't know!";

    Object[] identifiersStructs = new Object[2];

    Object[] identifiersAttributes = new Object[2];

    identifiersAttributes[PIT_ID] = "000000001";
    identifiersAttributes[PIT_ID_TYPE] = "EID";
    identifiersStructs[0] = new oracle.sql.STRUCT(
     identifiersStructDescriptor, conn, identifiersAttributes );

    identifiersAttributes[PIT_ID] = "CA9999999999";
    identifiersAttributes[PIT_ID_TYPE] = "SDL";
    identifiersStructs[1] = new oracle.sql.STRUCT(
     identifiersStructDescriptor, conn, identifiersAttributes );

    identifiers = new oracle.sql.ARRAY(
     identifiersArrayDescriptor, conn, identifiersStructs );
```

Example 15-1. Testing weakly typed JDBC object types (continued)

```
      personAttributes[PT_IDENTIFIERS] = identifiers;
      person = new oracle.sql.STRUCT(
       personStructDescriptor, conn, personAttributes );
      pstmt = conn.prepareStatement(
        "insert into person_ot values ( ? )");
      pstmt.setObject(1, person, Types.STRUCT);
      int rows = pstmt.executeUpdate( );
      pstmt.close( );
      pstmt = null;
      System.out.println(rows + " rows inserted");
      conn.commit( );
    }
    catch (SQLException e) {
      System.err.println("SQL Error: " + e.getMessage( ));
    }
    finally {
      if (cstmt != null)
        try { cstmt.close( ); } catch (SQLException ignore) { }
      if (pstmt != null)
        try { pstmt.close( ); } catch (SQLException ignore) { }
    }

    // insert a location
    try {
      // create struct descriptor for location type
      // not the table name!
      oracle.sql.StructDescriptor locationStructDescriptor =
       oracle.sql.StructDescriptor.createDescriptor(
         "LOCATION_TYP", conn );

      Object[] locationAttributes = new Object[6];

      stmt = conn.createStatement( );
      rslt = stmt.executeQuery(
       "select location_id.nextval from sys.dual");
      rslt.next( );
      location_id = rslt.getLong(1);
      rslt.close( );
      rslt = null;
      stmt.close( );
      stmt = null;
      locationAttributes[LT_LOCATION_ID] = new BigDecimal(location_id);
      locationAttributes[LT_PARENT_LOCATION_ID] = null;
      locationAttributes[LT_CODE] = "SEBASTOPOL";
      locationAttributes[LT_NAME] = "Sebastopol, CA, USA";
      locationAttributes[LT_START_DATE] =
       Timestamp.valueOf("1988-01-01 00:00:00.0");
      locationAttributes[LT_END_DATE] = null;

      location = new oracle.sql.STRUCT(
       locationStructDescriptor, conn, locationAttributes );
```

Example 15-1. Testing weakly typed JDBC object types (continued)

```
      pstmt = conn.prepareStatement(
        "insert into location_ot values ( ? )");
      pstmt.setObject(1, location, Types.STRUCT);
      int rows = pstmt.executeUpdate();
      pstmt.close();
      pstmt = null;
      System.out.println(rows + " rows inserted");
      conn.commit();
    }
    catch (SQLException e) {
      System.err.println("SQL Error: " + e.getMessage());
    }
    finally {
      if (rslt  != null)
        try { rslt.close();  } catch (SQLException ignore) { }
      if (stmt  != null)
        try { stmt.close();  } catch (SQLException ignore) { }
      if (pstmt != null)
        try { pstmt.close(); } catch (SQLException ignore) { }
    }

    // insert a person's location
    try {
      // Create struct descriptor for person location type
      // not the table name!
      oracle.sql.StructDescriptor personLocationStructDescriptor =
       oracle.sql.StructDescriptor.createDescriptor(
         "PERSON_LOCATION_TYP", conn );

      Object[] personLocationAttributes = new Object[4];

      personLocationAttributes[PLT_PERSON_ID] =
       new BigDecimal(person_id);
      personLocationAttributes[PLT_LOCATION_ID] =
       new BigDecimal(location_id);
      personLocationAttributes[PLT_START_DATE] =
       Timestamp.valueOf("1988-01-01 00:00:00.0");
      personLocationAttributes[PLT_END_DATE] = null;

      personLocation = new oracle.sql.STRUCT(
       personLocationStructDescriptor, conn, personLocationAttributes );

      pstmt = conn.prepareStatement(
        "insert into person_location_ot values ( ? )");
      pstmt.setObject(1, personLocation, Types.STRUCT);
      int rows = pstmt.executeUpdate();
      pstmt.close();
      pstmt = null;
      System.out.println(rows + " rows inserted");
      conn.commit();
    }
    catch (SQLException e) {
      System.err.println("SQL Error: " + e.getMessage());
```

Example 15-1. Testing weakly typed JDBC object types (continued)

```
    }
    finally {
      if (pstmt != null)
        try { pstmt.close(); } catch (SQLException ignore) { }
    }

    // Update the object using setValue()
    try {
      stmt = conn.createStatement();
      rslt = stmt.executeQuery(
        "select ref(p) from person_ot p " +
        "where last_name = 'O''Reilly' and first_name = 'Tim' ");
      rslt.next();
      personRef = rslt.getRef(1);
      rslt.close();
      rslt = null;
      stmt.close();
      stmt = null;

      person = (Struct)((oracle.sql.REF)personRef).getValue();

      Object[] personAttributes = person.getAttributes();

      personAttributes[P1_MOTHERS_MAIDEN_NAME] = null;

      person = new oracle.sql.STRUCT(
        ((oracle.sql.REF)personRef).getDescriptor(),
        conn,
        personAttributes);

      ((oracle.sql.REF)personRef).setValue(person);
      System.out.println("1 rows updated");
      conn.commit();
    }
    catch (SQLException e) {
      System.err.println("SQL Error: " + e.getMessage());
    }
    finally {
      if (rslt != null)
        try { rslt.close(); } catch (SQLException ignore) { }
      if (stmt != null)
        try { stmt.close(); } catch (SQLException ignore) { }
    }

    // Update the object using a PreparedStatement
    try {
      stmt = conn.createStatement();
      rslt = stmt.executeQuery(
        "select ref(p) from person_ot p " +
        "where last_name = 'O''Reilly' and first_name = 'Tim'");
      rslt.next();
      personRef = rslt.getRef(1);
      rslt.close();
```

Example 15-1. Testing weakly typed JDBC object types (continued)

```
    rslt = null;
    stmt.close( );
    stmt = null;

    person = (Struct)((oracle.sql.REF)personRef).getValue( );

    Object[] personAttributes = person.getAttributes( );

    personAttributes[PT_MOTHERS_MAIDEN_NAME] = "unknown";

    person = new oracle.sql.STRUCT(
     ((oracle.sql.REF)personRef).getDescriptor( ),
     conn,
     personAttributes);

    pstmt = conn.prepareStatement(
     "update person_ot p set value(p) = ? " +
     "where  ref(p) = ?");
    pstmt.setObject(1, person, Types.STRUCT);
    pstmt.setObject(2, personRef, Types.REF);
    int rows = pstmt.executeUpdate( );
    pstmt.close( );
    pstmt = null;
    System.out.println(rows + " rows updated");
    conn.commit( );
}
catch (SQLException e) {
    System.err.println("SQL Error: " + e.getMessage( ));
}
finally {
    if (rslt  != null)
      try { rslt.close( );  } catch (SQLException ignore) { }
    if (stmt  != null)
      try { stmt.close( );  } catch (SQLException ignore) { }
    if (pstmt != null)
      try { pstmt.close( ); } catch (SQLException ignore) { }
}

// Retrieve the object and display its attribute values
try {
  stmt = conn.createStatement( );
  rslt = stmt.executeQuery("select value(p) from person_ot p");
  while (rslt.next( )) {
    person = (Struct)rslt.getObject(1);
    System.out.println(person.getSQLTypeName( ));
    Object[] attributes = person.getAttributes( );
    System.out.println("person_id           = " +
     attributes[PT_PERSON_ID]);
    System.out.println("last_name           = " +
     attributes[PT_LAST_NAME]);
    System.out.println("first_name          = " +
     attributes[PT_FIRST_NAME]);
    System.out.println("middle_name         = " +
```

Example 15-1. Testing weakly typed JDBC object types (continued)

```
        attributes[PT_MIDDLE_NAME]);
      System.out.println("birth_date         = " +
       attributes[PT_BIRTH_DATE]);

      cstmt = conn.prepareCall(
       "{ ? = call PERSON_TYP.get_age( ? ) }");

      cstmt.registerOutParameter(1, Types.NUMERIC);
      // Pass the Struct person as the member SELF variable
      cstmt.setObject(2, person);
      cstmt.execute( );
      System.out.println("age              = " +
       new Long(cstmt.getLong(1)).toString( ));
      cstmt.close( );
      cstmt = null;

      cstmt = conn.prepareCall(
       "{ ? = call PERSON_TYP.get_age_on( ?, ? ) }");

      cstmt.registerOutParameter(1, Types.NUMERIC);
      // Pass the Struct person as the member SELF variable
      cstmt.setObject(2, person);
      cstmt.setObject(3, Timestamp.valueOf("1980-01-01 00:00:00.0"));
      cstmt.execute( );
      System.out.println("age on 1/1/1980    = " +
       new Long(cstmt.getLong(1)).toString( ));
      cstmt.close( );
      cstmt = null;

      System.out.println("mothers_maiden_name = " +
       attributes[PT_MOTHERS_MAIDEN_NAME]);

     identifiers = (Array)attributes[PT_IDENTIFIERS];
     if (identifiers != null) {
       Object[] personIdentifiers =
        (Object[])identifiers.getArray( );
       for (int i=0;i < personIdentifiers.length;i++) {
         System.out.println(
          ((Struct)personIdentifiers[i]).getSQLTypeName( ));
         Object[] idAttributes =
          ((Struct)personIdentifiers[i]).getAttributes( );
         System.out.println("id              = " +
          idAttributes[PIT_ID]);
         System.out.println("id_type         = " +
          idAttributes[PIT_ID_TYPE]);
        }
      }
    }
    rslt.close( );
    rslt = null;
    stmt.close( );
    stmt = null;
  }
```

Example 15-1. Testing weakly typed JDBC object types (continued)

```
    catch (SQLException e) {
      System.err.println("SQL Error: " + e.getMessage());
    }
    finally {
      if (rslt != null)
        try { rslt.close(); } catch (SQLException ignore) { }
      if (stmt != null)
        try { stmt.close(); } catch (SQLException ignore) { }
      if (cstmt != null)
        try { cstmt.close(); } catch (SQLException ignore) { }
    }
  }

  protected void finalize()
   throws Throwable {
    if (conn != null)
      try { conn.close(); } catch (SQLException ignore) { }
    super.finalize();
  }
}
```

The program starts in its main( ) method by instantiating a copy of itself and then executes its process( ) method. The process( ) method starts by creating a series of int constants that are used to identify the position of each database type's attribute in the array returned by the Struct object's getAttributes( ) method. Of course, these constants are not required; they are here only to keep us out of the trouble we could cause by not using the correct index for a particular attribute. Next, the program allocates additional variables that will be shared by the code that follows.

The program then proceeds by cleaning up any prior executions. This means it enters a try block where a Statement object is created and used to execute three DELETE statements in order to remove the rows the program is about to insert.

After deleting any previous work, the program goes to the first of three try blocks, in which data will be inserted using a Struct object. The first of the three try blocks inserts an object into the person_ot table. To insert a person, the program creates three descriptors. The first, identifiersArrayDescriptor, is used to create an Array object with person identifiers. The second, identifiersStructDescriptor, is used to create the Struct objects to hold the person identifier values that in turn are used as input for the creation of the Array. And the third, personStructDescriptor, is used to create the person Struct object to insert into the database. Next, an Object array is created to hold seven attributes. Then, a CallableStatement object is used to retrieve the next value from the person_id sequence for a primary key value by calling the person_typ static method get_id( ). The returned sequence value is stored in a long, person_id and is assigned to the first attribute of the person Struct. Then the remaining attributes of the Struct are assigned values using the constants declared earlier as the attribute identifiers.

Two Struct objects and one Array object are created by the identifiers program. To do this, the program creates two more Object arrays: one for two attributes and the second for two elements. The array identifersAttributes is assigned an id and id_type values. Then the array is used as input for an execution of the new operator with oracle.sql.STRUCT to create a Struct object for PERSON_IDENTIFIER_TYP. The newly created Struct object is stored as an element in the identifiersStructs array. This process of creating an identifier entry is repeated a second time. Now the identifiersStructs array holds two identifiers. Next, to create an Array object, identifiersStructs is passed into an execution of the new operator for oracle.sql.ARRAY.

Now that the Array, identifiers, exists, it is assigned to the person Struct as the seventh attribute. Next, a PreparedStatement object is created to insert the Struct object into the database, and the setObject() method is called, passing the Struct person along with the Types.STRUCT constant. Finally, the prepared statement is executed using the executeUpdate() method, which inserts the object into the person_ot object table.

In the next two try blocks, the same process is followed for a location_ot object and a person_location_ot object. At this point, in the database, there is a person object, a location object, and an intersection object (person_location) that tie the two together. Now that a person exists, the program proceeds in the next try block by modifying the newly inserted object using a Ref and the oracle.sql.REF object's setValue() method.

First, the program creates a Statement object to select the reference for the person from the database using the ref() database function. The accessor method for the ResultSet, getRef(), is used to retrieve the reference as a Ref, which is stored in the personRef variable. Next, the person object is retrieved from the database and placed into the Struct named person by casting personRef to an oracle.sql.REF and calling its getValue() method. Following that, the person Struct object's attributes are retrieved using its getAttributes() method. An attribute is then changed, and the person Struct is once again recreated using the oracle.sql.STRUCT constructor, as was done earlier when the row was inserted. Now that a modified Struct exists, the object is once again updated in the database by casting personRef to oracle.sql.REF and calling the setValue() method, passing the person Struct object as a parameter. The next try block also updates the person, but this time, it does so using a prepared statement.

Once again, the value for the person object is materialized using the getValue() method, modified, and then reconstructed. However, a PreparedStatement object is used to update the database. Pay close attention to the syntax used in the SQL statement:

```
update person_ot p set value(p) = ? where ref(p) = ?
```

The modified Struct, person, is used to set the value for the first placeholder. The previously retrieved Ref, personRef, is set against the second placeholder, which compares the value to the reference in the database. Accordingly, the program calls the setObject( ) method twice: the first time with the person Struct and the second time with personRef. At this point, we have inserted and modified the values in the database. The last try block selects the data and displays it on the screen.

The program proceeds in the last try block by creating a Statement object and executing a query that utilizes the value( ) database function to retrieve the row object from the database. In the while loop for the ResultSet object's next( ) method, the program calls the ResultSet object's getObject( ) method, casting the object to a Struct. Then an Object array variable is created and populated with the return value of the Struct object's getAttributes( ) method. Before the sixth attribute is encountered, a callable statement executes the type person_typ.get_age( ) member method. Then a second call gets the person's age on January 1, 1980. When the sixth attribute, identifiers, is encountered, it is cast and assigned to the Array identifiers. Next, another Object array variable is created, is named personIdentifiers, and is assigned the cast return value from the Array object's getArray( ) method. Then, for each element in the personIdentifiers array, a new Object array variable is created. Next, the personIdentifiers element is cast to a Struct, whereupon the getAttriibutes( ) method is executed to return the Struct object's attributes into the Object array. All of the returned attributes are echoed to the screen. After displaying the person object's values on the screen, the program terminates.

As you can see from this example, using the weakly typed SQL objects, Struct and Array, can be somewhat tedious. But if you're performing a data-processing-type task, they are more efficient than their strongly typed counterparts, which we'll talk about in Chapter 16. There is one thing that Struct, Array, and Ref did not allow us to do, and that is to call database object methods. To do that, we had to use a callable statement. Before we move on to Chapter 16, let's review Oracle's implementation of these weakly typed SQL objects.

Oracle's Implementations

The three JDBC interfaces we have examined in this chapter, java.sql.Struct, java.sql.Array, and java.sql.Ref, are implemented by the Oracle classes oracle.sql.STRUCT, oracle.sql.ARRAY, and oracle.sql.REF. In addition to the standard interface implementations, Oracle has two descriptor classes, oracle.sql.StructDescriptor and oracle.sql.ArrayDescriptor, used in conjunction with the STRUCT and ARRAY constructors to create new instances of the Struct and Array classes. This section documents the Oracle proprietary classes for the descriptors and the proprietary methods for all five classes.

ArrayDescriptor

The oracle.sql.ArrayDescriptor class extends java.lang.Object. An ArrayDescriptor object is input to the constructor for oracle.sql.ARRAY to create a new instance of ARRAY. It defines the SQL ARRAY characteristics as they are specified in the database. To create a new ArrayDescriptor, call the ArrayDescriptor class's createDescriptor() factory method, passing a database type name as a String and passing a Connection. The ArrayDescriptor class has the following constants:

```
TYPE_NESTED_TABLE
TYPE_VARRAY
```

The ArrayDescriptor class also has the following methods, all of which can throw a SQLException:

```
static ArrayDescriptor createDescriptor(String name, Connection conn)
int getArrayType()
String getBaseName()
int getBaseType()
long getMaxLength()
String getName()
```

ARRAY Implements Array

The oracle.sql.ARRAY class implements the java.sql.Array interface. An ARRAY not only implements an Array, but is also used with an ArrayDescriptor to create a new Array object in your Java program. Beyond the functionality defined by the java.sql. Array interface, the Array class also has the following proprietary constructor and methods, all of which can throw a SQLException:

```
ARRAY ARRAY(ArrayDescriptor type, Connection conn, Object elements)
OracleConnection getConnection()
ArrayDescriptor getDescriptor()
Datum[] getOracleArray()
Object getOracleArray(long index, int count)
String getSQLTypeName()
boolean isConvertibleTo(Class jClass)
int length()
Object toJdbc()
```

StructDescriptor

The oracle.sql.StructDescriptor class extends java.lang.Object. A StructDescriptor is input to the constructor for oracle.sql.STRUCT to create a new instance of Struct. It defines the characteristics of the data type in the database. To create a new Struct-Descriptor, call the StructDescriptor classes' createDescriptor() factory method, passing it the database object type name as a String and passing a Connection. The

StructDescriptor class has the following methods, all of which can throw a SQLException:

```
static StructDescriptor createDescriptor(String name, Connection conn)
int getLength( )
ResultSetMetaData getMetaData( )
String getName( )
```

STRUCT Implements Struct

The oracle.sql.STRUCT class implements the java.sql.Struct interface. A STRUCT not only implements a Struct, but is also used along with a StructDescriptor object to create a new Struct object in your Java program. Beyond the functionality defined by the java.sql.Struct interface, the Struct class also has the following proprietary constructor and methods, all of which can throw a SQLException:

```
STRUCT STRUCT(StructDescriptor type, Connection conn, Object attributes[])
OracleConnection getConnection( )
StructDescriptor getDescriptor( )
Datum[] getOracleAttributes( )
boolean isConvertibleTo(Class jClass)
Object toJdbc( )
```

REF Implements Ref

The oracle.sql.REF class implements the java.sql.Ref interface. A Ref is used as a pointer to an object row in the database. Besides implementing the java.sql.Ref interface, REF also has the following proprietary methods, all of which can throw a SQLException:

```
OracleConnection getConnection( )
StructDescriptor getDescriptor( )
STRUCT getSTRUCT( )
Object getValue( )
Object getValue(Dictionary map)
boolean isConvertibleTo(Class jClass)
void setValue(Object value)
Object toJdbc( )
```

Now you know how to use a Struct, Array, and Ref to insert objects into a database, update objects, delete objects, and select objects from a database. So let's move on to Chapter 16, where you'll learn to do the same with the strongly typed SQLData and CustomDatum interfaces.

Strongly Typed Object SQL

Strongly typed object SQL refers to the use of client-side custom Java classes to manipulate database-side SQL objects. The classes themselves are referred to as *custom* because a Java class is created to mirror its database counterpart. To mirror database objects you can use one of two approaches: the JDBC API's standard SQLData interface or Oracle's CustomDatum interface. With the SQLData interface, a database object is represented as a custom Java class that implements the SQLData interface; however, a collection is still represented by an Array object, and a reference is still represented by a Ref object. With the Oracle CustomDatum interface, a database object is represented as an Oracle custom class file that implements the CustomDatum and CustomDatumFactory interfaces. Unlike the SQLData interface, The CustomDatum interface supports all database object types, including references and collections.

For example, in Chapter 15 we used a Struct object to manipulate a database object, an Array object for collections, and a Ref object to hold a database reference. With strongly typed object SQL, you'll use a custom Java class to manipulate a database object, an Array object or another custom Java class for a collection, and a Ref object or yet another custom Java class to hold a database reference.

If you're concerned with portability, then you should use the SQLData interface. Otherwise, since the SQLData interface currently doesn't provide support for collections and references, or if you're performing a data-processing task, I'd use Oracle's CustomDatum interface.

In this chapter, we'll cover both the standard java.sql.SQLData and the Oracle oracle.sql.CustomDatum interfaces. Before we do, we'll spend some time in the next section covering how to use Oracle's JPublisher utility. JPublisher can be used to automatically generate the custom Java classes for both the SQLData and CustomDatum interfaces. It's important to take the time to read the next section because we use JPublisher throughout this chapter to generate the custom Java classes for the examples.

JPublisher

Oracle's JPublisher utility queries the database for the database object types you specify, and using the mapping options you specify, creates either a SQLData or a CustomDatum implementation of a Java class for each SQL object. JPublisher itself is a Java program that has a command-line interface. You specify its runtime parameters on the command line when you execute the program, but all the command-line options must be listed on one line, and this is an invitation for errors. Alternatively, instead of typing a long list of parameters on the command line, you can execute JPublisher using properties and input files. We'll start by covering all the command-line options, then discuss how most of them can be entered into a properties file, continue with input file syntax, and finish up with an outline of how to use JPublisher to generate a custom Java class.

Command-Line Options

Execute JPublisher by executing the *jpub* program at a host command prompt. Specify any command-line options by using the following syntax:

```
-option_name=value
```

which breaks down as:

option_name
Refers to one of the valid command-line options

value
A valid value for the corresponding *option_name*

 There should be no spaces following the switch character (-), nor around the equal sign (=).

Following are the options available for use with JPublisher along with descriptions of their possible values. Default values are underlined.

-builtintypes={jdbc|oracle}
Controls type mappings, such as the choice between standard Java classes such as String and Oracle Java classes such as CHAR, for nonnumeric, non-LOB, non-user-defined SQL or PL/SQL data types

-case={lower|mixed|same|upper}
Controls how JPublisher translates database type names to Java class and attribute names. lower, same, and upper are self-explanatory. For mixed, JPublisher uses the Java naming convention, removing any underscore (_) or dollar

sign (\$) characters but using their placement in the database type name to denote the beginning of different words to support capitalization.

-dir=*directory_name*

Controls where JPublisher writes the class files it generates. The default is the current directory.

-driver=*driver_name*

Controls which JDBC driver to use to access the database. The default is oracle. jdbc.driver.OracleDriver.

-encoding=*encoding_character_set*

Controls the character set encoding used when writing the class files. The default is the value in the system property file.encoding.

-input=*input_filename*

Specifies the name of a mapping file. A *mapping file* allows you to specify the data type mapping between SQL and Java in a file rather than on the command line.

-lobtypes={jdbc|oracle}

Controls the data type mapping between SQL and Java for the BLOB and CLOB SQL types.

-methods={true|false|named}

Controls whether JPublisher creates wrappers for a database type's static and member methods. When true or named, JPublisher creates *.sqlj* files as part of a CustomDatum interface class. CustomDatum classes are created because the SQLData interface does not provide a Connection object, which is required to make a stored procedure call, while the CustomDatum classes using SQLJ provide the required Connection object. When false, JPublisher creates *.java* files. Regardless, JPublisher always generates *.java* files for a reference, varying array, or nested table type. If the value is named, then only those methods listed in the input file are wrapped.

-numbertypes={bigdecimal|jdbc|objectjdbc|oracle}

Controls type mappings for the numeric types. The mapping types listed affect numeric data types differently, so they require some additional explanation:

jdbc

Maps most numeric types to primitive Java types such as short, int, long, float, double, etc. Choosing jdbc means you can't properly handle database NULL values in your program!

objectjdbc

Maps the numeric types to corresponding Java wrapper classes such as Short, Integer, Long, Float, Double, etc. This makes detecting database NULL values feasible.

bigdecimal

> Maps all numeric types to `BigDecimal`. Not too efficient, but it can handle any number Oracle throws its way.

oracle

> Maps all data types to their corresponding `oracle.sql.*` types and maps user-defined types to `CustomDatum`. Very efficient, but not portable.

`-omit_schema_names`

Controls whether the schema name is used in the generated classes. The default is to include the schema name.

`-package=java_package_name`

Specifies a Java package name to be included in the generated classes.

`-props=properties_filename`

Specifies the name of a properties file. A *properties file* allows you to specify the command-line options covered in this section in a file that in turn is read by JPublisher.

`-sql=type_name:super_class_name:map_class_name`
`-sql=type_name:map_class_name`

Specifies the name of a database object, an optional Java superclass name, and a Java class name for which to generate class files. You can use this option multiple times to specify multiple object types for which to generate classes:

type_name

> Identifies the name of the database type. If you're going to extend a superclass, then use the first format and specify a *super_class_name* that you will extend with a subclass: the *map_class_name*.

super_class_name

> The name of an intermediate class file that you will then extend.

map_class_name

> The name that will be used in the type map. Note that the case you specify overrides any other case settings.

`-url=database_url`

Specifies the database URL. The default value is `jdbc:oracle:oci8:@`.

`-user=username/password`

A username and password that have access to the database types for which you want to generate classes. This information must be specified in order to use JPublisher.

`-usertypes={jdbc|oracle}`

Controls mappings for user-defined types and determines whether the `SQLData` or `CustomDatum` interface is implemented by the generated classes. Selecting `jdbc` results in the use of the `SQLData` interface, while a value of `oracle` results in the use of the `CustomDatum` interface.

All of the properties in the previous list, except for -props, can be specified in a properties file. And for your sanity's sake, I hope you use one. To show you why I feel the way I do, I'll provide an example of a JPublisher command where I specify the properties on the command line. If you wish to create classes for the five object types introduced in Chapter 14 and wish for those classes to use SQLData interface implementations, use the following command at the host's command prompt:

```
jpub.exe -user=scott/tiger -methods=false -builtintypes=jdbc -lobtypes=jdbc -
numbertypes=objectjdbc -usertypes=jdbc -sql=LOCATION_TYP:JLocation:Location -sql=
PERSON_IDENTIFIER_TYPE_TYP:PersonIdentifierType -sql= PERSON_IDENTIFIER_TYP:
PersonIdentifier -sql=PERSON_TYP:JPerson:Person -sql=PERSON_LOCATION_TYP:
PersonLocation
```

Rather confusing, isn't it? There's more than ample opportunity to make a mistake when typing, isn't there? To better organize the process of generating custom classes using JPublisher, use a properties file to hold all the command-line options except -props and -sql. For the -sql property, use an input file. We'll examine both of these file types in the next two sections.

Property File Syntax

Instead of listing all the desired command-line options on the command line when you run JPublisher, you can put them in a properties file and specify the properties filename on the command line with the -props option. To enter options in a properties file, prefix them with jpub.. For example, to specify the -user option, type the following into a text file:

```
jpub.user=scott/tiger
```

For our earlier example, the contents of a properties file might look like this:

```
jpub.user=scott/tiger
jpub.methods=false
jpub.builtintypes=jdbc
jpub.lobtypes=jdbc
jpub.numbertypes=objectjdbc
jpub.usertypes=jdbc
jpub.input=sqldata.input
```

Be warned that trailing spaces on your property values will make them invalid—for example, "jdbc " with a trailing space character, is not recognized, but jdbc is recognized. If you make the mistake of leaving a trailing space character, you'll get an error message similar to this:

```
ERROR: Option -builtintypes=jdbc  is invalid
```

This error will drive you crazy trying to figure out what's wrong when your option setting looks right.

Input File Syntax

Instead of specifying the database types to generate classes on the command line, as we did in the earlier example, you can specify your class file generation options (those specified with the `-sql` option) in an input file that you in turn specify on the command line with the `-input` option. Alternatively, you can specify the input file in the properties file with the `jpub.input` property. An *input file* is a text file with the following syntax (items in brackets are optional):

```
SQL
  [schema.]{type_name | package_name}
[GENERATE
  [java_package_name.]java_super_class_name]
[AS
  [java_package_name.]java_map_class_name]
[TRANSLATE
   member_name AS java_name
[,member_name AS java_name...]]
```

which breaks down as:

schema

> The database object type's schema name.

type_name

> The database object type's name.

package_name

> The name of a database package.

java_package_name

> The name of the Java package to include in a generated class.

GENERATE

> A clause that determines the name of the class file that will be generated.

java_super_class_name

> The name of the class generated with the expectation that the class will be extended by *java_map_class_name*, which in turn will be manually coded by a programmer to extend *java_super_class_name*. If the GENERATE clause is omitted, then the AS clause's java_map_class_name is generated.

AS

> A clause that determines the name of a subclass if the GENERATE clause is used or the name of the generated class if the GENERATE clause is omitted.

java_map_class_name

> The name of the class that will subclass the generated class file if the GENERATE clause is used or the name of the class file that is generated if the GENERATE clause is omitted. It's also the class name that is used when modifying the class map in your Java program (more on this later).

TRANSLATE
> A clause that renames a type's static or member methods.

member_name
> The name of a type method.

java_name
> The name you wish to use for the method in the generated class.

Writing a Class That Extends a Generated Class

If you use the GENERATE clause, you need to write the subclass that will extend the superclass. When you do, your subclass must:

- Have a no argument constructor that calls the no argument constructor for the superclass. For a CustomDatum class, you must also have a constructor that takes a Connection object and passes it to the superclass, and you must have another constructor that takes a ConnectionContext object and passes it to the superclass.

- Implement the CustomDatum or SQLData interface. Your subclass activity does this automatically by inheriting from its parent class.

- Implement CustomDatumFactory if it's implementing the CustomDatum interface.

Now that you have some background on how JPublisher works, let's actually use it to generate a SQLData class for the type person_typ.

The SQLData Interface

The java.sql.SQLData interface allows you to create custom Java classes that mirror your user-defined database types. But, as my mother-in-law would say, "What do you get for that?" If you haven't used an object database before, using a database to store objects, that is, both data and methods, requires a shift in your thinking. Instead of just modeling the data around, and establishing relationships between, different things, you can complete the puzzle by including a thing's behavior. When you create a user-defined data type in the database, you can also include methods for its behaviors. You can continue to use relational SQL and retrieve the object data as though it were in tables, and execute object methods as though they were separate stored procedures, but with the SQLData interface, you don't have to. Instead, you can create a Java object that will mimic your database object and retrieve an object directly from the database into your Java program as an object. There is no longer any need to do any relational-to-object mapping in your Java program. Now you can use objects.

When you use SQLData, follow these steps:

1. Create custom Java classes to represent database user-defined data types.

2. Add the custom Java classes to the Connection object's type map.

3. For insert and update operations, use a `PreparedStatement` object with an appropriately formulated SQL statement.

4. Use the `getObject()` or `setObject()` accessor methods to get and set the object values as needed.

Since we will use JPublisher to write our custom Java classes, I will not go into any great detail about hand-coding them. However, I will briefly talk about the process for doing that in the next section.

Hand-Coding a SQLData Implementation

Writing your own `SQLData` classes is really not that difficult. The `SQLData` interface requires you to implement three methods:

```
String getSQLTypeName( )
void readSQL(SQLInput stream, String typeName)
void writeSQL(SQLOutput stream)
```

The `getSQLTypeName()` method returns the database type name. The `readSQL()` method uses the `SQLInput` stream that is passed to it from the JDBC driver to populate the attributes in the custom Java class. For each attribute in the database type, the appropriate `SQLInput` object readXXX() method is called in the same order as the attributes in the database type. For example, let's take `location_typ`. It's defined as:

```
create type LOCATION_typ as object (
location_id          number,
parent_location_id   number,
code                 varchar2(30),
name                 varchar2(80),
start_date           date,
end_date             date,
map member function get_map return varchar2,
static function get_id  return number );
/
```

Assuming that the class's variables are defined elsewhere in the class, a `readSQL()` method for this type would look something like this:

```
public void readSQL(SQLInput stream, String type)
  throws SQLException {
  locationId       = stream.readBigDecimal( );
  parentLocationId = stream.readBigDecimal( );
  code             = stream.readString( );
  name             = stream.readString( );
  startDate        = stream.readTimestamp( );
  endDate          = stream.readTimestamp( );
}
```

The `writeSQL()` method for the type, which writes the data back to the database, would look something like this:

```
public void writeSQL(SQLOutput stream)
  throws SQLException {
```

```
    stream.writeBigDecimal(locationId);
    stream.writeBigDecimal(parentLocationId);
    stream.writeString(code);
    stream.writeString(name);
    stream.writeTimestamp(startDate);
    stream.writeTimestamp(endDate);
  }
```

If you want the custom Java class to be useful, give it a set of applicable accessor methods so it follows the JavaBeans standard. Accordingly, for each attribute, create corresponding get and set methods. Putting it all together, you have the following class definition:

```
import java.sql.*;

public class SQLDataLocation implements SQLData, Serializable {
  private java.math.BigDecimal locationId;
  private java.math.BigDecimal parentLocationId;
  private String              code;
  private String              name;
  private java.sql.Timestamp  startDate;
  private java.sql.Timestamp  endDate;

  // A no argument constructor
  public SQLDataLocation() {
  }

  public void readSQL(SQLInput stream, String type)
   throws SQLException {
    locationId       = stream.readBigDecimal();
    parentLocationId = stream.readBigDecimal();
    code             = stream.readString();
    name             = stream.readString();
    startDate        = stream.readTimestamp();
    endDate          = stream.readTimestamp();
  }

  public void writeSQL(SQLOutput stream)
   throws SQLException {
    stream.writeBigDecimal(locationId);
    stream.writeBigDecimal(parentLocationId);
    stream.writeString(code);
    stream.writeString(name);
    stream.writeTimestamp(startDate);
    stream.writeTimestamp(endDate);
  }

  public String getSQLTypeName()
   throws SQLException {
    return "SCOTT.LOCATION_TYP";
  }

  public java.math.BigDecimal getLocationId() {
    return locationId;
  }
```

```java
    public java.math.BigDecimal getParentLocationId( ) {
      return parentLocationId;
    }

    public String getCode( ) {
      return code;
    }

    public String getName( ) {
      return name;
    }

    public java.sql.Timestamp getStartDate( ) {
      return startDate;
    }

    public java.sql.Timestamp getEndDate( ) {
      return endDate;
    }

    public void setLocationId(java.math.BigDecimal locationId) {
      this.locationId = locationId;
    }

    public void setParentLocationId(java.math.BigDecimal parentLocationId) {
      this.parentLocationId = parentLocationId;
    }

    public void setCode(String code) {
      this.code = code;
    }

    public void setName(String name) {
      this.name = name;
    }

    public void setStartDate(java.sql.Timestamp startDate) {
      this.startDate = startDate;
    }

    public void setEndDate(java.sql.Timestamp endDate) {
      this.endDate = endDate;
    }
}
```

But what if you have 100, or 500, or maybe even 1,000 types for which you need to create Java classes? Manually coding the classes can be an onerous and unproductive task, especially when you stop to consider that JPublisher can do the job for you.

Using JPublisher to Generate SQLData Classes

The process of creating custom Java classes for your database types with JPublisher is:

1. Create database object types.
2. Create a JPublisher mapping file, referred to as the input file.
3. Create a JPublisher properties file that points to the mapping file.
4. Execute JPublisher using the -props option.
5. Compile any *.sqlj* files created by JPublisher in order of dependence.
6. Compile any *.java* files created by JPublisher in order of dependence.

Creating database objects

We covered step 1, creating database objects, in Chapter 14. In that chapter, we created several types, so we won't repeat that step here. We ended up creating six types for our examples:

```
location_typ
person_identifier_type_typ
person_identifier_typ
person_identifier_tab
person_typ
person_location_typ
```

Let's proceed to step 2 and create a mapping file.

Creating a mapping file for SQLData

Of the six types mentioned previously, two, location_typ and person_typ, have methods. Since the SQLData interface does not support database object methods, we need to create a superclass using JPublisher and then later hand-code a subclass that implements their methods. So for these two types, we use the GENERATE clause to create a superclass. Then later, we create a subclass that implements JPublisher's generated class, which adds wrapper methods to call the database type's methods. For the other four types, we simply use the AS clause. Here's our mapping file, *sqldata.input*:

```
SQL LOCATION_TYP             GENERATE JLocation AS Location
SQL PERSON_IDENTIFIER_TYPE_TYP                AS PersonIdentifierType
SQL PERSON_IDENTIFIER_TYP                     AS PersonIdentifier
SQL PERSON_TYP               GENERATE JPerson  AS Person
SQL PERSON_LOCATION_TYP                       AS PersonLocation
```

The first line instructs JPublisher to generate a superclass JLocation that will be extended by the subclass Location from the database type LOCATION_TYP. Remember that although the case of the database data type is not important, the case of the GENERATE and AS clause's class names will be used in the classes themselves. The second line instructs JPublisher to generate the PersonIdentifierType class from the database data type PERSON_IDENTIFIER_TYPE_TYP. After executing JPublisher, you end up with five classes: JLocation, PersonIdentifierType, PersonIdentifier, JPerson, and PersonLocation. But what about the sixth type, PERSON_IDENTIFIER_TAB? When using the SQLData interface, you'll use a java.sql.Array for Oracle collections, just as we did in Chapter 15.

Now that we have the mapping, or input, file written, let's move on to the properties file.

Creating a properties file for SQLData

The properties file will allow you to list the properties you can pass on the command line in a text file. Using a properties file ensures that you use the same properties when generating all your classes. Here's the properties file *sqldata.properties*, which we'll use for generating the SQLData classes:

```
jpub.user=scott/tiger
jpub.methods=false
jpub.builtintypes=jdbc
jpub.lobtypes=jdbc
jpub.numbertypes=objectjdbc
jpub.usertypes=jdbc
jpub.input=sqldata.input
```

This breaks down as:

user
: Specifies the username and password to use when logging into the database.

methods
: Set to false because JPublisher does not support the creation of wrapper methods for the SQLData interface.

builtintypes
: Set to jdbc, so java.sql.String is used instead of oracle.sql.CHAR, and so forth.

lobtypes
: Also set to jdbc to get the JDBC LOB types and not the Oracle LOB types.

numbertypes
: Set to objectjdbc, so Java wrapper classes such as Integer and Double are used instead of the Java primitives such as int and double.

usertypes
: This is critical and determines whether JPublisher generates SQLData or CustomDatum classes. In this case, we specify jdbc to generate SQLData classes.

input
: Specifies the name of the input file.

As stated earlier, you can specify all these values on the command line. However, a properties file is a tidier approach.

Executing JPublisher

Now that you have an input and a properties file, you can generate the classes by executing JPublisher with the following command at the command prompt:

```
jpub -props=sqldata.properties
```

Given the input and properties we created earlier, you now have five new class source files:

JLocation.java
PersonIdentifierType.java
PersonIdentifier.java
JPerson.java
PersonLocation.java

You'll need to compile these generated classes before you attempt to use them in another program.

Examining JPublisher's output

Before we move on to using the classes generated by JPublisher, let's look at the source code that JPublisher created for the superclass JLocation.java:

```java
import java.sql.SQLException;
import oracle.jdbc.driver.OracleConnection;
import oracle.jdbc.driver.OracleTypes;
import java.sql.SQLData;
import java.sql.SQLInput;
import java.sql.SQLOutput;
import oracle.sql.STRUCT;
import oracle.jpub.runtime.MutableStruct;

public class JLocation implements SQLData
{
  public static final String _SQL_NAME = "SCOTT.LOCATION_TYP";
  public static final int _SQL_TYPECODE = OracleTypes.STRUCT;

  private java.math.BigDecimal m_locationId;
  private java.math.BigDecimal m_parentLocationId;
  private String m_code;
  private String m_name;
  private java.sql.Timestamp m_startDate;
  private java.sql.Timestamp m_endDate;

  /* constructor */
  public JLocation()
  {
  }
```

```java
public void readSQL(SQLInput stream, String type)
throws SQLException
{
    setLocationId(stream.readBigDecimal());
    setParentLocationId(stream.readBigDecimal());
    setCode(stream.readString());
    setName(stream.readString());
    setStartDate(stream.readTimestamp());
    setEndDate(stream.readTimestamp());
}

public void writeSQL(SQLOutput stream)
throws SQLException
{
    stream.writeBigDecimal(getLocationId());
    stream.writeBigDecimal(getParentLocationId());
    stream.writeString(getCode());
    stream.writeString(getName());
    stream.writeTimestamp(getStartDate());
    stream.writeTimestamp(getEndDate());
}

public String getSQLTypeName() throws SQLException
{
  return _SQL_NAME;
}

/* accessor methods */
public java.math.BigDecimal getLocationId()
{ return m_locationId; }

public void setLocationId(java.math.BigDecimal locationId)
{ m_locationId = locationId; }


public java.math.BigDecimal getParentLocationId()
{ return m_parentLocationId; }

public void setParentLocationId(java.math.BigDecimal parentLocationId)
{ m_parentLocationId = parentLocationId; }


public String getCode()
{ return m_code; }

public void setCode(String code)
{ m_code = code; }


public String getName()
{ return m_name; }

public void setName(String name)
{ m_name = name; }
```

```
      public java.sql.Timestamp getStartDate( )
      { return m_startDate; }

      public void setStartDate(java.sql.Timestamp startDate)
      { m_startDate = startDate; }

      public java.sql.Timestamp getEndDate( )
      { return m_endDate; }

      public void setEndDate(java.sql.Timestamp endDate)
      { m_endDate = endDate; }

  }
```

Overall, it's pretty similar to the SQLData interface code we hand-coded for type location_typ earlier. Nothing earth-shattering. And that's my point. Why should you write this generic code when your computer can do it for you? However, since the SQLData interface does not define database object method support, and therefore, JPublisher does not support the creation of wrappers for database object methods, you'll have to write some code after all. So let's take a look at extending a superclass.

Extending a generated superclass

Now that we have the classes generated by JPublisher, we need to create the subclasses Location and Person for JLocation and JPerson. Since the process is similar for both, and person_typ has more methods, I'll cover the Person class here.

Reviewing the criteria that we covered earlier for extending a JPublisher class, all we need to do in this instance is create a class that extends JPerson and has a no argument constructor that calls its parent class's no argument constructor. Accordingly, here's a minimal subclass:

```
  public class Person extends JPerson {

    public Person( ) {
      super( );
    }
  }
```

But what good is it to subclass JPerson unless we add some functionality? In the case of Person, we want to implement methods that call the member methods defined for person_typ in the database. The following is our fully coded subclass with all of person_typ type's methods implemented:

```
  import java.math.*;
  import java.sql.*;

  public class Person extends JPerson {
    private Connection conn = null;

    public Person( ) {
      super( );
    }
```

```
    // We've added a constructor that takes a connection so we
    // have one available to make stored-procedure calls
    public Person(Connection conn) {
      super( );
      setConnection(conn);
    }

    public BigDecimal getId( ) throws SQLException {
      BigDecimal id  = null;
      if (conn!=null) {
        Person thisPerson = this;
        CallableStatement cstmt = conn.prepareCall(
          "{? = call " + getSQLTypeName( ) + ".GET_ID( )}");
        cstmt.registerOutParameter(1, Types.NUMERIC);
        cstmt.execute( );
        id = cstmt.getBigDecimal(1);
      }
      return id;
    }

    public Integer getAge( ) throws SQLException {
      Integer age = null;
      if (conn!=null) {
        Person thisPerson = this;
        CallableStatement cstmt = conn.prepareCall(
          "{? = call " + getSQLTypeName( ) + ".GET_AGE( ? )}");
        cstmt.registerOutParameter(1, Types.NUMERIC);
        cstmt.setObject(2, thisPerson);
        cstmt.execute( );
        age = new Integer(cstmt.getInt(1));
      }
      return age;
    }

    public Integer getAgeOn(Timestamp date) throws SQLException {
      Integer age = null;
      if (conn!=null) {
        Person thisPerson = this;
        CallableStatement cstmt = conn.prepareCall(
          "{? = call " + getSQLTypeName( ) + ".GET_AGE_ON( ?, ? )}");
        cstmt.registerOutParameter(1, Types.NUMERIC);
        cstmt.setObject(2, thisPerson);
        cstmt.setTimestamp(3, date);
        cstmt.execute( );
        age = new Integer(cstmt.getInt(1));
      }
      return age;
    }

    // We've also added a setter method to set the connection
    // so one is available for the stored-procedure calls
    public void setConnection(Connection conn) {
```

```
        this.conn = conn;
    }

}
```

The first thing of importance in this definition for a `Person` class is that we've added a private variable `conn` to hold a `Connection` reference. Without a connection we can't execute the stored procedures using a callable statement. In conjunction with `conn`, we've added a second constructor that takes a `Connection` object as a parameter and stores it in `conn`, and we've also added a `setConnection( )` accessor method to set the connection. Now, when creating a new `Person` instance, we can use the alternate constructor to set the connection:

```
Person person = new Person(conn);
```

Or, if we have retrieved a person from the database, we can call the `setConnection( )` method to initialize the `Connection` in the `Person` instance.

The first method in the `Person` class is `getId( )`. `getId( )` is a wrapper method for the `person_typ` type's static method `GET_ID( )`. The static method `GET_ID( )` returns the next sequence value for the `personId` attribute. It's defined as `static` so that it is available when there is no instance of type `person_typ`. Of course, it has to be this way, because the method is used only when creating a new instance. Since `GET_ID( )` is a static method, it's called using its type name, `person_typ`. In our subclass, it has been implemented as an instance method, but it could have just as easily been a static method if we were to recode it to accept a `Connection` object. However, when we consider how it will be used, that is, to get the next ID value for the `personId` attribute, there is no need to make it a static function in Java.

The next method, `getAge( )`, is a wrapper class for the `person_typ` type's member method, `GET_AGE( )`. As defined in the database type, `GET_AGE( )` has no arguments, yet we pass an argument. So what's happening here? Since a member method requires an instance of its type in order to be executed, each member method has an implied first argument appropriately called `SELF`. What we're doing in `getAge( )` is passing the Java `this` reference to the member method as `SELF`.

The third method, `getAgeOn( )`, is a wrapper class for the `person_typ` type's member method `GET_AGE_ON( )`. `GET_AGE_ON( )` takes one argument, a `DATE` from which to calculate an age, but this time, we pass two arguments! Once again, that's because we pass the `this` reference as the implied first argument, `SELF`.

Notice that we've coded all three methods to fail silently if no `Connection` object is available by testing the existence of the `Connection` variable, `conn`, with an `if` statement.

One question that begs to be asked as a result of all this discussion is why would anyone want to execute methods in the database when they could possibly do so more efficiently in the client? The next section attempts to answer this question.

Database versus client method execution

Why would anyone execute a method in the database instead of writing code to execute the method on the client? Rather than take a one-sided stand, as the question implies, a better approach is to ask: "Where is the best place to execute a type's method?" With the first method, getId( ), there is no way to get a sequence's next value more efficiently in a client, and yet maintain control over how the sequence numbers are allocated, than in a database. Consequently, using a static type (user-defined database type) method is the best choice. However, using the member type methods getAge( ) and getAgeOn( ) instead of coding these in the custom Java class is questionable.

If it is possible to implement a method in a client's invocation of an object with exactly the same results that the database would produce, then the method in question can be coded in the Java class. However, keep in mind that we are now using the database as persistent storage for objects, not just for data. Any application that accesses the database should be able to use an object's methods as well as its data. This is a drastic departure from traditional relational database thinking. If a method is reproduced in another environment such as on the client, and later the functionality of said method is changed in the database, then the database and client implementations will be out-of-sync. On the other hand, if the method is wrapped and called from the database, it can never be out-of-sync.

There seems to be this pervasive impression that calling stored procedures, or making remote procedure calls, is inherently bad. Yet CORBA and Java, two of the most popular and growing technologies, are built around the concept of remote object invocation. Be very thoughtful when you decide how to implement database type methods in your Java classes.

Of course, there are always the no-brainer member methods, which perform a significant amount of database processing. These are best done in the database because doing so eliminates the network overhead involved in passing data back and forth between client and database. Regardless, I recommend that you always create wrapper methods that call a database object's methods in the database rather than attempt to recode those methods on the client. This allows you to move your object model into the database where it belongs.

Adding Classes to a Type Map

Now that we have a JPublisher SQLData class for each database type, it's time to put them to work. Unlike the built-in SQL data types, custom Java classes have no default SQL-to-Java data type mapping supplied by the driver. Instead, you, as the programmer, must provide the required mapping by adding your custom Java classes to a connection's type map. The type map for a connection is usually a hash table that holds keyword value pairs, with the database object type as the keyword and an empty instance of the custom Java class as the value.

After you provide an updated type map to your connection, use the getObject() and setObject() accessor methods as you would with any built-in SQL data type accessor to get and set values. When you add your custom Java classes to a connection's type map, a call to the getObject() method returns an instance of an object of the Java type you specified, and a call to setObject() expects an instance of the Java type you specified. If you don't update the type map, a call to the getObject() method gives you its default object, a Struct, while a call to a the setObject() methods expects a Struct. To add entries to a type map, follow these steps:

1. Get the existing type map from a Connection object.
2. Add your custom Java objects to the type map.
3. Replace the Connection object's current type map with the one you updated.

Getting an existing type map

When you first get a Connection object from DriverManager or from a DataSource object, the default type map is empty. So, at the time you wish to update a connection's type map, if you know that this is the first time it's being updated, it's not necessary to retrieve the existing type map. Instead, you can create a new Map object such as a HashTable, add your mapping entries to it, and use it to update the connection. However, it's easier and less problematic to just retrieve the existing type map, empty or not, from a connection. To retrieve an existing type map from a Connection object, use the getTypeMap() method, which has the following signature:

```
Map getTypeMap()
```

For example, to get the type map for the current connection named conn, use code similar to the following:

```
java.util.Map map = conn.getTypeMap();
```

Once you've retrieved the type map, you're ready to add mapping entries to it.

Adding mapping entries

To add new entries to a type map, use the Map object's put() method, passing the database type name and a copy of the class that implements the database type. To create a copy of a class, use the Class.forName() method. The put() method has the following signature:

```
Object put(Object key, Object value)
```

which breaks down as:

key

The key with which the specified value will be associated—in our case, the name of a database type

value

The value to be associated with the specified key—in our case, an instance of the appropriate custom Java class

returned Object

A copy of an existing Object value for the specified key, or null

For example, to add the custom Java class Location, which mirrors the database type LOCATION_TYP to the Map object retrieved earlier, your code will be similar to this:

```
map.put("SCOTT.LOCATION_TYP", Class.forName("Location"));
```

Here, the key, SCOTT.LOCATION_TYP, is the fully qualified name of the database object type upon which the LOCATION_OT object table was created. For the key's value, the Class.forName( ) method is called, passing the name of the Location class. Class.forName( ), in turn, instantiates a copy of the class. When you're finished adding mapping entries to the Map object, you're ready to update your connection with it.

Setting the updated type map

The last step in adding your custom Java classes to a type map is to update your connection's type map by using the Connection object's setTypeMap( ) method. The setTypeMap( ) method has the following signature:

```
setTypeMap(Map map)
```

in which map is the Map object to which you've added your desired entries. For example, to update the Connection object, conn, with the Map object, map, which we modified earlier, use the following code:

```
conn.setTypeMap(map);
```

Following is an example in which we retrieve the type map from Connection, conn, add the classes we created earlier, and then write the modified type map back to conn:

```
java.util.Map map = conn.getTypeMap( );
map.put("SCOTT.LOCATION_TYP",           Class.forName("Location"));
map.put(
 "SCOTT.PERSON_IDENTIFIER_TYPE_TYP",
 Class.forName("PersonIdentifierType"));
map.put("SCOTT.PERSON_IDENTIFIER_TYP", Class.forName("PersonIdentifier"));
map.put("SCOTT.PERSON_TYP",            Class.forName("Person"));
map.put("SCOTT.PERSON_LOCATION_TYP",   Class.forName("PersonLocation"));
conn.setTypeMap(map);
```

It's important to notice that we used the subclasses Location and Person, not the superclasses JLocation and JPerson, when adding entries to the type map.

Using getObject( ) with a Type Map

If all you do in your program is retrieve objects from a database, you have another option at your disposal. Instead of updating your connection's type map, you can create a new type map and pass it to one of the overloaded forms of the getObject( ) method. Here are the signatures for the two forms of the getObject( ) method that allow you to specify a type map:

```
Object getObject(int i, Map map)
Object getObject(String colName, Map map)
```

The first method takes the relative position of a column in the SELECT statement, starting with 1, as the first parameter, and a type map as the second parameter. The second method takes a column name (from the SELECT statement) as the first parameter and a type map for the second. These two methods allow you to use a type map to retrieve database objects without having to change your connection's type map.

Inserting an Object

Once you have your custom Java classes and an updated type map, you're ready to store an object in the database. In this section, we'll concentrate on inserting a new object into the database. The process for inserting an object is basically the same as it was when using a Struct object, but this time, you'll be using a custom Java class instead of a Struct. Because the process is basically the same, I won't get into as much detail here as I did in Chapter 15.

Assuming you have updated a connection with an updated type map that includes your custom Java classes, the process for inserting an object is:

1. Create a new instance of your custom Java class, setting the values for the new object where appropriate.
2. Formulate an INSERT statement for an object table where the VALUES clause has one placeholder for your new object.
3. Create a PreparedStatement object using your INSERT statement.
4. Use the setObject( ) method to set the value of the placeholder.
5. Execute the prepared statement.

Creating a new instance of a custom Java class

Creating a new instance of one of your custom Java classes is fairly straightforward. If you've been using Java for any period of time, you've already done this many times. To create a new instance, declare a variable of a custom Java class. Then assign it an instance of its custom Java class by using the new operator:

```
Person person = new Person(conn);
```

Here, we've created a new instance of a `Person` object with the new operator and assigned it to the variable person. In this case, we've used our alternative constructor that takes a connection as an argument, so we can later call the person object's getId( ) method to allocate a new primary key sequence. Now that we have a new person instance, we can use its accessor methods to set its attribute values. For example:

```
// Call the Person object's getId( ) method to get the next
// sequence value from the database for its primary key
long personId = person.getId( );
person.setPersonId(personId);

person.setLastName("O'Reilly");
person.setFirstName("Tim");
person.setMiddleName(null);
person.setBirthDate(
  Timestamp.valueOf("1972-03-17 00:00:00.0"));
person.setMothersMaidenName("Oh! I don't know!");

// The Oracle collection, PERSON_IDENTIFIER_TAB, must still be
// manipulated as a JDBC Array, but this time, we populate the
// Array object with our custom Java class personIdentifier
// instead of Struct
Object[] ids = new Object[2];
personIdentifier = new PersonIdentifier( );
personIdentifier.setId("EID");
personIdentifier.setIdType("000000001");
ids[0] = personIdentifier;
personIdentifier = new PersonIdentifier( );
personIdentifier.setId("SDL");
personIdentifier.setIdType("CA9999999999");
ids[1] = personIdentifier;
oracle.sql.ArrayDescriptor idArrayDescriptor =
oracle.sql.ArrayDescriptor.createDescriptor(
  "PERSON_IDENTIFIER_TAB", conn);
personIdentifiers = new oracle.sql.ARRAY(
  idArrayDescriptor, conn, ids );
person.setIdentifiers(personIdentifiers);
```

In this example, we first call the getID( ) method to allocate a new primary key value for the object. Next, we set the attribute values until we get to the Oracle collection PERSON_IDENTIFIER_TAB. The collection must still be manipulated using a JDBC Array object, but this time we populate the Array object with our custom Java class personIdentifier instead of with a Struct.

Formulating an INSERT statement

The next step is to formulate an INSERT statement to be used with a prepared statement to insert a new row into an object table. Since an object table has one column, which is based on a database user-defined type, an appropriate INSERT statement will contain one placeholder in the INSERT statement's VALUES clause:

```
insert into person_ot values ( ? )
```

Here, we've formulated an INSERT statement to insert a PERSON_TYP object into the PERSON_OT object table.

Creating a prepared statement object

If you've read the entire book up to this point, then creating a prepared statement is a no-brainer. See Chapter 11 if you need a refresher. To create a prepared statement, call the Connection object's prepareStatement( ) method, passing it a valid SQL statement:

```
PreparedStatement pstmt = conn.prepareStatement(
  "insert into person_ot values ( ? )");
```

Set the object value

Now gthat we have a prepared statement, we can set the VALUES clause placeholder using the PreparedStatement object's setObject( ) method:

```
pstmt.setObject(1, person);
```

Since the connection's type map was updated to map the database type PERSON_TYP to the Java class Person, the prepared statement's setObject( ) method can use this knowledge to automatically map the attributes in Person to PERSON_TYP using the SQLData interface's writeSQL( ) method.

Execute the prepared statement

The last step in inserting a database object is to execute the prepared statement. As we have done countless times before, we execute the prepared statement using the PreparedStatement object's executeUpdate( ) method:

```
int rows = pstmt.executeUpdate( );
```

After committing the INSERT statement, you can use SQL*Plus to verify the existence of the object in the PERSON_OT object table.

Retrieving an Object

Now that you know how to insert an object, let's take a look at how to retrieve one. Once again, the process for retrieving a database object is very similar to the process used in Chapter 15, except this time, you use your custom Java class instead of a Struct object.

Again, assuming that you have updated a connection with an updated type map that includes your custom Java class, the process for selecting an object from the database is:

1. Create a variable of your custom Java class's type to hold the retrieved object.
2. Formulate a SELECT statement against an object table using the database value( ) function, passing that function the alias for the table name.
3. Create a `Statement` or `PreparedStatement` object using your formulated SELECT statement.
4. Execute the SELECT statement.
5. Use the getObject( ) method to place the value of the row object into your custom Java class variable.

Creating a variable to hold your database object

Creating a variable to hold the database object when it is retrieved from the database is something we've been doing all along. This time, however, instead of creating a `String` to hold a VARCHAR2, or a `Long` to hold a NUMBER, or a `Timestamp` to hold a DATE, you create a variable that is your custom Java class's type to hold the corresponding database object. For example, to create a variable for database type PERSON_TYP, use the following code:

```
Person person = null;
```

This code creates a `Person` variable, `person`, that we'll use to hold a copy of the database object for type PERSON_TYP.

Formulating a SELECT statement

Now that we have the person variable, let's formulate a SELECT statement to retrieve an object from the database. Since an object table consists of one column of a specific user-defined data type, you must use the database value( ) function, passing it the object table's alias as in the SELECT statement to select a copy of an object from the database. For example:

```
select value(p) from person_ot p
```

Here, the object table `PERSON_OT` is aliased with the character p. Accordingly, the alias p is passed to the database value( ) function in order to retrieve a copy of a `PERSON_TYP` object from the database. For example, to select a copy of Tim O'Reilly's `Person` object from the database, use the following SELECT statement:

```
select value(p) from person_ot p
where  last_name  = 'O''Reilly'
and    first_name = 'Tim'
```

Creating a statement object

Now that we have a SELECT statement, we need to create a `Statement` or a `PreparedStatement` object to execute it. Since we formulated a SELECT statement for use with a `Statement` object, we'll create a `Statement`:

```
stmt = conn.createStatement();
```

Executing the SELECT statement

The next step in the process is to execute the SELECT statement. This is done using the `Statement` object's `executeQuery()` method:

```
ResultSet rslt = stmt.executeQuery(
  "select value(p) from person ot p " +
  "where last_name = 'O''Reilly' " +
  "and    first_name = 'Tim' ");
```

Getting an object value from a result set

The last step in the object-retrieval process is to get the object value from the result set and assign it to your local object variable. Since the type map has already been updated for the object, when you call a `ResultSet` object's `getObject()` method to retrieve the object, JDBC will automatically instantiate the appropriate class and return a reference to it. All you have to do is cast the result of the `getObject()` method to the appropriate type. For example, to retrieve a `Person` object, use the following code:

```
if (rslt.next())
  person = (Person)rslt.getObject(1);
```

At this point, we have a copy of the database object as an instance of a custom Java class. If we want to use the methods added to the subclass `Person`, we need to call the `Person` object's `setConnection()` method so a connection is available in the object instance. Now we are retrieving objects from the database!

Since we've covered the processes for inserting and selecting an object, we're ready to cover the process for updating an object.

Updating an Object

The process for updating an object is very similar to selecting and then inserting an object, with two exceptions. First, you retrieve an existing object and update one or more of its attributes. Second, you need to use a prepared UPDATE statement. Since we've covered all the necessary steps earlier, let's concentrate on formulating that UPDATE statement.

An UPDATE statement for an object requires you to use the database value( ) function on the lefthand side of the equals sign in the SET clause and a placeholder on the right:

```
update person_ot p
set value(p) = ?
```

Then, set the value of the placeholder using an updated copy of the database object:

```
pstmt.setObject(1, person);
```

The last thing to learn about manipulating database objects using SQLData is how to delete one.

Deleting an Object

Deleting a database object does not require the SQLData interface. All you need to do is formulate an appropriate DELETE statement using the object table's name and a WHERE clause. For example, to delete Tim O'Reilly's Person object, use the following DELETE statement:

```
delete person_ot
where  last_name  = 'O''Reilly'
and    first_name = 'Tim'
```

At this point, we're ready to put all you've learned into a working example.

A SQLData Example

Example 16-1 takes the SQLData classes that we've created so far and puts them to work, inserting, updating, and selecting data from the database. The program performs the following actions in order to exercise the use of the SQLData interface:

1. Updates the connection's type map
2. Deletes any old objects from prior executions of the program
3. Inserts a Person object into PERSON_OT
4. Inserts a Location object into LOCATION_OT
5. Inserts a PersonLocation object into PERSON_LOCATION_OT
6. Updates a Person object
7. Updates a Person object using a Ref object
8. Retrieves a Person object

Example 16-1. The TestSQLData interface

```
import java.io.*;
import java.math.*;
import java.sql.*;
import java.text.*;
import oracle.jdbc.driver.*;
```

Example 16-1. The TestSQLData interface (continued)

```java
public class TestSQLData {
  Connection conn;

  public TestSQLData() {
    try {
      DriverManager.registerDriver(new oracle.jdbc.driver.OracleDriver());
      conn = DriverManager.getConnection(
        "jdbc:oracle:thin:@dssw2k01:1521:orcl", "scott", "tiger");
    }
    catch (SQLException e) {
      System.err.println(e.getMessage());
      e.printStackTrace();
    }
  }

  public static void main(String[] args)
   throws Exception {
    new TestSQLData().process();
  }

  public void process() throws SQLException {
    BigDecimal        locationId        = null;
    BigDecimal        personId          = null;
    int               index             = 0;
    Location          location          = null;
    PreparedStatement pstmt             = null;
    ResultSet         rslt              = null;
    ResultSet         rslt2             = null;
    Statement         stmt              = null;
    Person            person            = null;
    PersonIdentifier  personIdentifier  = null;
    PersonLocation    personLocation    = null;
    java.sql.Array    personIdentifiers = null;

    // Update the connection's type map
    try {
      conn.setAutoCommit(false);

      java.util.Map map = conn.getTypeMap();
      map.put("SCOTT.LOCATION_TYP",
       Class.forName("Location"));
      map.put("SCOTT.PERSON_IDENTIFIER_TYP",
       Class.forName("PersonIdentifier"));
      map.put("SCOTT.PERSON_TYP",
       Class.forName("Person"));
      map.put("SCOTT.PERSON_LOCATION_TYP",
       Class.forName("PersonLocation"));
      conn.setTypeMap(map);
    }
    catch (ClassNotFoundException e) {
      System.err.println("Class Not Found Error: " + e.getMessage());
    }
    catch (SQLException e) {
```

Example 16-1. The TestSQLData interface (continued)

```java
      System.err.println("SQL Error: " + e.getMessage( ));
    }

  // Clean up a prior execution
  try {
    stmt = conn.createStatement( );
    stmt.executeUpdate(
     "delete person_location_ot where person_id = " +
     "( select person_id from person_ot " +
     "where last_name = 'O''Reilly' and first_name = 'Tim' )");
    stmt.executeUpdate(
     "delete location_ot " +
     "where code = 'SEBASTOPOL'");
    stmt.executeUpdate(
     "delete person_ot " +
     "where last_name = 'O''Reilly' and first_name = 'Tim'");
    stmt.close( );
    stmt = null;
    conn.commit( );
  }
  catch (SQLException e) {
    System.err.println("SQL Error: " + e.getMessage( ));
  }
  finally {
    if (stmt != null)
      try { stmt.close( ); } catch (SQLException ignore) { }
  }

  // Insert a person object
  try {
    // Use a special constructor to initialize the connection
    person = new Person(conn);

    personId = person.getId( );

    person.setPersonId(personId);
    person.setLastName("O'Reilly");
    person.setFirstName("Tim");
    person.setMiddleName(null);
    person.setBirthDate(
     Timestamp.valueOf("1972-03-17 00:00:00.0"));
    person.setMothersMaidenName("Oh! I don't know!");

    Object[] ids = new Object[2];
    personIdentifier = new PersonIdentifier( );
    personIdentifier.setId("EID");
    personIdentifier.setIdType("000000001");
    ids[0] = personIdentifier;
    personIdentifier = new PersonIdentifier( );
    personIdentifier.setId("SDL");
    personIdentifier.setIdType("CA9999999999");
    ids[1] = personIdentifier;
```

Example 16-1. The TestSQLData interface (continued)

```
  oracle.sql.ArrayDescriptor idArrayDescriptor =
  oracle.sql.ArrayDescriptor.createDescriptor(
    "PERSON_IDENTIFIER_TAB", conn );

  personIdentifiers = new oracle.sql.ARRAY(
    idArrayDescriptor, conn, ids );
  person.setIdentifiers(personIdentifiers);

  pstmt = conn.prepareStatement(
    "insert into person_ot values ( ? )");
  pstmt.setObject(1, person);
  int rows = pstmt.executeUpdate( );
  pstmt.close( );
  pstmt = null;
  System.out.println(rows + " rows inserted");
  conn.commit( );
}
catch (SQLException e) {
  System.err.println("SQL Error: " + e.getMessage( ));
}
finally {
  if (pstmt != null)
    try { pstmt.close( ); } catch (SQLException ignore) { }
}

// Insert a location
try {
  location = new Location(conn);

  locationId = location.getId( );

  location.setLocationId(locationId);
  location.setParentLocationId(null);
  location.setCode("SEBASTOPOL");
  location.setName("Sebastopol, CA, USA");
  location.setStartDate(
    Timestamp.valueOf("1988-01-01 00:00:00.0"));
  location.setEndDate(null);

  pstmt = conn.prepareStatement(
    "insert into location_ot values ( ? )");
  pstmt.setObject(1, location);
  int rows = pstmt.executeUpdate( );
  pstmt.close( );
  pstmt = null;
  System.out.println(rows + " rows inserted");
  conn.commit( );
}
catch (SQLException e) {
  System.err.println("SQL Error: " + e.getMessage( ));
}
finally {
  if (pstmt != null)
```

Example 16-1. The TestSQLData interface (continued)

```
      try { pstmt.close( ); } catch (SQLException ignore) { }
}

// Insert a person's location
try {
  personLocation = new PersonLocation( );

  personLocation.setPersonId(personId);
  personLocation.setLocationId(locationId);
  personLocation.setStartDate(
   Timestamp.valueOf("1988-01-01 00:00:00.0"));
  personLocation.setEndDate(null);

  pstmt = conn.prepareStatement(
   "insert into person_location_ot values ( ? )");
  pstmt.setObject(1, personLocation);
  int rows = pstmt.executeUpdate( );
  pstmt.close( );
  pstmt = null;
  System.out.println(rows + " rows inserted");
  conn.commit( );
}
catch (SQLException e) {
  System.err.println("SQL Error: " + e.getMessage( ));
}
finally {
  if (pstmt != null)
    try { pstmt.close( ); } catch (SQLException ignore) { }
}

// Update an object using standard JDBC
try {
  Ref personRef = null;
  stmt = conn.createStatement( );
  rslt = stmt.executeQuery(
   "select ref(p), value(p) from person_ot p " +
   "where last_name = 'O''Reilly' and first_name = 'Tim'");
  rslt.next( );
  personRef = (Ref)rslt.getObject(1);
  person = (Person)rslt.getObject(2);
  rslt.close( );
  rslt = null;
  stmt.close( );
  stmt = null;

  person.setMothersMaidenName(null);

  pstmt = conn.prepareStatement(
   "update person_ot p set value(p) = ? " +
   "where  ref(p) = ?");
  pstmt.setObject(1, person);
  pstmt.setRef(2, personRef);
```

Example 16-1. The TestSQLData interface (continued)

```
      int rows = pstmt.executeUpdate( );
      pstmt.close( );
      pstmt = null;
      System.out.println(rows + " rows updated");
      conn.commit( );
    }
    catch (SQLException e) {
      System.err.println("SQL Error: " + e.getMessage( ));
    }
    finally {
      if (rslt  != null)
        try { rslt.close( );  } catch (SQLException ignore) { }
      if (stmt  != null)
        try { stmt.close( );  } catch (SQLException ignore) { }
      if (pstmt != null)
        try { pstmt.close( ); } catch (SQLException ignore) { }
    }


    // Update an object using REF get/setValue( )
    try {
      Ref personRef = null;
      stmt = conn.createStatement( );
      rslt = stmt.executeQuery(
        "select ref(p) from person_ot p " +
        "where last_name = 'O''Reilly' and first_name = 'Tim'");
      rslt.next( );

      personRef = rslt.getRef(1);

      rslt.close( );
      rslt = null;
      stmt.close( );
      stmt = null;

      person = (Person)((oracle.sql.REF)personRef).getValue( );

      person.setMothersMaidenName("unknown");

      ((oracle.sql.REF)personRef).setValue(person);

      System.out.println("1 rows updated");
      conn.commit( );
    }
    catch (SQLException e) {
      System.err.println("SQL Error: " + e.getMessage( ));
    }
    finally {
      if (rslt  != null)
        try { rslt.close( );  } catch (SQLException ignore) { }
      if (stmt  != null)
        try { stmt.close( );  } catch (SQLException ignore) { }
    }
```

Example 16-1. The TestSQLData interface (continued)

```
  try {
    // Create and execute the object sql statement
    stmt = conn.createStatement();
    rslt = stmt.executeQuery("select value(p) from person_ot p");
    while (rslt.next()) {
      // Cast the object
      person = (Person)rslt.getObject(1);
      System.out.println(person._SQL_NAME);
      System.out.println("person_id          = " +
       person.getPersonId().longValue());
      System.out.println("last_name          = " +
       person.getLastName());
      System.out.println("first_name         = " +
       person.getFirstName());
      System.out.println("middle_name        = " +
       person.getMiddleName());
      System.out.println("birth_date         = " +
       person.getBirthDate());

      person.setConnection(conn);

      System.out.println("age                = " +
       person.getAge());
      System.out.println("age on 1/1/1980    = " +
       person.getAgeOn(Timestamp.valueOf("1980-01-11 00:00:00.0")));
      System.out.println("mothers_maiden_name = " +
       person.getMothersMaidenName());

      // Get the SQL Array
      personIdentifiers = person.getIdentifiers();
      // now use a result set
      rslt2 = personIdentifiers.getResultSet();
      while (rslt2.next()) {
        index = rslt2.getInt(1);
        personIdentifier = (PersonIdentifier)rslt2.getObject(2);
        System.out.println(personIdentifier._SQL_NAME);
        System.out.println("index              = " +
         index);
        System.out.println("id                 = " +
         personIdentifier.getId());
        System.out.println("id_type            = " +
         personIdentifier.getIdType());
      }
    }
    rslt.close();
    rslt = null;
    if (rslt2 != null) {
      rslt2.close();
      rslt2 = null;
    }
    stmt.close();
    stmt = null;
  }
```

Example 16-1. The TestSQLData interface (continued)

```
  catch (SQLException e) {
    System.err.println("SQL Error: " + e.getMessage());
  }
  finally {
    if (rslt != null)
      try { rslt.close();  } catch (SQLException ignore) { }
    if (rslt2 != null)
      try { rslt2.close(); } catch (SQLException ignore) { }
    if (stmt != null)
      try { stmt.close();  } catch (SQLException ignore) { }
  }
}

protected void finalize()
  throws Throwable {
  if (conn != null)
    try { conn.close(); } catch (SQLException ignore) { }
  super.finalize();
  }
}
```

Example 16-1, TestSQLData, starts in its main( ) method by instantiating a copy of itself and then executes its process( ) method. The process( ) method starts by allocating required variables, most notably location, personIdentifier, person, and personLocation. Each represents a custom SQLData class we created earlier. Then the program proceeds to the first of eight try blocks where it extracts the connection's type map, adds the custom Java classes, and saves the map.

Next, the program performs a little housekeeping by deleting any objects that were created by a previous execution of the program. After that, the program starts its third try block where it inserts a new Person object.

Now that we are using SQLData classes with our type methods implemented, the process of creating a new Person object is greatly simplified when compared to the use of the Struct object in the TestStruct program. The program first creates a new instance of a Person object using the alternate constructor that accepts a Connection object. Then it proceeds by calling the new Person object's getId( ) method to get the next primary key value for the object from the database. This is saved in the BigDecimal variable personId so it can be used later in the program. Then the Person accessor methods are called to set the new object's attributes. Before it can set the identifiers attribute, it must build a java.sql.Array for the collection. This time, however, that process is simplified by the use of the PersonIdentifier class. Two PersonIdentifier objects are created and stored in an Object array, which in turn is passed to the constructor for a new oracle.sql.ARRAY, along with an appropriate array descriptor to create the new Array. The resulting Array is then assigned to the Person object's identifiers attribute. Finally, a PreparedStatement object is created, and a setObject( ) method is called, passing the newly created Person object. Then the prepared statement is executed, inserting the Person object into the database.

A similar process is followed in the next two try blocks in order to add a location and a person's location. For the PersonLocation object, the default constructor is used, because the previously saved personId and locationId values are used as its primary key.

Next, the program proceeds with two more try blocks that retrieve and update the Person object. The first of the two update try blocks uses standard JDBC to update the object, while the second uses Oracle's REF object's proprietary getValue( ) and setValue( ) methods, which makes the REF act similar to a LOB locator, to update the object.

Finally, the last try block retrieves the person object from the database and echoes its contents to the screen. The program utilizes the Array object's getResultSet( ) method to treat the contents of the Array, identifiers, as a result set. Note that before the two member methods, getAge( ) and getAgeOn( ), are called, the program calls the Person object's setConnection( ) method to supply the retrieved object with the required Connection in order to use the member methods.

As you can see from Example 16-1, using SQLData greatly simplifies the storage and retrieval of an object to and from the database. But we still had to deal with the java.sql.Array interface for the Oracle collection. If you're not concerned about portability, then use the Oracle CustomDatum interface instead. With the CustomDatum interface, JPublisher not only creates an array for the Oracle collection, but also generates the wrapper methods for the type methods—in essence, a complete object solution. So let's take a look at Oracle's CustomDatum interface.

Oracle's CustomDatum Interface

In this section, you will learn how to use Oracle's CustomDatum interface classes to manipulate database objects. However, since we covered the SQLData interface in great detail, and there are minimal differences between the CustomDatum classes and the SQLData classes, I won't get into nearly as much detail as I did with SQLData.

Oracle's CustomDatum interface classes created by JPublisher are for one-stop shopping. When you use JPublisher with the option -usertypes=oracle, it creates custom classes for all the database data types you specify, including references and collections, and also creates wrapper methods for static and member type methods. In addition, if you use CustomDatum, no type map is required.

If you specify methods=true or methods=named, JPublisher generates .*sqlj* files instead of .*java* files. The .*sqlj* files then need to be compiled using SQLJ to create the corresponding .*java* files. The default constructor for the generated classes uses the SQLJ default Context for a connection—you don't want to use this. Instead, use one of the alternate constructors, that is, one that takes a Connection as an argument. Let's go ahead and start generating CustomDatum classes. Our first concern will be creating an appropriate input file.

Creating an Input File for CustomDatum

The mapping input file for generating CustomDatum classes is different from the one we used for SQLData. First, since JPublisher can generate the methods for us, we no longer need to subclass types LOCATION_TYP and PERSON_TYP. Second, even with the option case=mixed, JPublisher does not use the proper convention for naming Java methods, so we'll use the TRANSLATE clause to rename the methods manually. So here's the input file, *customdatum.input*:

```
SQL LOCATION_TYP                    AS LocationTyp
SQL PERSON_IDENTIFIER_TYPE_TYP AS PersonIdentifierTypeTyp
SQL PERSON_IDENTIFIER_TAB          AS PersonIdentifierTab
SQL PERSON_IDENTIFIER_TYP          AS PersonIdentifierTyp
SQL PERSON_TYP                     AS PersonTyp
 TRANSLATE GET_AGE                 AS getAge,
           GET_AGE_ON              AS getAgeOn
SQL PERSON_LOCATION_TYP            AS PersonLocationTyp
```

If we didn't translate GET_AGE to getAge, then JPublisher would name the method GetAge. But there's something missing. We haven't listed the static GET_ID methods from LOCATION_TYP and PERSON_TYP. Why? We intentionally leave out the GET_ID methods because there is a defect in JPublisher for Oracle 8.1.6 that prevents it from generating a wrapper for a static method with no arguments. There are only two workarounds. First, you can rewrite the GET_ID method to take a dummy argument. Or second, you can patch the generated *.sqlj* files, adding the code for the GET_ID methods, before you compile them into *.java* files. This defect is reportedly fixed in Oracle 8.1.7. So if you're using a later version of JPublisher, you need to add the TRANSLATE clauses for the rest of your methods to the input file. Now that we have an input file, let's move on to creating a properties file.

Creating a Properties File for CustomDatum

You need to change two options in the properties file in order to generate CustomDatum classes. The first is to use the option methods=named instead of methods=false. We use named so only the methods listed in the TRANSLATE clause of the input file are generated. This is part of the workaround for the JPublisher defect, but it's also a good idea to use named anyway. Then you can choose which methods to include in your Java classes. This is helpful if you decide to subclass a JPublisher-generated class to add client-side methods instead of calling those in the database. The second, and critical, change is to use the option usertypes=oracle instead of usertypes=jdbc. This is what directs JPublisher to create CustomDatum classes. Accordingly, here's the properties file, *customdatum.properties*:

```
jpub.user=scott/tiger
jpub.methods=named
jpub.builtintypes=jdbc
jpub.lobtypes=jdbc
jpub.numbertypes=objectjdbc
```

```
jpub.usertypes=oracle
jpub.input=customdatum.input
```

At this point, we have an input file and a properties file, so we can generate the classes by executing JPublisher with the following command at the command prompt:

```
jpub -props=customdatum.properties
```

JPublisher will then generate the following five *.sqlj* source files:

LocationTyp.sqlj
PersonIdentifierTypeTyp.sqlj
PersonIdentifierTyp.sqlj
PersonTyp.sqlj
PersonLocationTyp.sqlj

and create the following six *.java* source files:

LocationTypRef.java
PersonIdentifierTypeTypRef.java
PersonIdentifierTypRef.java
JPersonTypRef.java
PersonLocationTypRef.java

Since we need to patch the *PersonTyp.sqlj* and *LocationTyp.sqlj* files, we'll do that next. Here's the SQLJ code to add a wrapper method for GET_ID to the *LocationTyp. sqlj* file:

```
public java.math.BigDecimal getId ()
throws SQLException
{
  java.math.BigDecimal __jPt_result;
  #sql [_ctx] __jPt_result = { VALUES(LOCATION_TYP.GET_ID()) };
  return __jPt_result;
}
```

And here's the SQLJ code to add a wrapper method for GET_ID to the *PersonTyp.sqlj* file:

```
public java.math.BigDecimal getId ()
throws SQLException
{
  java.math.BigDecimal __jPt_result;
  #sql [_ctx] __jPt_result = { VALUES(PERSON_TYP.GET_ID()) };
  return __jPt_result;
}
```

After you've added the code to patch the *.sqlj* files, then you're ready to compile the *.sqlj* files into *.java* files.

If you're wondering how I knew how to code the two methods, I didn't. I copied a member method call from the *PersonTyp.sqlj* file and hacked the code. If you really want to know how to code using SQLJ, I suggest you investigate *Java Programming with Oracle SQLJ*, by Jason Price (O'Reilly).

Compiling SQLJ Files

Before you use SQLJ, you need to make sure its class file is on the `ClassPath`. In the Windows environment, you should have something like the following as part of your `ClassPath`:

```
C:\Oracle\Ora81\sqlj\lib\translator.zip; C:\Oracle\Ora81\sqlj\lib\runtime.zip;
```

Assuming you do have the correct `ClassPath` setting, compile the *.sqlj* files using SQLJ by typing the following commands at the command prompt:

```
sqlj LocationTyp.sqlj
sqlj PersonIdentifierTypeTyp.sqlj
sqlj PersonIdentifierTyp.sqlj
sqlj PersonTyp.sqlj
sqlj PersonLocationTyp.sqlj
```

This produces five more Java source files:

LocationTyp..java
PersonIdentifierTypeTyp..java
PersonIdentifierTyp..java
PersonTyp..java
PersonLocationTyp..java

You need to compile each of these five additional Java source files, and also the previously created Java source files, before attempting to use them in a program.

Now that we have all the supporting classes we need, let's put them all together in a working example.

A CustomDatum Example

Example 16-2, `TestCustomDatum`, is essentially the same as the `TestSQLData` program, but with a few significant differences:

- The program does not have to add any classes to the connection's type map. The Oracle driver recognizes and maps the `CustomDatum` classes automatically—well, almost.

- The program no longer uses the weakly typed `Array` class; instead, it uses the custom class `PersonIdentifierTab` created by JPublisher. This makes the creation of the `identifiers` attribute simpler and more easily understood.

- As you can see with the `insert a PersonLocation` try block, the `CustomDatum` constructor always takes a `Connection` object when used with JDBC.

- Do you remember when I said, "well, almost?" Well, an `OracleResultSet` is required to retrieve the classes using its proprietary method, `getCustomDatum( )`, which requires that a `CustomDatumFactory` object be passed as a parameter. This is what really takes the place of the need to modify the type map.

- The `getElement( )` method is used to retrieve the elements of the collection identifiers.

Example 16-2. The TestCustomDatum interface

```java
import java.io.*;
import java.math.*;
import java.sql.*;
import java.text.*;
import oracle.jdbc.driver.*;

public class TestCustomDatum {
  Connection conn;

  public TestCustomDatum( ) {
    try {
      DriverManager.registerDriver(new oracle.jdbc.driver.OracleDriver( ));
      conn = DriverManager.getConnection(
        "jdbc:oracle:thin:@dssw2k01:1521:orcl", "scott", "tiger");
    }
    catch (SQLException e) {
      System.err.println(e.getMessage( ));
      e.printStackTrace( );
    }
  }

  public static void main(String[] args)
   throws Exception {
    new TestCustomDatum().process( );
  }

  public void process( ) throws SQLException {
    BigDecimal           personId         = null;
    BigDecimal           locationId       = null;
    LocationTyp          location         = null;
    PreparedStatement    pstmt            = null;
    PersonLocationTyp    personLocation   = null;
    PersonIdentifierTab  personIdentifiers = null;
    PersonIdentifierTyp  personIdentifier = null;
    PersonTyp            person           = null;
    ResultSet            rslt             = null;
    Statement            stmt             = null;

    // Clean up a prior execution
    try {
      conn.setAutoCommit(false);

      stmt = conn.createStatement( );
      stmt.executeUpdate(
```

Example 16-2. The TestCustomDatum interface (continued)

```
      "delete person_location_ot where person_id = " +
      "( select person_id from person_ot " +
      "where last_name = 'O''Reilly' and first_name = 'Tim' )");
    stmt.executeUpdate(
      "delete location_ot " +
      "where code = 'SEBASTOPOL'");
    stmt.executeUpdate(
      "delete person_ot " +
      "where last_name = 'O''Reilly' and first_name = 'Tim'");
    stmt.close( );
    stmt = null;
    conn.commit( );
  }
  catch (SQLException e) {
    System.err.println("SQL Error: " + e.getMessage( ));
  }
  finally {
    if (stmt != null)
      try { stmt.close( ); } catch (SQLException ignore) { }
  }

  // Insert a person
  try {
    person = new PersonTyp(conn);
    personId = person.getId( );
    person.setPersonId(personId);
    person.setLastName("O'Reilly");
    person.setFirstName("Tim");
    person.setMiddleName(null);
    person.setBirthDate(Timestamp.valueOf("1972-03-17 00:00:00.0"));
    person.setMothersMaidenName("Oh! I don't know!");

    personIdentifiers =
      new PersonIdentifierTab(new PersonIdentifierTyp[2]);

    personIdentifier = new PersonIdentifierTyp(conn);
    personIdentifier.setId("FID");
    personIdentifier.setIdType("000000001");
    personIdentifiers.setElement(personIdentifier, 0);

    personIdentifier = new PersonIdentifierTyp(conn);
    personIdentifier.setId("SDL");
    personIdentifier.setIdType("CA9999999999");
    personIdentifiers.setElement(personIdentifier, 1);

    person.setIdentifiers(personIdentifiers);

    pstmt = conn.prepareStatement(
      "insert into person_ot values ( ? )");
    ((OraclePreparedStatement)pstmt).setCustomDatum(1, person);
    int rows = pstmt.executeUpdate( );
    pstmt.close( );
    pstmt = null;
```

Example 16-2. The TestCustomDatum interface (continued)

```
    System.out.println(rows + " rows inserted");
    conn.commit( );
}
catch (SQLException e) {
  System.err.println("SQL Error: " + e.getMessage( ));
}
finally {
  if (pstmt != null)
    try { pstmt.close( ); } catch (SQLException ignore) { }
}

// Insert a location
try {
  location = new LocationTyp(conn);
  locationId = location.getId( );
  location.setLocationId(locationId);
  location.setParentLocationId(null);
  location.setCode("SEBASTOPOL");
  location.setName("Sebastopol, CA, USA");
  location.setStartDate(
   Timestamp.valueOf("1988-01-01 00:00:00.0"));
  location.setEndDate(null);

  pstmt = conn.prepareStatement(
   "insert into location_ot values ( ? )");
  ((OraclePreparedStatement)pstmt).setCustomDatum(1, location);
  int rows = pstmt.executeUpdate( );
  pstmt.close( );
  pstmt = null;
  System.out.println(rows + " rows inserted");
  conn.commit( );
}
catch (SQLException e) {
  System.err.println("SQL Error: " + e.getMessage( ));
}
finally {
  if (pstmt != null)
    try { pstmt.close( ); } catch (SQLException ignore) { }
}

// Insert a person's location
try {
  // CustomDatum always need a Connection
  personLocation = new PersonLocationTyp(conn);
  personLocation.setPersonId(personId);
  personLocation.setLocationId(locationId);
  personLocation.setStartDate(
   Timestamp.valueOf("1988-01-01 00:00:00.0"));
  personLocation.setEndDate(null);

  pstmt = conn.prepareStatement(
   "insert into person_location_ot values ( ? )");
  ((OraclePreparedStatement)pstmt).setCustomDatum(1, personLocation);
```

Example 16-2. The TestCustomDatum interface (continued)

```
    int rows = pstmt.executeUpdate( );
    pstmt.close( );
    pstmt = null;
    System.out.println(rows + " rows inserted");
    conn.commit( );
  }
  catch (SQLException e) {
    System.err.println("SQL Error: " + e.getMessage( ));
  }
  finally {
    if (pstmt != null)
      try { pstmt.close( ); } catch (SQLException ignore) { }
  }


  // Update person using a PreparedStatement
  try {
    PersonTypRef personRef = null;
    stmt = conn.createStatement( );
    rslt = stmt.executeQuery(
      "select ref(p), value(p) from person_ot p " +
      "where last_name = 'O''Reilly' and first_name = 'Tim'");
    rslt.next( );
    personRef = (PersonTypRef)
     ((OracleResultSet)rslt).getCustomDatum(
      1, PersonTypRef.getFactory( ));
    person = (PersonTyp)
     ((OracleResultSet)rslt).getCustomDatum(
      2, PersonTyp.getFactory( ));
    rslt.close( );
    rslt = null;
    stmt.close( );
    stmt = null;
    person.setMothersMaidenName(null);

    pstmt = conn.prepareStatement(
      "update person_ot p set value(p) = ? " +
      "where  ref(p) = ?");
    ((OraclePreparedStatement)pstmt).setCustomDatum(1, person);
    ((OraclePreparedStatement)pstmt).setCustomDatum(2, personRef);
    int rows = pstmt.executeUpdate( );
    pstmt.close( );
    pstmt = null;
    System.out.println(rows + " rows updated");
    conn.commit( );
  }
  catch (SQLException e) {
    System.err.println("SQL Error: " + e.getMessage( ));
  }
  finally {
    if (rslt  != null)
      try { rslt.close( );  } catch (SQLException ignore) { }
    if (stmt  != null)
      try { stmt.close( );  } catch (SQLException ignore) { }
```

Example 16-2. The TestCustomDatum interface (continued)

```
  if (pstmt != null)
    try { pstmt.close( ); } catch (SQLException ignore) { }
}

// Update person using REF get/setValue( )
try {
  PersonTypRef personRef = null;
  stmt = conn.createStatement( );
  rslt = stmt.executeQuery(
   "select ref(p) from person_ot p " +
   "where last_name = 'O''Reilly' and first_name = 'Tim'");
  rslt.next( );
  personRef = (PersonTypRef)
   ((OracleResultSet)rslt).getCustomDatum(
    1, PersonTypRef.getFactory( ));
  rslt.close( );
  rslt = null;
  stmt.close( );
  stmt = null;
  person = personRef.getValue( );
  person.setMothersMaidenName("unknown");
  personRef.setValue(person);
  System.out.println("1 rows updated");
  conn.commit( );
}
catch (SQLException e) {
  System.err.println("SQL Error: " + e.getMessage( ));
}
finally {
  if (rslt  != null)
    try { rslt.close( );  } catch (SQLException ignore) { }
  if (stmt  != null)
    try { stmt.close( );  } catch (SQLException ignore) { }
}

try {
  stmt = conn.createStatement( );
  rslt = stmt.executeQuery("select value(p) from person_ot p");
  while (rslt.next( )) {
    person = (PersonTyp)
    ((OracleResultSet)rslt).getCustomDatum(
     1, PersonTyp.getFactory( ));
    System.out.println(person._SQL_NAME);
    System.out.println("person_id          = " +
     person.getPersonId( ));
    System.out.println("last_name        = " +
     person.getLastName( ));
    System.out.println("first_name       = " +
     person.getFirstName( ));
    System.out.println("middle_name      = " +
     person.getMiddleName( ));
```

Example 16-2. The TestCustomDatum interface (continued)

```
            System.out.println("birth_date          = " +
              person.getBirthDate( ));
            System.out.println("age                 = " +
              person.getAge( ));
            System.out.println("age on 1/1/1980     = " +
              person.getAgeOn(
                Timestamp.valueOf("1980-01-01 00:00:00.0")));
            System.out.println("mothers_maiden_name = " +
              person.getMothersMaidenName( ));
            personIdentifiers = person.getIdentifiers( );
            if (personIdentifiers != null) {
              System.out.println(personIdentifiers._SQL_NAME);
              for (int i=0;i < personIdentifiers.length( );i++) {
                System.out.println(personIdentifier._SQL_NAME);
                System.out.println("id                  = " +
                  personIdentifiers.getElement(i).getId( ));
                System.out.println("id_type             = " +
                  personIdentifiers.getElement(i).getIdType( ));
              }
            }
          }
          rslt.close( );
          rslt = null;
          stmt.close( );
          stmt = null;
        }
        catch (SQLException e) {
          System.err.println("SQL Error: " + e.getMessage( ));
        }
        finally {
          if (rslt != null)
            try { rslt.close( );  } catch (SQLException ignore) { }
          if (stmt != null)
            try { stmt.close( );  } catch (SQLException ignore) { }
        }
      }

  protected void finalize( )
    throws Throwable {
    if (conn != null)
      try { conn.close( ); } catch (SQLException ignore) { }
    super.finalize( );
    }
  }
```

At this point, you can store and retrieve objects in the database and call object methods.

Now we'll move on to Part V, which will cover more global topics such as transactions, detection and locking, performance, and troubleshooting.

Essentials

Part V covers the essentials that every application programmer using a database should know about but is sometimes afraid to ask:

"It's so obvious, right?"

"Well, no, it's not!"

Here, we'll cover what database transactions are, their scope, and Oracle's use of implicit locking. We'll also cover distributed transactions. Then we'll look at several strategies and tactics you can employ to ensure data integrity. Next, we'll investigate performance issues. And finally, we'll take a lighthearted look at troubleshooting. While not strictly JDBC, these are essential topics that every JDBC programmer should understand.

CHAPTER 17

Transactions

So far we've been talking about all the ways to connect to a database and how to manipulate data in a database, but we haven't said much about transactions. If your JDBC connection is in auto-commit mode, which it is by default, then every DML statement is committed to the database upon its completion. That may be fine for simple applications, but there are three reasons why you may want to turn off auto-commit and manage your own transactions:

- To increase performance
- To maintain the integrity of business processes
- To use distributed transactions

First, if you are performing batch insert, update, or delete operations, then turning off auto-commit and committing results manually at reasonable intervals will improve performance. Note that I said "at reasonable intervals." If you perform more operations per transaction than can fit into a rollback segment, the database takes additional time to increase the rollback segment to hold your uncommitted transaction statements, and that impairs performance.

The second reason why you may want to manage your own transactions is to maintain the integrity of your business processes. For example, if a customer places an order for some merchandise, the information you'd need to store for that order would include a list of items to purchase, billing and shipping information, and an authorized credit card charge. This information would likely be stored in several different tables. Without a manually managed transaction, it's possible to enter part of the order, and then the system fails. The rest of the order information is then lost. This results in an incomplete business transaction.

The third reason why you may want to manage your own transactions is to take advantage of the benefits of distributed systems. If you have to acquire information from, or update, several different systems, perhaps of unrelated technology, then you can use Oracle database links to perform a distributed transaction. Alternatively, you can use an XA connection, which is a connection based on the X/Open XA Architecture that supports distributed transaction processing.

In this chapter, we'll look at how to enable manual-transaction support, the scope of transactions, and their implications for the visibility of database changes. We'll finish with a discussion of the distributed transaction support provided by Oracle's JDBC implementation. So let's get started with a look at how to enable manual transactions.

Manual Transactions

To enable manual-transaction support instead of the auto-commit mode that the JDBC driver uses by default, use the Connection object's setAutoCommit( ) method. If you pass a boolean false to setAutoCommit( ), you turn off auto-commit. You can pass a boolean true to turn it back on again. For example, if you have a Connection object named conn, code the following to turn off auto-commit:

```
conn.setAutoCommit(false);
```

Disabling auto-commit is simple enough, but what are the implications of handling transactions manually? When is a particular transaction complete, and when does a new one start? And what effects does a manual transaction have on the implicit locking mechanism of an Oracle database? Let's begin by defining the scope of a transaction.

Transaction Scope

An existing transaction ends, and a new transaction starts, at the moment a commit or rollback command is issued. Assuming you've turned off auto-commit, a COMMIT statement makes permanent any changes you've made to the database using INSERT, UPDATE, or DELETE statements since the last time a COMMIT or ROLLBACK statement was executed. With JDBC, commit your changes manually by calling the Connection object's commit( ) method. Calling the commit( ) method sends a COMMIT to the database. The commit( ) method takes no arguments but may throw an SQLException. However, it's very rare for a commit to result in an exception. For example, to commit changes for the Connection named conn, use the following code:

```
conn.commit( );
```

On the other hand, a rollback command irrevocably discards, or undoes, any INSERT, UPDATE, or DELETE statements you've executed since the last time a COMMIT or ROLLBACK statement was executed. To roll back, use the Connection object's rollback( ) method. For example, to roll back updates to the database made using the Connection named conn, use the following code:

```
conn.rollback( );
```

One last note: while auto-commit is off, if a Connection is closed without committing or rolling back, or if any DDL is executed, then any uncommitted changes are automatically committed.

Implicit Locking and Visibility

It's important for you to understand the implications that a transaction has on implicit locking and visibility. Implicit locking refers to how Oracle automatically locks a database row during an insert, update, or delete operation. To help you understand the effects of implicit locking, I've created a table, TEST_TRANS, that has two columns: COL1, which is the table's primary key, and COL2. Figure 17-1 is a timeline for SQL statements against table TEST TRANS. On the left are SQL statements entered from the same transaction and session. On the right are the effects of those SQL statements on the other session.

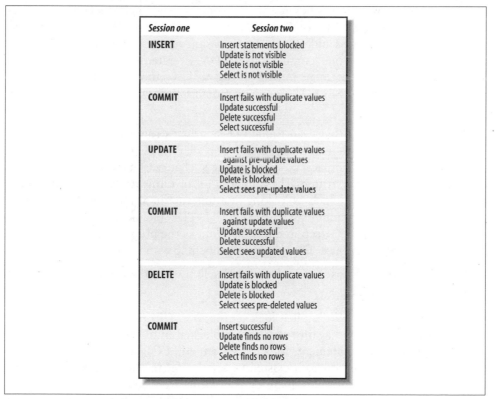

Session one	Session two
INSERT	Insert statements blocked Update is not visible Delete is not visible Select is not visible
COMMIT	Insert fails with duplicate values Update successful Delete successful Select successful
UPDATE	Insert fails with duplicate values against pre-update values Update is blocked Delete is blocked Select sees pre-update values
COMMIT	Insert fails with duplicate values against update values Update successful Delete successful Select sees updated values
DELETE	Insert fails with duplicate values Update is blocked Delete is blocked Select sees pre-deleted values
COMMIT	Insert successful Update finds no rows Delete finds no rows Select finds no rows

Figure 17-1. Implicit locking during manual transactions

To begin, session one performs an insert on table TEST_TRANS:

```
insert into test_trans ( col1 ) values ( 'X' )
```

From the moment the INSERT statement is successfully executed, Oracle places an implicit lock on the new row. Since the new row has not been committed, it is not visible to an UPDATE, DELETE, or SELECT statement from session two. However, if attempts are made in session two to insert a row with the same primary key, that session will be blocked indefinitely until the first transaction is either committed or rolled back. When session one commits, the INSERT statement in session two will fail with a duplicate key error. After the commit, session one's new row is visible to an UPDATE, DELETE, or SELECT statement from session two.

Session one now executes an UPDATE statement against the newly inserted and committed row:

```
update test_trans set col2 = 'A' where col1 = 'X'
```

Oracle once again places an implicit lock on the row. This time, an INSERT statement from session two with the same primary key will fail immediately. Furthermore, because of the implicit lock, any DML statement issued from session two will see a copy of the row as it was before it was updated by session one's UPDATE statement. However, an UPDATE or DELETE statement from session two against the same row will be blocked indefinitely until session one commits or rolls back its changes. When session one commits its UPDATE statement, then any blocked UPDATE or DELETE statement in session two will execute immediately. After the commit, any subsequent SELECT statement from session two will see the new row values.

A major concern here is that even though session one's row was locked, when the lock was released through a commit, session two's UPDATE statement did not take into consideration the impact of session one's changes. Instead, session one's changes were simply overwritten. The only way to solve this problem is to use some form of change detection, such as looking at a timestamp, at an updatestamp, or at all the columns you are modifying with your UPDATE statement. We'll cover more of this issue in Chapter 18. Keep in mind that you, as the programmer, are responsible for preventing this type of situation from happening with your code.

Session one continues by executing the following DELETE statement:

```
delete test_trans where col1 = 'X'
```

Oracle once again places an implicit lock on the row. This time, any insert, update, or delete from session two against that row is blocked until session one commits or rolls back its DELETE statement. Meanwhile, any SELECT statement from session two continues to see the row as it existed before the delete. When session one commits its DELETE statement, any INSERT statements from session two that use the same primary key will be successful. Any UPDATE, DELETE, or SELECT statement from session two will find no rows to affect.

For this scenario, I've assumed that Oracle's default transaction isolation level, which is read committed, is used. Oracle also supports a serializable level.

Isolation Levels

When applied to transactions, the term *isolation level* refers to how well one transaction is isolated from another. Oracle's default transaction isolation level is *read committed*. You can get the current isolation level for a connection by using the Connection object's getTransactionIsolation( ) method. You can set the transaction isolation level by calling the Connection object's setTransactionIsolation( ) method and passing one of the two valid constants: TRANSACTION_READ_COMMITTED or TRANSACTION_SERIALIZABLE. Oracle's *read serializable* isolation level will give you a consistent view of data from multiple tables since the last commit or rollback. Essentially, you see a snapshot of the tables as they existed when the transaction started. This is as opposed to read committed, which allows you to see changes during your transaction as soon as other transactions commit.

Distributed Transactions

A *distributed transaction* is a set of two or more individual transactions, or branches, managed externally by a transaction manager and committed or rolled back as a single, global transaction. When it comes to distributed transactions, you have two choices of how to implement them. If you need to implement a distributed transaction between two or more Oracle databases, you can use database links. When using database links, you act as though your distributed transaction is just another local transaction and let Oracle's two-phase commit mechanism take care of the distributed transaction process transparently. But what if you want to manage a transaction between an Oracle and a Sybase database? Or with a credit card processing center? For cases such as these, you can use the JDBC 2.0 optional package's XAConnection object instead of a standard Connection object.

Oracle's XA functionality implements the JDBC 2.0 optional package's support for distributed transactions. Although distributed transaction functionality is typically supported by an application server, such as one that supports Enterprise JavaBeans (EJB), this does not mean that you can't take advantage of the XA infrastructure to manage your own distributed transactions.

To create an XAConnection object, use an XADataSource. For the most part, Oracle's XADataSource is configured just like, and allocates connections just like, the DataSource and ConnectionPoolDataSource objects we covered in Chapter 7. Therefore, I won't cover much about establishing a connection using the XA facility, because you can refer to Chapter 7 and the Oracle API for most of what you need to know. Further, XA is typically implemented in a middle-tier application server, and, as an application developer, you typically use it in a somewhat transparent way. For example, if you develop EJB, the EJB container uses the XA infrastructure to manage distributed transactions for your EJB. So for most of us, the XA classes are of little use. Given that, we won't spend much time on this topic. Instead, just to ensure that you are familiar with distributed transaction concepts, I'll simply provide an example of an XADataSource and an XAConnection in a sample program.

Let's take a moment to cover the typical steps taken for a distributed transaction using XA with two data sources:

1. Each data source, or branch, of the distributed transaction gets an XAConnection object, which represents a physical connection to a transaction manager, such as a database, from its XADataSource object.

2. Using the XAConnection object, each branch gets a Connection object that will be used to perform SQL manipulations.

3. Again, using the XAConnection object, each branch gets an XAResource object, which will be used to coordinate the distributed transaction with the other branches.

4. A global transaction ID is created that will be used to create Xid objects for each branch to coordinate a distributed transaction.

5. For each branch, a branch transaction ID is created that will be used along with the global ID to create an Xid object for each branch.

6. An Xid object is created for each branch using an ID format identifier, a global ID, and a branch ID.

7. Each branch starts its leg of the distributed transaction by using the XAResource object's start( ) method, passing it the branch's Xid object. Next, any desired SQL statements are executed. The branch's leg is then ended by calling the XAResource object's end( ) method.

8. After each branch of a distributed transaction completes its SQL operations, it each calls its XAResource object's prepare( ) method to prepare for a global commit or rollback operation.

9. If all branches report a successful prepare phase, then each branch calls its XAResource object's commit( ) method. Otherwise, it calls its XAResource object's rollback( ) method.

Now that you have the big picture of how distributed transactions are implemented using XA, let's look at the details. We'll start with the optional package's XADataSource interface.

XA Data Sources

The XADataSource interface is implemented with the OracleXADataSource class and uses the same properties as the DataSource and ConnectionPoolDataSource classes we discussed in Chapter 7. XADataSource objects are factories for XAConnection objects, which in turn are factories for Connection and XAResource objects. Instead of the two overloaded getConnection( ) methods found in the DataSource interface, the

XADataSource interface has two overloaded getXAConnection( ) methods with the following signatures. Keep in mind that they, like all JDBC methods, can throw a SQLException.

```
XAConnection getXAConnection( )
XAConnection getXAConnection(String username, String Password)
```

You can configure JNDI to allocate XADataSource objects just as we did for DataSource objects in Chapter 7. After you've created an XADataSource object, your next step is to allocate an XAConnection using one of the two getXAConnection( ) methods.

XA Connections

An XAConnection extends PooledConnection and is implemented by the OracleXAConnection class. An XAConnection represents a physical database connection. Seeing that an XAConnection object extends a PooledConnection, it inherits all of the PooledConnection methods:

```
addConnectionEventListener( )
close( )
getConnection( )
removeConnectionEventListener( )
```

In addition to the PooledConnection methods, the XAConnection interface defines one more method, getXAResource( ). Following is the additional method signature. As usual, the method can throw a SQLException.

```
XAResource getXAResource( )
```

Like the connection returned by a PooledConnection object, the Connection object returned by an XAConnection is not the same type of Connection object returned by DriverManager. At least, they are not the same internally. However, the two Connection objects implement the same Connection interface, so they appear to be the same. The difference is that the close( ) method of a Connection object from an XAConnection object returns a connection to XAConnection, an intermediary that provides the hooks for distributing a transaction and does not necessarily close the physical connection to a database. Calling XAConnection object's close( ) method actually closes the physical connection to a database.

XA IDs

The Xid interface, which is implemented by the OracleXid class, is composed of a 4-byte format identifier, a 64-byte distributed transaction ID that is shared among all the Xid objects involved in a distributed transaction, and a 64-byte transaction branch ID for each branch of a distributed transaction. A transaction manager in a middle-tier application server can use the Oracle OracleXid constructor to create a new Xid object, passing the constructor a format ID, a global or distributed transaction ID, and a branch transaction ID. The Xid interface has three getter methods:

```
getFormatId( )
getGlobalTransactionId( )
getBranchQualifier( ).
```

XA Resources

An XAResource object, which is implemented by OracleXAResource, does the actual multiphase commit for a distributed transaction. To do a multiphase commit, use a global transaction ID represented by an Xid object together with appropriate methods from XAResource. The XAResource methods have the following signatures, and all of the methods can throw an XAException:

```
void commit(Xid xid, boolean onePhase)
void end(Xid xid, int flags)
void forget(Xid xid)
void prepare(Xid xid)
Xid[] recover(int flag)
void rollback(Xid xid)
void start(Xid xid, int flags)
```

With Version 8.1.6, the forget( ) and recover( ) methods are not implemented.

Using an XAResource object, you typically start, end, prepare, and commit or roll back a transaction. When using a Connection object from an XAConnection, you cannot use the connection's commit( ) or rollback( ) methods. Instead, you must use the XAResource object's commit( ) or rollback( ) methods. If you do inadvertently use a Connection object's commit( ) or rollback( ) method, you'll get a SQLException. A transaction manager, typically your database, uses XAResource objects to coordinate the individual transactions, or branches, of a distributed transaction. When you perform a distributed transaction, you start a transaction branch, execute some DML statements, end the branch, and then repeat those steps for as many branches as is required. Then prepare each branch to commit, and then commit the changes.

To start a new transaction branch and associate it with a distributed transaction, use the start( ) method, passing it an Xid along with the XAResource object's constant TMNOFLAGS as a second parameter. The start( ) method transparently associates a branch with a distributed transaction, because the Xid object passed to it has a common global ID. Here is a list of all the XAResource constants that can be used with the start( ) method:

TMNOFLAGS
> Starts a new transaction branch

TMJOIN
> Adds to an existing transaction branch

TMRESUME
> Resumes a previously suspended branch

To end a transaction branch, use the end( ) method, passing it an Xid and one of the following XAResource constants as a second parameter. Which constant you should pass depends on whether your SQL manipulations were successful.

TMSUCCESS
> The transaction was successful.

TMFAIL
> The transaction failed.

TMSUSPEND
> Suspends the transaction branch.

To prepare a branch for a two-phase commit, use its XAResource object's prepare( ) method, passing it the branch's Xid. The prepare( ) method returns one of the following XAResource constants:

XA_RDONLY
> This result notifies the application that the connection supports only read-only activities such as SELECT statements.

XA_OK
> This result notifies the application that the update prepared successfully.

A call to prepare( ) may throw an XAException if an error is encountered during any of the branches being prepared.

To commit the prepared changes in a transaction branch, call its XAResource object's commit( ) method, passing the transaction branch's Xid and a boolean to direct the commit method to use a one-phase (true) or two-phase (false) commit protocol. The default, if you don't pass a boolean, is to do a two-phase commit. To roll back the changes in a transaction branch, call the rollback( ) method, passing the transaction branch's Xid.

To determine whether two branches have the same resource manager, call the XAResource's sameRM( ) method, passing it another XAResource object. The sameRM( ) method returns a boolean. A true return value means that both branches indeed use the same resource manager. With this information, you can direct two branches to use the same resource manager.

Now that we've talked about XAResource and have referred to an XAException several times, let's discuss XAException objects.

XA Exceptions

XA methods throw an XAException, which is implemented by OracleXAException. Besides the standard getMessage( ) method that all exceptions have, the OracleXAException class also defines a getXAError( ) method that returns one of the XA error message constants defined in XAException. There's also a getOracleError( ) method that returns the number of the Oracle error. Table 17-1 maps common XAException error code constants to their Oracle error equivalents.

Table 17-1. XA-to-Oracle error codes

XAException constant	Oracle error code and message
XAER_RMFAIL	ORA-03113 end-of-file on communication channel.
XAER_RMFAIL	ORA-03114 not connected to ORACLE.
XAER_NOTA	ORA-24756 transaction does not exist.
XA_HEURCOM	ORA-24764 transaction branch has been heuristically committed.
XA_HEURRB	ORA-24765 transaction branch has been heuristically rolled back.
XA_HEURMIX	ORA-24766 transaction branch has been partly committed and aborted.
XA_RDONLY	ORA-24767 transaction was read-only and has been committed.
XA_RETRY	ORA-25351 transaction is currently in use.
XA_RMERR	All other error codes.

Now that you have an overview of Oracle's support for XA, let's take a look at some implementation details.

classpath and imports

To use XA, you not only need the Oracle driver file *classes12.zip*, but you must also have the Java Transaction API file *jta.zip* in your classpath. Then you must add the following import statements to your Java program:

```
import oracle.jdbc.pool.*;
import oracle.jdbc.xa.OracleXid;
import oracle.jdbc.xa.OracleXAException;
// If yours is a client-side, middle-tier program:
import oracle.jdbc.client.*;
// Or for a server-side, database resident program:
import oracle.jdbc.server.*;
import javax.transaction.xa.*;
```

If your Java code will reside in the database, and yet access a remote database, then don't use the imports. Instead, use the fully qualified names for both the client-side (the part that will access the remote database) and server-side portions of your program. At this point, we're ready to look at a working example of a program using XA to perform a distributed transaction.

An XA Example

Now that we've covered Oracle's implementation of XA, let's see it in action. The following DDL is for four tables: cart, item, shipping, and billing. If you have two databases available, then create the cart and item tables on the first database, then create the shipping and billing tables on the second database. Otherwise, create all four tables on the same database.

```
create table cart (
cart      number  not null primary key,
ordered   date    not null )
tablespace users pctfree 20
storage (initial 4K next 4K pctincrease 0)
/

create table item (
item      number        not null  primary key,
cart      number        not null,
quantity  number        not null,
descr     varchar2(30)  not null,
each      number        not null )
tablespace users pctfree 20
storage (initial 4K next 4K pctincrease 0)
/

create table shipping (
cart      number        not null  primary key,
name      varchar2(30)  not null,
address1  varchar2(30)  not null,
address2  varchar2(30),
city      varchar2(30)  not null,
state     varchar2(30),
country   varchar2(30)  not null,
postal    varchar2(30)  not null,
carrier   varchar2(30)  not null,
service   varchar2(30)  not null )
tablespace users pctfree 20
storage (initial 4K next 4K pctincrease 0)
/

create table billing (
cart      number        not null  primary key,
name      varchar2(30)  not null,
card      varchar2(30)  not null,
expires   date          not null,
amount    number        not null )
```

```
    tablespace users pctfree 20
    storage (initial 4K next 4K pctincrease 0)
    /
```

Update the database URLs and schema names used in the SQL statements in
Example 17-1 to show where you placed the tables. Also check usernames and passwords, then compile Example 17-1 and execute it.

Example 17-1. TestXA

```java
import java.sql.*;
import javax.sql.*;
import javax.transaction.xa.*;
import oracle.jdbc.xa.OracleXid;
import oracle.jdbc.xa.OracleXAException;
import oracle.jdbc.xa.client.*;

public class TestXA {
  OracleXADataSource xaDSLocal  = null;
  OracleXADataSource xaDSRemote = null;

  public TestXA() {
    // Create two XA data sources. Normally, the application server
    // would do this for you, or your program would use JNDI
    try {
      xaDSLocal = new OracleXADataSource();
      xaDSLocal.setURL("jdbc:oracle:thin:@dssw2k01:1521:orcl");
      xaDSLocal.setUser("scott");
      xaDSLocal.setPassword("tiger");

      xaDSRemote = new OracleXADataSource();
      xaDSRemote.setURL("jdbc:oracle:oci8:@dssw2k01");
      xaDSRemote.setUser("scott");
      xaDSRemote.setPassword("tiger");
    }
    catch (SQLException e) {
      System.err.println(e.getMessage());
      e.printStackTrace();
    }
  }

  public static void main(String[] args)
   throws Exception {
    new TestXA().process();
  }

  public void process() throws SQLException {
    boolean        allOk       = true;
    Connection     connLocal   = null;
    Connection     connRemote  = null;
    int            rows        = 0;
    Statement      stmt        = null;
    XAConnection   xaConnLocal = null;
    XAConnection   xaConnRemote = null;
    XAResource     xarLocal    = null;
```

Example 17-1. TestXA (continued)

```
XAResource      xarRemote    = null;
Xid             xidLocal     = null;
Xid             xidRemote    = null;

try {
  xaConnLocal  = xaDSLocal.getXAConnection( );
  xaConnRemote = xaDSRemote.getXAConnection( );

  connLocal    = xaConnLocal.getConnection( );
  connRemote   = xaConnRemote.getConnection( );

  xarLocal     = xaConnLocal.getXAResource( );
  xarRemote    = xaConnRemote.getXAResource( );

  // Create the Xids
  // Create the global ID
  byte[] globalTransactionId = new byte[64];
  globalTransactionId[0]    = (byte)1;

  // Create the local branch ID
  byte[] branchQualifierLocal = new byte[64];
  branchQualifierLocal[0]     = (byte)1;
  xidLocal = new OracleXid(
   0x1234, globalTransactionId, branchQualifierLocal);

  // Create the remote branch ID
  byte[] branchQualifierRemote = new byte[64];
  branchQualifierRemote[0]     = (byte)2;
  xidRemote = new OracleXid(
   0x1234, globalTransactionId, branchQualifierRemote);

  // Start the local branch of the distributed transaction
  xarLocal.start(xidLocal, XAResource.TMNOFLAGS);

  // Perform DML
  long cart = System.currentTimeMillis( );

  stmt = connLocal.createStatement( );
  rows = stmt.executeUpdate("insert into cart values " +
   " ( " + Long.toString(cart) +
   ", to_date( '20010317', 'YYYYMMDD' ) )");
  System.out.println(rows + " carts inserted");

  rows = stmt.executeUpdate("insert into item values " +
   " ( " + Long.toString(cart + 1) + ", " + Long.toString(cart) +
   ", 1, 'St. Patrick''s Day Banner', 19.99 )");
  System.out.println(rows + " items inserted");

  rows = stmt.executeUpdate("insert into item values " +
   " ( " + Long.toString(cart + 2) + ", " + Long.toString(cart) +
   ", 12, '4 Leaf Clover Party Hats', 4.49 )");
  System.out.println(rows + " items inserted");
```

Example 17-1. TestXA (continued)

```
stmt.close( );
stmt = null;

// End the local branch of the distributed transaction
xarLocal.end(xidLocal, XAResource.TMSUCCESS);

// Start the remote branch of the distributed transaction
xarRemote.start(xidRemote, XAResource.TMNOFLAGS);

stmt = connRemote.createStatement( );
rows = stmt.executeUpdate("insert into shipping values " +
  " ( " + Long.toString(cart) + ", 'Don Bales', " +
  " '137 Universal Drive', null, 'Oracle', 'AZ', 'USA', " +
  " '11130', 'UPS', 'Next Day' )");
System.out.println(rows + " shippings inserted");

rows = stmt.executeUpdate("insert into billing values " +
  " ( " + Long.toString(cart) + ", 'Don Bales', " +
  " 'Visa', to_date( '25250101', 'YYYYMMDD' ), 79.87 )");
System.out.println(rows + " billings inserted");

stmt.close( );
stmt = null;

// End the remote branch of the distributed transaction
xarRemote.end(xidRemote, XAResource.TMSUCCESS);

// Prepare both branches for a two-phase commit
int local  = xarLocal.prepare(xidLocal);
int remote = xarRemote.prepare(xidRemote);

if (local == XAResource.XA_OK)
  System.out.println("local XA_OK");
else if(local == XAResource.XA_RDONLY)
  System.out.println("local XA_RDONLY");

if (remote == XAResource.XA_OK)
  System.out.println("remote XA_OK");
else if(remote == XAResource.XA_RDONLY)
  System.out.println("remote XA_RDONLY");

allOk = true;

if (!((local  == XAResource.XA_OK) |
      (local  == XAResource.XA_RDONLY)))
  allOk = false;
if (!((remote == XAResource.XA_OK) |
      (remote == XAResource.XA_RDONLY)))
  allOk = false;

// Commit or roll back
if (local  == XAResource.XA_OK) {
```

Example 17-1. TestXA (continued)

```
      if (allOk) {
        System.out.println("commit Local");
        xarLocal.commit(xidLocal, false);
      }
      else {
        System.out.println("rollback Local");
        xarLocal.rollback(xidLocal);
      }
    }

    if (remote  == XAResource.XA_OK) {
      if (allOk) {
        System.out.println("commit Remote");
        xarRemote.commit(xidRemote, false);
      }
      else {
        System.out.println("rollback Remote");
        xarRemote.rollback(xidRemote);
      }
    }
    // This is the end of the distributed transaction

    // Close the resources
    connLocal.close();
    connLocal = null;

    connRemote.close();
    connRemote = null;

    xaConnLocal.close();
    xaConnLocal = null;

    xaConnRemote.close();
    xaConnRemote = null;
  }
  catch (SQLException e) {
    System.err.println("SQL Error: " + e.getMessage());
  }
  catch (XAException e) {
    System.err.println("XA Error: " +
      ((OracleXAException)e).getOracleError());
  }
  finally {
    if (stmt != null)
      try { stmt.close(); } catch (SQLException ignore) { }
    if (connLocal != null)
      try { connLocal.close(); } catch (SQLException ignore) { }
    if (connRemote != null)
      try { connRemote.close(); } catch (SQLException ignore) { }
    if (xaConnLocal != null)
      try { xaConnLocal.close(); } catch (SQLException ignore) { }
    if (xaConnRemote != null)
```

Example 17-1. TestXA (continued)

```
        try { xaConnRemote.close( ); } catch (SQLException ignore) { }
    }
  }

  protected void finalize( )
   throws Throwable {
    super.finalize( );
   }
}
```

The TestXA program in Example 17-1 starts by creating two different XADatasource objects. Then, using each XADatasource object's getXAConnection( ) method, the program retrieves two physical connection objects in the form of XAConnections. Using the XAConnection objects, the program proceeds by retrieving a Connection object and an XAResource object from each XAConnection object. Next, the program creates a global transaction ID, two branch transaction IDs, and finally, two Xid objects. These Xid objects are used to identify the transaction branches as the program continues. The fact that they both contain the same global ID is what ties the two branches together in one distributed transaction.

After creating the Xid objects, the program starts its first transaction branch by calling the XAResource object's start( ) method, passing the local Xid. Next, it performs several DML statements and ends the transaction branch by calling the XAResource object's end( ) method. The program continues by starting the remote transaction branch, performing DML statements, and then ending that branch. At this point, the data manipulations are finished, and the program is ready to prepare to commit the distributed transaction.

To prepare the distributed transaction, the program calls the XAResource object's prepare( ) method for both the local and remote branches. Then the return codes from the prepare methods are tested for success, and the appropriate XAResource object's commit( ) or rollback( ) methods are called as required to commit or roll back the transaction. Finally, the program cleans up its resources by closing first the Connection objects and then the XAConnection objects.

If you run into errors while running TestXA, you may have inadvertently left a distributed transaction in an inconsistent state. To correct such a problem, log into the server as username SYS using SQL*Plus and execute the following rollback statement:

```
    rollback force 'globalTransactionId';
```

In this rollback statement, replace *globalTransactionId* with the ID of the inconsistent transaction as reported by the TestXA program.

CHAPTER 18

Detection and Locking

As I pointed out in Chapter 17 when discussing Oracle's implicit locking mechanism during a transaction, just because you lock a resource before updating it does not prevent someone else from corrupting your update with his or her own update. As a matter of fact, database locks unto themselves do not solve the problem of multiuser data access integrity. Instead, you as the programmer are responsible for employing a methodology that will prevent application users from overwriting each other's data.

In this chapter, we'll look into the problem of multiuser update integrity and at how you can use locks with detection (a *pessimistic* approach) or update detection (an *optimistic* approach) to ensure the integrity of data in a multiuser application. First, we'll examine the locking options available when utilizing an Oracle database. Then we'll review the reasons why locks alone don't solve the update integrity problem. We'll continue by exploring detection techniques, that is, detecting that a change has taken place outside the current session and transaction. Next, we'll discuss several pessimistic, high-contention approaches to solving the problem of maintaining data integrity. Finally, we'll discuss an optimistic approach. Since there's a popular notion that locking alone ensures data integrity, let's start by examining Oracle's locking mechanisms in order to debunk this notion.

Oracle's Locking Mechanisms

Oracle provides three locking mechanisms. The first is the implicit locking that automatically takes place when you execute an INSERT, UPDATE, or DELETE statement. The second is the ability to lock rows for an update by first selecting the desired rows using the FOR UPDATE clause in a SELECT statement. The third is the LOCK TABLE command. Let's review implicit locking first.

Implicit Locking

As we discussed in Chapter 17, if you execute an INSERT, UPDATE, or DELETE statement for a particular row, then the database implicitly locks that row until you commit or roll back the current transaction. This means that if you perform DML on a table with a primary key constraint or unique index, and you are not in auto-commit mode, another user in another session with its own transaction can see the database as it existed before you started your transaction. You may be thinking to yourself, "Well, that's good, then they can't step all over my data." But you're wrong. All implicit locking does is prevent the second user from updating the row in question until your transaction ends. At that point, her update can overwrite any changes you made without her ever knowing that you've made them.

If you, as the first user, insert a new row, a second user inserting, updating, or deleting a row with the same primary key or unique index value will wait indefinitely until you end your transaction. At that time, if the second user is inserting, her insert will fail with a primary key constraint violation. However, if the second user is updating or deleting, her update or delete will be successful.

If you update a particular row instead of inserting a row, then a second user updating or deleting the same row will once again wait indefinitely until your transaction ends.

And finally, if you delete a row, then a second user updating or deleting the same row will wait until your transaction ends, at which point, her update or delete will succeed, but it will succeed without affecting any rows.

In none of these instances will the second user have any indication that your actions had changed the row between the time when your SQL statement's implicit lock took place and the time when the second user's statement executed. No detection at all! This lack of detection is the data integrity problem we're concerned about. Now, let's look at an example of explicit locking.

Row Locking

Using Oracle's FOR UPDATE clause in a SELECT statement, you can prelock any desired rows before updating them. The rows you lock with your SELECT statement will remain locked until you end your transaction with a commit or rollback. For example, to lock all the rows in the person table with a last name of "O'Reilly," use a SELECT statement such as the following:

```
select *
from   person
where  last_name = 'O''Reilly'
for update;
```

Of course, using FOR UPDATE means you have an extra step to perform in your program; you'll have to add a SELECT statement before each UPDATE or DELETE to explicitly lock the rows you intend to affect. This will allow you to detect if another user has already locked the desired rows by making your program wait to acquire the lock. However, this will still not solve the integrity problem completely, because you won't see if rows you are about to INSERT have already been inserted. In addition, your SELECT statement will wait indefinitely until it can acquire a lock. So, for the FOR UPDATE clause to be useful as a means of detecting if another session has a lock on something for which you wish to acquire a lock, you'll have to use it with the NOWAIT modifier.

If you execute a SELECT statement with FOR UPDATE NOWAIT, and it can't acquire a lock immediately, it will generate an SQLException with the Oracle error "ORA-00054: resource busy and acquire with NOWAIT specified." You can then use the generation of this error to control how you respond when a row you want is already locked by another session. Using explicit locks to maintain update integrity requires a great deal of additional programming effort and works only if every application that updates the database uses the technique. And that's unlikely!

Table Locking

Now that you know how to explicitly lock rows, let's look at how to lock an entire table. Locking an entire table is a very high-contention action. Regardless of locking mode, no other user on the system will be able to modify the table until you end your transaction, so use this approach only as a last resort. In 15 years of using Oracle and building applications, I have had only one instance in which it was necessary to lock an entire table. The LOCK TABLE command syntax is:

```
lock table table_name in mode [nowait]
```

which breaks down as:

table_name
    The name of the table you wish to lock

mode
    One of five possible lock modes:

        share
        share update
        exclusive
        row share
        row exclusive

nowait
    An optionally specified modifier that makes the LOCK TABLE command return an error if it cannot acquire the lock immediately

Although you can lock an entire table, another user can still queue an update that will wait until your transaction is finished with no knowledge of the changes you are making while the table is locked, and hence, no update detection. By now you must be coming to the realization that locking alone does not ensure data integrity. But just in case you aren't fully convinced, let's take a look at an example that proves my point.

Locks Alone Don't Solve the Problem

The easiest way to demonstrate that locks alone don't solve the data integrity problem is to open two SQL*Plus sessions and issue some SQL statements to show how one user can overwrite another user's updates. For this experiment, we'll use the TEST_TRANS table created in Chapter 17. If that doesn't exist, and you want to follow along, you'll need to create it now. Recall that TEST_TRANS has two columns: COL1, which is the table's primary key, and COL2. Both are VARCHAR2 columns. Let's start our experiment by inserting a new row into TEST_TRANS from session one:

```
SQL> insert into test_trans values ( '1', 'X' );

1 row created.
```

Then let's commit:

```
SQL> commit;

Commit complete.
```

Next, still from session one, let's update the row we just inserted:

```
SQL> update test_trans set col2 = 'Y' where col1 = '1';

1 row updated.
```

Now, from session two, let's select the row from TEST_TRANS where COL2 is equal to X:

```
SQL> select * from test_trans where col2 = 'X';

C C
- -
1 X
```

At this point, session two knows that the row with a primary key equal to 1 has a value of X. Let's now say that session two wants the row to have a value of Z in COL2. Unbeknownst to session two, however, the row no longer has a value of X in COL2. Session one has changed the value of COL2 to Y, but session two can't see that change because session one has not committed the change. As far as session two is concerned, the row has the value X. To change that value to Z, session two executes the following UPDATE statement:

```
SQL> update test_trans set col2 = 'Z' where col1 = '1';
```

After issuing this statement, session two waits indefinitely until session one commits, thus releasing its lock. So let's proceed by committing session one's transaction:

```
SQL> commit;

Commit complete.
```

Now session two's update succeeds, and session two also commits its changes:

```
1 row updated.

SQL> commit;

Commit complete.
```

If you requery the row from session one, you'll see that the value is not Y, which was just set in session one, but is instead Z. While this value seems legitimate to session two, it's probably not the result the session one user expected to see after having just changed the value to Y. What went wrong? Session two had no opportunity to detect that the row with a value of 1 in COL1 and a value of X in COL2 no longer had a value of X in COL2, because the original value of COL2 was not used in the WHERE clause of the UPDATE statement it issued to change the value to Z. To solve this problem, we need to include the original value of COL2 in the WHERE clause as a form of update detection.

Detection

Detection, in our current discussion, is the ability to detect if data you are about to modify has changed since the point when you selected it to be updated. There are several tactics you can employ for detection. Let me clarify that we are no longer discussing locking, but detection. Detection is mutually exclusive of locking.

The first two detection tactics we will discuss are pessimistic. By *pessimistic*, I mean it is assumed that a user in another session will most likely modify all the columns of a row of data you just selected to be updated by your program. One pessimistic detection approach is to use an updatestamp. As an alternative to using an updatestamp, you can compare all the columns of a table, or attributes of an object, to their original values in the WHERE clause of any UPDATE statement that you issue.

The third detection tactic is *optimistic*. It operates under the premise that a user in another session is not likely to modify the same data that you intend to modify. It entails comparing only modified columns or attributes in a WHERE clause.

Let's examine each tactic in detail, beginning with an updatestamp.

Using an Updatestamp

An updatestamp is a number column in a table or a number attribute in an object. The database increments its value by 1 each time you modify a given row or object.

That way, you can compare the updatestamp you retrieved from the database to its current value to detect a modification of the row or object by another session.

The benefit of using an updatestamp is that it makes formulating a WHERE clause for an UPDATE statement fairly simple. Typically, you need to include only the primary key and the updatestamp in the WHERE clause. The drawback is that you have to add code to your application, or even to the database in the form of triggers, to increment the updatestamp every time a row or object is updated.

Adding an updatestamp to a row or object also means that you have to add an additional column or attribute to every table or object type you use in your database. If you find this to be undesirable, you can use the second detection method, in which you compare all columns and attributes of the table (or object) that you are updating to their original values in the WHERE clause of your UPDATE statement.

An Updatestamp Versus a Timestamp

In databases other than Oracle, you might be able to add an additional column or attribute of a timestamp data type and then have the database update the timestamp every time a row or object is updated. Then, you can compare the value of the timestamp in the database to the original value you retrieved prior to your update in the SQL statement's WHERE clause. However, this does not work with Oracle because Oracle's timestamp data type, DATE, holds values only down to the second. In addition, if you create a custom data type, such as a number, to hold the time value down to milliseconds, you'll find that Oracle can still perform several hundred updates within that time frame. So a feasible approach is to use an updatestamp.

Comparing All Columns or Attributes to Their Original Values

A second detection tactic is to compare all the columns (or attributes) in the table (or object) that you are updating to their original values. You do this as part of your UPDATE statement in the WHERE clause; so the UPDATE statement fails if someone else has modified the row in question. With reference to my earlier example, when session two retrieved the row in which COL2 contained an X, it found that COL1 was equal to 1. To rewrite session two's UPDATE statement to include detection, add a comparison of COL2 to its original value. For example:

```
update test_trans
set col2 = 'Z'
where col1 = '1' and col2 = 'X';
```

Execute this UPDATE statement from session two in the earlier example, and no rows will be affected. The reason no rows will be affected is because COL2 has been modified by session one and is no longer equal to X. You can use the fact that the executeUpdate( ) method returns 0 for the number of rows affected to determine that the update was not successful. You then know that the row was changed between the time you selected it and the time you attempted your update.

The benefit to using all columns or attributes in a WHERE clause is that you don't have to add an additional updatestamp column or attribute to your tables and objects. The drawback is that you have to formulate a more complex, and larger, WHERE clause. If a table has 20 columns, you have to compare all 20 columns to their original values.

One problem with both pessimistic methods of detection is that they prevent more than one user from updating a row in a table at any point in time without an update failure, in the sense that a second updator will always fail. Accordingly, we call these low-concurrency methods. The fact that they essentially check on an entire row or object is what makes them pessimistic.

Comparing Modified Columns or Attributes to Their Original Values

The third method, which provides a high level of concurrency, is to compare only modified columns to their original values. To facilitate a high amount of concurrency, that is, the ability for multiple users to update the same row or object without update failure, you can detect changes that are relevant only to your UPDATE statement by including only the primary key and the modified columns in the WHERE clause of the UPDATE statement. For example, let's use the person table we created in Chapter 8. Let's assume that we insert a row:

```
insert into person (
        person_id,
        last_name,
        first_name,
        middle_name,
        birth_date,
        mothers_maiden_name )
values (
        1,
        'O''Reilly',
        'Tom'
        null,
        to_date( '19800315', 'YYYYMMDD' ),
        'Unknown' );
```

Let's further assume that two sessions select the values of the row just inserted. After both sessions select the row, session one executes the following UPDATE statement and commits:

```
update person
set     first_name = 'Tim'
where   person_id  = 1
and     first_name = 'Tom';
```

Session two then executes the following UPDATE statement and commits:

```
update person
set    birth_date = to_date( '19800317', 'YYYYMMDD' )
where  person_id  = 1
and    birth_date = to_date( '19800315', 'YYYYMMDD' );
```

Both statements will execute successfully. The trickery here is that while these two UPDATE statements both update the same row, they each modify different columns in that row. As a result, they don't overwrite each other's changes during the update. This technique of using the primary key and modified columns provides the highest amount of concurrency, the least amount of update failure, and prevents unintended corruption of data due to lack of detection. Since it allows more than one user to update a row, I consider it an optimistic approach. The downside of this tactic is that the formulation of WHERE clauses becomes quite complex to code.

Now that you've seen what locking and detection can do individually, let's examine how to combine them to effectively protect the integrity of updates in a multiuser environment.

Data Integrity Solutions

Whenever more than one user accesses a database, there is the possibility that one user will inadvertently overwrite another user's data. As we have seen from this chapter's earlier discussions, locks alone do not guarantee data integrity. Indeed, some form of change detection is also needed. In this section, we'll take what we've learned about locking and detection and formulate two pessimistic solutions and one optimistic solution to maintaining data integrity.

Pessimistic Data Integrity Solutions

Let's start our discussion of maintaining data integrity by taking a look at two pessimistic approaches. The first is to use row locking by selecting a row FOR UPDATE NOWAIT before updating it. The second is to use implicit locking and detection.

SELECT FOR UPDATE NOWAIT

If every user of a database uses the technique of selecting a row FOR UPDATE with NOWAIT, then data integrity will be maintained, because a second user will not be able to acquire a lock on the data until the first has committed his changes. But what about detection? Detection is implicit in the fact that an application will get an SQLException with Oracle error "ORA-00054" if it cannot immediately lock the desired row. A row that can't be locked is one that is already being modified by someone else. Hence, the contention between updates is detected before it even exists.

Although the SELECT FOR UPDATE NOWAIT approach works well, it has major concurrency and coding drawbacks. First, as soon as one user locks a row FOR UPDATE, it remains locked until that person commits or rolls back. This means that if he selects a row, then go on vacation for two weeks leaving his computer running, the row remains locked until he returns and commits or rolls back. Now that's a great deal of contention for the same row of data! A workaround to this problem is to retrieve a row to present its data to a user and then re-retrieve the row FOR UPDATE NOWAIT after the user has made changes. Then, compare the original values returned by the first query to those returned by the reselect just before updating the row. This brings us to another drawback: this method can require a great deal of extra coding. Finally, there is also the fact that every user of the database must play by the rules in order for this technique to work. A less contentious tactic is to use pessimistic detection with implicit locking. Let's examine that tactic next.

Pessimistic detection and implicit locking

Pessimistic detection is the use of an updatestamp or of all columns of a table (or all attributes of an object) in a SQL statement's WHERE clause to detect if changes have occurred in a target row or object. Implicit locking happens automatically when any INSERT, UPDATE, or DELETE statement is executed. If you combine implicit locking with the use of an updatestamp or with the checking of all columns, you will maintain data integrity. The drawback to this approach is straightforward: any change to a row by another session after the row has been selected in your session will result in an update failure. You'll then have to notify your software user that he will need to start over, essentially reselecting the data and updating once again.

With the technique described in this section, you get lower contention, because locks occur only when a change has taken place, but you trade contention for update failures. Since you'll create a simple WHERE clause, the construction of which is predictable, the coding burden is minimized, but you trade WHERE clause complexity for the need to notify the user that an update has failed. Overall, this is a better technique than using explicit locking when you have a large application with many users. An even better tactic for a large application, however, is to use an optimistic data integrity solution.

An Optimistic Data Integrity Solution

An optimistic solution to the multiuser data integrity problem is to combine optimistic detection with implicit locking. In this scenario, you store the original values of columns or attributes when you retrieve a row or an object and use them in a dynamically constructed WHERE clause when you later update that row or object. In the WHERE clause, you compare the values of the primary key, and any modified columns or attributes, to their original values. If the original and new values all match, you know that no other user has updated the same columns that you yourself are updating. While dynamic coding of the WHERE clause requires a good deal of programming, the fact that you employ implicit locking along with optimistic detection provides the highest level of concurrency while reducing the number of update failures. This technique works regardless of how other applications use the database. You still have to code update failure notification, but your program's users will not see many such messages.

Which Approach to Use?

So which data integrity approach is the right tactic for you? Many development tools employ the pessimistic approaches but suffer when a second or third tool is used to develop against the same database. With an optimistic approach you can't get into data integrity trouble regardless of what other tools are used. Ultimately, you have to decide based on how differing technologies access the same database. Personally, I always choose an optimistic approach. Then I don't have to be concerned about scalability.

Now that you're an expert at detection and locking and have several tactics you can employ to maintain data integrity, let's move on to Chapter 19, in which we'll examine myths and facts of JDBC performance.

Performance

Performance is usually considered an issue at the end of a development cycle when it should really be considered from the start. Often, a task called "performance tuning" is done after the coding is complete, and the end user of a program complains about how long it takes the program to complete a particular task. The net result of waiting until the end of the development cycle to consider performance includes the expense of the additional time required to recode a program to improve its performance. It's my opinion that performance is something that is best considered at the start of a project.

When it comes to performance issues concerning JDBC programming there are two major factors to consider. The first is the performance of the database structure and the SQL statements used against it. The second is the relative efficiency of the different ways you can use the JDBC interfaces to manipulate a database.

In terms of the database's efficiency, you can use the EXPLAIN PLAN facility to explain how the database's optimizer plans to execute your SQL statements. Armed with this knowledge, you may determine that additional indexes are needed, or that you require an alternative means of selecting the data you desire.

On the other hand, when it comes to using JDBC, you need to know ahead of time the relative strengths and weaknesses of using auto-commit, SQL92 syntax, and a `Statement` versus a `PreparedStatement` versus a `CallableStatement` object. In this chapter, we'll examine the relative performance of various JDBC objects using example programs that report the amount of time it takes to accomplish a given task. We'll first look at auto-commit. Next, we'll look at the impact of the SQL92 syntax parser. Then we'll start a series of comparisons of the `Statement` object versus the `PreparedStatement` object versus the `CallableStatement` object. At the same time we'll also examine the performance of the OCI versus the Thin driver in each situation to see if, as Oracle's claims, there is a significant enough performance gain with the OCI driver that you should use it instead of the Thin driver. For the most part, our discussions will be based on timing data for 1,000 inserts into the test performance table TESTXXXPERF. There are separate programs for performing these 1,000 inserts using the OCI driver and the Thin driver.

The performance test programs themselves are very simple and are available online with the rest of the examples in this book. However, for brevity, I'll not show the code for the examples in this chapter. I'll only talk about them. Although the actual timing values change from system to system, their relative values, or ratios from one system to another, remain consistent. The timings used in this chapter were gathered using Windows 2000. Using objective data from these programs allows us to come to factual conclusions on which factors improve performance, rather than relying on hearsay.

I'm sure you'll be surprised at the reality of performance for these objects, and I hope you'll use this knowledge to your advantage. Let's get started with a look at the testing framework used in this chapter.

A Testing Framework

For the most part, the test programs in this chapter report the timings for inserting data into a table. I picked an INSERT statement because it eliminates the performance gain of the database block buffers that may skew timings for an UPDATE, DELETE, or SELECT statement.

The test table used in the example programs in this chapter is a simple relational table. I wanted it to have a NUMBER, a small VARCHAR2, a large VARCHAR2, and a DATE column. Table TESTXXXPERF is defined as:

```
create table TestXXXPerf (
id          number,
code        varchar2(30),
descr       varchar2(80),
insert_user varchar2(30),
insert_date date )
tablespace users pctfree 20
storage( initial 1 M next 1 M pctincrease 0 );

alter table TestXXXPerf
add constraint TestXXXPerf_Pk
primary key ( id )
using index
tablespace users pctfree 20
storage( initial 1 M next 1 M pctincrease 0 );
```

The initial extent size used for the table makes it unlikely that the database will need to take the time to allocate another extent during the execution of one of the test programs. Therefore, extent allocation will not impact the timings. Given this background, you should have a context to understand what is done in each section by each test program.

Auto-Commit

By default, JDBC's auto-commit feature is on, which means that each SQL statement is committed as it is executed. If more than one SQL statement is executed by your program, then a small performance increase can be achieved by turning off auto-commit.

Let's take a look at some numbers. Table 19-1 shows the average time, in milliseconds, needed to insert 1,000 rows into the TESTXXXPERF table using a Statement object. The timings represent the average from three runs of the program. Both drivers experience approximately a one-second loss as overhead for committing between each SQL statement. When you divide that one second by 1,000 inserts, you can see that turning off auto-commit saves approximately 0.001 seconds (1 millisecond) per SQL statement. While that's not interesting enough to write home about, it does demonstrate how auto-commit can impact performance.

Table 19-1. Auto-commit timings (in milliseconds)

Auto-commit	OCI	Thin
On	3,712	3,675
Off	2,613	2,594

Clearly, it's more important to turn off auto-commit for managing multistep transactions than for gaining performance. But on a heavily loaded system where many users are committing transactions, the amount of time it takes to perform commits can become quite significant. So my recommendation is to turn off auto-commit and manage your transactions manually. The rest of the tests in this chapter are performed with auto-commit turned off.

SQL92 Token Parsing

Like auto-commit, SQL92 escape syntax token parsing is on by default. In case you don't recall, SQL92 token parsing allows you to embed SQL92 escape syntax in your SQL statements (see "Oracle and SQL92 Escape Syntax" in Chapter 9). These standards-based snippets of syntax are parsed by a JDBC driver transforming the SQL statement into its native syntax for the target database. SQL92 escape syntax allows you to make your code more portable—but does this portability come with a cost in terms of performance?

Table 19-2 shows the number of milliseconds needed to insert 1,000 rows into the TESTXXXPERF table. Timings are shown with the SQL92 escape syntax parser on and off for both the OCI and Thin drivers. As before, these timings represent the result of three program runs averaged together.

Table 19-2. SQL92 token parser timings (in milliseconds)

SQL92 parser	OCI	Thin
On	2,567	2,514
Off	2,744	2,550

Notice from Table 19-2 that with the OCI driver we lose 177 milliseconds when escape syntax parsing is turned off, and we lose only 37 milliseconds when the parser is turned off with the Thin driver. These results are the opposite of what you might intuitively expect. It appears that both drivers have been optimized for SQL92 parsing, so you should leave it on for best performance.

Now that you know you never have to worry about turning the SQL92 parser off, let's move on to something that has some potential for providing a substantial performance improvement.

Statement Versus PreparedStatement

There's a popular belief that using a PreparedStatement object is faster than using a Statement object. After all, a prepared statement has to verify its metadata against the database only once, while a statement has to do it every time. So how could it be any other way? Well, the truth of the matter is that it takes about 65 iterations of a prepared statement before its total time for execution catches up with a statement. This has performance implications for your application, and exploring these issues is what this section is all about.

When it comes to which SQL statement object performs better under typical use, a Statement or a PreparedStatement, the truth is that the Statement object yields the best performance. When you consider how SQL statements are typically used in an application—1 or 2 here, maybe 10–20 (rarely more) per transaction—you realize that a Statement object will perform them in less time than a PreparedStatement object. In the next two sections, we'll look at this performance issue with respect to both the OCI driver and the Thin driver.

The OCI Driver

Table 19-3 shows the timings in milliseconds for 1 insert and 1,000 inserts in the TESTXXXPERF table. The inserts are done first using a Statement object and then a PreparedStatement object. If you look at the results for 1,000 inserts, you may think that a prepared statement performs better. After all, at 1,000 inserts, the PreparedStatement object is almost twice as fast as the Statement object, but if you examine Figure 19-1, you'll see a different story.

Table 19-3. OCI driver timings (in milliseconds)

Inserts	Statement	PreparedStatement
1	10	113
1,000	2,804	1,412

Figure 19-1 is a graph of the timings needed to insert varying numbers of rows using both a Statement object and a PreparedStatement object. The number of inserts begins at 1 and climbs in intervals of 10 up to a maximum of 150 inserts. For this graph and for those that follow, the lines themselves are polynomial trend lines with a factor of 2. I chose polynomial lines instead of straight trend lines so you can better see a change in the performance as the number of inserts increases. I chose a factor of 2 so the lines have only one curve in them. The important thing to notice about the graph is that it's not until about 65 inserts that the PreparedStatement object outperforms the Statement object. 65 inserts! Clearly, the Statement object is more efficient under typical use when using the OCI driver.

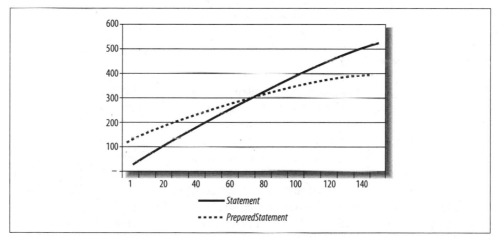

Figure 19-1. OCI driver timings

The Thin Driver

If you examine Table 19-4 (which shows the same timings as for Table 19-3, but for the Thin driver) and Figure 19-2 (which shows the data incrementally), you'll see that the Thin driver follows the same behavior as the OCI driver. However, since the Statement object starts out performing better than the PreparedStatement object, it takes about 125 inserts for the PreparedStatement to outperform Statement.

Table 19-4. Thin driver timings (in milliseconds)

Inserts	Statement	PreparedStatement
1	10	113
1,000	2,583	1,739

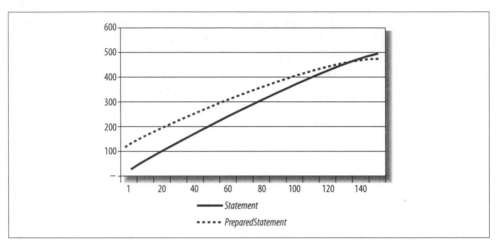

Figure 19-2. Thin driver timings

When you consider typical SQL statement usage, even with the Thin driver, you'll get better performance if you execute your SQL statements using a Statement object instead of a PreparedStatement object. Given that, you may ask: why use a PreparedStatement at all? It turns out that there are some reasons why you might use a PreparedStatement object to execute SQL statements. First, there are several types of operations that you simply can't perform without a PreparedStatement object. For example, you must use a PreparedStatement object if you want to use large objects like BLOBs or CLOBs or if you wish to use object SQL. Essentially, you trade some loss of performance for the added functionality of using these object technologies. A second reason to use a PreparedStatement is its support for batching.

Batching

As you saw in the previous section, PreparedStatement objects eventually become more efficient than their Statement counterparts after 65–125 executions of the same statement. If you're going to execute a given SQL statement a large number of times, it makes sense from a performance standpoint to use a PreparedStatement object. But if you're really going to do that many executions of a statement, or perhaps more than 50, you should consider batching. Batching is more efficient because it sends multiple SQL statements to the server at one time. Although JDBC defines batching capability for Statement objects, Oracle supports batching only when Prepared-Statement objects are used. This makes some sense. A SQL statement in a PreparedStatement object is parsed once and can be reused many times. This naturally lends itself to batching.

The OCI Driver

Table 19-5 lists Statement and batched PreparedStatement timings, in milliseconds, for 1 insert and for 1,000 inserts. At the low end, one insert, you take a small performance hit for supporting batching. At the high end, 1,000 inserts, you've gained 75% throughput.

Table 19-5. OCI driver timings (in milliseconds)

Inserts	Statement	Batched
1	10	117
1,000	7,804	691

If you examine Figure 19-3, a trend line analysis of the Statement object versus the batched PreparedStatement object, you'll see that this time, the batched Prepared-Statement object becomes more efficient than the Statement object at about 50 inserts. This is an improvement over the prepared statement without batching.

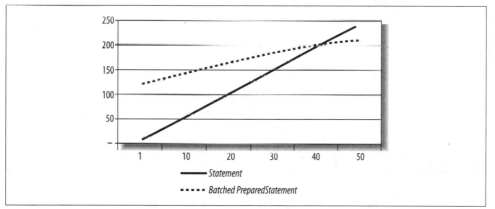

Figure 19-3. OCI driver timings for batched SQL

 There's a catch here. The 8.1.6 OCI driver has a defect by which it does not support standard Java batching, so the numbers reported here were derived using Oracle's proprietary batching.

Now, let's take a look at batching in conjunction with the Thin driver.

The Thin Driver

The Thin driver is even more efficient than the OCI driver when it comes to using batched prepared statements. Table 19-6 shows the timings for the Thin driver using a Statement object versus a batched PreparedStatement object in milliseconds for the specified number of inserts.

Table 19-6. Thin driver timings (in milliseconds)

Inserts	Statement	Batched
1	10	117
1,000	2,583	367

The Thin driver takes the same performance hit on the low end, one insert, but gains a whopping 86% improvement on the high end. Yes, 1,000 inserts in less than a second! If you examine Figure 19-4, you'll see that with the Thin driver, the use of a batched PreparedStatement object becomes more efficient than a Statement object more quickly than with the OCI driver—at about 40 inserts.

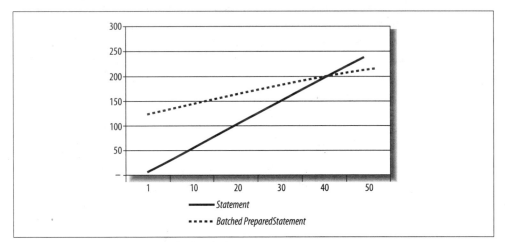

Figure 19-4. Thin driver timings for batched SQL

If you intend to perform many iterations of the same SQL statement against a database, you should consider batching with a PreparedStatement object.

We've finished looking at improving the performance of inserts, updates, and deletes. Now let's see what we can do to squeak out a little performance while selecting data.

Predefined SELECT Statements

Every time you execute a SELECT statement, the JDBC driver makes two round trips to the database. On the first round trip, it retrieves the metadata for the columns you are selecting. On the second round trip, it retrieves the actual data you selected. With this in mind, you can improve the performance of a SELECT statement by 50% if you predefine the SELECT statement by using Oracle's defineColumnType() method with an OracleStatement object (see "Defining Columns" in Chapter 9). When you predefine a SELECT statement, you provide the JDBC driver with the column metadata using the defineColumnType() method, obviating the need for the driver to make a round trip to the database for that information. Hence, for a singleton SELECT, you eliminate half the work when you predefine the statement.

Table 19-7 shows the timings in milliseconds required to select a single row from the TESTXXXPERF table. Timings are shown for when the column type has been predefined and when it has not been predefined. Timings are shown for both the OCI and Thin drivers. Although the defineColumnType() method shows little improvement with either driver in my test, on a loaded network, you'll see a differentiation in the timings of about 50%. Given a situation in which you need to make several tight calls to the database using a Statement, a predefined SELECT statement can save you a significant amount of time.

Table 19-7. Select timings (in milliseconds)

Driver	Statement	defineColumnType()
OCI	13	10
Thin	13	10

Now that we've looked at auto-commit, SQL92 parsing, prepared statements, and a predefined SELECT, let's take a look at the performance of callable statements.

CallableStatements

As you may recall, CallableStatement objects are used to execute database stored procedures. I've saved CallableStatement objects until last, because they are the slowest performers of all the JDBC SQL execution interfaces. This may sound counterintuitive, because it's commonly believed that calling stored procedures is faster than using SQL, but that's simply not true. Given a simple SQL statement, and a stored procedure call that accomplishes the same task, the simple SQL statement will always execute faster. Why? Because with the stored procedure, you not only have the time needed to execute the SQL statement but also the time needed to deal with the overhead of the procedure call itself.

Table 19-8 lists the relative time, in milliseconds, needed to call the stored procedure TESTXXXPERF$.SETTESTXXXPERF(). This stored procedure inserts one row into the table TESTXXXPERF. Timings are provided for both the OCI and Thin drivers. Notice that both drivers are slower when inserting a row this way than when using either a statement or a batched prepared statement (refer to Tables 19-3 through 19-6). Common sense will tell you why. The SETTESTXXXPERF() procedure inserts a row into the database. It does exactly the same thing that the other JDBC objects did but with the added overhead of a round trip for executing the remote procedure call.

Table 19-8. Stored procedure call timings (in milliseconds)

Inserts	OCI	Thin
1	113	117
1,000	1,723	1,752

Stored procedures do have their uses. If you have a complex task that requires several SQL statements to complete, and you encapsulate those SQL statements into a stored procedure that you then call only once, you'll get better performance than if you executed each SQL statement separately from your program. This performance gain is the result of your program not having to move all the related data back and forth over the network, which is often the slowest part of the data manipulation process. This is how stored procedures are supposed to be used with Oracle—not as a substitute for SQL, but as a means to perform work where it can be done most efficiently.

OCI Versus Thin Drivers

Oracle's documentation states that you should use the OCI driver for maximum performance and the Thin driver for maximum portability. However, I recommend using the Thin driver all the time. Let's take a look at some numbers from Windows 2000. Table 19-9 lists all the statistics we've covered in this chapter.

Table 19-9. OCI versus Thin driver timings (in milliseconds)

Metric	OCI	Thin
1,000 inserts with auto-commit	3,712	3,675
1,000 inserts with manual commit	2,613	2,594
1 insert with Statement	10	10
1,000 inserts with Statement	2,804	2,583
1 insert with PreparedStatement	113	113
1,000 inserts batched	1,482	367
SELECT	10	10
Predefined SELECT	10	10
1 insert with CallableStatement	113	117
1,000 inserts with CallableStatement	1,723	1,752
Totals	12,590	11,231

As you can see from Table 19-9, the Thin driver clearly outperforms the OCI driver for every type of operation except executions of `CallableStatement` objects. On a Unix platform, my experience has been that the `CallableStatement` numbers are tilted even more in favor of the OCI driver. Nonetheless, you can feel completely comfortable using the Thin driver in almost any setting. The Thin driver has been well-tuned by Oracle's JDBC development team to perform better than its OCI counterpart.

CHAPTER 20

Troubleshooting

In this chapter, we'll finish up by taking a look at common stumbling blocks for JDBC programmers using Oracle. Then we'll look at the tools available to help determine the source of your grief when your programs don't work, and conclude with a look at what Oracle has to offer in the near future. Let's start with the "gotchas," those pesky details that'll drive you crazy if you don't pay attention to detail.

The "Gotchas"

You know them! Those little details that are documented, but for some reason, you ignore them until they pop up their ugly heads and say, "Gotcha!" Until you've had your own round with them, you often pay no heed to the letter of the documentation. Even worse, sometimes the documentation is wrong! In the next few sections, we'll look at the most common stumbling blocks and resource killers. Let's begin where all new Java programmers suffer, the "Class not found" message.

Class XXX Not Found

"Class XXX not found" is a classic compile-time error message that tells you that one of the class names in your source code is not identifiable. It's likely that you've misspelled a class name and even more likely that you're missing an `import` statement. For example, if you remove the `import` statement for the `java.sql` package from Example 2-1, you'll get the following error messages when you compile that program:

```
TestOCIApp.java:6: Class SQLException not found in throws.
   throws ClassNotFoundException, SQLException {
                                  ^
TestOCIApp.java:11: Class Connection not found.
  Connection conn =
  ^
TestOCIApp.java:12: Undefined variable or class name: DriverManager
    DriverManager.getConnection(
    ^
```

```
TestOCIApp.java:15: Class Statement not found.
    Statement stmt = conn.createStatement( );
       ^
TestOCIApp.java:16: Class ResultSet not found.
    ResultSet rset = stmt.executeQuery(
       ^
TestOCIApp.java:20: Variable rset may not have been initialized.
    rset.close( );
       ^
6 errors
```

Wow! Six errors simply because you forgot to add import java.sql.*; to your source file. If you get a "Class not found" message for a class, and you're not sure what your import statement for that class should be, open up the API documentation and search for the class you are using. The package name will be documented with the class.

Typically, when you import a package, you can begin with the import keyword, follow it with the package name, and then append .* to import all classes in the package. Sometimes, however, that doesn't work as you expect. For example, if you want to use the Date class from the java.util package and the java.sql package in the same program, you'll probably use an import statement for the package you use a lot of classes from, i.e., java.sql.*;, and then fully qualify the class name for the class from the other package in order to resolve ambiguity. For example, you might import java.sql.*, use Date for the value returned from the database, and use the fully-qualified java.util.Date to refer to the Date class from the java.util package.

Next, let's look at what happens when you're missing class files at runtime.

A Missing JDBC Jar File

You may be able to successfully compile your program without a "Class not found" error, but when you run it you may get a ClassNotFoundException. To understand what's wrong, you must understand that JDBC is defined as a set of interfaces. These interfaces are resolved at runtime by DriverManager, which loads the appropriate implementation of the database and JDBC version you are using. If the necessary class files that implement the JDBC interfaces can't be loaded at runtime, then the program will generate an exception such as the following:

```
Exception in thread "main" java.lang.ClassNotFoundException: oracle.jdbc.driver.
OracleDriver
        at java.net.URLClassLoader$1.run(URLClassLoader.java:202)
        at java.security.AccessController.doPrivileged(Native Method)
        at java.net.URLClassLoader.findClass(URLClassLoader.java:191)
        at java.lang.ClassLoader.loadClass(ClassLoader.java:290)
        at sun.misc.Launcher$AppClassLoader.loadClass(Launcher.java:286)
        at java.lang.ClassLoader.loadClass(ClassLoader.java:247)
        at java.lang.Class.forName0(Native Method)
        at java.lang.Class.forName(Class.java:124)
        at TestOCIApp.main(TestOCIApp.java, Compiled Code)
```

This type of ClassNotFoundException is typically a problem when you are missing the appropriate java library jar (or zip) file in your class path. For Oracle 8.1.6, that file is *classes12.zip*. In fact, I generated the previous error message by removing *classes12. zip* from the class path and executing a JDBC program. Double-check your class path, your package library structure, and the spelling of any dynamically loaded class any time you get a ClassNotFoundException.

A Bad Database URL

After you've successfully compiled your program and dynamically loaded the JDBC driver, your next likely headache is a malformed database URL. The database URL you specify is used by DriverManager to find and use the appropriate implementation classes. If you make a mistake when formulating a database URL such that DriverManager cannot find a matching implementation, you'll get the rather annoying "No suitable driver" message. For example, the following error is the result of misspelling oracle as xracle in jdbc:xracle:oci8:@dssnt01:

```
Exception in thread "main" java.sql.SQLException: No suitable driver
        at java.sql.DriverManager.getConnection(DriverManager.java:477)
        at java.sql.DriverManager.getConnection(DriverManager.java:137)
        at TestOCIApp.main(TestOCIApp.java, Compiled Code)
```

To generate the next example, I used the URL jdbc:oracle:oci9:@dssnt01, which misspells the subprotocol name oci8 as oci9. This time, DriverManager can't find the subprotocol in the loaded driver, oracle.jdbc.driver.OracleDriver, so the driver itself generates the "Invalid Oracle URL" message to warn you that the subprotocol name is not supported:

```
Exception in thread "main" java.sql.SQLException: Invalid Oracle URL specified:
OracleDriver.connect
        at oracle.jdbc.dbaccess.DBError.throwSqlException(DBError.java:114)
        at oracle.jdbc.dbaccess.DBError.throwSqlException(DBError.java:156)
        at oracle.jdbc.dbaccess.DBError.check_error(DBError.java:775)
        at oracle.jdbc.driver.OracleDriver.connect(OracleDriver.java:143)
        at java.sql.DriverManager.getConnection(DriverManager.java:457)
        at java.sql.DriverManager.getConnection(DriverManager.java:137)
        at TestOCIApp.main(TestOCIApp.java, Compiled Code)
```

As you can see from these last two examples, you must be exact when specifying database URLs. There's no margin for error, only anguish as you stare blankly at your code and wonder what in the heck is wrong with Oracle's JDBC driver when it doesn't work. Then, minutes later, you come to the painful conclusion that, like most programmers, you can't type or spell worth a damn. I myself have at least three favorite spellings for the word oracle, but DriverManager recognizes only one. Be careful and double-check your database URLs.

Explicitly Closing JDBC Objects

If you don't like memory leaks, running out of cursors, or running out of connections, then you'd better call the close( ) method on any Oracle JDBC resource you open. Contrary to to standard JDBC documentation, Oracle JDBC objects—such as Connection, Statement, ResultSet, PreparedStatement, and CallableStatement—do not have finalizer methods. If you don't explicitly call the close( ) method for each of these objects as soon as you are done with them, your programs are likely to run out of resources, and you're likely to go mad wondering why.

Go one step further and be certain that the close( ) method gets called; always code a finally clause for any try-catch block making JDBC calls. In that finally clause, close any JDBC resources that will no longer be needed should an error occur. In addition to invoking the close( ) method on a resource, assign it a null afterwards, so that it will immediately become eligible for garbage collection. Doing these things will keep your programs nice and tidy, and keep you from wanting to pull your hair out.

Running Out of Connections

Even if you're a good programmer and close all your resources after you're finished using them, there's still a chance that you can run out of connections. Platform limitations may prevent you from opening more than 16 OCI connections per process. There are several things you can check if you find you can't open a connection. First, see if you've exceeded the maximum number of processes specified in the server initialization file. If so, that means you have to dig out the DBA manual. Second, verify that your operating system's per-process file descriptor limit has not been exceeded by examining your operating system's settings. If it has, then once again, you have to dig out the manual.

Boolean Parameters in PL/SQL

If you write stored procedures using PL/SQL and make use of boolean parameters, you won't be able to call these stored procedures using JDBC. That's because Oracle does not support a SQL BOOLEAN data type. The workaround is to create wrapper functions or procedures that return another data type instead of BOOLEAN. For example, instead of returning a BOOLEAN true or false, you might return integers 1 and 0. Yes, it's an ugly solution, but it works. When you write your wrapper function or procedure, you can take advantage of PL/SQL's ability to do method overloading, and therefore, use the same function or procedure name but replace your BOOLEAN parameters with NUMBERs.

The Evil CHAR Data Type

Don't use the CHAR data type. Use the VARCHAR2 data type instead. Why? Because using CHAR, which is fixed-length and right-padded with spaces, leads to all kinds of grief. Let's take a look at two specific problems you will encounter if you use CHAR.

The first problem involves comparing a CHAR column with a VARCHAR2 column in a SQL statement's WHERE clause. The comparison semantics used when a CHAR value is involved may surprise you and may lead to unexpected, and undesired, results. Consider, for example, a CHAR(13) column in which you store the value "O'Reilly". Because the column is a CHAR column, it is right-padded with spaces, and the actual value is "O'Reilly   ". A VARCHAR2(13) column, on the other hand, has the value "O'Reilly" (no padding). When you compare the CHAR(13) "O'Reilly   " with the VARCHAR2(13) "O'Reilly", such as you might do when joining two tables, you'll find that Oracle doesn't consider the two values to be equal, and your join fails. Even though you initially stored the same value ("O'Reilly") into both columns, they aren't seen as equal because of the difference in data types. To work around this problem, you have to use a function on one of the two columns. You can use rtrim( ) on the CHAR(13) column or rpad( ) on the VARCHAR(13) column. You also need to use the setFixedCHAR( ) method instead of setString( ) when setting values for a CHAR column in a WHERE clause. Either way, you negate the possibility of using an index for your join, and your performance goes out the window. If that doesn't turn your stomach, then maybe the next problem will.

The second problem with the CHAR data type is if it is used as an IN OUT or OUT variable in a stored procedure. By default, Oracle's JDBC drivers will right-pad any CHAR value with enough spaces to make the value 32,767 bytes in length. Ugh! You can work around this problem by using the Statement object's setMaxFieldSize( ) method. But this sets the maximum field size for all character data types, which can lead to other problems. So the real solution is to simply avoid using CHAR data types.

Unsupported Features

Oracle's JDBC implementation is quite complete except for a handful of fairly insignificant features. These features are part of the JDBC specification but are not implemented by Oracle. Even though they are not significant, it's important for you to know what these features are, so you don't think that you have a bug in a program when what you are really encountering is a problem from an attempt to use an unimplemented feature.

Named Cursors

A named cursor allows you to use a SQL-positioned UPDATE or DELETE using the cursor's name. However, with Oracle, the `ResultSet` object's `getCursorName()` method and the `Statement` object's `setCursorName()` method are not supported. If you call this method, you'll get a `SQLException`.

SQL92 Join Syntax

SQL92 join syntax is not supported. You need to use Oracle's join syntax. For outer joins you need to use Oracle's syntax involving the (+) character sequence. To left outer join you need to append (+) to the column on the lefthand side of the equal sign (=) for the columns specified in a WHERE clause. For a right outer join you need to append (+) to the righthand columns in a WHERE clause. The (+) character sequence denotes the optional table.

For example, to right outer join table A to table B on column code, your SQL statement will look something like this:

```
select a.name,
       b.descr
from   A,
       B
where  a.code = b.code(+);
```

This SELECT statement will return all names from table A with all available descr values from table B.

PL/SQL Boolean, Table, and Record Types

The PL/SQL data types, BOOLEAN, RECORD, and TABLE, are not supported by JDBC. To use BOOLEAN types, you'll need to create a wrapper stored procedure that passes integer values instead of BOOLEAN values. As for RECORD and TABLE data types, it is best to store such values in a temporary table from the stored procedure in which you desire to pass these values and then retrieve them using a SELECT statement in the calling program.

IEEE 754 Floating-Point Compliance

Oracle's NUMBER data type does not comply with the IEEE 754 standard that Java follows. Instead of complying with the standard, NUMBER guarantees 38 digits of precision, and 0, negative infinity, and positive infinity have an exact representation. This variation from the standard can cause minor differences in computations between Oracle and Java.

Oracle's JDBC does not consistently represent the Java NaN (Not a Number) constant for a float or double and does not throw a SQLException if you try to store a float or double with the NaN value, so don't store this value from your Java programs.

Catalog Arguments to DatabaseMetadata

Since Oracle needed a means to pass package names and does not have multiple catalogs, the catalog field is used to pass package names in calls to the DatabaseMetaData object's getProcedures() and getProcedureColumns() methods. If you specify an empty string ("") for a catalog using either method, you'll get standalone functions and procedures, which have no package name. If you pass null or "%", you'll get both standalone and packaged functions and procedures. Otherwise, pass a package name pattern using the SQL wildcard characters (either % or _) to retrieve the functions and procedures for a particular package or set of packages.

SQLWarning

Oracle JDBC drivers support SQLWarning only for scrollable ResultSets.

Debugging

So far in this chapter, I've tried to build an awareness of those things that can cause common problems when using JDBC with Oracle. Now it's time to become familiar with good programming practices and with the features available to help debug your JDBC programs. The first of these is handling a thrown SQLException.

Handling SQLExceptions

With JDBC, error conditions are communicated via a thrown SQLException. Errors can originate in the database or in your client application. Either way, they throw a SQLException. Therefore, it's good programming practice to always block each SQL operation with a try-catch-finally clause. In the catch clause you catch a SQLException. When a SQLException occurs, you have four methods available to you to get further information about the error:

getMessage()
> Returns the error message associated with a SQLException. If the message originates in the database, it will be prefixed by ORA-*XXXXX*, in which *XXXXX* represents an Oracle error number. If an error originates from the JDBC driver, the error message returned by getMessage() won't have an ORA-*XXXXX* prefix.

getErrorCode()
> Returns the five digits of an ORA-*XXXXX* number from the Oracle error whether the error occurred in your client application or the database.

---

getSQLState( )
> Returns a five-digit SQL state code if the error originated from the database. Otherwise, this method returns null.

printStackTrace( )
> Prints the current program stack to standard error.

Of these four methods, getMessage( ) is the most useful. When you combine it with a standard message format of your own design that identifies the name of the class and shows which SQL statement was executed, you can provide very meaningful information for debugging purposes. In order to provide a copy of the SQL statement that was executed, you need to create a String variable or better yet, a StringBuffer variable prior to your try-catch-finally clause to hold the contents of your SQL statement. Then it will be available for printing in your catch block. Example 20-1 demonstrates what we've been discussing. A variable named sql is created prior to the try-catch-finally clause to hold the SQL statement.

Example 20-1. Handling a thrown SQLException

```java
import java.sql.*;

class HandlingSQLExceptions {

 public static void main (String args[])
   throws ClassNotFoundException, SOLException {

   Class.forName("oracle.jdbc.driver.OracleDriver");
// Or you can use:
// DriverManager.registerDriver(new oracle.jdbc.driver.OracleDriver( ));

   Connection conn =
    DriverManager.getConnection(
     "jdbc:oracle:thin:@dssw2k01:1521:orcl","scott","tiger");
   System.out.println("Connection opened.");

   StringBuffer sql = new StringBuffer( )
   sql.append("select 'Hello Thin driver tester '||USER||'!' result ");
   sql.append("from    xdual");
   Statement stmt = null;
   ResultSet rset = null;
   try {
    stmt = conn.createStatement( );
    rset = stmt.executeQuery(sql);
    while(rset.next( ))
     System.out.println(rset.getString(1));
    rset.close( );
    rset = null;
    stmt.close( );
    stmt = null;
   }
   catch (SQLException e) {
    System.err.println("SQLException: " + e.getMessage().trim( ));
    System.err.println("in HandlingSQLExceptions while executing: ");
```

Example 20-1. Handling a thrown SQLException (continued)

```
  System.err.println(sql);
 }
 finally {
  if (rset != null) try { rset.close(); } catch (SQLException ignore) { }
  if (stmt != null) try { stmt.close(); } catch (SQLException ignore) { }
 }
 conn.close();
 System.out.println("Connection closed.");
 }
}
```

In Example 20-1, the JDBC statements for creating and executing the SQL statement, along with the JDBC statements for retrieving the data from the result set, are all in the same try block. In the example, I've purposely misspelled the name of the table dual as xdual to cause a SQLException. When the program executes, the code in the catch block produces the following error message:

```
SQLException: ORA-00942: table or view does not exist
in HandlingSQLExceptions while executing:
select 'Hello Thin driver tester '||USER||'!' result from xdual
```

The kind of information in this message is what you'll need to debug your programs. Now that you have a framework for handling a thrown SQLException, let's look at another facility that may help you: connection logging.

Logging DriverManager Connections

Connection logging is a facility provided by DriverManager that allows you to write a log of your JDBC activities to a host's filesystem. If you're having problems with establishing a connection, connection logging may be helpful. Enable connection logging by calling the DriverManager object's setLogWriter() method, passing it a PrintWriter object. For example, to enable DriverManager connection logging to System.err, code the following:

```
DriverManager.setLogWriter(new java.io.PrintWriter(System.err));
```

Set the log writer before you try to establish a connection. Then, when you attempt to establish a connection, DriverManager will log its actions to the specified stream. Here's the output from a successful connection:

```
DriverManager.getConnection("jdbc:oracle:thin:@dssw2k01:1521:orcl")
    trying driver[className=oracle.jdbc.driver.OracleDriver,oracle.jdbc.driver.
OracleDriver@e8af3995]
getConnection returning driver[className=oracle.jdbc.driver.OracleDriver,oracle.jdbc.
driver.
OracleDriver@e8af3995]
```

If you misspell thin as thim, you'll get output such as the following:

```
DriverManager.getConnection("jdbc:oracle:thim:@dssw2k01:1521:orcl")
    trying driver[className=oracle.jdbc.driver.OracleDriver,oracle.jdbc.driver.
OracleDriver@e8af3efc]
```

```
getConnection failed: java.sql.SQLException: Invalid Oracle URL specified:
OracleDriver.connect
```

This time we've specified a port number other than the port on which the listener is listening:

```
DriverManager.getConnection("jdbc:oracle:thin:@dssw2k01:1525:orcl")
    trying driver[className=oracle.jdbc.driver.OracleDriver,oracle.jdbc.driver.
OracleDriver@e8a23f8b]
getConnection failed: java.sql.SQLException: Io exception: The Network
Adapter could not establish the connection
```

Due to the overhead of using connection logging, I suggest you use it only for troubleshooting. It's worth noting that you get only slightly more information from connection logging than you do from a call to printStackTrace().

Logging DataSource Connections

You can enable the same logging facility for a DataSource as for a DriverManager by calling the DataSource object's setLogWriter() method, passing it a PrintWriter object. The pattern is the same as that used for the DriverManager object's setLogWriter() method. If you get your DataSource from a JNDI server, you must set the log writer for each DataSource after you get it from JNDI, even if you set it before it was serialized into the JNDI directory. This is because the PrintWriter object is transient, and therefore, cannot be serialized. Here's abbreviated output from a successful connection:

```
DRVR OPER Enabled logging (moduleMask 0x0fffffff, categoryMask 0x0fffffff)
DRVR DBG1 User us scottURL is jdbc:oracle:thin:
@(DESCRIPTION=(ADDRESS=(PROTOCOL=tcp)(PORT=1521)(HOST-dssw2k01))(CONNECT_
DATA=(SID=orcl)))
DRVR FUNC OracleConnection.OracleConnection(access, ur="jdbc:oracle:thin:
@(DESCRIPTION=(ADDRESS=(PROTOCOL=tcp)(PORT=1521)(HOST=dssw2k01))(CONNECT_
DATA=(SID=orcl)))", us="scott", p="tiger",
db="(DESCRIPTION=(ADDRESS=(PROTOCOL=tcp)(PORT=1521)(HOST=dssw2k01))(CONNECT_
DATA=(SID=orcl)))", info)
DRVR FUNC OracleConnection.initialize(ur="jdbc:oracle:thin:
@(DESCRIPTION=(ADDRESS=(PROTOCOL=tcp)(PORT=1521)(HOST=dssw2k01))(CONNECT_
DATA=(SID=orcl)))", us="scott", access)
. . .
DRVR DBG1 After execute: valid_rows=1
DRVR DBG2 defines:  oracle.jdbc.dbaccess.DBDataSet@e705c891
  DBDataSet.m_dynamic=false
  DBDataSet.m_arrayDepth=10 (valid only when m_dynamic=false)
  DBDataSet.types.length=1
    types[0].type= VARCHAR  (max_length=56)
  DBDataSet.data.length=1
    data[0].items[0] has 31 bytes:
    48 65 6c 6c 6f 20 54 68 69 6e  20 64 72 69 76 65 72 20 74 65
    73 74 65 72 20 53 43 4f 54 54  21
    data[0].items[1] has 0 bytes:

    data[0].items[2] has 0 bytes:
```

```
data[0].items[3] has 0 bytes:

data[0].items[4] has 0 bytes:

data[0].items[5] has 0 bytes:

data[0].items[6] has 0 bytes:

data[0].items[7] has 0 bytes:

data[0].items[8] has 0 bytes:

data[0].items[9] has 0 bytes:

DRVR FUNC OracleResultSetImpl.next( ): closed=false
DRVR DBG1 closed=false, statement.current_row=-1, statement.total_rows_visited=0,
statement.max_rows=0, statement.valid_rows=1, statement.got_last_batch=true
DRVR FUNC OracleStatement.getStringValue(getColumn=true, index=1)
DRVR FUNC OracleStatement.getBytesInternal(getColumn=true, index=1)
DBCV FUNC DBConversion.CharBytesToString(bytes[], nbytes=31)
DBCV DBG2 DBAccess bytes: (31 bytes):
  48 65 6c 6c 6f 20 54 68 69 6e  20 64 72 69 76 65 72 20 74 65
  73 74 65 72 20 53 43 4f 54 54  21
DBCV DBG2 UCS-2 bytes (62 bytes):
  00 48 00 65 00 6c 00 6c 00 6f  00 20 00 54 00 68 00 69 00 6e
  00 20 00 64 00 72 00 69 00 76  00 65 00 72 00 20 00 74 00 65
  00 73 00 74 00 65 00 72 00 20  00 53 00 43 00 4f 00 54 00 54
  00 21
DRVR FUNC OracleResultSetImpl.next( ): closed=false
DRVR DBG1 closed=false, statement.current_row=0, statement.total_rows_visited=1,
statement.max_rows=0, statement.valid_rows=1, statement.got_last_batch=true
DRVR FUNC OracleResultSetImpl.internal_close( )
DRVR FUNC OracleResultSetImpl.internal_close( )
DBAC FUNC DBDataSet.DBDataSet(conn, nrows=0)
DRVR FUNC OracleResultSetImpl.internal_close( )
DRVR OPER OracleStatement.close( )
DRVR OPER OracleConnection.close( )
```

The complete log file is actually eight pages long! It provides a great deal of information about the connection and the SELECT statement's execution, including the Oracle character set to UCS-2 conversion. Considering the size of the output file, enabling logging equates to a substantial performance hit.

Net8 Tracing

If you use the OCI driver, you can configure Net8 to trace your database communications. You can enable Net8 tracing on both the client and the server. Keep in mind, however, that enabling Net8 tracing translates into a substantial performance hit.

Client-Side Tracing

To enable client tracing, you add four parameters to your *sqlnet.ora* file, which is located in your *$ORACLE_HOME\network\admin* directory. The first of the four parameters is TRACE_LEVEL_CLIENT, and you can set it to one of the following four values:

> 0 or OFF
> 4 or USER
> 10 or ADMIN
> 16 or SUPPORT

For example, to turn tracing on and get the most amount of information, specify the following:

```
TRACE_LEVEL_CLIENT = SUPPORT
```

To turn tracing off, which you definitely want to do after your debugging session is complete, use 0 or OFF:

```
TRACE_LEVEL_CLIENT = OFF
```

The second parameter, TRACE_DIRECTORY_CLIENT, is used to specify the directory for the client-side trace files. Typically, this parameter is set as:

```
TRACE_DIRECTORY_CLIENT = $ORACLE_HOME/network/trace
```

You can, however, select any directory you wish as the destination directory for trace files.

 On Windows machines, do not set TRACE_DIRECTORY_CLIENT to the root directory of a drive (e.g., c:\). If you do so, you won't get any trace files even with tracing turned on.

The third parameter is TRACE_UNIQUE_CLIENT. This parameter can be set to ON or OFF. If you set it to OFF, then each session will use and overwrite the trace file. If it is set to ON, then the driver will append the process ID to the last parameter, TRACE_FILE_CLIENT, to create a unique trace filename for each session. For example, to overwrite the trace file with each session, specify the following:

```
TRACE_UNIQUE_CLIENT = OFF
```

The last parameter, TRACE_FILE_CLIENT, allows you to specify the name of the overwritten trace file, or a trace file prefix if you are going to set TRACE_UNIQUE_CLIENT to ON. For example, to set the overwritten trace file name to CLIENT.TRC, specify the following:

```
TRACE_FILE_CLIENT = CLIENT.TRC
```

Or if you want to use TRACE_UNIQUE_CLIENT, specify something like this:

```
TRACE_FILE_CLIENT = CLI
```

For troubleshooting JDBC, you want to use client-side tracing at the SUPPORT level with TRACE_UNIQUE_CLIENT set to OFF. When you do this, you get an exceptionally large trace file, but it contains packet images, so you can see exactly what has been sent between your application and the server. Example 20-2 shows a small portion of a trace file produced when executing TestOCIApp from Chapter 2.

Example 20-2. Sample support-level trace listing

```
nsdofls: sending NSPTDA packet
nspsend: entry
nspsend: plen=217, type=6
nttwr: entry
nttwr: socket 380 had bytes written=217
nttwr: exit
nspsend: 217 bytes to transport
nspsend: packet dump
(1256) nspsend: 00 D9 00 00 06 00 00 00  |........|
(1256) nspsend: 00 00 11 78 0A B8 DB 66  |...x...f|
(1256) nspsend: 05 01 00 00 00 01 00 00  |........|
(1256) nspsend: 00 11 69 0B B8 DB 66 05  |..i...f.|
(1256) nspsend: 01 00 00 00 01 00 00 00  |........|
(1256) nspsend: 03 5E 0C 61 81 00 00 00  |.^.a....|
(1256) nspsend: 00 00 00 98 4C 6B 05 3E  |....Lk.>|
(1256) nspsend: 00 00 00 30 A5 65 05 0A  |...0.e..|
(1256) nspsend: 00 00 00 00 00 00 00 54  |.......T|
(1256) nspsend: A5 65 05 00 00 00 00 00  |.e......|
(1256) nspsend: 00 00 00 00 00 00 00 00  |........|
(1256) nspsend: 00 00 00 00 00 00 00 00  |........|
(1256) nspsend: 00 00 00 00 00 00 00 00  |........|
(1256) nspsend: 00 00 00 00 00 00 00 56  |.......V|
(1256) nspsend: A5 65 05 73 65 6C 65 63  |.e.selec|
(1256) nspsend: 74 20 27 48 65 6C 6C 6F  |t 'Hello|
(1256) nspsend: 20 4F 43 49 20 64 72 69  | OCI dri|
(1256) nspsend: 76 65 72 20 74 65 73 74  |ver test|
(1256) nspsend: 65 72 20 27 7C 7C 55 53  |er '||US|
(1256) nspsend: 45 52 7C 7C 27 21 27 20  |ER||'!' |
(1256) nspsend: 72 65 73 75 6C 74 20 66  |result f|
(1256) nspsend: 72 6F 6D 20 64 75 61 6C  |rom dual|
(1256) nspsend: 00 01 00 00 00 00 00 00  |........|
(1256) nspsend: 00 00 00 00 00 00 00 00  |........|
(1256) nspsend: 00 00 00 00 00 00 00 00  |........|
(1256) nspsend: 00 00 00 00 00 01 00 00  |........|
(1256) nspsend: 00 00 00 00 00 04 00 00  |........|
(1256) nspsend: 00 00 00 00 00 00 00 00  |........|
nspsend: normal exit
nsdofls: exit (0)
snsbitts_ts: entry
snsbitts_ts: acquired the bit
snsbitts_ts: normal exit
nsdo: nsctxrnk=0
snsbitcl_ts: entry
```

Example 20-2. Sample support-level trace listing (continued)

```
snsbitcl_ts: normal exit
nsdo: normal exit
```

As you can see, the trace file shows you the exact contents of the packet communication between the application and the server. In this case, you can see that the application executed a SQL SELECT statement against the dual table.

Server-Side Tracing

If you can't use the OCI driver on the client, you can still get a trace file by turning on the trace facility on the server. The server-side trace facility works exactly like the client side's, except that the parameters have the word CLIENT replaced by SERVER. Otherwise, the same settings apply.

To enable server-side tracing, you must edit *sqlnet.ora* on your server machine. When you enable tracing on the server, you'll get trace files for all sessions connecting to the server; thus, you might actually wish to use unique filenames with which you set TRACE_FILE_SERVER to a file prefix, and Oracle adds a session number suffix. This means you need to capture your session number in your program so you can identify the correct tracing file. Here's an example of server-side settings:

```
TRACE_LEVEL_SERVER = SUPPORT
TRACE_DIRECTORY_SERVER = $ORACLE_HOME/network/trace
TRACE_UNIQUE_SERVER = ON
TRACE_FILE_SERVER = SESS-
```

Wait for the Cure

One way of solving a problem is to simply wait for the cure. With each new release of Oracle's JDBC drivers, new features are added. Functionality you desire may not yet exist, but it may arrive in the near future. So let's look at useful features you'll find in Oracle8*i* 8.1.7 and Oracle9*i*.

Oracle8i Release 3 (Version 8.1.7) Features

With Release 3 of Oracle8*i*, several new features have been added to Oracle's JDBC support. Here's a short list showing some of the more important ones:

Statement caching
    SQL statements are cached to prevent the overhead of repeated cursor creation.

Access to scalar-based PL/SQL tables
    You can now pass PL/SQL tables created with scalar data types as OUT parameters in stored procedures.

Complete XA support
    XA Recover and XA Forget methods are implemented.

Fixed wait scheme for connection caching
This new scheme makes a requestor wait indefinitely if the maximum limit has been reached for a connection pool.

Thin driver 56-bit Encryption
The Thin driver now supports 56-bit encryption.

Oracle9i Features

Oracle8*i* Release 3 is the last update to Oracle8*i*. Oracle9*i* is just out, with improvements to object-relational SQL that allow you to move your application's object model into the database. Here's a short list of Oracle9*i*'s more important enhancements and new features:

Support for Unicode with NCHAR datatypes
JDBC drivers can measure strings the same way users do, using UCS-2 semantics. The NCHAR types are redefined to hold Unicode data.

Support for object type inheritance
Database types can be extended. Lack of type inheritance in Oracle's object implementation has been a stumbling block for moving an application's object model into the data. With inheritance, making incremental changes to an object should no longer require recreating an object table.

Support for multilevel collections
You can have collections inside of collections. Single-level collections have also been a stumbling block for Oracle's object implementation. Now an application's object model can be completely implemented using Oracle.

Support for SQL accessible objects
Java mapping for database types is now supported in the type DDL. This means Java objects can be directly inserted, updated, deleted, and selected through the JDBC driver.

Connection management extensions for the OCI driver
These management extensions improve resource consumption of the pooled connection facilities.

Support for returning REF cursors from Java stored procedures
You can create REF cursors within a Java stored procedure and return those REF cursors to your Java program through JDBC

XA support for pre-Version 8.1.6 databases
Support for XA now extends to Oracle version 8.0 or higher

As of *i*AS release 9.0.2, EJB does not run inside the database server JVM.

The CustomDatum interface is being superseded by the ORAData interface. They are functionally the same except that the ORAData interface expects a connection object obtained through the DataSource interface.

That's it. I hope you've found the answers to any of your JDBC questions here in this book. If not, consider sending me an email message at *don@donaldbales.com* so I can include a solution to your JDBC programming problem in the next edition.

Create great programs!

Index

Symbols

? (question mark)
    locating parameters, 310
    placeholders in prepared statements, 217
/ (slash character), creating tables, 155

A

absolute( ) method, positioning cursors, 201
ACCEPTED value
    SQLNET.CRYPTO_CHECKSUM_
        SERVER and, 108
    SQLNET.ENCRYPTION_SERVER
        parameter and, 104, 106
accessor methods
    prepared statements and, 218–227
    result sets, 181–198
actions parameter, 98
adaptive applet tags, 51–53
addBatch( ) method, 167
Advanced Security (Oracle), 102–112
    authentication, 103
    data encryption, 103–107
    DataSource object and, 120
afterLast( ) method, positioning cursors, 202
ALTER TABLE statement, 155
API (JDBC), 3–5
APPLET tag (HTML), 39
applets, 14
    database connections, 34–58
    methods called by browser when
        loading, 35–38
    packaging, 38–44
    sandboxes and, 44–56

application database connections, 11–33
    examples for, 25–33
architecture (two-tier), 6
ARRAY data type, 220
ArrayDescriptor object, 363
arrays, 345–348
    ARRAY object, implementing, 363
    creating, 345–348
ASCII methods, storing character data, 273
attributes, 136
    comparing to values, 432–434
auto-commit mode, 94, 439
    executeUpdate( ) method, using, 158

B

baseName attribute, 77
batching, 230–243, 442
    Oracle, implementation, 237–243
    standard implementation, 231–237
beforeFirst( ) method, positioning
        cursors, 201
BFILE data type, 143, 178, 220, 286–294
    deleting, 291
    inserting, 288–291
    methods for, 294
    selecting, 292–294
    tables, creating, 288
    updating, 291
bfilename( ) database function, 288
BIGINT data type, 220
binary data, 143
    storing characters in, 273
BINARY data type, 220

We'd like to hear your suggestions for improving our indexes. Send email to *index@oreilly.com*.

executing prepared statements, 387
stored procedures, executing, 316
EXPLAIN PLAN facility, 437

F

Firewall-1, supporting Net8-compliant
firewalls, 58
firewalls
connections, establishing, 56–57
Net8-compliant, 57
first( ) method, 201
FIXED_RETURN_NULL_SCHEME
value, 124
FIXED_WAIT_SCHEME value, 124
FLOAT data type, 220
FOR UPDATE clause, 427, 434
framework, testing, 438
functions (standalone), 303

G

GENERATE clause, 371, 375
getAge( ) method, 382
GET_AGE_ON( ) method, 381
getAgeOn( ) method, 381, 382
getAsciiOuputStream( ) method, 277
getAsciiStream( ) method
LONG data types and, 300
storing character data, 273
getAttributes( ) method, 342, 360
getBigDecimal( ) method, 184
getBinaryOutputStream( ) method, 249
getBinaryStream( ) method
LONG data types and, 300
retrieving BLOB data, 268
getBlob( ) method, 249, 254
getBufferSize( ) method, 249
getBytes( ) method
LONG data types and, 300
LONG RAW, using, 300
getCatalogName( ) method, 191
getCharacterOutputStream( ) method
inserting CLOBs, 274–277
storing character data, 273
getCharacterStream( ) method
LONG data types and, 300
storing character data, 273
getClob( ) method, 282, 284
getColumnClassName( ) method, 191

getColumnCount( ) method, getting column
information, 190
getColumnDisplaySize( ) method, 191
getColumnLabel( ) method, 191
getColumnName( ) method, 191
getColumnType( ) method, 191
getColumnTypeName( ) method, 191
getConcurrency( ) method, 200
getConnection( ) method, 25, 79, 93
DataSource object, getting connections
from, 115
encryption and, 105
server-side internal driver, using, 89
using database URLs with usernames and
passwords, 22
getCursorName( ) method, 453
getDouble method, 184
getErrorCode( ) method, 32, 454
getFetchDirection( ) method, 201
getGreeting( ) method, 91
server-side Thin drivers, using, 96
getId( ) method, 382
get_id( ) method, 360
executing, 350
getInt( ) method, 184
getMessage( ) method, 32, 454
XA exceptions and, 420
getNextException( ) method, 33
getNumParameters( ) method, 94
getObject( ) method
object values, getting from result sets, 389
type maps, 385
adding classes to, 383
getParameters( ) method, 94
getPrecision( ) method, 191
getProcedureColumns( ) method, 305, 454
getProcedures( ) method, 454
getRef( ) method, 361
getResultSet( ) method, 149, 167
getRow( ) method, 201
getScale( ) method, 191
getSchemaName( ) method, 190
getSQLState( ) method, 32, 455
getSQLTypeName( ) method, 372
getString( ) method
LONG data types and, 300
getTableName( ) method, 190
getType( ) method, 200
getUpdateCount( ) method, 149

getValue( ) method, 361
    object methods, calling, 350
    object values, retrieving, 342
getXAResource( ), 417
getXXX( ) methods, 181–198
.gif files, using locators to load into
        databases, 250
global unique identifier (GUID), 336
GROUP BY clause, 218
GUID (global unique indentifier), 336

H

hosts (TCP/IP address), 22
HTML (Hypertext Markup Language)
    adaptive applet tag, 51–53
    packaging applets, 39
HttpSessionBinding interface, 71
Hunter, Jason (author), 87
Hypertext Markup Language (see HTML)

I

identifiers attribute, 360
IEEE 754 standard, 453
if statements, 154
IllegalAccessException exception type, 63
implicit locking, 413, 428
    pessimistic detection and, 435
import statements, 420
    connecting to a database, 19
IN parameters, 315
includeSynonyms driver property, 25
init( ) method
    applets, loading, 35
    servlet connections, 60
        per-transaction, 61–63
input files
    CustonDatum, creating for, 399
    syntax, 370
-input option, 367
InputStream object, selecting CLOBs, 283
INSERT statement, 156–158
    formulating, 387
    implicit locking and, 428
        pessimistic detection, 435
    locking mechanisms and, 427
    SQL statements, formulating, 217
    testing frameworks and, 438
    transaction scope and, 412, 414
insertRow( ) method, 207
InstantiationException exception type, 63

INSTEAD OF triggers, creating, 329–333
INTEGER data type, 220
integrity (data), 107–109
    example of, 109
internal database connections, 88–101
internal drivers, 13
    server-side, 88–94
internal_login driver property, 24
inUse attribute, 77
isAfterLast( ) method, 201
isAutoIncrement( ) method, 191
isBeforeFirst( ) method, 200
isCaseSensitive( ) method, 191
isCurrency( ) method, 192
isDefinitelyWritable( ) method, 192
isFirst( ) method, 201
isInUse( ) method, 77
isLast( ) method, positioning cursors, 202
isNullable( ) method, 191
isolation levels, 415
isReadOnly( ) method, 192
isSearchable( ) method, 192
isSigned( ) method, 192
isWritable( ) method, 192

J

J2EE (Java 2 Enterprise Edition), 6
    Thin drivers, installing, 17
jar files, 449
Java
    classes, creating, 375, 385
    exception handling in, 30
    stored procedures, executing, 93
Java 2 Enterprise Edition (see J2EE)
Java API, 3
.java files
    CustomDatum and, 398
    generating SQLData classes, 375
Java Naming and Directory Interface (see
        JNDI)
Java Native Interface (JNI), 15
Java Servlet Programming (Hunter and
        Crawford), 87
Java Virtual Machine (see JVM)
JavaBeans (see EJB)
JavaScript, using the adaptive applet tag, 51
java.sql.PreparedStatement
    CLOBs, inserting, 278–282
    structs, inserting, 341
java.sql.SQLData interface, 371

REQUESTED value
   SQLNET.CRYPTO_CHECKSUM_
      SERVER and, 108
   SQLNET.ENCRYPTION_SERVER
      parameter and, 104, 106
REQUIRED value
   SQLNET.CRYPTO_CHECKSUM_
      SERVER and, 108
   SQLNET.ENCRYPTION_SERVER
      parameter and, 104
ResultSet object, 150, 167, 176–215
   accessor methods and, 181–198
   cursor positioning, 176
   data types and, 177–181
   object values from, 389
   OracleResultSet and, 214
   scrolling and updating, 198–214
   SELECT statements and, 199
ResultSetMetaData object, 190–198
   example, 192–198
reusePooledConnection, 123
rollback( ) method, 426
ROLLBACK statement, 412
row locking, 428
row prefetch extension, 174
ROWID data type, 179, 220
rows, inserting/updating in result sets, 207
runMonitor( ) method, 84

S

sameRM( ) method, returning boolean
      values, 419
samples directory for Oracle client
      software, 16
sandboxes (applets), 44–56
   sockets, getting permissions, 47–56
scope (transactions), 412
scrollability (ResultSet object), 200
Secure Socket Layer (SSL), 111
SecurID protocol, 103
SecurIT (SLM), 58
security (sockets), 48
SELECT statement, 199, 342
   executing, 168–170, 389
   formulating, 388
   locators, retrieving, 249
   objects, creating, 389
   predefined, 444
   row locking and, 428
   transaction scope and, 414
serverName DataSource property, 114

servers, enabling encryption on, 104
server-side
   driver types, 88–99
      internal drivers, using, 89–94
      Thin drivers, using, 95–99
   Thin drivers, using, 13
servlets, 7, 14
   connection strategies, 60–86
   database connections, 59–87
session connections for servlets, 60, 67–75
session-bound wrappers, 70–75
SessionLogin servlet, 85
setAsciiStream( ) method, 278, 283
   LONG data types and, 300
   storing character data, 273
   using, 282
setBinaryStream( ) method, 260
   LONG data types and, 300
setBytes( ) method, 260
   BLOBs, inserting, 263–266
   limiting data sizes, 227
   LONG RAW data type and, 295, 300
setCacheScheme( ) method, 123
setCharacterStream( ) method, 278, 283
   LONG data types and, 300
   storing character data, 273
   using, 279
setConnection( ) method, 389
setFixedCHAR( ) method, 224
setLogWriter( ) method, 457
setLong( ) accessor method, 260
setObject( ) method, 260, 279, 361
   BLOB, inserting, 266
   object values, setting, 387
   structs, inserting, 341
   type maps, adding classes to, 383
setOracleObject( ) method, 223
setQueryTimeout( ) method, 99
setRowPrefetch( ) method, 174
setString( ) methods, limiting data sizes, 227
setTypeMap( ) method, 384
setValue( ) method, 361
setVerbose( ) method, 84
setXXX( ) methods, 216
sid (System Identifier), 22
signatures (stored procedures), 303–305
   describing, 305–308
signed by, 48
size limiations for binary/character data, 227
slash character (/),creating tables, 155

About the Author

Donald Bales is a computer applications consultant specializing in the analysis, design, and programming of distributed systems, systems integration, and data warehousing. Donald has over 16 years of experience with Oracle as both a developer and a database administrator and over 6 years of experience with Java. He is currently working on the migration of medical and industrial hygiene systems to a web environment for a major energy company.

When he is not developing applications, Donald can often be found working with horses, playing the piano, or playing the bagpipes. Donald has had several careers and has at various times been a mechanic, a general contractor, Mr. Mom, a developer, and currently a consultant. He has a Bachelor of Science degree in Business from Elmhurst College in Elmhurst, Illinois. Donald currently resides in Downers Grove, Illinois with his wife Diane, his daughter Kristyn, their two cats Booger and Scooter, and their horse Breezy. Donald can be contacted by email at *don@donaldbales.com*.

Colophon

Our look is the result of reader comments, our own experimentation, and feedback from distribution channels. Distinctive covers complement our distinctive approach to technical topics, breathing personality and life into potentially dry subjects.

The animals on the cover of *Java Programming with Oracle JDBC* are hummingbird moths. As its name suggests, this moth looks much like a hummingbird at a glance. It feeds by hovering in front of a flower and sipping nectar through its proboscis (its feeding structure) in much the same way as the hummingbird. However, at a closer look, the insect's antennae mark it as a moth. Belonging to the family Sphingidae, this moth is commonly called "hummingbird," "sphinx," or "hawk moth."

The hummingbird moth is a strong flyer, with a rapid wingbeat. Most are medium to large moths with heavy bodies, with wing spreads up to five inches. Although few are active in the daytime, most fly on cloudy days or at dusk. Though most don't cause damage to garden plants, some feed on tomatoes and tobacco when in caterpillar form. The tomato hornworm, for example, feeds on potato, tomato, and tobacco plants, and can cause severe economic loss in those crops. Leaves provide an additional source of food for the moth.

Matt Hutchinson was the production editor and copyeditor for *Java Programming with Oracle JDBC*. Leanne Soylemez and Rachel Wheeler provided quality control. Joe Wizda wrote the index. Edie Shapiro provided production assistance.

Ellie Volckhausen designed the cover of this book, based on a series design by Edie Freedman. The cover image is from *Animal Creation, Volume 2*. Emma Colby produced the cover layout with QuarkXPress 4.1 using Adobe's ITC Garamond font.

David Futato designed the interior layout. Neil Walls converted the files from Microsoft Word to FrameMaker 5.5.6 using tools created by Mike Sierra. The text font is Linotype Birka; the heading font is Adobe Myriad Condensed; and the code font is LucasFont's TheSans Mono Condensed. The illustrations that appear in the book were produced by Robert Romano and Jessamyn Read using Macromedia Free-Hand 9 and Adobe Photoshop 6. The tip and warning icons were drawn by Christopher Bing. This colophon was written by Sarah Sherman.

Whenever possible, our books use a durable and flexible lay-flat binding. If the page count exceeds this binding's limit, perfect binding is used.